D0024432

POST-COLONIAL DRAMA

Post-colonial Drama: Theory, practice, politics is the first full-length study to examine how performance practices intersect with and develop an understanding of post-colonial theories. Addressing the specific ways in which performance has been instrumental in resisting the continuing effects of imperialism, this study considers how post-colonial theatre acts as an important form of cultural capital.

Gilbert and Tompkins' discussion ranges across a variety of plays from Australia, Africa, Canada, New Zealand, the Caribbean, and other former colonial regions. Critiquing anthropological approaches to drama, they call for a culturally specific approach to the analysis of plays from both Western and non-Western societies.

Post-colonial Drama combines a rich cluster of post-colonial and performance theories with close attention to the play texts themselves. It will be invaluable reading for all students, teachers, and theorists of drama.

Helen Gilbert teaches Drama and Theatre studies at The University of Queensland, Australia, and directs experimental performance work. She has published a number of critical articles on post-colonial drama and performance theory. **Joanne Tompkins**, formerly Head of the Department of Theatre and Drama at La Trobe University, Melbourne, now lectures in English and Drama and Theatre Studies at The University of Queensland. She has published work on Australian, Canadian, and New Zealand literatures, and on post-colonial theory and drama.

POST-COLONIAL DRAMA

Theory, practice, politics

Helen Gilbert
and
Joanne Tompkins

London and New York

Thomas J. Bata Library
TRENT UNIVERSITY
WITHDRAWN
PETERBOROUGH, ONTARIO

PR9083 .G55 1996

First published 1996
by Routledge
11 New Fetter Lane, London EC4P 4EE

Simultaneously published in the USA and Canada
by Routledge
29 West 35th Street, New York, NY 10001

Routledge is an International Thomson Publishing company

© 1996 Gilbert and Tompkins

Typeset in Baskerville by Keystroke, Jacaranda Lodge,
Wolverhampton
Printed and bound in Great Britain by
TJ Press (Padstow) Ltd, Padstow, Cornwall

All rights reserved. No part of this book may be reprinted
or reproduced or utilized in any form or by any electronic,
mechanical, or other means, now known or hereafter
invented, including photocopying and recording, or in any
information storage or retrieval system, without permission
in writing from the publishers.

British Library Cataloguing in Publication Data
A catalogue record for this book is available from the British Library

Library of Congress Cataloguing in Publication Data
A catalogue record for this book has been requested

ISBN 0–415–09023–7
ISBN 0–415–09024–5 (pbk)

CONTENTS

v

ILLUSTRATIONS

ACKNOWLEDGEMENTS

This project has become much larger than we originally envisaged. As such a project grows, however, so do its absences – both primary and secondary texts. We have endeavoured to discuss well-known playwrights and to introduce readers to less internationally recognised writers, but there will inevitably be significant writers and/or plays left unmentioned.

Our research in various parts of the world was greatly assisted by many academics, playwrights, and theatre practitioners. Among them, we would like to thank in particular:

- *in Australia*: Gareth Griffiths, Veronica Kelly, Jacqueline Lo, Geoffrey Milne, Helen Tiffin.
- *in Canada*: Susan Bennett, Diane Bessai, Gary Boire, Diana Brydon, Alan Filewod, Ann Jansen, Daniel David Moses, Native Earth Theatre Company, Denis Salter, and Jerry Wasserman.
- *in New Zealand*: John Anderson, Sebastian Black, David Carnegie, Murray Edmond, Stuart Hoar, Hone Kouka, Phillip Mann, Howard McNaughton, Vincent O'Sullivan, Roma Potiki, Apirana Taylor, Lisa Warrington, Mark Williams, and Playmarket.
- *in South Africa*: David Attwell, Hilary Blecher, Annette Combrink, Dorothy Driver, Mikki Flockemann, Stephen Gray, Michael Green, Temple Hauptfleisch, Maishe Maponya, Martin Orkin, Barney Simon, Ian Steadman, and Clarke's Bookshop in Cape Town.
- *in the Caribbean*: Banyan, Ken Corsbie, Rawle Gibbons, Tony Hall, Beverly Hanson, Albert La Veau, Dani Lyndersay, Pauline Matthie, Judy Stone, Trinidad Theatre Workshop, and Earl Warner.

- *in the United States*: Rhonda Cobham-Sander, J. Ellen Gainor, Renu Juneja, and Elaine Savory (Fido).

We would not have been able to undertake our overseas research without the generous financial support of La Trobe University Faculty of Humanities, Monash University, the Australian Academy of Humanities, and the Australian Research Council. The librarians at La Trobe University and Monash University helped us gain access to numerous obscure texts. Julie Orlowski and Melissa Fisher were very helpful and resourceful with what seemed like constant computer problems and questions. Talia Rodgers at Routledge has been most helpful and supportive throughout the project. Without our research assistants we could not have completed this book: Susie Ezzy, Pauline Hopkins, Anna Johnston, Susan Luckman, Lisa Male, Simone Murray, and Heather Wearne have all worked on various stages of this project. Special thanks are due to Christy Collis for close editing and excellent investigative work. Any errors or omissions are, of course, ours, not theirs. Veronica Kelly and Alan Lawson provided editorial assistance, help with ideas, computers, references and referencing, as well as useful complementary texts. Thanks also to Joan Ward for encouragement and emotional support.

Thanks to the following for permission to publish photographs and diagrams: David George for the photograph of *The Tempest*; David Diamond, Headlines Theatre, Sherri-Lee Guilbert, and Hal B. Blackwater for the *No' Xya'* photograph; Ellis Bartkiewicz, Tarragon Theatre, Stephen Ouimette, Colin Fox, and Ed McNamara for the photograph of Sharon Pollock's *Generations*; the estate of Brian Brake and Hodder Moa Beckett Publishers for the photograph of Maurice Shadbolt's *Once on Chunuk Bair*; Victoria University Press and Michael Tubberty for the photograph of Stuart Hoar's *Squatter*; Jeff Busby for the photograph of Jimmy Chi and Kuckles' *Bran Nue Dae*; Kee Thuan Chye for the photograph of *1984 Here and Now*; and Currency Press, Geoffrey Lovell, and Michael Fuller for the photograph of Jack Davis's *The Dreamers*. Every effort has been made to acknowledge the photographs and diagrams in this book, but in several cases we have not discovered to whom credit is due. We would be happy to acknowledge anyone more fully in any subsequent edition/s of this book.

Our partners, Cameron Browne and Alan Lawson, deserve particular thanks for their long-suffering support and tolerance when others would have long since given up.

INTRODUCTION:
RE-ACTING (TO) EMPIRE

In 1907, *The Theatre*, a short-lived Sydney newspaper, reported on 'Seditious Drama' in the Philippines. It noted that the Filipinos, governed at that time by the United States, had 'turned their stage to a seditious purpose, though the authorities [had] not seen fit to censor it, except for the more daring of the dramas intended to stir up the native spirit' (1907: 17). As a common device to thwart American propaganda, the Filipinos used politicised costumes:

> [They are] so coloured and draped that at a given signal or cue the actors and actresses rush together, apparently without design, and stand swaying in the centre of the stage, close to the footlights, their combination forming a living, moving, stirring picture of the Filipino flag. Only an instant or so does the phantom last, but that one instant is enough to bring the entire house to its feet with yells and cries that are blood-curdling in their ferocious delight, while the less quick-witted Americans in the audience are wondering what the row is about.
>
> (ibid.: 17)

Such a display, understood in political terms by the Filipinos in the audience and *mis*understood by the Americans – the targets of the act of political resistance – provides an example of theatre's politicality in a post-colonial context in which performance functions as an anti-imperial tool. This book focuses on the methods by which post-colonial drama resists imperialism and its effects. We isolate possible ways to read and view theatre texts from around the post-colonial world as well as ways to interpret the strategies by which playwrights, actors, directors, musicians, and designers rework a historical moment or a character or an imperial text or even a theatre building.

1

POST-COLONIALISM

At a time when the prefix 'post' has been affixed to almost every concept, state of being, or theory (for instance, postmodernism, post-feminism, post-structuralism, post-industrialism), the hazards of using a term with such a prefix are great. While it risks being relegated to the increasingly less useful and less meaningful 'post-box' of trite expressions, 'post-colonial', we feel, is a relevant term, and certainly more relevant than its alternatives: the dated and homogenising Commonwealth Literature; New Literatures in English, very few of which are 'new'; and, as the Modern Languages Association terms them, Literatures other than British and American, a categorisation which perpetuates these litera-tures' already well-ingrained marginalisation from the countries who have historically declared themselves as constituting the metropolitan cultural centre or mainstream. Post-colonialism is often too narrowly defined. The term – according to a too-rigid etymology – is frequently misunderstood as a temporal concept meaning the time after colonisation has ceased, or the time following the politically determined Independence Day on which a country breaks away from its governance by another state. Not a naive teleological sequence which supersedes colonialism,[1] post-colonialism is, rather, an engagement with and contestation of colonialism's discourses, power structures, and social hierarchies. Colonisation is insidious: it invades far more than political chambers and extends well beyond independence celebrations. Its effects shape language, education, religion, artistic sensibilities, and, increasingly, popular culture. A theory of post-colonialism must, then, respond to more than the merely chronological construction of post-independence, and to more than just the discursive experience of imperialism. In Alan Lawson's words, post-colonialism is a 'politically motivated historical-analytical movement [which] engages with, resists, and seeks to dismantle the effects of colonialism in the material, historical, cultural-political, pedagogical, discursive, and textual domains' (1992: 156). Inevitably, post-colonialism addresses *reactions to* colonialism in a context that is not necessarily determined by temporal constraints: post-colonial plays, novels, verse, and films then become textual/cultural expressions of resistance to colonisation. As a critical discourse, therefore, post-colonialism is both a textual effect and a reading strategy. Its theoretical practice often operates

2

on two levels, attempting at once to elucidate the post-coloniality which inheres in certain texts, and to unveil and deconstruct any continuing colonialist power structures and institutions. While the time frames of both post-colonialism and post-modernism generally intersect, and postmodern literary devices are often found in post-colonial texts, the two cannot be equated. Part of postmodernism's brief is the dismantling of the often unwritten but frequently invoked rules of genre, authority, and value. Post-colonialism's agenda, however, is more specifically political: to dismantle the hegemonic boundaries and the determinants that create unequal relations of power based on binary oppositions such as 'us and them', 'first world and third world', 'white and black', 'coloniser and colonised'. Postmodern texts are certainly political, but post-colonial texts embrace a more specifically political aim: that of the continued destabilisation of the cultural and political authority of imperialism. Post-colonialism, then, has more affinity with feminist and class-based discourses than with postmodernism, even if post-colonialism and postmodernism employ similar literary tropes.

Within its specific agenda, post-colonialism's effects can be wide-ranging. Post-colonial literature is, according to Stephen Slemon, 'a form of cultural criticism and cultural critique: a mode of disidentifying whole societies from the sovereign codes of cultural organisation, and an inherently dialectical intervention in the hegemonic production of cultural meaning' (1987: 14). Post-colonial *theatre's* capacity to intervene publicly in social organisation and to critique political structures can be more extensive than the relatively isolated circumstances of written narrative and poetry; theatre practitioners, however, also run a greater risk of political intervention in their activities in the forms of censorship and imprisonment, to which Rendra in Indonesia, Ngũgĩ wa Thiong'o in Kenya, and countless South African dramatists can attest. While banning books is often an 'after the fact' action, the more public disruption of a live theatre presentation can literally 'catch' actors and playwrights in the act of political subversion.

Post-colonial studies are engaged in a two-part, often paradoxical project of chronicling similarities of experience while at the same time registering the formidable differences that mark each former colony. Laura Chrisman cautions that criticism of a nation's contemporary literature cannot be isolated from the imperial history which produced the contemporary version of the nation (1990: 38). Shiva Naipaul, a Trinidadian writer, puts it more succinctly: 'No literature is free-floating. Its vitality springs, initially, from its rootedness in a specific type of world' (1971: 122). Post-colonial criticism must carefully contextualise the *similarities* between, for example, the influence of ritual on the Ghanaian and Indian theatrical traditions, at the same time as it acknowledges significant *divergences* in the histories, cultures, languages, and politics of these two cultures. It is the particular attention to 'difference' that marks post-colonialism's agency. Alan Lawson and Chris Tiffin situate the politics and possibilities of difference in a useful construction:

> 'Difference', which in colonialist discourse connotes a remove from normative European practice, and hence functions as a marker of subordination, is for post-colonial analysis the correspondent marker of identity, voice, and hence empowerment. Difference is not the measure by which the European episteme fails to comprehend the actual self-naming and articulate subject. Moreover, difference demands deference and self-location . . . : not all differences are the same.
>
> (1994: 230)

A theory of post-colonialism that fails to recognise this distinction between 'differences' will recreate the spurious hierarchies, mis-readings, silencings, and ahistoricisms that are part of the imperial enterprise. Critiques of post-colonialism are frequently responses to arguments based primarily on attempts to homogenise texts, histories, and cultures.

Much discussion surrounds which countries ought to be considered part of the post-colonial world. Since former states of the Soviet Union have adopted the expression to refer to post-glasnost, 'post-colonialism' is not specific to a particular imperial regime, even though it often refers to the former colonies of the British Empire, the focus – with some exceptions – of this study. The British Empire was the largest modern empire, and its vestiges still exist today in a reconfigured organisation of former commonwealth states which oversees political alliances and trade discussions among the former colonies. Many of these former colonies now possess a linguistic heritage that is based on the English language. While English is not the only language of post-colonial writing[2] – in fact the incorporation of a variety of tongues

4

is vital to post-colonial literatures – it is the base language of most of the texts discussed here.

Debates within the field of post-colonialism are themselves fraught with division and difference, as the divergences between several recent critical texts illustrate. The most important theoretical treatment to date is *The Empire Writes Back: Theory and Practice in Post-Colonial Literatures* (1989) by Bill Ashcroft, Gareth Griffiths, and Helen Tiffin, which introduces many approaches to post-colonial literatures, concentrating particularly on language. This text was followed in 1995 by their *The Post-Colonial Studies Reader*. The post-colonial reader edited by Patrick Williams and Laura Chrisman, *Colonial Discourse and Post-Colonial Theory* (1993), is one of many readings of the field that questions the claim that various regions and/or constituencies have to the post-colonial umbrella.[3] Heavily privileging Edward Said's *Orientalism* and the construction of the Oriental 'other' as the core text/concept of the field, this reader discounts settler colonies where, among other locations, Said's Orientalism can be said to be inadequately historicised, or even inapplicable. Generally overlooking indigenous peoples from the settler-invader regions, this reader delimits the post-colonial world to an organisation that is curiously devoid of the controversy and paradox that is inevitable and constructive in the experience of post-imperial states. The essentialist[4] arguments that many critics have adopted concerning who may and may not participate in post-colonial discourse often amount to disagreements concerning power versus impotence, and particularly contests over who can claim a more impressive victim position; the irony in these disputes is that such struggles merely invert (unproductively) the hegemony upon which imperialism is based. It seems more reasonable and productive to capitalise on the differences between former colonies while not losing sight of their similarities.

Chris Tiffin and Alan Lawson argue that 'Imperial textuality appropriates, distorts, erases, but it also *contains*' (1994: 6). The imperial project contains cultures/subjects in order to control them, but no former colony is as simply circumscribed as colonial discourse would have it: each post-colonial political, historical, linguistic, and cultural situation inevitably becomes much more convoluted than is figured by the coloniser. Discussions of some of these intricacies have been drawn out, further complicated, and fruitfully enhanced by, among other theorists, Homi Bhabha, whose work elucidates the ambivalent psychological positioning of both the colonised *and* the coloniser. Contrary to the assumptions inherent in the binary opposition of coloniser and colonised, Bhabha (1984) maintains that the colonised is never *always impotent*; the coloniser is never *always powerful*. The ambivalence inherent in these binaries assists in breaking down the constructed limitations of all binary oppositions. In, for instance, the binary of 'white' and 'black', 'white' is not only defined in terms of 'blackness', but its reliance upon a conceptual knowledge of blackness also perpetually destabilises the power invested in 'white' and not in 'black'. Bhabha's work offers valuable assistance in dismantling binaries (and their correlative power structures) by recognising their inevitable ambivalences. As Ashcroft, Griffiths, and Tiffin point out, 'The term, "post-colonial" is resonant with all the ambiguity and complexity of the many different cultural experiences it implicates' (1995: 2).

There are at least two types of former colonies among the remains of the British Empire. The first, settler-invader colonies, are comprised of land masses that were, at the time of initial imperial explorations, proclaimed (usually with the full knowledge of the presence of indigenous people) to be empty, nearly empty, or peopled by compliant 'natives'.[5] As settlers invaded the territories, usually driving out the local inhabitants, massacring them, or pressing them into service, these colonies could conveniently forget about the presence of 'natives' altogether. The particular position that such settler-invader colonies (Australia, Canada, New Zealand/Aotearoa,[6] and in some cases, South Africa) occupy is extremely problematic: they neither quite satisfy the requirements for acceptance into the 'first' and 'old' world of Europe, nor are they 'poor' enough to be included in the economically and politically determined 'third world', a term that is still used on occasion to define the post-colonial world. The settler-invader colonies are located in an awkward 'second world' position (Lawson 1994) that is neither one nor the other; they have been colonised by Europe at the same time that they themselves have colonised indigenous peoples who experienced (and frequently continue to experience) the constraints on freedom, language, religion, and social organisation that also litter the histories of many of the second type of former colony, the 'occupation' colonies. These include India, parts of South-East Asia, west and central Africa, and many islands of the Caribbean.[7] The settler-invader colonies share many similar subject positions, and historical and geographical elisions with the 'occupation' colonies (which are often considered to be more *bona fide* post-colonial cultures than settler-invader societies). The depth to which imperial rhetoric has been established in both types of colonies complicates attempts to remove the constraints of subordination, inferiority, and insignificance that the colonised subject inevitably experiences.

POST-COLONIALISM AND DRAMA

This study considers plays from Australia, Canada, India, Ireland, New Zealand, various countries in Africa, parts of South-East Asia, and the Caribbean. Ireland, Britain's oldest colony, is often considered inappropriate to the post-colonial grouping, partly because it lies just off Europe. Yet Ireland's centuries-old political and economic oppression at the hands of the British – and its resistance to such control – fits well within the post-colonial paradigm. We do not consider the United States, also once a British colony, as post-colonial because the political and military might that the United States wields in its role as global 'super-power' has long since severed its connections with the historical and cultural marginality that the other former colonies share. American *neo-imperialism* and the neo-imperial activities of several former colonies are, however, not exempt from examination here. Neo-imperialism, which frequently takes the form of apparently mutually lucrative industrialisation projects, tourism, or aid programmes, typically repeats many of the same power games and struggles of initial imperial endeavours. For a very different reason, this text does not analyse Indian drama to any great detail. Since its history/practice is extremely complex, it is impossible to do justice to Indian drama in a broadly comparative study.[8] Moreover, the varieties of drama, dance, languages, and cultures that have influenced Indian theatre are too vast to consider in a text other than one devoted to just India. For the same reason, some sectors of Asia will not be considered as fully here as the drama from other parts of the former empire. Many of our arguments are nevertheless valid in these contexts and we hope that readers will find this an opportunity to test our theories, rather than to condemn this text for any perceived 'anomalies'.

When Europeans settled a colony, one of the earliest signs of established culture/'civilisation' was the presentation of European drama which, according to official records, obliterated for many years any indigenous performance forms:[9] in 1682, for instance, a playhouse was established in Jamaica and functioned until slaves were freed in 1838 (Wright 1937: 6). India boasted a proliferation of grand proscenium arch theatres from 1753, and five full-size public theatres by 1831, the popularity of which prompted the erection of many rival private theatres financed by rajahs (Mukherjee 1982: viii; Yajnik 1970: 86). Neither the Jamaican theatre nor the Indian theatres were designed for the indigenous peoples or transported slaves; rather, they were built for the entertainment of the British officers. The first play staged in Canada was Marc Lescarbot's 1606 *Théâtre Neptune en la Nouvelle France*, presented by French explorers. It included words in various native Canadian languages, as well as references to Canadian geography, within a more typically French style of play (Goldie 1989: 186). The nature of theatre designed for colonial officers and/or troops (and the nature of colonialism itself) required that the plays produced in these countries be reproductions of imperial models in style, theme, and content. Various elements of 'local colour' were of course included, so that an early settler play might position a native character in the same way that the nineteenth-century British theatre figured the drunken Irishman: as an outsider, someone who was in some central way ridiculous or intolerable. While it may have appeared that the deviations from the imperial plots were generally isolated to issues of setting and occasional minor characters, sometimes the plays produced in the colonies transformed mere 'local colour' into much more resistant discourses. In the case of Australia, the performance of the first western play in 1789, George Farquhar's *The Recruiting Officer*, provided an early opportunity for political resistance. The cast, composed of transported convicts, used the play's burlesque trial and military theme as an apt expression of life in a colony that was itself predicated on punishment, and they also wrote a new epilogue to Farquhar's play, calling attention to their plight. Colonial theatre, then, can be viewed ambivalently as a potential agent of social reform and as an avenue for political disobedience.

Even though Ola Rotimi, a Nigerian playwright, maintains that drama is the best artistic medium for Africa because it is not alien in form, as is the novel (1985: 12), most post-colonial criticism overlooks drama, perhaps because of its apparently impure form: playscripts are only a part of a theatre experience, and performance is therefore difficult to document.[10] Given that dramatic and performance theories, particularly those developed in conjunction with Brechtian, feminist, and cultural studies criticism, have much to offer post-colonial debates about language, interpellation, subject-formation, representation, and forms of resistance, this marginalisation of drama suggests a considerable gap in post-colonial studies. Examining drama through the conceptual frameworks developed in post-colonial studies involves more than a simple and unproblematic transposition of reading strategies because some of the signifying systems through which plays 'mean' are vastly different to those of texts not designed for performance. Hence, although this study seeks to demonstrate how its subject area might be illuminated by the chosen theoretical approach, it also aims to extend the current limits of that approach. In this respect, theories of drama and performance have much to add to debates about how imperial power is articulated and/or contested.

Our field of inquiry falls into three main sections that address post-colonial performance: dramatic language (vocal and visual, as expressed through the performing body), the arrangement of theatrical space and time, and the manipulation of narrative and performative conventions of drama. Within this field, we inevitably focus on the connections between form and content which a politicised approach to theatre always recognises.

INTERCULTURALISM AND ANTHROPOLOGICAL APPROACHES TO THEATRE

The drama from the 'outposts of empire' has not been entirely ignored by critics from the centres of Europe and the United States: theatre anthropologists and interculturalists have examined the theatre forms and styles of other cultures and often embraced the possibilities inherent in adopting them for use in a western context. Yet an anthropological approach to drama (such as that espoused by Victor Turner, Eugenio Barba, and Richard Schechner) is designed to enumerate the similarities between all cultures without recognising their highly significant differences. In this style of analysis, several plays and/or theatre cultures are usually compared in order to highlight the likenesses in various rituals or practices, which Anuradha Kapur deems a result of postmodernism:

> In mounting an attack on mimesis, postmodernism claims as its territory non-mimetic forms from all over the world. Thus theatre from the 'Third World' comes to be defined by

the needs and uses of postmodernism; forms from different
cultural contexts become evacuated of subject matter and
are seen as a series of formal options.

(1990: 27)

Interculturalism and postmodernism intersect at the point of
ahistorical, acultural synthesis that can also be perceived to be
neo-colonial, particularly as practised in the United States. An
example from Gautam Dasgupta, a critic located in New York, is
revealing: writing of interculturalism, he invokes the ethos of the
Indian *Vedas* and the refrain from a recent American pop song.
Arguing that interculturalism recognises personal as well as public
spheres of influence, he concludes without obvious irony that
'We are the world' (1991a: 332). This imperialist notion that the
United States *is* the world emanates from an insidious pop song
that, while ostensibly raising money for starving people in Africa,
reinscribes western (particularly American) privilege/power, by
stressing the west's capacity to do good works. This type of intercultural approach is obviously self-centred: it often involves the
parasitical activity of taking that which seems useful and unique
from another culture and leaving that host culture with little
except the dubious opportunity to *seem to have been* associated with
a powerful and influential nation(s). Not all intercultural theorists
are ethnocentric: Rustom Bharucha (1993) and others are acutely
aware of the political ramifications of failing to acknowledge
a country's historical, political, and cultural specificity. Bharucha
attacks critics and practitioners such as Schechner, Barba, and
Peter Brook for mining 'exotic' – usually 'third world' – cultures
for theatrical raw materials, much in the way that multinational
corporations have been known to exploit materials and cheap
labour from the developing world, conveniently overlooking the
safety and security of the local people and the pollution of their
land. As well as ignoring the differences among and between
peoples who have been colonised, the anthropological approach
to theatre also moves perilously close to universalist criticism
whereby a text is said to speak to readers all around the world
because it espouses, for example, universal principles of life. Texts
which apparently radiate such 'universal truths' have usually been
removed from their social and historical setting. Although it is a
favourite catch-cry of theatre critics, the 'universal theme' allows
no appreciation of cultural difference.

10

MARKERS OF POST-COLONIAL DRAMA

The apparent unity of the British Empire (iconised by such devices as the vast pink surfaces on many classroom maps indicating the dominion of the Queen of England) has been substantially denied by post-colonial texts. Often, post-colonial literatures refuse closure to stress the provisionality of post-colonial identities, reinforcing Helen Tiffin's comment that 'Decolonization is process, not arrival' (1987a: 17). The absence of a 'conclusion' to the decolonising project does not represent a failure; rather it points to the recombinant ways in which colonised subjects now define themselves. Situated within the hybrid forms of various cultural systems, such subjects can usefully exploit what Diana Brydon calls 'contamination' (1990), whereby the influence from several cultures can be figured as positive rather than negative, as for instance, is miscegenation.

For the purposes of this study, we define post-colonial performance as including the following features:

- acts that respond to the experience of imperialism, whether directly or indirectly;
- acts performed for the continuation and/or regeneration of the colonised (and sometimes pre-contact) communities;
- acts performed with the awareness of, and sometimes the incorporation of, post-contact forms; and
- acts that interrogate the hegemony that underlies imperial representation.[11]

Building on existing work done in the separate fields of post-colonial and performance studies, this book develops specific post-colonial performative and theoretical frameworks in relation to selected plays from a range of countries. It does not attempt to categorise texts, regions, types of plays, historical approaches to drama; to identify the major playwrights of different countries; or to discuss national theatre traditions separately, country by country.[12] Readers should be able to use the frameworks we establish as reading strategies for interpreting a range of post-colonial playtexts, and for deconstructing imperialist thought, practices, and regimes. One of the aims of this book is to teach readers and audiences to re-see or re-read texts in order to recognise their strategic political agendas, since, as Ian Steadman notes in the context of South African theatre, 'the real potential

11

of dramatic art lies in its ability to teach people *how* to think' widely (1991: 78), beyond the narrow parameters of the status quo, of political oppressiveness, and even of political correctness. To this end, we are particularly concerned with the intersection of dramatic theory with theories of race in post-colonial contexts; in the varieties of feminisms, including many forms of third world feminism through which the gendered body can be described; in the body, the voice, and the stage space as sites of resistance to imperial hegemonies; and in the deployment of theatricalised cultural practices such as ritual and carnival to subvert imposed canonical traditions. Accordingly, Chapter 1 outlines a process of canonical counter-discourse through which imperial/classical texts are no longer automatically privileged at the expense of other discourses. Chapter 2 contextualises ritual and carnival, two forms that intersect with and reconfigure drama in decidedly non-western ways. How history and language are articulated in post-colonial drama and how they reshape theatrical texts are the focus of Chapters 3 and 4. Historical recuperation is one of the crucial aims and effects of many post-colonial plays, which frequently tell the other side of the conquering whites' story in order to contest the official version of history that is preserved in imperialist texts. Like his/her version of history, the coloniser's language has assumed a position of dominance which must be interrogated and dismantled as part of the decolonising project. Theatrical manipulations of the English language can significantly amplify the political effects of a play, since, according to Bill Ashcroft, post-colonial adaptations of English have managed to 'relocate the "centre" of the English language by *decentring* it' (1987: 117). Other modes of communicating, such as song and music, also destabilise the political position of spoken English as the dominant transmitter of meaning. The body in its various colonial and post-colonial contexts is explored in Chapter 5, which pays particular heed to the ways in which theatre can recuperate the disintegrated and dissociated body characteristic of colonialism. Finally, Chapter 6 surveys contemporary manifestations of neo-imperialism, with a particular focus on the effects of tourism and the globalisation of the media.

The colonised subject exists in a complex representational matrix, variously situated between opposing forces (in the settler-invader cultures) or figured in opposition to the imperial powers (in occupation cultures as well as in indigenous cultures within

12

settler-invader countries). Theatre's three-dimensional live context further complicates representations of the colonised subject so that interpreting post-colonial drama requires a careful analysis of multiple sign systems. This text takes up such issues to provide ways of re-acting to the imperial hegemonies that continue to be manifest throughout the world.

NOTES

1 Our distinction between 'colonialism' and 'imperialism' follows the definitions Edward Said has delineated in *Culture and Imperialism*: '"imperialism" means the practice, the theory, and the attitudes of a dominating metropolitan centre ruling a distant territory; "colonialism", which is almost always a consequence of imperialism, is the implanting of settlements on distant territory' (1994: 8). While both imperialism and colonialism can also take place on local territory (witness Ireland in the British Empire), these terms are generally useful. Imperialism, then, is the larger enterprise, but colonialism can be more insidious.

2 The former colonies of Spain, France, and Portugal, to name just a few, exercise similar resistant strategies to imperial forces, using hybrid forms of the dominant, colonising languages.

3 See also Hodge and Mishra (1991).

4 'Essentialism', when combined with Spivak's modifying adjective, 'strategic' (1988: 205), becomes a tool by which marginalised peoples can deliberately foreground constructed difference to claim a speaking position. Otherwise, essentialism problematically appeals to absolute difference without an awareness of 'similarity' in the broader historical and cultural paradigm.

5 This term must be clarified. While all people born in a particular place are 'natives' of that country, we use 'native' to refer more specifically to the indigenous inhabitants of the settler-invader colonies, those people who were already living in a particular location when the Europeans arrived. 'Indian', the historical name for indigenous North Americans, is a misnomer instituted by Christopher Columbus who thought, on seeing their skin colour, that he had indeed found the easier route to India that he was seeking. This term has been fortified by Hollywood-type representations of indigenous peoples in 'Cowboy and Indian' movies. 'First Nations' is a term adopted by Canada's indigenous people in a politically astute move that reminds other North Americans that the land was already occupied when Europeans claimed it. More recently, 'Aboriginal Canadians' has been used to underscore that chronology: the term 'aboriginal' means 'from the beginning'. In contrast to the Aborigines of Australia, Aboriginal Canadians have chosen this name themselves rather than having had it given to them by white invaders. In the North American context, we use 'Indian' in the same way that Daniel Francis uses it in *The Imaginary*

Indian (1992): to signify white *representations* of natives. We use 'native' or 'First Nations' or 'indigenous peoples' to represent the people themselves.

6 New Zealand is frequently also recognised by its Maori name, 'Aotearoa', meaning 'the land of the long white cloud'.

7 The Caribbean region is a special case, comprised of islands/territories which have been at once both settler and occupation colonies. After imperial campaigns largely annihilated indigenous inhabitants of the area, the European colonists repopulated many islands with slave and indentured labour from Africa, India, and other places. Most of these colonies were then governed from afar until the latter half of the twentieth century, setting up different relationships than with other settler societies. We use the term 'West Indies' to indicate the English-speaking (ex)colonies of the area, while 'Caribbean' refers to the wider cultural/geographical region.

8 Indian theatre history dates back to the *Natyashastra*, the ancient Sanskrit theory of drama, which was written down by Bharata approximately fifteen hundred years ago. Bharata did not know how long the *Natyashastra* had already existed as an oral text before he transcribed it (Rangacharya 1971: 2). It is also very difficult to study Indian theatre texts since few are published in English.

9 In all probability, they were still happening underground.

10 Our definition of drama and our theoretical discussions also incorporate other performance events (such as dance) even though most of the texts we examine are 'plays'.

11 In order to schematise our study, this generalised definition is inevitable. There are undoubtedly many examples of post-colonial performance which exceed the parameters outlined and we encourage readers to pursue such works.

12 While we attempt to ground our analyses of plays in their (different) historical contexts, it is not always possible for a variety of reasons. Particular texts and their production histories can be explored independently through reviews, articles, interviews, and books focused on individual playwrights and/or specific national theatres.

1

RE-CITING THE CLASSICS: CANONICAL COUNTER-DISCOURSE

CONSTANCE: Have you known God to be called Shakespeare?
DESDEMONA: Shake
            Spear? He might be a pagan god of war.
                                    (Ann-Marie MacDonald,
            Goodnight Desdemona (Good Morning Juliet) (1990: 36))

COUNTER-DISCOURSE AND THE CANON

For generations during (and often after) imperial rule, the formal education of colonial subjects was circumscribed by the concerns and canons of a distant European centre. Because of its supposed humanistic functions, 'English Literature' occupied a privileged position in the colonial classroom, where its study was designed to 'civilise' native students by inculcating in them British tastes and values, regardless of the exigencies of the local context.[1] Accordingly, William Wordsworth's poem, 'I Wandered Lonely as a Cloud', was taught to uncomprehending West Indians, Kenyans, and Indians who had never seen a daffodil. George Ryga takes up this particular example in *The Ecstasy of Rita Joe* (1967)[2] when the native Canadian girl, Rita Joe, cannot remember the poetry from her teacher's syllabus. The lines the teacher quotes and expects to hear in echo blur into meaninglessness as the poetry and social studies lessons intermingle when Rita Joe perceives the teacher to order, 'Say after me! "I wandered lonely as a cloud, that floats on high o'er vales and hills . . . when all at once I saw a crowd . . . a melting pot"' (1971: 90). This outdated and ethnocentric model of literary education was abolished several decades ago in most former colonies around the world where educational systems now strive to reflect local histories and cultures. The hegemony of the

15

imperial canon is, nevertheless, still in evidence in many post-colonial societies, as manifest not only in the choice of curricula material and the relative worth assigned to European texts but also through the ways in which such texts are taught – usually without serious consideration of their ideological biases.

Given the legacy of a colonialist education which perpetuates, through literature, very specific socio-cultural values in the guise of universal truth, it is not surprising that a prominent endeavour among colonised writers/artists has been to rework the European 'classics' in order to invest them with more local relevance and to divest them of their assumed authority/authenticity. Helen Tiffin terms this project 'canonical counter-discourse' (1987a: 22), a process whereby the post-colonial writer unveils and dismantles the basic assumptions of a specific canonical text by developing a 'counter' text that preserves many of the identifying signifiers of the original while altering, often allegorically, its structures of power. The staging of the 'intact' canonical play offers one kind of counter-discourse which might, through a revisionist perform-ance, articulate tensions between the Anglo script and its localised enunciation. Rewriting the characters, the narrative, the context, and/or the genre of the canonical script provides another means of interrogating the cultural legacy of imperialism and offers renewed opportunities for performative intervention. These are not, however, strategies of replacement: there is no attempt to merely substitute a canonical text with its oppositional reworking. Counter-discourse seeks to deconstruct significations of authority and power exercised in the canonical text, to release its strangle-hold on representation and, by implication, to intervene in social conditioning. This chapter addresses various forms of canonical counter-discourse in post-colonial theatre and outlines the ways in which performance itself can be counter-discursive.

Not all texts that refer to canonical models are counter-discursive. Intertextuality – where one text makes explicit or implicit reference to other texts or textual systems – does not necessarily entail a *re*writing project. While all counter-discourse is intertextual, not all intertextuality is counter-discursive. By definition, counter-discourse actively works to destabilise the power structures of the originary text rather than simply to acknowledge its influence. Such discourse tends to target imposed canonical traditions rather than pre-existing master narratives which 'belong' to the colonised culture. Hence, when Vijay Mishra comments that 'we may indeed claim that all Indian literary, filmic and theatrical texts endlessly rewrite *The Mahabharata* (1991: 195), he is using 'rewriting' less as a marker of counter-discourse than of intertextuality: all other narratives in India have as context and influence *The Mahabharata* but the master text itself is not particularly targeted for strategic reform. A specific example of this kind of rewriting occurs in Stella Kon's *The Bridge* (1980) which is self-consciously shaped by another influential Indian epic, *The Ramayana*. Kon's Singaporean drama, with its additional intertextual references to Peter Weiss's *Marat/Sade*, uses *The Ramayana* as a play-within-a-play for the patients of a Help Service Centre who are trying to overcome drug dependence. Kon maintains the traditional (pre-contact) structures of the epic, dramatising it as part of the contemporary play so that the two levels of narrative can comment on each other. Excerpts from *The Ramayana*, in which Rama searches for the kidnapped Sita who has been captured by a demon, are performed in full traditional costume and music, as Rama '*mimes hunting, with stylised dance movements*' (1981: 7) while the Cantor sings the story for the boys who watch on stage; the audience, meanwhile, watches both sets of action. As the boys succeed in beating their drug habits, they are allowed to participate in the building of a human bridge that will enable Rama to cross the sea to rescue Sita. Thus *The Bridge*'s use of *The Ramayana* facilitates a greater (contemporary) understanding of the epic and elicits its continued relevance to the society as a dramatic archive and a point of cultural reference. The play holds up to question not only the western preference for naturalism as the dominant theatrical mode but also the hegemony of positivist approaches to rehabilitation and social control. The post-coloniality of *The Bridge* and many other works that employ *The Ramayana* or *The Mahabharata* rests not on a rewriting of the originary narrative but on the juxtaposition of a local 'classic' to its imperial counterpart, a tactic that avoids the reifying inscription of European texts and their performance conventions. While this demonstrates the need to differentiate between the influence of imposed and inherited canons, it is also important to recognise that some traditional narratives simultaneously work in ways that uphold the imperial agenda because of class, caste, race, and/or gender bias.

Some plays simply contemporise classical texts and therefore fail to fit the definition of canonical counter-discourse. Two examples of contemporary versions of Euripides' *The Bacchae* include *Mr.*

O'Dwyer's Dancing Party (1968) by the New Zealand poet and playwright, James K. Baxter, and *A Refined Look at Existence* (1966) by the Australian, Rodney Milgate. Both these plays localise the temporal and spatial setting of Euripides' drama, but their updating of the plot overshadows any attempt to decentre imperial hegemonies; rather, these two texts merely make the British Empire more accessible to the former colonies in the twentieth century. Although Milgate casts Pentheus as an Aborigine, he misses a significant opportunity to use him to centralise the issue of race relations in Australian society of the 1960s. Instead, the portrayal of 'Penthouse', the Aboriginal Pentheus, becomes racist, and 'Donny's' (Dionysus') attempts to seek revenge on his family reveal a protagonist even more self-absorbed than Euripides' original. Similarly, Baxter's play, which focuses on boredom in a number of 1960s marriages in Remuera, New Zealand, is not a strategic post-colonial reworking of a canonical text but merely a somewhat misogynist updating. As contemporary versions of a Greek play with Australian and New Zealand reference points, *A Refined Look at Existence* and *Mr. O'Dwyer's Dancing Party* are only moderately successful, and certainly dated.

Those plays which do articulate oppositional reworkings of the European canon almost always incorporate performative elements as part of their anti-imperial arsenal. As a genre, drama is particularly suited to counter-discursive intervention *and* equally useful for its expression, since performance itself replays an originary moment. In other words, the rehearsal/production of a play is a continued reacting – which may or may not be interventionary – of and to an originary script. Thus counter-discourse is always possible in the theatrical presentation of a canonical text, and even expected in some cases: for instance, it is rare to see a contemporary production of William Shakespeare's *The Tempest* that does not refigure Caliban in ways which demonstrate how the racial paradigms characteristic of Renaissance thought are no longer acceptable to most late twentieth-century audiences, especially in non-western societies. The numerous layers of meaning and coded information that a performance communicates (information which cannot be expressed in the same way by fiction or poetry) are each themselves, singly or combined with others, capable of acting counter-discursively. Among these semiotic codes are costume, set design, theatre design (or the design of the space co-opted as a theatre), lighting, music, choreography, verbal and gestural languages (including accent and inflection), casting choices, and a number of extra-textual factors such as historical contexts, how the stars are billed, and the economics of ticket prices.[3] Hence the staging of a scene, for example, or the costuming of a character can immediately provide additional layers of signification that call the assumptions of the canonical text into question, whether by subverting its usual codes, as in parody, or by appropriating those representational signs normally reserved for the dominant group/ culture. Even in the face of fixed dialogue and/or plot closure, manipulation of a play's performative codes and contexts can productively shift the power structures that seem predetermined in the originary script.

SHAKESPEARE'S LEGACY

Among the many post-colonial reworkings of canonical texts, Shakespeare's plays figure prominently as targets of counter-discourse. The circulation of 'Shakespeare's Books' within educational and cultural spheres has been a powerful hegemonic force through-out the history of the British Empire,[4] and is one which continues to operate in virtually all former colonies of England. In India, Canada, Australia, South Africa, New Zealand, and the West Indies, Shakespeare was for generations the most popular playwright, indeed the only playwright deemed worthy of attention. The Shakespeare 'industry' – as it impacts on the educational systems, the critical discourses, and the theatrical culture of a society – often operates in ways that sustain ideas, values, and even epistemologies which are foreign to the receivers and therefore of limited rel-evance, except in maintaining the interests of imperialism. As Jyotsna Singh has argued in reference to India, 'Shakespeare kept alive the myth of English cultural refinement and superiority – a myth that was crucial to the rulers's [*sic*] political interests' (1989: 446).[5] Martin Orkin points to a similar situation in South Africa:

> Students have been and still are taught Shakespeare and examined on him in ways that entail the assumption of an idealised past; the focus is upon character and interiority, obsession with the 'timeless' and the transcendental, all of which, it may be argued, encourage in students a particular view of the subject and attitudes of withdrawal and sub-mission to existing hierarchies.
>
> (1991: 240)

Shakespeare, then, becomes complicit in justifying apartheid. Not just a symptom of imperialism in South Africa, such approaches to 'The Bard' – whose nickname attests to his function as a cultural shibboleth – have been endemic everywhere that the Shakespeare myth has taken hold, affecting the critical examination of the man, the plays, and the performances.

Not surprisingly, the ideological weight of Shakespeare's legacy is nowhere felt more strongly than in the theatre, where his work is still widely seen as the measure of all dramatic art, the ultimate test for the would-be actor or director, the mark of audience sophistication, and the uncontested sign of 'Culture' itself. Within this regulatory system, the meaning of any particular Shakespearian play tends to be fixed so that non-canonical productions are even today criticised for not being true to 'authorial intent'. In 1992, for example, the Australian-based Bell Shakespeare Company lost school bookings after receiving several negative reviews for its frank portrayal of homosexuality in *The Merchant of Venice*. The homophobia expressed by such responses is only part of the discomfort with a production judged, apparently, to misread Shakespeare. The tendency to deem Shakespeare's worth 'self-evident' and his application 'universal' not only naturalises a particular Eurocentric (and patriarchal) world view but also paralyses the development of local theatrical traditions. The Australian critic, Penny Gay, alludes to this problem when she asks the rhetorical question: 'How can one aspire to write plays when Shakespeare has already, incontrovertibly, written the greatest dramas in the English language?' (1992: 204). For the post-colonial dramatist/critic, this is a politically charged question because the 'univocal and monolithic significance' of Shakespeare (Campbell 1993: 2) perpetuates notions of a theatre which is always already constituted within imperial epistemology, and thus closed to other(ed) knowledges. Decolonising that theatre must involve the reopening of such closures and the dismantling of Shakespeare as a transcendental signifier for theatre practice and criticism alike.

The proliferation of the Shakespeare industry has had a major impact not only on the theatrical repertoires of colonised countries but also on approaches to acting, directing, and other aspects of performance. In theatre training, as in the colonial education system, pupils were until recently invariably exhorted to master 'The Master' in order to prove their talents.[6] This practice had significant implications for the (re)formation of the voice, stance, expressions, and gestures of the non-Anglo actor, especially in societies with strong indigenous performance cultures. As Tiffin argues in reference to school and public eisteddfod recitations, performative reproductions of the English script functioned to discipline the body of the colonial subject while suppressing signifiers of alterity:

> The 'local' body was erased not just by script and perform-
> ance, but by the necessary assumption on the part of both
> audience and performer that speakers and listeners were
> themselves 'English'. Recitation performance is thus itself
> metonymic of the wider processes of colonialist interpella-
> tion, in the reproduction, at the colonial site, of the locally
> embodied yet paradoxically disembodied imperial 'voice', in
> a classic act of obedience.
>
> (1993a: 914)

As our reference to Ryga's *Rita Joe* has already demonstrated, however, recitation also implies a gap between the canonical text and its distant reproduction. While this gap often becomes a site of subversion in performative counter-discourse, historically it has served to make the shortcomings of colonial theatre acutely visible. In particular, the use of Shakespeare as the gold standard of dramatic art was instrumental in constructing the inferiority of the non-European actor since his/her rendition of the Shakespearian text could never be 'authentic'. As Homi Bhabha observes, 'to be Anglicized is *emphatically* not to be English' (1984: 128).

This shaping of the theatre practices of colonised countries according to an imposed foreign standard can be seen as one manifestation of what Gayatri Spivak has termed the 'epistemic violence' of imperialism: its attack on other cultures' ways of knowing and representing themselves (1985: 251). In attempting to redress the situation, post-colonial performance texts often violate the canon, setting up an agonistic encounter between local and received traditions. A case in point is the theatre of Utpal Dutt, the noted Bengali actor, director, and playwright who revolutionised theatrical approaches to Shakespeare in India during the 1950s. In an attempt to undermine both the elitism and the Anglocentrism associated with the Shakespearian theatre of the time, Dutt took translations of such plays as *Macbeth* to the rural masses, dispensing with the conventions of the proscenium stage and infusing his productions with the ritual traditions of *jatra*, the folk theatre of Bengal (see Bharucha 1983: 61–3). By using Shakespearian texts in this manner, Dutt's work presented a way not only of indigenising the imperial canon but also of disrupting its cultural clout.

A more pointed violation of canonical authority occurs in the Apotheosis scene of Derek Walcott's *Dream on Monkey Mountain* (1967) where Shakespeare, along with other chief promulgators of white western culture, is tried and hanged for crimes against humanity. Despite the vehemence of this particular attack, however, Walcott is not suggesting that colonised cultures should never perform canonical texts. As he argues in his essay, 'Meanings', post-colonial performance praxis requires a fusion of influences to form a distinctive theatrical style which does not privilege the Eurocentric model – in his case, 'a theatre where someone can do Shakespeare or sing Calypso with equal conviction' (1973: 306). Walcott's later play, *A Branch of the Blue Nile* (1983), which dramatises efforts to forge such a theatre in Trinidad, stages performers who are acutely aware of how they have been positioned by Shakespeare's pervasive influence over dramatic representation. In preparing for a production of *Antony and Cleopatra*, Sheila, who is to play Cleopatra, feels unequal to the part because her skin is too dark to pass as Mediterranean. The 'ambitious black woman', she learns, has no place on Shakespeare's stage, or at least not in the role of his great queen: 'Caroni isn't a branch of the river Nile, and Trinidad isn't Egypt, except at Carnival, so the world sniggers when I speak her lines' (1986: 285). Although the relationship between Sheila and Chris (who plays Antony) develops in ways which rework the story of Shakespeare's famous lovers, the real counter-discursivity of *A Branch of the Blue Nile* lies in its questioning of received performance conventions, a project enhanced by the use of multiple metatheatrical frameworks and an ongoing dialogue about the function of theatre in the society. Among the other group members, Gavin articulates most clearly the dilemma of the colonial actor who must validate his craft by mastering Shakespeare in a major metropolitan centre: 'I went up there [New York] to be an actor and found out that I was a nigger, so I could have spared myself the airfare' (ibid.: 249). As he has learnt only too well, the universality of theatre is a myth; its governing force is 'economics, and economics means race' (ibid.: 224). Eventually, the text fulfils Walcott's formula for an indigenous theatre when the actors (with Marilyn having taken over Sheila's role) present a comic new 'dialectical' version of *Antony and Cleopatra* by hybrid-ising Shakespearian forms with local ones:

> MARILYN/CLEOPATRA: 'Hast thou the pretty worm of Nilus
> there,
>   That kills and pains not?'
> GAVIN/CLOWN: 'Madam, I have him, but 'tain't go be me
> who go ask you handle him, because one nip from this
> small fellow and basil is your husband; the little person will
> make the marriage, in poison and in person, but the
> brides who go to that bed don't ever get up.'
>
> (ibid.: 262)

This dialogue not only questions the presumed immortality of The Bard's famous heroine but also goes some way towards the larger task of dismantling what the Indian critic, Leela Gandhi, has termed 'the imperishability of Shakespeare's empire' (1993: 81).

Walcott's interest in metatheatre as a way of examining the problems involved in developing a performance aesthetic specific to the needs of the local culture is common to other post-colonial reworkings of Shakespeare, and to much of the wider body of drama under discussion in this book. Metatheatre[7] reminds us that any performance stages the necessary provisionality of represen-tation. Although often playfully postmodern as well as strategic, it should not be seen as simply part of the postmodern intertextual experiment. By developing multiple self-reflexive discourses through role playing, role doubling/splitting, plays within plays, interventionary frameworks, and other metatheatrical devices, post-colonial works interrogate received models of theatre at the same time as they illustrate, quite self-consciously, that they are acting out their own histories/identities in a complex replay that can never be finished or final. In all this, the question of how Shakespeare might be fully appropriated remains disturbingly relevant. Louis Nowra's *The Golden Age* (1985) demonstrates how this may be possible by stressing Australian populist over classical interpretations of the theatrical canon. This text incorporates many metatheatrical moments, among them an inset play performed by the 'lost' tribe of forest people descended from ex-convicts, gold miners, and an actor. When found by Francis and Peter in the wilds of Tasmania, the tribe presents to their guests a play that is not Shakespeare's *King Lear* but Nahum Tate's folk version of the story, the 'happy' *Lear*, enacted in précis and further bastardised through pastiche and parody. The conversion from tragedy to comedy effects one level of translation in the actors' presentation of the play while their energetic and even histrionic performance implements another. The tribe's improvisation is a direct contrast to the somewhat static recitation which opens the play: a scene from Euripides' *Iphigenia in Tauris* set in a crumbling Greek temple that is located in the palatial gardens of colonial Hobart and built by convict labour. Elizabeth Archer complains that 'It took the Parthenon two thousand years to crumble; it took our temple less than a hundred' (Nowra 1989: 33). The play suggests that the veneration of an unadapted classical Greek culture is alien to Australia, which must derive new forms and models that depict an Australian way of life, not a transplanted European experience. Taken together, the performances of Tate's *Lear* and the Greek play emphasise the epistemic split between a regulated classical society and its colonial offshoot. As Nowra demonstrates, a successfully indigenised canon can be made to speak the experiences of the colonised subject rather than those of the imperialist. This text, like many post-colonial counter-discursive plays, uses selected portions of master narratives, instead of concentrating on one rewriting project.

Murray Carlin's *Not Now, Sweet Desdemona* (1968) also addresses the question of how to replay the Shakespearian text. His canonical target, *Othello*, is an obvious focus for counter-discursive interpretations because it centralises racial issues, presenting miscegenation as not just a metaphorical threat to the white society but as an actualised event. By using the rehearsal of *Othello* to frame its narrative, this metatheatrical play explores the ways in which two actors, a white woman from South Africa and a black West Indian man, come to terms with playing their roles, a task complicated by the fact that the two are lovers outside the context of the play. Their exploration of race in Shakespeare's play is circumscribed by the political and social implications of apartheid – particularly of the Immorality Act which prohibited sexual acts between even consenting adults of different racial categories – their responses to it, and their responses to each other. 'Othello's' reading of the play as inherently about race conflicts with 'Desdemona's' assumption that it dramatises love and marriage. The South African Desdemona must acknowledge that within a system hierarchised along racial categories, the power of the white woman outweighs virtually all of Othello's military authority. This realisation forces the actors to rehearse a much less conventional *Othello*, and perhaps more crucially, to re-evaluate their own relationship in the context of this power dynamic. Carlin's temporal and political relocation of *Othello* thus writes a play which takes on the history of racism that Shakespeare's text helped to institutionalise, and then reproblematises it in the contemporary situation of apartheid. In this respect, *Not Now, Sweet Desdemona* stages a deliberately political act designed to destabilise both the imperial power of the invoked canonical tradition and the currency of its associated discourses.

REPLAYING *THE TEMPEST*

The Tempest remains the text most widely chosen for counter-discursive interrogations of the Shakespearian canon. A number of factors account for this choice: the play's figuration of racial binaries and the threat of miscegenation; its representation of the New World 'other' as opposed to the European 'self', troped as a form of the nature/culture dichotomy; and its pervasive interest in power relationships involving dominance, subservience, and rebellion (see Brydon 1984). Interpreted as a fable of the colonial experience, *The Tempest* offers, in the movements of resistance to Prospero's power, several sites for potential intervention in the imperial process through politicised readings and reworkings of the text. The originary site of this potential resistance to imperialism can be found in the text of *The Tempest* itself which, as Paul Brown points out, can be reread as 'not simply a reflection of colonialist practices but an intervention in an ambivalent and even contradictory discourse' (1985: 48). Applying Bhabha's theories of the colonial stereotype, Brown argues that Prospero's narrative, which seeks to legitimise *a posteriori* his usurpation of the island, is continually destabilised by its necessary production of Caliban as the 'other' who must be mastered in the name of civility:

> Colonialist discourse voices a demand for order and disorder, producing a disruptive other in order to assert the superiority of the coloniser. Yet that production is itself evidence of a struggle to restrict the other's disruptiveness to that role. Colonialist discourse does not simply announce a triumph for civility, it must continually produce it and this work involves struggle and risk.
>
> (ibid.: 58)

Hence, in its interpellation of Caliban as a colonial subject, Prospero's discourse opens up the possibility of insurrection and the dispersal of his own power.

Long before revisionist criticism intervened in interpretative responses to *The Tempest*, productions of the text had demonstrated, albeit sometimes tentatively, that performance plays a powerful role in the counter-discursive project. In his extensive survey of the play's stage history, Trevor Griffiths cites, for example, a nineteenth-century burlesque called *The Enchanted Isle* (1848) which featured Caliban as an anti-slavery campaigner, and an 1838 production in which he was portrayed with sufficient empathy to prompt one reviewer to declare that Prospero was partly to blame for his slave's behaviour (1983: 160–1). Contemporary productions of *The Tempest* which give serious consideration to its colonial themes stress this challenge to Prospero's authority, a threat also inherent in his relationships with many other characters in the play. In the so-called New World, Caliban has frequently become the quintessential figure of resistance in a local struggle for political and cultural decolonisation, while even in the imperial centre, some emphasis on colonialism has been expected since Jonathan Miller's influential London revival of the play in 1970. Miller cast black actors as Caliban and Ariel to represent examples of differing native responses to European invasion,[8] and, even more radically, incorporated all of the other characters into his revisionary interpretation by transforming the Miranda/Ferdinand/Prospero relationship and Caliban/Stephano/Trinculo scenes into yet further expression of the main theme of colonialism.

Skylight Theatre's 1989 production of *The Tempest* in Earl Bales Park, Toronto, provides a more recent example of a performative counter-discourse shaped to fit the contingencies of local history. Directed by Lewis Baumander, the action was set on the Queen Charlotte Islands off the coast of British Columbia, and Caliban and Ariel, characterised as representatives of the Haida nation, were played by the prominent native actors, Billy Merasty and Monique Mojica. While Caliban's buffoonery may not have been as subversive as post-colonial practices urge, it did strike a chord in the predominantly non-native audience: as Helen Peters argues, the nervous laughter which greeted his antics 'comes of a bad conscience' (1993: 200) among Canadians accustomed to ridiculing drunken 'Indians'. The production's more enabling counter-discourse was located in set design and choreography, and, in particular, in the character of Ariel who functioned to integrate the native themes/images of the performance. As well as using Haida motifs in the set to demonstrate the vitality and complexity of indigenous cultures in pre-colonial Canada, the production stressed the spiritual power of the Haida world in its figuring of Ariel as Raven, one of the many manifestations of the native trickster spirit. Through the 'magic' of Ariel/Raven, *The Tempest*'s masque scene was refigured as an Indian potlatch when feathered and masked dancers began the banquet with a purification of the smokehouse, followed by traditional gift-giving and feasting. That the potlatch was banned by Canadian law for over half a century made this choice particularly apposite for the performative recuperation of traditional elements of native culture. At the same time, the masque became a powerful expression of the colonial encounter through the presentation of the Europeans as guests from hell whose presence initiated the death of native peoples and the destruction of their culture, an outcome visualised in Baumander's production by the skeletal remains highlighted after the ceremonies.

A more problematic reworking of *The Tempest*'s performative codes was evident in the 1987 production of the play in Bali, directed by David George and Serge Tampalini, and performed by Australian students in collaboration with Balinese dancers and musicians. Although George claims that his company's 'intentions were to demonstrate cultural respect' for the Balinese customs (1989–90: 23), this theatrical event maintained, on one level at least, elements of the intercultural approach we have associated with neo-imperialism. Since Australian actors played all the main parts while Bali and the Balinese provided a 'scenic backdrop' for the action, the production tended to reinforce some of the hierarchies implicit in Shakespeare's text, and to exoticise non-western performance conventions such as the *wayang kulit* (shadow-puppet play) or the various Balinese dances. As Leigh Dale notes, a photograph published with one of George's articles about the production pictures the archetypal imperial gaze of Miranda, who stares at one of the dancers – a woman – positioned outside what appears to be a temple set in the jungle clearing (1993: 107). Moreover, even while George parodied the western cultural invasion of Bali by casting the clowns Stephano and Trinculo as an Australian tourist and an American film-maker, for the most part he avoided emphasising the colonialist themes of

The Tempest. In fact, the production depoliticised representations of Caliban, who was played by a Sri Lankan Australian but then bleached of racial signification in a move designed to preserve the happy myth of cross-cultural harmony. As George himself admits, 'if the audience for one instant, identifies [Caliban] as a brown man enslaved and persecuted by this bunch of white imposters, we'll have to make a quick exit from Bali' (ibid.: 29). Hence the production focused on magic and art in order to stress the connections between Shakespeare's world and contemporary Bali, and in doing so to revitalise a play that George felt could only be a 'fairy story' in Australian culture:

> Alchemy remains alive in Bali. Our original interest in the play was to see whether inspiration from another culture could effect a revival of the play's original power – whether Indonesian theatre could restore to us one of our own classics. Indonesian (specifically Balinese) culture shares with Shakespeare . . . a similar belief in the power of theatre to influence real life, to alter perceptions, cause hallucinations, influence natural events.
>
> (1988: 22)

This statement reveals the directors' impulse to use the art/magic of Balinese theatre to rejuvenate a European classic primarily for the benefit of the Australians involved in the production.

These examples demonstrate the possibilities, and the perils, involved in (re)producing a canonical play in a post-colonial context. The radical instability of the originary play as a cultural artefact illustrates Tony Bennett's point that interpretation is 'not a question of what texts mean but of what they might be *made* to *mean* politically' (1982: 229). Performative counter-discourse is the most difficult form to document since it is often unscripted and therefore transitory; none the less, it offers a powerful mode of critiquing the imperial canon through politicised deployments not only of the voice, body, and costume, but also of the whole semiotic network of the *mise-en-scène*. While such strategies can work in contradistinction to the play's plot and ethos, they can also re-inscribe western privilege – whether intentionally or not – by setting up unequal relations of power in the production and/or reception of the theatrical event. In order to avoid this kind of neo-imperialism, it is imperative to contextualise each intercultural exchange or, as Bharucha urges, to confront 'the

Plate 1 Balinese dancer, Prospero, and Miranda. *The Tempest*, directed by David George and Serge Tampalini, 1987

Source: Photo: Reprinted with the permission of David George

politics of its location' (1993: 240). What is thus called for in performative counter-discourse is a praxis which goes beyond the reworking of representational systems to take account of the wider relationship between the source text and its redefined target culture.

As a point of discursive entry for post-colonial practice, *The Tempest*'s legacy has a critical presence as well as a dramatic presence. In the early 1950s, following the publication of O. Mannoni's *Prospero and Caliban: The Psychology of Colonization* (1950) and Frantz Fanon's *Black Skin, White Masks* (1952), Prospero's enslavement of Caliban was established as a key paradigm in colonialist discourse, and, accordingly, as an important critical target. Shortly afterwards, *The Pleasures of Exile* (1960) by George Lamming and *Caliban Without Prospero* (1974) by Max Dorsinville explored the dialectical nature of the Caliban/Prospero relationship, arguing for a more interactive model of colonial power structures and generally rejecting Mannoni's tenets that oppression and dependence are the inevitable outcomes of the coloniser/colonised encounter. Roberto Fernández Retamar's 'Caliban' (1974; republished 1989) takes a more revolutionary stand, reclaiming the once-evil Caliban as a Cuban post-colonial subject who overthrows the imperial regime and takes back his island. Using as a basis the work of the Uruguayan critic, José Enrique Rodó, who favoured South and Central American identification with Ariel, Retamar insists that Caliban is the only possible representative figure for Cuba, the Caribbean, and Central America. Disputing the suggestion that Caliban is always already constructed within imperialist tropologies, Retamar argues that appropriating this figure amounts to 'adopt-[ing] with honor something that colonialism meant as an insult' (1989: 16).

Retamar's blueprint for a Calibanic counter-discourse has been widely taken up in the substantial body of *Tempest*-centred literature and criticism that has emerged from post-colonial societies in the last few decades. Although rewrites of *The Tempest* and critical reactions to them are too numerous to detail here, most authorities agree that black and native writers – from African, Caribbean, Afro-American, or Amerindian societies – tend to focus on the Prospero/Caliban relationship and to suggest that subversion lies in Caliban's appropriation of the coloniser's language or creation of his own, the redefinition of rape and appetite to implicate the coloniser, and the destruction of a binary system of logic in which black is defined by white, chaos by order, and savagery by civility (see Brydon 1984; Nixon 1987; Ashcroft *et al.* 1989: 189–91). In contrast, writers from settler cultures such as Australia and Anglophone Canada[9] seem more inclined to dramatise a dispersal of Prospero's power without necessarily centralising race relations, and to rework the coloniser's relationship with the land. This general pattern of response leads to the eventual consolidation of a 'black' identity while the settler subject remains marked by ambivalence and radical instability.

First staged in 1969, *Une tempête*, by Aimé Césaire, was the earliest influential post-colonial rewriting of *The Tempest* in dramatic form.[10] This play anticipated Retamar's interest in the particular relevance of Caliban as a potential site of insurgence for a counter-canonical Afro-Caribbean literature. Césaire, a Martinican poet and one of the founders of the negritude movement, conceived his 'adaptation' of Shakespeare's play as an explicit attempt to 'de-mythify' the allegorical tale so that its colonialist themes could be writ large.[11] In collaboration with the French director, Jean-Marie Serreau, Césaire reworked the discursive structures of *The Tempest* to expose Prospero's 'magic' as merely superior technology – anti-riot arsenal – and to celebrate Caliban as a rebel hero even while maintaining, for the most part, the play's original plot and characterisation. Staged in anti-naturalistic style with a range of contemporary and historical images projected onto huge screens, *Une tempête* renovated Shakespeare's text both theatrically and thematically. The result is an allegory of a different kind, one which follows the trajectory of the master/slave relation by taking its action to the brink of colonialism's demise. It is no coincidence that Césaire's play was written at a time when many Caribbean, as well as African, countries were achieving independence from their European colonisers. At the end of *Une tempête*, there is neither reconciliation nor retreat for Prospero, who, decrepit and weak, faces the imminent rebellion of a bellicose Caliban no longer under his control.

Césaire brings race into focus as a key issue in colonialism by specifying in his list of characters that Caliban is a black slave while Ariel is a mulatto. Their divergent responses to enslavement, as detailed in an added dialogue at the beginning of the second act, are linked to racial difference; Caliban urges 'freedom now' by whatever means while Ariel advocates neither violence nor submission but a patient waiting-game until Prospero's conscience leads him to repair his wrongs. At the same time as it delineates these two characters along racial lines, *Une tempête* refuses notions of a fixed racial (or gender) identity by contextualising the action with a prologue in which the *compère* of the show invites each of the actors to take up any mask/role randomly. According to Robert Livingston, 'The effect of the mask play is to de-essentialize the construction of race, to set up a tension between the racial script and its performance [so that] the actors come to occupy allegorical roles rather than to create unified characters' (1995: 193).

Césaire's text minimises the roles of Ferdinand and Miranda while giving Caliban a strong and resonant voice with which to speak/act his opposition to Prospero's rule. From his first appearance, Caliban defies his master's authority by stating that he will no longer answer to a name which insults him. Instead he calls himself X (a deliberate allusion to the American black activist, Malcolm X) as an overt reminder that his name/identity has been stolen. This refusal to be interpellated as the linguistic subject of the master narrative represents a crucial intervention into colonial relations as expressed in *The Tempest*. Having situated himself outside the parameters of linguistic control, Caliban/X maintains a powerful position from which to 'curse' his oppressor. At the end of the play, in a long catalogue of the injustices forced upon him, Caliban denounces both Prospero and the wider colonial enterprise as a sham. On another level, the entire text occupies a subversive position in relation to language control. Although 'translated' into another imperial tongue – French – the dialogue does not simply transpose the linguistic conventions of Shakespeare's play. Instead, Césaire hybridises the master's language by introducing Creole, Swahili, and English, and largely abandons the verse structures of the canonical text and their associated hierarchies of usage – lofty verse for the coloniser's dialogue and prose for his subject. The African rhythms of Caliban's songs to the Yoruba god of thunder, Shango, add to the development of a dramatic language appropriated to fit the contingencies of a post-colonial context.

In its retrieval of Caliban's African roots, *Une tempête* bolsters the slave's ability to counter his master's power over representation. This is particularly evident in the masque scene when another Yoruba figure, the trickster *dieu-diable* (devil-god) Eshu, arrives at Caliban's behest to disrupt the spectacle, precipitating the hasty exit of Greek and Roman deities – Juno, Iris, and Ceres – who are disgusted and offended by his 'vulgar' antics. In Shakespeare's play, the betrothal masque represents Prospero's version of utopia, dispelling anti-masque forces like those of the storm and the harpies' banquet. The dance of the nymphs and reapers thus enacts ritualised social harmony, while its portent of a bounteous harvest appropriates the New World as a pastoral retreat. Moreover, this dance desexualises the body by linking the forthcoming union of Miranda and Ferdinand with images of the fruition of nature, while denying illegitimate sexual desire by excluding Caliban from the spectacle. In contrast, Césaire's version of the masque is anything but sanitised as Eshu drinks and dances with tumultuous energy, chanting a ribald song that draws on explicit phallic imagery. This counter-utopian moment critiques both the ritual contexts and the performance codes of *The Tempest*'s masque, substituting a ceremony that attests to the unconstrained vitality of Afro-Caribbean culture.

Whereas political independence is the subtext of Césaire's play, David Malouf's *Blood Relations* (1987), which relocates *The Tempest* to contemporary Western Australia, enacts a less revolutionary brand of politics while still presenting as a form of social critique. Hybridising Shakespeare's *dramatis personae* to produce slightly different kinds of counter-discourse, Malouf focuses on the racial and territorial consequences of two centuries of European settlement. The subversiveness of his characters lies not only in their imperfect imitations – their contaminations – of the canonical models but also in the complex genealogical relationships which connect the various 'family' members. Here Caliban, the part-Aboriginal Dinny, is both the colonial subject of Willy/Prospero and his bastard son; hence, the 'other' is inescapably a part of the coloniser's self and a constant reminder of his miscegenation. Willy's identity is further contaminated by the appearance of the ghosts of Tessa (Prospero's absent wife) and her lover Frank/Antonio, both of whom call into question Willy's self-authorising history. Malouf's instruction for the ghosts to be played by the actors performing Cathy/Miranda and Edward/Ferdinand enacts another slippage between characters. Role doubling, a specifically performative technique, harnesses the idea of hybridity in ways which fictional rewrites of *The Tempest* cannot approximate. Once two (or more) different characters have been introduced through the same actor, each carries traces of the other throughout the play, a process which thwarts the formation of an unproblematically delineated character. The refractions and reverberations of identity suggested by this technique are extended through a further layer of irony in the evocation of each character's Shakespearian counterpart. Whereas the doubling (and, at the same time, the fracturing) of Desdemona and Othello in Carlin's *Not Now, Sweet Desdemona* works to break down the assumptions implicit in apartheid South Africa's Immorality Act, the doubling in *Blood Relations* is designed to give voice to many, but ultimate authority to none. Metatheatrically, role doubling exposes the arbitrariness of all roles and foregrounds the illusionistic nature of representation, making 'seeing double' a process by which the audience can follow the multiple movements of the text *vis-à-vis* its own enunciation and its intertextual interrogations of Shakespeare's theatre.

Whereas *The Tempest*'s closure attempts to contain disruptive energies that have threatened Prospero's rule and thus his identity throughout the play, *Blood Relations* illustrates that the dispersal of power is inevitable. Hence, Willy's self-created subject position as unimpeachable patriarch is first rendered provisional by satire and direct interrogation, then suspended via death. The semiotics of Malouf's staging further suggest that a unified sense of self is not possible: in a potent expression of hybridity, a triple figure composed of Willy/Prospero, Dinny/Caliban, and Kit/Ariel emerges to represent, visually, the split subjectivity of the non-indigenous Australian. Finally, Willy becomes the objectified other, his presence palpable only through scattered ashes and the inscrutable crates of stones which are all that remain of his dreams of absolute power. The coloniser, the play seems to suggest, must eventually face the consequences of what Césaire calls the 'boomerang' effect of colonisation: its decivilising of both oppressor and oppressed (1976: 26).

Like Césaire, Malouf is particularly concerned to interrogate the utopian vision expressed in Shakespeare's masque. Hence, *Blood Relations* refigures this metatheatrical moment to convey conflict rather than harmony through a carnivalesque magic show layered with ironic and apocalyptic overtones. Kit engineers the show despite Willy's opposition, then foregrounds the dance as homosexual display, eclipsing the young lovers' performance as the 'happy couple'. During their movements, the characters' dialogue operates as a running metacommentary on the dancing itself, stressing its theatricality, a manoeuvre which provides the spectator with a method for deconstructing the illusionistic devices of representation. Meanwhile, by declining an invitation to join the dance and staging his own 'show' instead – a recitation of Caliban's 'This island's mine' speech from *The Tempest* – Dinny refuses the inscriptions of white ritual movement on his body and holds the whole performance, and its Shakespearian prototype as well, up to scrutiny. In contrast to the easy appropriation of nature imaged in Shakespeare's masque – and in Gonzalo's speech about the New World (2.1.145-62) – *Blood Relations* demonstrates that the harvest vision, with the coloniser as husbandman, never comes to fruition. Willy's antipodean 'island' is a rocky outcrop on a remote and barren coastal strip that separates two seemingly infinite voids: the desert and the sea. Instead of offering a 'brave new world' for the enactment of utopian settlement myths, Malouf's text represents nature as neither sympathetic nor controllable, resisting the Virgilean myth of the pastoral perpetuated by its canonical model. Despite Willy/Prospero's effort to colonise the landscape, nature in its various guises shapes the contours of the performance text so that he quickly loses control of his carefully staged drama as the weird musical sounds of place and the vagaries of the weather (the tempest) intervene.

Malouf's interest in the discursive legacy of Shakespearian representations of the landscape is shared by Canadian dramatist John Murrell whose *Tempest* play, *New World* (1984) is set on the southwest coast of Vancouver Island, British Columbia. While Murrell does rework (and parody) *The Tempest*'s iconography by suggesting that this particular isle falls something short of Eden, his play's primary focus remains on the redemptive possibilities of the new world – variously described as fresh, blank, raw, wet, brash, and open – to rejuvenate a tired and cynical old-world consciousness. Despite being set in an area well known for its active Haida culture, *New World*, unlike Baumander's production of *The Tempest*, shows little cognisance of Canada's indigenous peoples. Instead, it is informed by a pastoral mode which functions ideologically to appropriate an alien landscape for the settler subject, at the same time repudiating an Anglo-European culture anaesthetised by modernity. Within this framework, there are only limited opportunities to decentre the imperialist epistemologies which have provoked – or compelled – other dramatists such as Césaire or Malouf to rewrite *The Tempest*.

CRUSOE AND FRIDAY

Daniel Defoe's *Robinson Crusoe* has also been a focal point in the project of 'writing back' to the imperial centre because, as 'Biodun Jeyifo notes, it is 'a classic "megatext" of Eurocentrism' (1989: 114). For Caribbean writers in particular, Defoe's novel, along with *The Tempest*, is held responsible for establishing and maintaining the New World tropologies that have led to the subordination of black peoples in a master/slave dialectic. Read critically, both texts depict the profound interpellation of the racial other into western discourse; hence, the Crusoe/Friday and Prospero/Caliban relationships act as symbolic touchstones for the larger colonial enterprise.

Derek Walcott's *Pantomime* (1978) resituates *Robinson Crusoe* in a new temporal setting but maintains its original geographic locale. The play's action unfolds in a guest house on the West Indian island of Tobago, thereby alluding to the ways in which the Crusoe story has perpetuated an exoticised vision of the Caribbean that still circulates in western discourses – the legacy of Defoe's book is evident even today in the local tourist industry in Trinidad which promotes one day trips to Tobago as 'Crusoe's Dream'. Unlike fictional reworkings of the novel such as J.M. Coetzee's *Foe* and Sam Selvon's *Moses Ascending*, *Pantomime* alters the genre of the original text as one of its major counter-discursive strategies. Thus the play sets up a context which displaces the centralised voice of Defoe's narrator while harnessing the theatrical power of local performance traditions. As part of this focus on genre, Walcott's version also responds to other rewrites of *Robinson Crusoe* that have appeared since 1719.

In the late eighteenth and nineteenth centuries, *Robinson Crusoe* was a very popular story for pantomime in which, following generic convention, the Friday character was usually played by a woman. Race then becomes invisible in favour of the more powerful signifier of (white) gender. Walcott's play draws attention to this substitution by substituting back again, only here the roles of Crusoe and Friday are continually negotiated rather than simply given. Harry Trewe, a pantomime actor, used to perform *Robinson Crusoe* on the London stages, with his ex-wife playing Friday, and he is still obsessed about her ability to continually outshine him. When Trewe persuades his black servant, the ex-calypsonian Jackson Phillip, to mount a reprise of the pantomime, he finds himself upstaged once again because this 'Friday' not only insists that his

36

own history will be heard but even demands that Trewe take a turn at playing the slave. Both men have their separate interpretations of the Crusoe story (outside Defoe's novel) before they enact the pantomime; Trewe's is a romantic, clichéd, rhyming song about Crusoe's isolation on a deserted island beach while Phillip's version is a calypso tune that foreshadows a possible social reorganisation: 'But one day things bound to go in reverse, / With Crusoe the slave and Friday the boss' (1980: 177). This challenge to the racial hierarchy notwithstanding, the conflicting content of the two characters' narratives is perhaps less important in this play than the differences in their performance styles, which become the central site of *Pantomime*'s revisionary project.

Arrogating the power of naming, when Phillip plays the black man he calls himself Thursday. More radically, he eschews the stock British forms of pantomime and insists on replaying the Crusoe story in his calypso style. He declares that he will employ both 'tradegy' and 'codemy' (ibid.: 139) and then goes on to enact his part with ebullient energy, unsettling Trewe who prefers a more restrained mode of performance. The disruptive force of Phillip's parodic style is nowhere more evident than in the long and detailed mime sequence which illustrates Trewe's version of Crusoe's landing on the island. By staging the scene with excessive attention to detail, the calypsonian exposes the Crusoe myth as a farce, his carnivalesque performance prompting Trewe to call off the whole show. On a metatheatrical level, this scene provides a space for the actor playing Phillip to showcase his talents since the success of the mime sequence depends largely on improvisational comedy, which in turn depends on an acute awareness of audience response.[12] Elsewhere, the pantomime relies on slapstick humour, gender- and race-swapping, and verbal and visual puns to convey its interest in performance as a site of struggle between cultures. There are also more serious moments when Walcott's text adopts a sharp critical edge to communicate the violence inherent in the Crusoe/Friday history. A case in point is Phillip's description of the colonial enterprise:

> Three hundred years I served you breakfast in . . . in my white jacket on a white verandah, boss, bwana, effendi, bacra, sahib . . . in that sun that never set on your empire I was your shadow, I did what you did, boss, bwana, effendi, bacra, sahib . . . that was my pantomime.
>
> (ibid.: 112)

Here, Phillip sketches the dynamics of the master/slave relation-ship as a performance, stressing the power of the imperialist but also suggesting that the slave can play his/her role without becoming reduced to it. In this respect, Phillip remains acutely aware of the performativity of the other pantomime he plays as servant/factotum to Trewe, a role he sheds the moment his daily work shift is finished.

In *Pantomime*, acting is ultimately a means to power. Phillip estab-lishes himself as the more consummate actor not only because he excels at the performer-oriented art of the pantomime but also because he understands the constructedness of his role. Overall, the play stages a political re-enactment of the Crusoe and Friday myth in order that its tropologies be challenged and changed. Only when Trewe accepts Phillip's art as valid and relinquishes the directorial role that he assumes, will the two be able to act together with integrity. The hybridising of the two performative approaches within Walcott's text results in a shape-shifting Creole theatre that displaces the authority of western classical styles. As Jeyifo notes, 'The performance idioms of the English music hall and the Trinidadian calypsonian carnival become vehicles of thorough going textual revisions of Defoe's classic novel and deconstructive assault on a vast array of cultural systems and codes which have defined the encounter of the colonizer and the colonized' (1989: 115).

CLASSICAL GREEK INFLUENCES

While classical Greek theatre has undoubtedly exerted less influence on post-colonial drama than has Shakespeare, it is nevertheless an important target for canonical counter-discourse, especially in African countries, such as Nigeria, where contemporary theatre practices maintain strong roots in ritual and festival. As well as providing numerous local deities which might be invoked to rework the Greek pantheon of gods, the traditional contexts of much African drama also supply a performance culture which can be used to interrogate classical models. In particular, indigenous songs, dances, stories, and ceremonies demonstrate the viability of forms of narrative construction and verbal/visual representation that differ from the dominant conventions of contemporary western theatre as it has evolved over the centuries, largely leaving its ritual roots behind.

Since it stages so convincingly the destruction of a tyrant by supernatural forces, Euripides' *The Bacchae* is an ideal text for appropriation by marginalised groups: Pentheus is easily refigured as an agent of colonialism – or, in the case of feminist rewritings of the play, as a patriarchal force to be overthrown.[13] The most significant post-colonial revision of this text is Wole Soyinka's *The Bacchae of Euripides*,[14] which was commissioned by Britain's National Theatre in 1973. This play incorporates Yoruba cosmology in its rewriting of dramatic form, hybridising genres to refuse the primacy of the western tragic mode. Dismissed by many reviewers as a violation of the original (see Bishop 1988: 77), Soyinka's version resituates the action in a war-time African setting (Nigeria's post-independence civil wars are but one historical referent for this text), adds wedding feasts, and alters the ending. The play also employs a promiscuous performance style to dramatise effectively its ritual elements, music hall routines, masque scenes, and festival celebrations. This 'violation', like Walcott's arraignment of Shakespeare, is a conscious 'crime' designed to draw attention to the ways in which colonised societies might exploit what Frantz Fanon calls imperialism's 'contamination' of all its subjects. By violating purist versions of classical master narratives, texts such as Soyinka's open up a space for the performance of local histories and mythologies.

Among the many deviations from its canonical model, *The Bacchae of Euripides* foregrounds dance as a motif of disjunction with the original text. The play's dances take many forms, their variety and multiplicity reinforcing the importance of movement as a signifying practice. The music-hall steps executed by Kadmos and Tiresias during a farcical dialogue about the 'first collapsible thyrsus in Attica' (1973: 254) are but one kind of addition. Others include the wedding jigs and a savagely suggestive routine in which the drunken Hippoclides, a Soyinkan invention, ritualistically dances his bride away. The play also highlights dance as part of the procession that heralds the ritual flogging for the sacrifice to Dionysos, and the procession in the wedding service. Following the stylised mime of the hunt, Agave and her Maenads perform a soft, graceful Maypole dance which becomes more frenzied as she realises the implications of the dancing. The most impressive form of dance, however, is the earthquake that the slaves and Dionysos are able to summon up on stage, conjuring visually and aurally the remarkable force that can easily be channelled into political

39

upheaval. Slow, fast, solo, or group based, the hybridised dances of *The Bacchae of Euripides* suggest the variety of (performative) powers commanded by Ogun, the Yoruba god on whom Soyinka's Dionysos is modelled.[15] The dancing returns the power of the past to the people, the power that Pentheus' cruel governance had denied them. All the different forms of dancing also image an end to the political and historical structures that empire had imposed on the region – both specifically in Nigeria and more widely throughout Africa – and which power-hungry rulers like Pentheus retained: dancing is liberation. Not only is Pentheus conquered, but other imperial manifestations of his rule are also banished when the dance's power takes effect.

Soyinka's play inserts two mimed wedding scenes conjured by Ogun/Dionysos which are intended to be a lesson to Pentheus, who is blind to their meanings. In the first scene, a bridegroom who refuses the wedding conventions of the West dances to Dionysos' tune, which prompts his would-be father-in-law to abruptly call off the marriage. The father-in-law, more concerned with the trappings of wealth and the imitation of western social and political fashions, is distinguished from the bridegroom, whose association with the local provides a moral for the scene. The second mime enacts the Biblical miracle of the marriage at Canaan, but here the refilling of the wine jugs represents the renewal of spiritual energies that must also accompany an Ogunian philosophy of life, the philosophy that Pentheus has denied. Both scenes sustain images of horror and excess; the linking signifier of the wine intensifies Dionysos' insistence on balance in life, which will help maintain individual integrity, and, far more significant in the Yoruba culture, communal integrity.

The ironic addition of the wedding mimes in Soyinka's text recalls the Jacobean genre of the masque and also alludes to many comedies' prominent figuring of weddings, good tidings, and personal and national happiness, particularly for the monarch. Soyinka's version of this symbolic metatheatrical event offers Pentheus more than just homage: it suggests the way to ensure salvation, happiness, and political stability, but Pentheus pays no attention. References to Shakespeare's dream plays, *A Midsummer Night's Dream* and *The Tempest*, make explicit that the dreams staged in *The Bacchae of Euripides* are not merely entertainment. Instead they indicate that Ogun's magic is more potent than Prospero's or Ariel's, and that Pentheus ought to take Dionysos' directions very seriously. The canonical form and usage of the masque is further subverted by the Ogunian requirement of a sacrifice: the tyrannical ruler must die to restore the critical balance. This god-driven philosophy is different again from the counter-discourse in fellow Nigerian Ola Rotimi's *The Gods Are Not to Blame* (1968), which, in its rewriting of Sophocles' *Oedipus Rex*, limits the gods' interference in everyday life to moments when corrective action must repair destruction wrought by humans.

The most crucial distinction between the Greek and the Yoruba versions of *The Bacchae* is the ending. In Soyinka's play, the final image is a red glow from Pentheus' head which Kadmos interprets to be blood. Agave soon discovers the blood to be wine and everyone takes a restorative drink. The tragedy of the situation is not undermined; rather, the ritual also demonstrates the importance of rejuvenating other emotions and energies through Pentheus' death, an event which represents community good and the restoration of harmony, rather than the tragic fate that death usually signifies. After being located outside the community during his tyrannical rule, Pentheus is finally repositioned within that community: he is 'the centre of their communion, the symbol of their victory over the old regime and of their power to transform what remains into a new, more human order, building a future of plenitude, well-being and renewal in which all can share' (Wilkinson 1991: 81). The ritual of Pentheus' death and the various other rituals – such as Tiresias' flogging and the mimed wedding ceremonies – along with the hybridising of genre all help to produce a careful reworking of *The Bacchae*, rather than a contemporary Nigerian rendering of a Greek 'classical' text. Soyinka's play disrupts the comedy–tragedy binary and the influence exerted by the Greek panoply of gods. Instead, a Yoruba god offers a more appropriate philosophy. Ogun – in his disguise as Dionysos – is more powerful than Pentheus, and, ultimately, than Euripides' play.

Sophocles' *Antigone* has also received considerable counter-discursive attention because it disputes the state's definition of justice and champions a figure who is imprisoned for maintaining her sense of moral and legal principle. The differences between two systems of justice and the triumph of the stronger power over the weaker can easily be articulated in a colonial context. *The Island* (1973), by Athol Fugard, John Kani, and Winston Ntshona, resituates *Antigone* on Robben Island, the high-security prison

41

island off the coast of Cape Town in South Africa. Since the play depicted prison conditions at a time when such representations were forbidden, it was the predictable target of government intervention. As Orkin notes, 'Even Fugard . . . was afraid of censorship, refusing to commit *The Island* to script form until it had been performed abroad' (1991: 151). The play's performances in Port Elizabeth were cancelled, and the Cape Town première was watched by police who threatened to charge all involved (threats which were not acted upon) (ibid.: 152). In *The Island*, two inmates rehearse a passage from *Antigone* for a prison concert, using Sophocles' play to articulate the injustices of the law as it is practised in their society. To make absolutely clear the connection between the Antigone story and the story of apartheid, Winston – playing Antigone – breaks role in the final moments of the play-within-the-play, resuming his usual identity to enact a powerful protest addressed to his fellow prisoners (whom the paying audience 'play'). Here the performance functions not simply as a metaphor for wider action but also as action itself, the links between theatre and 'real life' being reinforced by the fact that Fugard's co-dramatists are also the actors in *The Island* and that they keep their own names, John and Winston. At the same time, by extending the playing space of the Antigone story from the stage to the whole of the theatre and, beyond that, into the outside life of the actors, the play reminds us that their endeavour must always be read in the context of their location: any freedom that these men may obtain from incarceration is mediated by their release into the 'prison' of apartheid.

The specific location of Antigone in South Africa is the strength of *The Island*, while *Odale's Choice* (1962), by Edward Kamau Brathwaite, which also sets *Antigone* in Africa, deliberately chooses an unspecified region. At the base of this geographic vagueness is Brathwaite's mission to find in Africa an 'authentic' ancestral homeland for West Indians of African origin, a project directly opposed to Walcott's vision of a new home forged in the rich hybridity that is the unique heritage of all Caribbeans. The narrative relocation of the Antigone story thus takes on mythic resonances in Brathwaite's version rather than foregrounding local politics, and there is added emphasis on *choice* as a moral category which opposes oppression – in this case, Odale's choice not only to disobey Creon but also to refuse his pardon and hence to choose death as an emphatic act of free will. While the production note to the published play points out that 'The theme is timeless: the defiance of tyranny' (1967: 3), Brathwaite nonetheless indigenises his rewriting of *Antigone* by having the soldiers who do Creon's bidding speak a form of West Indian Creole. That the play was written for black actors and first performed in the newly independent Ghana inevitably politicises its content further. Within these counter-discursive sites – language, race, and geography – *Odale's Choice* stages other, less central moments of focus.[16]

REWORKING CHRISTIAN MYTHS

The forced conversion of colonised peoples to Christianity throughout the empire precipitated what Walcott has called 'one race's quarrel with another's God' (1970b: 13). As a master narrative which has assisted and justified the imperial project, the Bible – and particularly its institutional significations and uses – necessarily figures among the chief canonical texts targeted for strategic reform. In their discussion of the Canadian novel *Not Wanted on the Voyage*, Ashcroft, Griffiths, and Tiffin argue that Timothy Findley's version of the Biblical story of Noah's Ark 're-enter[s] the Western episteme at one of its most fundamental points of origination to deconstruct those notions and processes which rationalized the imposition of the imperial world on the rest of the world' (1989: 104). A similar interest in attacking the foundational structures of western culture underlies the reworking of various Biblical myths in post-colonial drama, particularly in the settler-invader cultures where the proselytising activities of Christian missionaries have had catastrophic effects on indigenous cultures. In Australia and Canada, for example, the enforced relocation of indigenous peoples from their traditional homelands to Christian schools/missions has been part of an overall strategy designed to undermine tribal and familial solidarity, to appropriate land for white settlers, and to achieve the effective destruction of indigenous races. Such histories illustrate Greenblatt's point that the 'rhetorical task of Christian imperialism' is to 'bring together commodity conversion and spiritual conversion' (1991: 71). Uncle Herbie, one of the Aboriginal characters in Jack Davis's *In Our Town* (1990), puts it even more plainly: 'Wetjala cunning fella alright. When they come here they had the Bible and we had the land, [now] they've got the land and we've got the Bible' (1992: 44).

Davis's earlier play, *No Sugar* (1985), draws on the Biblical story of King Herod's massacre of the innocents to recuperate the black history repressed in official versions of European settlement in Australia. Set in the late 1920s, the play focuses on a detribalised family sent by the police to a mission under the pretext that they must have access to good health care and education. Two massacres are detailed: the first in a story told by the black tracker, Billy Kimberley, during a corroboree, and the second as part of an address by Mr Neville, Chief Protector of Aborigines, to the Royal Western Australian Historical Society. While Neville appears somewhat sympathetic, the juxtaposition of these two scenes, especially in performance,[17] highlights the differences between Aboriginal and European epistemologies and suggests that the white version of history has been censored, a proposition supported by the surreptitious murder (massacre) of Aboriginal babies at the mission. Such Biblical allusions are strengthened through Sister Eileen's reading of the Herod story at Sunday school; at this point, however, Davis stresses that Christian teachings must speak to Aboriginal experience as the farcical school lesson emphatically does not. Davis's wider play, on the other hand, fully appropriates the Bible's discursive tropes and is even so bold as to re-situate the Christian myth of the nativity of Jesus. In a related endeavour, Canadian Métis writer Yvette Nolan uses Biblical sources in her play, *Job's Wife* (1992), to allegorise the story of a white woman about to miscarry her part-native baby. Here, God appears to the incredulous woman in the figure of a native man who eventually carries her unborn child away to the spirit world. Whereas the ending of Nolan's play stages a grim image of aborted possibility, Davis's final focus is on the young Aboriginal couple, Joseph and Mary, whose escape from the mission with their newly-born baby promises a hopeful future. By using these allegorical frameworks, both dramatists tap into the narrative archive of their predominantly white audiences while simultaneously questioning the racial and cultural biases of a religion which has had profound and lasting effects on indigenous communities.

Most post-colonial texts which (mis)use the master narratives of Christianity to illustrate imperialism's effect on native cultures 'translate' the Bible's content and rework its forms so that the word of God is transmitted through oral story-telling rather than liturgical readings. This process establishes what Bhabha calls 'partial knowledges' through a splitting and doubling that under-mines the authority of colonialist discourse (1985: 102) by replacing the codes, conventions, and cultural associations of the canonical text with those of a distinctively different local one. Louis Nowra's *Capricornia* (1988) dramatises a particularly effective subversion of Christian mythology when Tocky, the part-Aboriginal protagonist, 'translates' the story of David and Goliath into an oral performance in Pidgin, much to the consternation of her teacher, the stern and humourless Mrs Hollower. As she translates, Tocky incorporates more and more gestures into her narrative until finally it becomes a full-blown carnivalesque parody before Mrs Hollower stops her, proclaiming that 'the word of God needs no translation' (1988: 31). The teacher's intervention is an uncomfortable recognition of the subversive power of her student's performance, especially as opposed to her own toneless recitation. What Mrs Hollower objects to most is Tocky's over-literal enactment of a text which largely derives its authority and 'truth value' (in the Foucaultian sense) from the historical contingency of its closure in written form.

The particularly misogynist nature of much Judeo-Christian doctrine makes it a common subject for feminist counter-discourse, although this is often divorced from, rather than informed by, critiques of colonialism. *The Serpent's Fall* (1987), by Sarah Cathcart and Andrea Lemon, combines Aboriginal and ancient Greek mythologies in an attempt to dislodge imperial patriarchy from its moorings in the Biblical story of Adam and Eve. The particular mythologies recuperated are chosen for their emphasis on female power, and although their origins are very different, they are productively juxtaposed in a discontinuous narrative that also emphasises points of common experience among Aboriginal and Greek women positioned in the margins of mainstream Australian culture.[18] The play's premise is that Christianity has effected a cleavage between woman and the serpent – a figure of exceptional powers in many cultures – which becomes emblematic of her split from the land, and, ultimately, of the gap between Aboriginal and contemporary western epistemologies. The text opens with an overt interrogation of the myth of Genesis and then develops this deconstructive project throughout, radically revisioning the Bible's iconography through a focus on the disruptive *and* creative energies of both Medusa and the Aboriginal Rainbow Serpent. In so far as it uses some of the images and myths circulating in Australian culture to devise a 'tribal' story told by one person

45

through dancing, singing, explication, and impersonation, to an audience which is actively included in the tale, the play resembles in structure and enactment an Aboriginal oral narrative. This provides a self-reflexive focus on the transformative powers of the artist/actor/story-teller figure, and, consequently, on the notion of theatrical transformation itself. As well as converting the myth of 'The Fall of Man' into the tragedy of 'The Serpent's Fall', the performance text of this monodrama posits the possibility of rewriting the body (in Cixous's terms) against the more subtle discourses of power engendered in the Biblical myth of Genesis.

The tyranny of the Bible has affected not only minority groups in settler colonies but also majority populations in areas where Christianity continues to dilute the influence of local religions long beyond the official withdrawal of colonial rule. *Woza Albert!* (1981) by Percy Mtwa, Mbongeni Ngema, and Barney Simon (mis)uses the Bible to demonstrate its covert racism and to protest against apartheid. The play also targets fundamentalist Afrikaaners, urging them to recognise the inhumanity of a socio-political system which refuses to acknowledge the basic rights of all people. The belief that to suffer is edifying – expressed in the beatitude 'blessed are ye when men revile ye and persecute ye' – is one of the main Christian doctrines attacked for upholding the status quo through the promise of an eternal reward for the persecuted. *Woza Albert!* is much more interested in the here-and-now consequences of inequality and in breaking the cycle of oppression instituted by imperial Christianity and sustained by the social and material order of the society. An immediate success among black and, ironically, white audiences, the play stages the fantasy of the Second Coming of Jesus Christ who returns to earth as a black man, Morena, in contemporary South Africa. In due course, Morena is incarcerated at Robben Island but he simply walks away across the waters of Cape Town's bay. Attempts to torpedo him only effect the spectacular destruction of the island, a powerful symbol of bondage for black South Africans. 'Divine justice' is thus reimaged as the apocalyptic overthrow of imperial systems. Morena himself re-appears in a cemetery and, in a subversive replay of the Biblical story of Lazarus, proceeds to raise from the dead key militant leaders murdered or otherwise persecuted in their struggle for freedom against the prison of apartheid. The final movement of *Woza Albert!* is towards an imminent revolution in the social order.

The Bible has spawned a number of other 'classic' texts which provide suitable loci for revisionary interrogations of Christian doctrine. In this respect, medieval drama is a particularly apposite target for theatrical counter-discourse. Obotunde Ijimere's *Everyman* (1966), a version of the medieval morality play, reconstitutes the original text's moral lesson into a Yoruba story-telling exercise for the community benefit in Nigeria, rather than dramatising a personal invitation to live a good life according to Christian teachings. In Ijimere's version, Everyman's journey has repercussions for the next generation, as his last wish is for his spirit to return in his daughter's unborn child. Ijimere's allegorical world is both human-centred and god-controlled, in keeping with Yoruba cosmology. Only one personified object appears at the end of Everyman's life – Good Deeds – unlike in the original play, which presents most of Everyman's potential companions as material objects. The medieval drama is rewritten here to explore more locally relevant concepts of life, death, community, and spirituality, while the Yoruba interpretation of how one lives a good life denies the authority of the Christian missionary impositions in, and radical reconstructions of, Nigerian life in the eighteenth and nineteenth centuries, and even into the contemporary period.

REPLACING THE CANON

These examples are only the beginnings of many other possible rewritings of canonical texts. There are, as well, many plays that rework texts which are already counter-discursive, especially in settler colonies where the canon has had a different impact on indigenous and non-indigenous groups. One particularly resonant example is *The Rez Sisters* (1986) by Tomson Highway, a native Canadian playwright. At one level, this play reworks Michel Tremblay's *Les Belles Soeurs* (1968 in French, 1973 in English), which itself focused on the dislocation and placelessness experienced by seven Québécois women living in the east end of Montréal – dislocation in terms of their families, their futures, and their society within the larger realm of Canadian politics. Borrowing the Greek chorus motif, *Les Belles Soeurs* stages Québec of the 1960s as a spiritual wasteland; the use of the Greek theatrical trope in a Canadian play intensifies this feeling *and* underlines the society's abandonment by the gods. The Catholic Church's stultifying effects on family and social formations are, for Tremblay, the basis of this disintegration, and any solution to the political and social malaise in Québec must be generated by the people. Highway transposes a similar story to a reservation in northern Ontario, where the women do not remain in situations as futile as those Tremblay depicts. While both writers create women with strong stage presences, Highway's native characters gain greater control over their lives and destinies with the help of Nanabush, the central figure in Cree and Ojibway religions. Here, mythical figures return to the women's world, informing it in ways that Christian and/or classical gods cannot.

Mustapha Matura's *Playboy of the West Indies* (1984) resituates J.M. Synge's 'classic', *Playboy of the Western World* (1907), in the Caribbean, transforming the folk traditions of the Irish country pub into the carnival traditions of the Trinidadian rum shop. Synge's play itself removed the focus of attention from the imperial centre, privileging instead the characters of rural Ireland and dramatising their stories in local dialect. According to Sandra Pouchet Pacquet, the setting of Matura's *Playboy* in pre-independence Trinidad on Discovery Day (originally a holiday to honour Columbus which has since been abandoned in favour of Emancipation Day) gives the fable a specific historical context in the colonial moment; hence, 'issues of discovery and self-definition in the play parallel a regional quest that subsequently becomes an island quest for freedom and independence' (1992: 91). Both plays capitalise on the pub as a suitable locale for the expression of their respective vernacular languages but the festival atmosphere of Matura's version takes Synge's interest in the metaphoric richness of the local dialect one step further, especially through the bawdy humour associated with calypso. *Playboy of the West Indies* and *The Rez Sisters*, twice removed from the canonical centre, both enact further dislocations of imperial power as well as demonstrating the changing influences on post-colonial cultures.

In New Zealand, canonical counter-discourse seems to take yet another form: examining the icon of Katherine Mansfield. Here, very few theatre texts act counter-discursively, while an enormous number of texts (short story and poetry as well as drama) refer to Mansfield, who has significantly shaped New Zealand's literary traditions. Many of these texts are merely hagiographic, but others, especially Vincent O'Sullivan's *Jones and Jones* (1988), demonstrate less 'heroic' sides to Mansfield by pushing her off centre-stage and highlighting her friend/servant, Ida Baker, and the relationship between them. In contrast, *The Rivers of China* (1987), by expatriate

New Zealander Alma De Groen, presents Mansfield as a 'text' that must be recreated against the containment of critical co-option and appropriation. By choosing this particular historical figure as her focus for a feminist reworking of history, De Groen provides a paradigm of the colonial woman writer immured in the territo-rialised spaces of the imperial patriarchal canon. Critiques that focus on Mansfield's 'mastery' of the short story form or the uni-versality of her themes pay little attention to the feminist aspects of her work, and even less to the political and material effects of her position as expatriate colonial subject writing in England and living with her English editor-husband. *The Rivers of China* takes up these issues, questioning the constitutive framework that has coloured much discussion of Mansfield's work since her death. And since Mansfield makes an express point of her identity as a New Zealander, the play reminds us that her work might be more properly considered in its historical specificity rather than assigned to the homogenising universal (that is, British) canon.

The canon itself is always an unstable category and a contentious classification, generally referring to texts that are considered worthy of reading and studying, indeed the texts that ought to be read and studied, to the concomitant exclusion of other texts. Traditionally composed of works by Anglo-European male writers, the canon has become an obvious site for attacks from those whom it excludes: women, people of colour, homosexuals, and non-Europeans being the more obvious examples. As issues of 'value' and 'value judge-ments' are no longer as clear cut as they were in the heyday of the British Empire – the days of Matthew Arnold's touchstones – other kinds of texts and discourses have become increasingly relevant as targets of potential rewriting. Hollywood movies, in particular, are identifiable signifiers of the post-1950s American domination of world culture, and thus are appropriate systems for discursive deconstruction. Displacing power-laden signifiers and/or axiomatic ways of seeing questions the bases on which a culture's authority/authenticity rests. The rewriting of movie texts in native Canadian plays such as Monique Mojica's *Princess Pocahontas and the Blue Spots* (1990) and Margo Kane's *Moonlodge* (1990) is far more likely to strike chords of recognition than another revision of a Greek classic. By refusing and refuting negative stereotypes, Mojica's and Kane's plays create some space for contemporary native women to express their subjectivities. Eliminating singular, all-encompassing identities, these plays dismantle the maelstrom of images that have

defined the 'Indian', and force audiences to recognise the constructedness of these images. As these two examples illustrate, the
definition of canonical counter-discourse will, in all likelihood,
continue to be less centred on the traditional British literary
canon, as the master narratives are increasingly created by cinema,
television, videos, and other forms of media.
Criticism has often contributed to the misreading of counter-
discourse. Parisian critics, for example, summarised Césaire's *Une
tempête* as a 'betrayal' of Shakespeare (see Nixon 1987: 575) while
Malouf's version of *The Tempest* was dismissed by some as merely
parodic. African texts in particular have been subject to reviews
that refuse to acknowledge the possibility of intelligence, artistic
merit, and political savvy. Such misreadings have also carried over
into plays which are not attempting to rework the canon. Critics
in the early years of post-colonial studies often assumed that many
African texts were merely second-rate imitations of European
models; hence, any play premised on a hierarchy of gods risked
being assessed according to the closed conventions of Greek
theatre and likely found wanting. Soyinka's early work and that of
his compatriot, J.P. Clark-Bekederemo, attracted such misguided
criticism which ensured that readers and audiences did not see the
performance structures and cosmologies foregrounded. To a large
degree, that situation has changed now, but the overwhelming
expectation on the part of many ethnocentric western critics is
that any god must be a Greek or a Christian god. Conversely, many
allusions employed by counter-canonical texts are simply not
noted. Tomson Highway found that the Hera and Zeus story in
his play, *Dry Lips Oughta Move to Kapuskasing* (1989), was overlooked by virtually all reviewers and critics. In other words, they
did not recognise their own apparently originary myths. Using
this as a critique of Canadian settler society, Highway claims that
such omissions illustrate just how distanced contemporary white
cultures are from their roots – no matter how they choose to
define those origins.
    Put simply, canonical counter-discourse destabilises the power/
knowledge axis of imperialism. There are many counter-discursive
possibilities even within one culture's encounter with the master
narratives which have impacted upon its history. Whatever the
route taken, the subversion involved in these practices can free up
a space for the colonial subject to renegotiate an identity that
is not necessarily constituted by the authority of the coloniser's

perspective of the past, present, or future. The classical, Shake-spearian, and Biblical worlds circumscribe European literatures but they cannot circumscribe post-colonial literatures in the same way. Canonical counter-discourse is one method by which colonised cultures can refuse the seamless contiguity between a classical past and a post-colonial present that the empire strives to preserve.

NOTES

1 For a persuasive account of how the study of English Literature contributed to the socio-political consolidation of the British Empire, see, for example, Viswanathan's *Masks of Conquest: Literary Study and British Rule in India* (1989).

2 Dates given after play titles refer to the first production except where this information has been unavailable, in which case the publication date is provided. Quoted references are to the published text as listed in the bibliography.

3 For discussion of the many semiotic codes which affect theatrical representation, see Pavis (1982), Elam (1980), Carlson (1990), and Tompkins (1992b).

4 See, for instance, Mead and Campbell, eds, *Shakespeare's Books: Contemporary Cultural Politics and the Persistence of Empire* (1993).

5 See also Loomba's book, *Gender, Race, Renaissance Drama* (1991).

6 In his overview of Jamaican theatre history, Wycliffe Bennett points to a graphic example of how theatre and education reinforce each others' canonical biases: at the first local drama festival for schools in 1950, all thirty-one of the presentations were chosen from Shakespeare (1974: 7).

7 On one level, any intertextual reference between plays is meta-theatrical. Our use of the term here applies to those techniques which overtly and self-consciously invoke other theatre texts in order to comment on representation itself.

8 Caliban had been played by black actors prior to Miller's production, but generally in ways designed to reinforce connotations of 'savagery' and libidinal appetite, and to foreground contrasts between Caliban and Ariel, who was usually played by a white actor (male or female). See Hill's study of American productions of *The Tempest* for further details (1984: 2–5).

9 Brydon (1984) has identified a pattern of *Tempest* rewrites in Anglophone Canadian fiction wherein Miranda is remodelled as a protest figure, creating a suitable fable for the settler society's impulse to reject her role as the dutiful daughter of empire. Francophone rewrites, on the other hand, choose a Calibanic model of resistance which highlights dissension between Québécois and Anglophone Canadians. See Zabus (1985) or Dorsinville (1974) for further discussion.

10 In his discussion of *Une tempête*, Pallister (1991) cites an 1878 play,

Caliban, by Ernest Renan, which depicts Caliban's eventual over-throwing of Prospero's rule. It is unclear, however, whether Césaire had read this relatively unknown play when he wrote his own version of *The Tempest*.

11 It should be noted that Césaire's play predates by some years the new historicist interest in the colonial contexts of Shakespeare's work, as discussed by critics such as Greenblatt (1976) and Hulme (1986). It is also possible that Miller's London production of *The Tempest* was influenced by *Une tempête*.

12 The late Wilbert Holder, who played Jackson Phillip in the première season of *Pantomime* in Trinidad as well as in subsequent productions in the United States, foregrounded this metatheatricality with a compelling improvisation of Crusoe's adventures. See *Pantomime* video (1979c).

13 Examples include Churchill and Lan's *A Mouthful of Birds* (1986) and Duffy's *Rites* (1969), plays which are beyond the ambit of this study.

14 See Sotto (1985) for the most complete study of the play, its inspiration, an account of the comparisons between the two texts, and an assessment of Soyinka's reading of Euripides.

15 Ogun is the god of wine, war, roads, and metals.

16 More recently, the Antigone story has been taken up by a number of Irish writers, including Brendan Kenelly, Tom Paulin, and Aidan Matthews. According to the critic, Christopher Murray, this interest in re-writing Sophocles' legend was kindled by the radical political and social upheaval of the mid-1980s, and in particular, by the controversial Criminal Justice Bill of 1984, seen by Irish liberals as a draconian law which limited the rights of suspects (1991: 129). Taken as a group, the Irish reworkings of *Antigone* appear to equivocate in their exploration of both Creon's and Antigone's versions of justice (see Roche 1988; Murray 1991) and thus their points of contact/conflict with the canonical model are sometimes less clear cut than the examples discussed here.

17 The published text of *No Sugar* does not place these scenes in adjacency; however, recent performances of the play in Melbourne (1988) and Perth (1990) rearranged the scene order (with Davis's approval) to make a strategic point of Neville's insensitivity.

18 The play is careful to distinguish between ancient Greek 'civilisation' and the traditions and cultures of modern Australian Greeks.

2

TRADITIONAL ENACTMENTS: RITUAL AND CARNIVAL

> We black Africans have been blandly invited to submit
> ourselves to a second epoch of colonialisation – this
> time by a universal-humanoid abstraction defined and
> conducted by individuals whose theories and prescrip-
> tions are derived from the apprehension of *their* world
> and *their* history, *their* social neuroses and *their* value
> systems.
>
> (Soyinka 1976b: x)

This new discursive colonisation which Soyinka critiques has had at
least two effects on theatre activity in Africa and other non-western
countries: the rejection of culturally specific drama by many western
critics for not adhering to normative (usually Anglo-European or
American) conventions,[1] and the imposition of western forms in
non-western settings. Regarding the latter, Robert Serumaga, a
Ugandan playwright, observes that received performance practices,
like imported colonial systems, are inherently ideological: 'the
theatre of Europe came to Africa and established itself in complete
ignorance of and indifference to [indigenous] traditions' (qtd in
Graham-White 1974: 89). Criticism of African theatre continues to
be largely circumscribed by western critics' inability to comprehend
– or even, in some cases, to be *willing* to comprehend – different
sets of assumptions.[2] Many such critics have also insisted – however
inadvertently – that African drama be classified as a contained,
known entity that is 'authentic' or 'pure' according to a predetermined western definition of authenticity and the exotic/erotic.[3]
Such impositions have, as Joseph Okpaku points out, 'frozen [African
literature] in this anachronistic mode and thereby deprived [it] of
the opportunity to grow and develop along with the growth and

development of . . . African society' (qtd in Bishop 1988: 63). The west has similarly restricted definitions of Indian drama which, Rustom Bharucha observes, is only of interest to the majority of western analysts if it is 'traditional' (1983: xi).

This simultaneous interest in and disavowal of traditional performance is closely related to the misguided perception that such theatre is 'primitive' and/or simplistic. Apart from being more complex than most western commentators generally allow, traditional enactments have special functions in post-colonial societies and are often key sites of resistance to imposed values and practices.[4] Rooted in folk culture, these enactments are not only mnemonic devices that assist in the preservation of history but are also effective strategies for maintaining cultural difference through specific systems of communication – aural, visual, and kinetic – and through specific values related to local (often pre-contact) customs. In the Caribbean, traditional elements derived from African, or in some cases, Indian, folk culture performed the added function of 'indigenising'[5] colonised peoples uprooted from their homelands and forced to adapt to a new environment as slaves or indentured labourers.

When traditional performance elements are incorporated into a contemporary play, they affect the play's content, structure, and style, and consequently, its overall meaning/effect. This process, which usually involves a departure from the techniques and assumptions of realism, stretches colonial definitions of theatre to assert the validity (and the vitality) of other modes of representation. As a way of appropriating received forms of drama and adapting them to fit the local experience, the meshing of performance conventions is one form of what Sylvia Wynter has called folklore's 'cultural guerilla resistance against the Market economy' (1970: 36). The result is a theatrical practice in which the community and the social order are given prominence. Yet, a politically motivated theatre based on traditional enactments also moves beyond its origins while not undermining them. As Edouard Glissant argues of Caribbean drama, when 'The folkloric background [is] represented, reflected on, given a cultural thrust, [and so] raised to the level of consciousness', it emerges as a new form of self-critical culture (1989: 198). This facility for self-evaluation is crucial; otherwise, drama influenced by such practices as ritual and carnival – the two 'traditions' discussed in this chapter – will be perceived as a static art form. Within post-colonial frames of reference, the concept of tradition far exceeds the quaintness, the fixity, and ultimately, the dismissibility which it represents in highly industrialised societies.

RITUAL

One of the most enduring – and most appropriated and misunderstood – markers of cultural difference and stability in both Africa and India is ritual. Frequently associated with theatre, ritual remains the event/practice which attracts the most attention in the west because of its 'difference'. Yet the difference between African or Indian rituals and western forms of worship and/or entertainment and/or representation are too often overlooked in critical analysis which attempts to mark only similarities. The theatre anthropologist, Victor Turner, argues that ritual forms the basis of all theatre activity (as well as other sorts of worldly action and interaction). This urge to map definitively all known rituals worldwide and to extract their commonalities seems to lose sight of the purpose of specific rituals and of the all-important differences among various ritual actions; for instance, Richard Schechner deliberately does not distinguish between secular 'rituals' like sports events and sacred devotional rituals (1989). Likewise, his theory overlooks the forms and meanings of specific rituals among, say, the Hausa people, which cannot be equated with those of the Igbo. Attempts to find both ritual and drama in as many situations/cultures as possible do not provide a greater understanding of either: instead, both ritual and drama are reduced to criteria that support Turner's (and other theatre anthropologists') homogenising arguments. Turner sees a universal evolution of performance following a 'liminal' to 'liminoid' pattern, where 'liminal' is more presentational and 'liminoid' is more representational. He asserts that liminal 'performances' occur in 'technologically simpler societies' (1989: 14), which leads to the rather problematic evolutionist argument that suggests the advancement of humanity from a primitive, uncivilised state towards western, industrialised perfection. Schechner supports this view in 'Magnitudes of Performance', where he constructs the 'Performance Event–Time–Space Chart' to log 'ritual performances' as diverse as a bar mitzvah, a performance art piece, a Ph.D. oral examination, the election of a pope, a murder trial, and the *puja* (prayer) at a Hindu temple (1989: 20–1). Many of these events are rites of passage which create a sense of theatre, but the ways in which each is situated within its community or setting are vastly different. Schechner's diverse rituals cannot, then, be as synonymous as he would wish; his scheme ascribes ritual status to so many activities that ritual becomes diluted to the point of being any meaningful activity that has a sense of ceremony, an actant, and an audience.

This chapter outlines a more specific definition of ritual and explores its use in post-colonial drama and performance. Discussing ritual's connection with drama is made all the more difficult by the many differing opinions about the origin of drama in, for instance, Africa. Some follow Turner's lead by advocating that contemporary drama grew out of rituals, while others maintain that the two developed simultaneously.[6] Given the numerous cultures and heritages within Africa, signified by the presence of over eight hundred different languages (Götrick 1984: 19), the intersections between ritual and drama necessarily vary in each tradition. It is perhaps easier to understand ritual (and its importance in a community) if it is compared to drama and its function in society. In the Igbo context, M.J.O. Echeruo observes that 'drama is to the society what ritual is to religion: a public affirmation of an idea; a translation into action of a *mythos* or plot just as ritual is the translation of a faith into external action' (1981: 138). Ritual and drama are often similar in their transformative, translational qualities, but they are emphatically not the same.

Some critics see all theatrical events as ritualistic: Ola Rotimi, for instance, says, 'I don't call [theatre] a recreational pastime. I see theatre as a serious, almost religious, undertaking and I try to impress upon [actors and students] the sobriety which participation in theatre demands' (1985: 17). Not all drama is ritual, however, and not all ritual is drama even though ritual usually employs elements of dramatic performance. A consideration of ritual in post-colonial contexts requires a reconsideration of drama itself. While western drama is based, to some extent, on the principles of Aristotelian mimesis, African drama is not. Kacke Götrick's analysis of the Apidan theatre of the Yoruba people leads her to determine that existing definitions of drama predicated on mimesis are demonstrably false in relation to most African theatre forms; 'instead, a new definition of drama is needed, which includes enactments that are at the same time presentational and representational, that are efficacious, and that are conceived of as a duality by the appropriate spectators, comprising reality and fiction simultaneously' (1984: 130–1). As well as pointing towards a more appropriate way of looking at non-western drama, this statement also assists in defining ritual, since ritual can satisfy all of Götrick's markers except the last: fiction. Ritual usually presents a reality – that is, something conceived as a real situation – even if some of its performative practices depend on the stylisation and simplification of that reality. For instance, the *egungun* or ancestral death cult of the Yoruba people is based on the ancestors' protection of the living. When the *egungun* practitioner's presence is subsumed by the ancestors, he (usually he) speaks in a 'croaky voice' (ibid.: 38). That voice in itself signals both the presence and the vast cosmological realm of the ancestors. Ritual tends to prefer presentational actions (showing, telling, dancing, drumming, singing, and other forms of communication that maintain some distance between performer and subject) over representational actions (imitation, impersonation, and other forms of mimesis that suggest the seamless unity of performer and subject) but often includes both. In some African rituals, a human *represents* a god but does not necessarily *become* a god, while in others, depiction of a god transcends both presentation and representation: Götrick explains, for example, that the *egungun* practitioner 'does not symbolize the ancestors, it *is* the spirit of the ancestors' (ibid.: 38). Such a transcendence – or manifestation – usually involves a transition or transformation through which the performer becomes the vehicle for the actions of a god or ancestral spirit. Manifestational ritual performances are metonymic in so far as the performer's actions become an attribute of the god/spirit invoked.

Whatever performative tropes it uses, ritual is always efficacious for the community and enacted for a particular audience to preserve the order and meaning of anything from harvests to marriage, birth, and death. Unlike drama, which is mostly a re-enactment (even of a 'true' story), ritual is never fiction. Generally, then, ritual comprises:

• presentational acts that often incorporate the representational, and sometimes manifestational acts which transcend both;
• acts that are believed to be real, not fictional or play, even if aspects of play are incorporated into the ritual;[7]
• acts that are performed by 'knowledgeable human agents'

(Drewal 1992: xiii)[8] for a specific audience which knows how to act or participate in response;

• acts that are performed for the continuance and regeneration of a specific community often at a particular time, usually through a spiritual dimension; and

• acts that are based in history and work to preserve history but which are not necessarily impervious to change.[9]

The community service that ritual performs will most likely have entertaining consequences, but entertainment is not necessarily its goal. The secular context, while important, is submerged by the more crucial spiritual or sacred dimension.

One of the common assumptions about ritual is that it embodies an ostensibly pure, pre-contact reality; ritual, however, is not static. Yoruba ritual, for instance, 'is molded and remolded by creative performer/interpreters. . . . [It] is shaped by the competitive pulls and tugs of a multitude of manipulators' (Drewal 1992: 28), including the forces of colonialism. Given its inherent adaptability, ritual – like other modes of performance, communication, and worship – can never be recaptured in its 'original' pre-colonial form. The combining of ritual with other cultural forms can, however, provide new performative events and practices that acknowledge the changes wrought by colonialism. Soyinka, among other writers, interweaves elements of western drama with Yoruba ritual to situate ritual more prominently in a contemporary world. The resulting hybridity and 'contamination' can provide a constructive way of locating ritual in a post-imperial context. Drewal cites the example of a Catholic priest, Father Valentine Awoyemi, who employs Yoruba rituals in conjunction with Christian rituals: 'that is the only way Christian religion can make sense among the Yoruba. . . . Christianity is the object being operated upon, not traditional religion' (ibid.: 168). This blending involves, for example, Father Valentine making theological connections between the *Ebibi* festival and the Biblical Passover to 'bring out the values he believes Catholicism shares with traditional Yoruba religion' (ibid.: 169).

The relationship between this Judeo-Christian ritual and the Yoruba ritual is intricate, tenuous, and mutable, much like the relationship between ritual and theatre. In some instances, however, the adaptation of a ritual is much less interactive or culturally sensitive. As a function of western society's spiritual commodification, ritual is frequently packaged for tourists in a manner which apparently replicates anthropological voyeurism. The rituals enacted for these tourists have been emptied of their sacred signification, however, and remain theatre, not ritual. In various places in Australia, notably Darwin, visitors can pay to watch an Aboriginal corroboree which is performed daily at sunset. While it may serve an important function in familiarising white Australians and overseas tourists with a fragment of traditional Aboriginal cultures, that corroboree no longer performs its ritualistic purpose; it also becomes an exoticised spectacle for uninitiated, paying spectators. Likewise, the Maori *haka*, or war cry, is regularly 'performed' by New Zealand rugby players (Pakeha [white], Maori, and Pacific Islander players) at the beginning of their international matches. In this instance, the *haka* has taken on new secular ritual connotations, and does not provide the wonted spiritual protection or regeneration; instead, it exemplifies New Zealand Pakeha appropriation of Maori customs for the purpose of constructing a nationalist rhetoric.

In a less neo-colonial context, Ossie Enekwe finds that 'ritual can easily be transformed into theatre and vice versa – in a number of ways. A ritual becomes entertainment once it is outside its original context or when the belief that sustains it has lost its potency' (1981: 155). This apparently easy transformation from ritual to drama blurs the boundaries between the two events and risks undermining the sacred nature of the ritual. The distinctions between ritual and theatre must be acknowledged if either is to have agency. When ritual is to be presented on stage, 'it must needs be re-presented, that is, re-interpreted in the dramatic context. Its justification becomes theatrical, not religious, and as "theatre" it is given a different form, another god' (Gibbons 1979: 91). Further, not all rituals can be immediately relocated into a westernised theatre practice. Andrew Horn rightly maintains that ritual.

> may in some ways be theatre, [but] ritual is not drama. . . .
> [Ritual] has developed in a divergent direction, towards
> magical communication between man and the natural forces
> rather than worldly communication among men. It would
> greatly facilitate the understanding of both ritual and drama
> – religion and art – if generic distinctions between them are
> kept distinct.
>
> (1981: 197)

Certainly, ritual and drama can intersect when each has particular locations, actions, and implements that can apply to the other. Horn schematises this possible intersection in a diagram which maintains a distinction between drama and ritual, but recognises the potential for overlap between them (see Figure 1).

Further complicating an examination of ritual is the fact that while ritual often adopts a theatrical context, its meaning tends to be altered when it is placed consciously within a play: its combination with drama devices that are designed primarily to entertain necessarily changes the ritual. This process is well illustrated by the Hausa theatre of Niger which customarily employs ritual, particularly in *Gaadoo K'arhin Allaa*, the most well-known Hausa play, written in 1973 by the Zinder troupe, Amadou 'Dan Bassa. The play centres on the enthronement of a *sarki*, or regional chief (Beik 1987: 15), but this theatrical representation of the ritual is not quite the same as an actual enthronement ceremony. A Hausa audience recognises that the play represents the *sarki* ritual but is *not* ritual; thus the distinction between ritual and drama – despite some intersection – is maintained. In many cases,

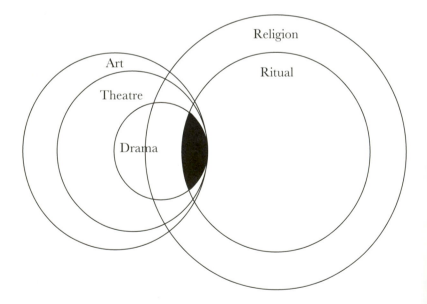

Figure 1 Horn's diagram detailing the intersection of art, theatre, drama, religion, and ritual

dramatised rituals keep some sacred elements/functions, but they are also secularised as part of a larger activity that is arts and entertainment based. While this does not necessarily deny the sacred quality of the ritual, it does force it to interact with the secular. The resultant coexistence of ritual and drama preserves and disseminates traditional forms and practices. Nevertheless, even when ritual's overlap with drama appears to associate the two very closely, they must be recognised as distinct practices.

Ritual and the body

Many of the requirements for ritual are similar to those of drama: actor(s), audience, costume, space, language(s), and a specified amount of time. When ritual takes place in drama, its codes accrete additional signification as part of both the theatrical and the ritual spectacle. Ritual can, however, impose restrictions on these performative signifiers or otherwise highlight certain characteristics not normally part of their systems of representation. Actants in a ritual are often distinguishable from actors in a play not only by their functions but also by their approaches to the performance. The transformation of a human actant into a god figure (the basis of many rituals) necessitates perhaps more preparation (or a different kind of preparation) than the transformation of an actor into the role of a theatrical character. While both ritual and theatre employ human actors/actants, Adedeji notes that ritual and non-ritual forms of characterisation differ in significant ways:

> In ritual drama the dramatic element is manifest when the individual or group in ecstasy aimed at communion with the metaphysical or divine power displays a pronounced character. There is a kind of awareness which drives the individual to reach out in order to attain this close communion, and by working himself up, steps outside himself and portrays a character which reflects his emotional state. In secular drama, however, the individual submerges his own personality and assumes a new character or role which is then presented.
>
> (1966: 88)

In naturalistic theatre, the body undergoes a conscious and voluntary transformation so that one person (the actor) 'becomes' a completely different – likely fictional – character. This process is based on conceptions of the body as a composite signifier which can be trained to convey the desired characteristics through facial expression, gesture, posture, movement, and so on. Human transformation in ritual appears to rely on 'a deeper awareness of body as symbol, as a "vessel" of meanings' (Gibbons 1979: 49) even though the actant(s) may also be highly trained performers whose craft, executed properly, is necessary for the manifestation of the gods/spirits. Ritual transformation can also involve considerable spectacle and metamorphosis, usually related to the intense concentration of individual (and often communal) energy – spiritual, physical, and/or emotional. As well as being able to create other temporal spaces (for example, the realm of the ancestors/gods), ritual actants can affect their own physical welfare and alter their own emotional consciousnesses, as well as those of their audience. Some rituals, particularly those of ancestral cults in the Caribbean, achieve transformation by spirit possession, which is significantly more complex than the illusionism that comprises most European drama traditions. Often involuntary, though still requiring complex preparation, spirit possession is generally manifested through vigorous physical movement/dance, producing a 'force' which is expressed in the tension maintained between control and frenzy. Although transformations that occur in ritual may rely to some extent on the assistance of illusion, they are not predicated on such 'unreality': ritual's transformations are concrete metamorphoses – however short in duration – that have the specific function of community preservation.

In its ability to traverse the human/spirit divide, the ritual body confounds the rational processes of imperial discourse and thus refuses capture and containment. Ritual renders the body open and mutable while often requiring or producing highly formalised actions, such as dance or processional movement, which display the ritual force as energy in action. Dance is particularly important, not only as a celebration of the physical (as in much western theatre) but also as a performed statement of transformation or possession. In many cases, the spirits are actually conjured through dancing, assisted by the power of the drum which is first felt in the dancer's feet as they contact the earth. The dancer's body expands, claims and/or creates space, marks it ritually, and so exerts power over his/her physical environment. Theatrical practice can translate the principles of ritual movement into a strongly physical interpretation of a role. The object, however, is not to achieve actual transformation or possession; instead, ritual drama seeks to express the mythos of the community by 'confront[ing] the audience with its own centre in as articulate a form as possible' (Gibbons 1979: 84).

Ritual and costume

If ritual is sacred, its associated costumes and paraphernalia are also sacred and not to be used randomly (or even seen in some cases) at non-ritual times or places. Like the uniform of the Christian clergy, a military officer, or a prison warden, non-western ritual clothing carries with it various unspoken authorities and can be read, therefore, as a potentially powerful tool for post-colonial cultures. While it may serve as a body covering, its signified meanings (and therefore its effects) extend far beyond the utilitarian. Because ritual costumes are symbolic as well as functional, stripping or denuding (a common practice in imperial regimes) is a significant act. The connotations of particular costumes/masks are of course specific to the context and culture in which they are used but there are a number of common practices. Masks are mostly used to create archetypes and to help establish ancestral links; thus, in ritual transformation, the masked[10] performer is animated by the spirit/god he or she depicts. As Christopher Balme remarks, 'The mask as a totem means that it is not just an aesthetic but is a religious cult object of considerable spiritual power for the wearer/possessor' (1992: 186). Masking in post-colonial drama often marks a theatre that is both spiritual and political in reference. While a mask conceals the face of the actor, it also reveals the site of culture, and the significance and power invested in the mask outside the context of the play. In contemporary African texts, the use of a ritualised mask generally signifies a shift away from imperial expectations and a return to traditional values, and an overturning of colonising, western influences. It also asserts the continuation of traditional or indigenous ritualised religious practices despite the influence of Christian missionaries.

Ritual and music

The ritual soundscape, often composed of music, verse, chants, and other affective forms of communication, propels the activity from naturalistic representation to ritualistic manifestation. Such traditional and transitional languages reserved for ritual occasions heighten the sacredness and specificity of the particular event. In many African and Afro-Caribbean rituals, the rhythm of the drum – the most significant musical instrument – is no mere accompaniment but one of the principal forces guiding the action: it shapes the dance and song and helps summon spiritual power(s). Verbal languages tend to be less significant for their literal meanings than for their ritual functions: songs of invocation and dismissal, for example, effect the appearance and exit of a god, while dirges ensure the safe passage of a dead person's spirit into the ancestors' realm. The process of naming takes on special significance in ritual because it is seen to confer indisputable identity and (sometimes) status. This is related to a belief in the magic power of words but it also depends on the proper completion of ritual procedures. Basic oral sounds or phonic elements are frequently stressed, producing an incantatory or mesmeric effect. Choral effects, another common feature of ritual, add to the archive of traditional forms which might inspire a linguistic rebellion against the norms of imposed verbal languages. In several respects, then, stylised ritual languages can undermine the authority of imperial discourse and avoid its reliance on semantic logocentrism. When a ritual that employs an indigenous language is situated within a play which uses a European language, the ritual takes on further emphasis as a culturally discrete activity that is enacted for the continued well-being of the initiated community.

Ritual in time and space

The ritual time scale differs significantly from theatrical and clock time. If theatrical time can be lengthened or shortened as required by the narrative, time in ritual often encompasses divine dimensions such as the ancestors' time, time after death, or time before birth. Movements through time in ritual can operate as a fluid interchange for related actions or as a rupture that suddenly transports the participant(s) from one temporal location to another. Although such manipulations of time also occur in drama, their justification is generally artistic rather than conceptual. By drawing on notions of a time (or timelessness) that is qualitatively different and often perceived as separate, ritual plays situate their subjects and actions within non-western epistemologies, thereby escaping the teleological assumptions of linear time.

Spatial considerations, which can interact with time, are also at issue in ritual. The space in which a ritual is conducted generally requires preparation and it may remain sacred after the ritual is completed. Like drama, ritual also creates its own conceptual plastic space/place that may be more symbolic than practical. Incorporated into a play, ritual space may require a disjunction from specifically theatre space, or there may be a need for at least some reorganisation of the usual spatial relationships facilitated by the proposed venue. As Rohmer notes about a production of Soyinka's *Death and the King's Horseman* (1976), 'the conditions of a theatre in the round and the spatial integration of the foyer [generally a non-acting space] avoid the conventional and paralyzing illusionism which is so easily created by the proscenium arch form' (1994: 58–9). In this case, removing the play from constraints of naturalistic theatre space (and thus intervening in the assumptions that space endorses) opens up audiences to engaging with the re-enacted ritual as an event distinguishable from the drama. Soyinka has commented that ritual theatre 'establishes the spatial medium not merely as physical area for simulated events but as a manageable contraction of the cosmic envelope within which man . . . fearfully exists' (1976a: 176). Generally preferring an arena-style or round playing space for his plays, Soyinka maintains that the community of spectators can participate more efficaciously when they inhabit a space that is not generally associated with secular theatre.

The kind of spectator response encouraged by ritual drama should not be confused with the sometimes gimmicky forms of what is blithely termed 'audience participation' in westernised theatre. As Peter Brook insists, participation occurs when there is an emotional, spiritual, and cognitive relationship between the actor(s) and the audience, a genuine relationship which is not necessarily overtly expressed: 'the audience that answers back may seem active, but this may be quite superficial – true activity can be invisible, but also indivisible' (1968: 144). Through its inherent metatheatricality, ritual drama aims to make the processes of participation conscious and therefore potentially powerful as part of a larger communal project that images liberation from cultural oppression. Such drama is distinct from virtually all contemporary western plays that involve the more colloquial ritual form of ritualised or repeated events.

RITUAL-CENTRED PLAYS

Ritual in post-colonial plays can be generally associated with at least one of two categories (aside from the references to a ritual at the end of a play to purify the community or repair the damage following the performance event). The first type of drama centres on a ritual (or sometimes a number of related rituals) which determines and structures the action, and often impacts upon the style of the performance. In such plays, theatrical and ritual transformations are of prime importance. Fatima Dike's *The Sacrifice of Kreli* (1976), dramatises two rituals designed to reinvigorate the contemporary community through the re-enactment of traditional practices. Set in 1885 in Bomvanaland (known now as the Transkei), the play is about the Gcaleka nation who have been forced from their land and into dire circumstances by the white settlers. The first ritual, a sacrifice to the god Mendu, takes place offstage and fails to have the desired effects. Some participants blame the intrusion of Soga (the first black Christian minister) and his travelling companion, Southey (a journalist), but one of the warriors, Sabela, reminds the group that 'what the British have done to [them] has no power over [their] ancestors. The customs must be carried out' (1978: 41). The failure of the ritual results in general dissatisfaction and insurrection among the warriors and necessitates a further sacrifice, the human sacrifice of the diviner, Mlanjeni. This second sacrifice, in which Mlanjeni is sewn into a bull's skin to die as the sun shrinks the skin, is much more significant (given Mlanjeni's position and history in the community) and becomes a central focal point of the play. The prophecy that Mlanjeni makes with his dying breath is a positive one: 'They say there is a way' (ibid.: 79). Through this ritual, the community is revived, its people encouraged to return to their lands and 'defend the honour of what [they] are' (ibid.: 79).

Even if all their facets are not explicitly portrayed on stage, the rituals that form the core of *The Sacrifice of Kreli* function not only as the major focus of the fictional community but also as a parable for contemporary struggles against apartheid. Designed to demonstrate the possibilities for articulating resistance to apartheid on African terms, this play's use of ritual is exceptional rather than typical in South African theatre. Nevertheless, its rituals ensure that one of the region's pre-contact histories is recuperated for modern-day black South Africans, regardless of tribal affiliation.

At the same time, the staging of these rituals directs both the king, Kreli, and the play's audience to contest white authority and its encroachments on Gcaleka land. Describing a community working together for the benefit of all (despite differences of opinion), the play's ritual allegorically sets up a model of cultural action: Mlanjeni's final prophecy and Kreli's interpretation of those words revive a sense of honour and pride in/for South Africa's blacks who have felt defeated by apartheid's constraints and humiliations. Kreli determines that Mlanjeni's prophecy instructs the Gcaleka nation to refuse intimidation by and subordination to whites. The elastic temporal and spatial frames of this dramatised ritual expand the play's theatrical and metaphorical frames of reference. Hence the ritual has significant agency and a regenerative effect for all its participants: it reinforces the community on stage and, in turn, the community in the audience who are also exhorted to fight apartheid and maintain their honour.

Another play which highlights the fact that colonialism has not destroyed local pre-contact customs or traditions is Soyinka's *Death and the King's Horseman*. A discussion of ritual in theatre must invariably include Soyinka; he is only one of many writers to employ ritual, but he is the most well-known and he has also theorised his use of it in his *Myth, Literature and the African World* (1976). Femi Osofisan maintains that *Death and the King's Horseman* is the play in which 'Soyinka succeeds most in recreating the complete, credible world of African ritual [because] here the ritual form is not merely recast, but the playwright invests it with a dialectic, and his personal vision intervenes for a crucial interrogation of history' (1982a: 77). That dialectic is predicated on a comparison of two ritual structures: those of the Yoruba and the British. *Death and the King's Horseman* is based on an incident that took place in Oyo, Nigeria in 1946.[11] The play focuses on Elesin, the King's Horseman, who is preparing to die ritualistically so that he can accompany the King, who died thirty days earlier, into the realm of the ancestors. Elesin's failure to do so will result in the King cursing his people for the humiliation they have caused him. Thus, Elesin's duty to die is inextricably associated with the continued health and viability of his community, but this is not recognised by the colonial District Officer who seeks to intervene because he considers the ritual barbaric. Elesin's ritual centres on a dance which, undertaken in a trance state, leads to death. He is, however, detained in this world by earthly pursuits when he decides to take a wife on his last night before the ritual instead of focusing all his energies on preparing for death. This is the action – not the District Officer's meddling – that disturbs the ritual, rendering it incomplete, and therefore ineffective. To ensure the community's safety, Elesin's son, Olunde, dances to death instead, leaving Elesin humiliated and without a purpose or place in both this world and the next. This main ritual is contrasted to several British ritualised events, including a masqued ball. The two cultures/rituals are paralleled structurally but not, ultimately, in purpose or power. To attend the masqued ball, the District Officer and his wife, Simon and Jane Pilkings, appropriate confiscated *egungun* costumes, the sacred garb for a ritualistic death cult. They are certain that the *egungun* clothing will ensure their winning the prize for best costume, and they are boldly impervious to their servants' horror at their actions. One desecrated sacred ritual assists in the success of a secular ritualised event. The impatient 'civiliser', Simon Pilkings, shows no respect for the sacred costumes because he can only read the Yoruba rituals as primitive and regressive. The play suggests, however, that these rituals have survived the onslaught of colonialism to outweigh easily what are to some degree their British equivalents.

Olunde's ritual death to correct his father's failed ritual can be read aesthetically, religiously, culturally, and, more importantly, politically. David Moody regards this corrective action as a ritual recuperation of performative agency and, consequently, cultural power:

> Olunde is 'actor' in both senses of the word: here we see per-
> formance as politics. Finally, he is also 'activist'; his death,
> senseless from the logic of the colonizer's economy, is literally
> pure 'play': a bodily sign of a culture's refusal to die. From the
> Pilkings' point of view, Olunde's death is a great waste; they
> had invested so much education in him! However, Olunde
> understands the importance of the sign; and performs, quite
> physically, the reappropriation of his society's rites, and rights
> of passage.
>
> (1991: 100)

The fact that Olunde's ritual is not performed on stage does not diminish the impact of the ritual moment and its political ramifications. There is ample evidence in the play to suggest the importance invested in the various Yoruba rituals: the costumes, the praise-singer's words, the community's readiness, the beginnings of Elesin's trance dance, and Olunde's dead body are all shown/staged quite clearly. This is entirely appropriate, given – in all likelihood – the audience's unreadiness to participate in the ritual itself (as opposed to its dramatised interpretations) at any deeper level. It is in the actual 'performance' of the ritual within the structure of the play that ritual and drama differ most significantly: a play's performance is generally based in entertainment, albeit likely with other intentions and effects; whereas ritual's 'performance' is carefully constructed to preserve community welfare, even if entertainment is a by-product. In *Death and the King's Horseman*, having the ritual offstage also prevents it from being construed as a merely theatrical device.[12] The use of diegetic space rather than mimetic space reinforces the idea that ritual's temporal and spatial parameters extend beyond those of drama.

Dennis Scott's *An Echo in the Bone* (1974) presents a West Indian death ritual, the Nine Night ceremony,[13] which honours someone recently dead and frees his/her spirit of the past so that a transition into the afterlife can be completed. As Renu Juneja explains, this ritual 'is not only evidence of cultural continuities with Africa but is also associated with direct political resistance' since it involves spirit possession (sometimes called *myal*), which was seen in colonial society as anti-white (1992b: 99). Scott initially sets his play in Jamaica in 1937, and then uses the Nine Night ritual to structure the main action in which nine episodes from the past (from three hundred years to two days before the ceremony) are presented to the audience and to the ritual participants, the ten people on stage. The ceremony itself unfolds over one evening in an old barn and, apart from a short preparation scene which gathers together the participating characters, all events 'take place' within this ritual framework. As the action proceeds, moments in slave and colonial history are juxtaposed to the more specific history of the dead man, Crew, and to the other characters' interactions in the fictional present. In this way, Scott combines the time and space of the living and the dead, collapsing phenomenological parameters into the intensified time/space of ritual performance. The play thus retrieves the past as a function of the contemporary moment and also suggests that re-enactments of history can achieve the necessary release from the psychological and spiritual (if not always the actual physical) legacies of slavery and racism. Particularly important here is the replaying of Crew's murder of the white plantation owner, Mr Charles, which becomes a rite of purification designed to counter the oppression endured by Crew and his enslaved compatriots. According to Errol Hill's introduction to the play, this act of murder is highly symbolic: 'It absolves the past record and looks hopefully towards the future. It typifies a cleavage between two dispensations: the old one of master–slave relationship and the new one of multi-racial brotherhood' (1985b: 13). Paradoxically, it is equally crucial that the final part of the ritual stages an alternative past in which the murder is averted. This does not alter the 'truth' of what has been presented but ensures that history need not become deterministic. As Rachel declares at the end of the play when she has come to terms with her husband's suicide, 'No matter what is past, you can't stop the blood from drumming, and you can't stop the heart from hoping. We have to hold on to one another. That is all we can do' (Scott 1985: 136).

The performative techniques called for in *An Echo in the Bone* also follow the conventions of the Nine Night ceremony. The ritual's focal point is possession, which 'induces a change of persona in the possessed individual without any obvious change in facial makeup or dress' (Hill 1985b: 11). By staging possession, the play enables the ritual participants to be transformed into the various historical characters presented. Rawle Gibbons, director of the Trinidad production of the play in 1976, describes how he approached this aspect in the second act, which, he argues, is propelled primarily by Rachel's trance (as opposed to the previous level of action induced by her son's possession):

> [Rachel] ritually greet[ed] each of her players who then demonstrated signs of possession. . . . Once possessed, the cast of Rachel's drama, dance to the table/altar set upstage centre, and each appropriates some symbol of the role he [*sic*] will be playing in the coming sequence. . . . After this ritual identification the characters walked or danced to their positions in a manner that more clearly state[d] what role they had adopted. . . . All these actions are supported in song by the characters who are not possessed through Rachel.
>
> (1979: 94–5)

Of course, such rapid role transitions are not only the prerogative of ritual theatre, but their justification, in this instance, is spiritual as well as theatrical, situating the idea of performative transformation within the wider cultural beliefs of the represented group and the projected audience. This technique also sets up a dialectical tension between the various roles played by the one actor as part of his/her character's ritual experience. Since Scott specifies that all of the ritual participants are black, their representations of white figures are particularly loaded because they foreground a racial gap between the signifier and the signified, thus diminishing the ultimate authority of the whites whose dialogue and actions are nonetheless explicitly illustrated. Possession also functions as a form of verification of the oral histories re-enacted, since manifest ancestral spirits are believed to tell the truth. That the otherwise mute drummer, Rattler, is able to assume a speaking character while possessed is part of the power of this manifest 'truth' as well as a potent statement about imperialism's silencing of black histories.

An Echo in the Bone, like several other plays with a central ritual, depends on metatheatre to clarify relationships between the different levels of action. The distribution of ganja among the characters and the preparation of the ritual site by spilling rum are small but significant acts designed to notify the audience that a different kind of performance is about to occur. In keeping with ritual's emphasis on affective arousal, the drumming is particularly important as a way of achieving transitions between various enacted scenes and also signifying such changes to the viewer. The more specific metatheatrical aspect, the use of multiple plays-within-a-play (including the overall Nine Night ceremony and its many historical 'flashbacks'), removes naturalistic frameworks, emphasises the epic sweep of the racial memory activated by the ritual, and encourages examination of the structural and thematic links between various performative levels. Moreover, each historical scene requires a further conceptual (spatial and temporal) alteration which repositions the original action and the larger play so that the audience must continually re-evaluate their understanding of both the ritual and its dramatic functions. As with *The Sacrifice of Kreli*, the viewer in/of *An Echo in the Bone* responds to the metatheatre on two levels: to the ritual 'insert' and to the allegorical frame play.

As Scott's play demonstrates, ritual re-enactment is a way of 'possessing' the past, of finding a home within the fractures of a history marked by dislocation and slavery and a present complicated by continued race/class inequities. *QPH* (1981), by the Sistren Theatre Collective, also uses a 'dead-wake' ceremony to

recover the past of the Jamaican people but focuses more specifically on women's histories, confining its time scale to the twentieth
century and incorporating many monologues in which the main
characters tell their stories directly to the audience. This particular
technique reflects the play's development from interview material
gathered from a number of inmates who had been living in the
Kingston Almshouse when part of it was destroyed by fire in 1980,
killing over a hundred and fifty women. Shaped by the structure
and performance conventions of the *Etu* ritual, *QPH* dramatises
the lives of Queenie (a preacher), Pearlie (a prostitute), and Hopie
(a domestic), three old women who met in the Almshouse after
years of poverty, exploitation, and neglect. Sistren's choice of ritual
is particularly apposite since *Etu* tends to be more women-centred
than many other equivalent rituals such as the Nine Night ceremony.[14] Not only are women the main participants, but the ritual
is usually guided by the Queen, the lead dancer, who 'shawls' other
dancers to invoke in them the spirit of the deceased. The dance
itself uses pelvic movement to symbolise fertility and rebirth,
further stressing the regenerative powers of women. In the play,
Queenie, who survives the fire, plays the Queen, raising Pearlie
and Hopie from the dead, so that the three 'relive' fragments from
their past. As well as presenting its dramatic action through the
frameworks of the *Etu* ritual, *QPH* actually verges on becoming
the ritual in so far as its distinctions between 'reality' and fiction
are deliberately blurred: in the theatre, the play *is* a remembrance
ceremony for the many fire victims buried without any memorial,
and in this respect each performance requires appropriate prep-
arations, including the sprinkling of the four corners of the stage
with rum. When *QPH* was performed, members of the audience
also protected themselves thus against the spirits evoked.[15] The
ritual/drama ends with a call for the recognition of the many
old women whose stories have been represented by the three main
figures: as Queenie says, 'We old, but remember, the old have the
key to the future, cause we hold the secrets of the past' (qtd in
Allison 1986: 11).

RITUAL ELEMENTS/RITUAL CONTEXTS

While the texts we have discussed foreground ritual, even if the
specific rituals are not entirely staged for the audience, a second
type of play uses ritual more as an incidental activity, a backdrop

for the action. Rather than being the central thematic and/or structural focus, ritual supports the action in such a play and tends to be used as part of a larger recuperation of tradition/history, as an expression of hybridisation, as a device to establish setting/ context, or as a performative model for various sections of the action/dialogue. Quite often, such ritual elements are closely linked with the political thrust of the play, adding agency to its over- all effect as an expression of post-colonial culture. A case in point is Mbongeni Ngema's *Township Fever* (1991 [1992]), a play about striking South African rail workers, which incorporates a Zulu protection ritual staged to disperse throughout the auditorium the smoke that each striker must breathe. The ritual prepares them for the dangers they face and adds a spiritual dimension to the strike, emphasising the inhumanity of the conditions under which they worked.[16]

The Broken Calabash (1984), by Tess Onwueme, is set against a backdrop of the Igbo *Ine* festival which marks the beginning of the harvest, and includes various rituals that help the community prepare for the new yam season. The specific ritual staged is a dance in which the young people of the village, cross-dressed in European clothing, perform comic scenes/movements for the entertainment *and* edification of their community. Adopting the costumes of the opposite sex, the dancers parade in the town square created on stage so that the audience can witness the effect of their exaggerated 'double' (cross-cultural and cross-gender) transformation. The Town Crier encourages all youths to partici- pate and explains the ritual's purpose as he advises them that the evil of the old year must be purged:

> Therefore, you must heartily satirize those sons and daughters of iniquity who, year in, year out, pollute our land by their ways and deeds. . . . Anyone singled out as the polluter of our land must pay the final debt to the gods. Only if the gods are pleased can we then eat the new yam.
>
> (1993: 37)

The dance, then, deploys the grotesque body of the (cultural) transvestite in a purification rite which is predicated on a healthy rejection of over-zealous attempts to imitate the by-products of western culture, symbolised here by European clothing. While the Town Crier inveighs against such western 'polluters', the play itself attempts to situate the ritual in a correlative site *with* the westernised lifestyles that are becoming dominant globally. One of the main characters, Courtuma, cannot understand how 'tradition' – very closely tied to patriarchal authority in this case – can coexist with such things as western face make-up and the Christianity in which his daughter, Ona, is dabbling. Hence, he is unable to appreciate or respect his daughter's choice to seek solace in both Igbo and/or western entertainments and forms of worship. Ona counters, 'We all wear more than one face at a time in this society' (ibid.: 25), but the impasse between father and daughter results in Courtuma's suicide, which threatens the new yam season and the community's welfare. Onwueme thus critiques the hegemony of a tradition which clearly subjects young women to the dictates of their male elders; yet, at the same time, she contextualises the clash between tradition and modernity, and celebrates aspects of the folk culture by staging some of its forms. The performance text's particular reinforcement of the place of ritual in a society in transition allegorically allows for the accommodation of change since, for instance, the calabash cannot be repaired once it is broken.

Ritual in Jack Davis's *No Sugar* is much more of a recovery exercise than in *The Broken Calabash*, and it functions less as a context for the action than as a momentary transformation for Aborigines already detribalised by the forces of imperialism. Here, the corroboree, the ritual most commonly staged in Aboriginal plays, enables all the initiated males to express their cultures and histories together via song, music, dance, and story-telling. Even Billy, the black tracker who otherwise guards the remaining men, participates fully in the ceremony, thereby transgressing his usual ('white') role of 'politjman' or police agent. The corroboree that the men enact has been necessarily altered as a result of these characters being forcibly relocated to missions: the men are not in their usual location, they are partly dressed in European clothes, and the quality of the *wilgi* (ceremonial paint) they use on their bodies is not quite right. Nevertheless, the corroboree serves valuable functions: it gives the men an opportunity to tell (and thereby to perpetuate) their dreaming stories, and it educates the audience (both black and white) in Aboriginal history. The dance itself can also be seen as a symbolic reclamation of the land, as was potently illustrated in the 1990 Perth production of the play in which the ritual inscriptions of the dancers' footprints on the sand remained visible for some time after the corroboree had finished.

This ritual successfully challenges white history and thwarts the colonisers' attempts to constrict Aborigines, both physically by consigning them to the camps and metaphorically by attempting to destroy their cultures. The corroboree's placement within a larger piece of theatre that establishes appropriate frameworks/codes for a ritual re-enactment avoids the reifying processes implicit in the 'tourist-centred' spectacles described earlier.

Ritual can be re-enacted – to some degree – *in* theatre; as well, ritual and theatre can coexist: in parts of India, for instance, there may be a ritual event in the context of a Hindu devotional drama that, while significant, does not reclassify the play as ritual. Another possibility, common in Hindu drama, involves 'preliminary rituals which remove obstacles in the way of successful performance (usually by making offerings to Ganesha), [or] sanctify the stage or playing space' followed later by concluding rituals such as 'a simple prayer or dance offering to the gods, asking their forgiveness for any mistakes or anything displeasing in the performance' (Richmond *et al.* 1990: 123). Ritual frames these Hindu plays, associating their specific theatrical activities more closely with sacred or devotional rites. Native North American theatre and Maori theatre frequently begin or end with such a ritualistic moment: Maori plays often include a ceremonial welcome or blessing while in indigenous North American plays, a sacred circle or ceremony invokes the gods or spirits to honour the participants or to ask for protection from evil. The Spiderwoman troupe (composed of three sisters from the United States) conclude their performances with an honouring song for the spirits. In *The Book of Jessica* (1981), the Canadian writer, Maria Campbell, explains the importance of protecting the actors from the spirits by 'doing [the] circle every morning and every night' to begin and end rehearsals, particularly during difficult sessions (Griffiths and Campbell 1989: 40). The signification of specific, community-based ritual actions that are designed for particular social benefit, and that can be accommodated within a performance context that does not significantly alter their meaning, intersect here with the ways in which theatre communicates its dramatic images/narratives.

The emphasis on recuperating indigenous ritual traditions from both the erasures of imperial history and the exoticising impulses of contemporary western culture is clearly evident in *No' Xya'* (*Our Footprints*) (1990), a play devised by David Diamond and the Headlines Theatre Company of Vancouver in close collaboration with the Gitksan and Wet'suwet'en Hereditary Chiefs. The playwrights – or rather, playmakers – also incorporated a number of rituals to produce a docudrama about native land claims against the provincial government of British Columbia in 1984. The Dance of the Salmon, for example, is a ritual re-enactment designed to illustrate (through metaphor) the tribal structures and migratory patterns of the original inhabitants of the land. Like the subsequent dance which focuses on a caribou hunt, this ritual is performed by the contemporary characters in full costume and totemic masks, giving spiritual weight to their claim for jurisdiction over ancestral territories. The play's action is also punctuated by traditional songs recorded by the elders of the Gitksan and Wet'suwet'en tribes and only to be used as part of a rehearsal/performance that has had proper ritual preparation.[17] Accordingly, *No' Xya'* frames its action with a ceremonial opening: the audience is brought into the playing area to the sounds of traditional singing/music and then told that 'The doors are closed' (1991: 50). This simple statement – the first line of the play – makes the viewers aware that they have entered a ritual space. As the lights come up, white feathers (a sign of peace) are released into the auditorium while a tribal Chief sanctifies the stage by walking its perimeter and pounding his cane down on its four corners. Only after this ritual has been completed can the dramatised action begin. At the end of the performance, in keeping with the gift-giving tradition of the Feast Hall (or potlatch), each audience member is given a tree and invited to speak with the attendant representatives of the Gitksan and Wet'suwet'en peoples. Hence, although the structure of the overall performance/ritual remains the same each night, the outcome of the play is flexible and depends largely on the audience's participation.

As demonstrated by many of the plays discussed, the political dimension of ritual intersects with the sacred, not least because many rituals were officially banned by imperial agents. Such forbidden events became subversive activities under colonial rule and can now function as symbols of liberty for an independent post-colonial system, especially when ritual is contextualised by and/or located in a particular community. It follows, then, that a theatre practice informed by ritual aims to do more than merely keep the spectator aesthetically engaged. Like other forms of political theatre, it foregrounds belief systems and demands some kind of active response. And while ritual is a central way of transforming and simultaneously maintaining the spiritual and social

Plate 2 Ritual costumes in *No' Xya'*. Sherri-Lee Guilbert (top) and Hal
B. Blackwater in 'Dance of the Salmon'
Source: Reprinted with the permission of Playwrights' Canada Press, Toronto,
David Diamond, and Headlines Theatre Company, 1990. Photo: Chris Cameron

health of a society, it has also shaken the geographic boundaries that colonisation erected, as illustrated throughout the African diaspora by the increasing emphasis on ritual-based traditional enactments in theatre practice and in more general forms of cultural expression. Necessarily, such enactments do not remain static but transform to fit the contingencies of the new context and of the indigenising process. In the Caribbean, one of the most obvious and prominent of these transformations of cultural signifiers has been Carnival.[18]

CARNIVAL

The performative elements of a society's secular festivals, like those of its religious/sacred rituals, provide an important archive for a post-colonial theatre praxis which aims to articulate the specificities of local experience. Typically, such festivals are derived from pre-colonial traditions which have been altered in response to changing circumstances and contexts. Because they tend to be relatively open in structure, secular festivals often become highly syncretic events which incorporate many elements of the colonising culture even while expressing difference and/or dissent from them. In theatrical terms, they offer a repertoire of stock roles and situations which might inspire a society's drama and, perhaps more importantly, a style of performance that decentres imperial conventions. Characteristically exuberant, non-naturalistic, and self-consciously theatrical, drama based on festival enactments calls attention to public space, communal activity, and vernacular languages. Its subjects are positioned within a distinctive local history, thereby foregrounding the various cultural influences at play. Like ritual drama, festival drama also works towards revitalising the folk culture even while adapting its specific tropes.

The Trinidad Carnival is a paradigmatic example of a secular event which has exerted a strong influence on the drama of its region. Although the current commercialisation of this festival has undoubtedly diluted its protest against the inequities of a social system founded on class- and race-based hierarchies, Carnival remains an important source of inspiration for theatre practitioners in the Caribbean. Intertwined with its development over the past two centuries is a long history of struggle against slavery and colonial rule, and it is this specific background, as much as the inherent subversiveness of Carnival,[19] that makes it a particularly suitable model for a 'home-grown' post-colonial drama. In this respect, Errol Hill argues that Trinidad's Carnival may resemble those of other countries 'but it is essentially a local product in form, content and inner significance' (1972c: 5). As a spectacular performance which celebrates the transformative functions of costume, role-play, language, music, and dance, Carnival also demonstrates the rich theatricality of Trinidadian culture while proffering a range of folk characters and themes that might be reinvigorated on the contemporary stage.

Although Carnival in Trinidad began as a pre-Lenten festival observed by the French settler-elite class in the eighteenth century, it was subsequently appropriated by the masses, shaped by various African-based customs (especially those associated with harvest festivals), and thus transformed into an expression of black culture.[20] As Hill notes, celebrations commemorating freedom from slavery formed the ritual beginnings of an indigenised Carnival and often accounted for the serious elements that appeared in the early street masquerades (ibid.: 23). For many decades after emancipation, Carnival commenced with canboulay (from the French, *cannes brûlées*), a midnight procession in which ex-slaves carried flaming torches (*flambeaux*) through the streets accompanied by drumming, dancing, and singing.[21] As a 're-enactment of the drama of bondage' (Juneja 1988: 88), canboulay remembered the brutalities of the colonial experience at the same time as it asserted the black population's right to take part in a festival from which they had previously been debarred. That planters disguised as estate blacks (*negue jardin*) had themselves been in the habit of staging a similar scene at Carnival makes canboulay even more significant as a subversive practice because it demonstrates that a masquerade designed to degrade its subject can be taken over, invested with new meanings, and deployed as an empowering strategy.

Once it had been fully appropriated by the black lower classes (causing the white and coloured classes to withdraw their partici-pation), Carnival became a vehicle for rebellion against colonial authority. For poor urban blacks in particular, Carnival represented more than a licensed inversion of accepted norms; it embodied an ongoing struggle against inequity and oppression. The spirit of protest was evident not only in the traditional calypso lyrics and the various masquerades which satirised white society, but also in a pattern of disorderly behaviour that culminated in riots during

79

the 1881 and 1884 Carnivals. Not surprisingly, such eruptions of violence fuelled ruling-class hostilities towards what was deemed a 'vulgar' festival, but authoritarian efforts to suppress the event remained ineffectual and were often absorbed into the content of the masquerades through parody and satire (ibid.: 90). This ability to neutralise the political power of its detractors has undoubtedly contributed to the longevity of carnival culture in the Caribbean. Improvisation, which has long been a defining characteristic of Carnival, also accounts for its rapid response to social pressures. The quintessential example here is the evolution of the steelband following the 1883 ban on African drums. In search of substitute percussive instruments, masqueraders initially resorted to the shack shack (a calabash rattle), then devised an orchestra of bamboo sticks, before finally settling on discarded oil drums (pans) which they tempered and tuned to make original music. When authorities imposed a similar ban on steelbands during World War Two, the panmen defied the law, clashing with police and turning their music into a form of open protest.[22] Juneja argues that the history of the steelband demonstrates the 'resilience and startling creativity of an economically deprived people' as well as the element of resistance that had always characterised the Trinidad Carnival (ibid.: 91).

Ritualised forms of conflict – both physical and verbal – became an important part of the post-emancipation Carnival. Some of these combative elements were derived from the slave folk culture and subsequently shaped into flamboyant displays designed to challenge the repressive forces of law and order. In particular, the stick fight emerged as a prominent feature of Carnival in the second half of the nineteenth century. Previously a form of sport among plantation slaves, stick fighting was taken up by the dispossessed urban masses and foregrounded as one of the defining elements of the jamet[23] or yard culture. The jamets, excluded from mainstream society because of their colour, lack of education, and poverty, formed yard bands for the purposes of gambling, fighting, and exploiting women, deliberately cultivating an image which reversed the norms of respectability. During Carnival, stick-fighting bands were praised by the shantwelle (predecessor of the modern-day calypsonian) and a chorus as they marched through the streets engaging in mock and real combat. The most common structure for the stick fight, the calinda or *bois bataille*, comprised intricate dance steps as well as attacking and defensive manoeuvres which required considerable skill and rehearsal. Hill maintains that the fighter (*batonye*) 'was first a performer conscious that his play was watched by a critical audience' and adds that the 'stick-fighting argot – the challenges and rebuttals – is a picturesque, metaphoric language, the stuff of which dramatic dialogue is made' (1972c: 27).

The verbal cousins of the stick fighters, the English Pierrots and the Pierrot Grenades, came to the fore as principal masqueraders in the Carnival after stick fighting declined with the suppression of canboulay parades towards the end of the nineteenth century. Whereas the batonniers had moulded the stick fight into a finely honed display of physical movement, the Pierrot characters paraded their linguistic skills. The English Pierrot, an upper-class figure not averse to duelling with whips or sticks as well as language, displayed his[24] erudite learning in speeches characterised by inflated rhetoric and grandiose boasts. The Pierrot Grenade, on the other hand, was a 'low-born' character, a jester who spoke the Patois of the underprivileged and depended solely on his wits to survive. He entertained the audience with topical commentary, satire, and burlesque, and invented word-destruction exercises as a parody of grandiloquence (see Gibbons 1979: 164–9; Creighton 1985: 61–6). Like later speech-based masquerades such as the Midnight Robber, a bandit who harangued his audiences with lengthy monologues until they paid a ransom,[25] the Pierrots exploited the dramatic qualities of language, using it as a mode of action rather than a countersign of thought. Although the style and function of their speeches differed, both characters' linguistic performances were rooted in the colonial experience; taken together, they demonstrate a characteristic ambivalence towards imposed language and education systems which were simultaneously mocked and celebrated. As Helen Tiffin observes, 'The Carnival confrontation between the two kinds of Pierrots dramatized the ironies inherent in competing oral performances which on the one hand re-produce and on the other traduce Anglo-imperialist scribal tradition' (1993a: 915).

While there are many other traditional conventions and characters worthy of comment – the Dame Lorraine (a transvestite who used dance to satirise the upper classes) and the Jab Molassi (fearsome devils carrying chains and pitchforks) are cases in point – this brief account of Carnival shows the ways in which the Trinidadian version of a common secular festival contains within its history a theatre of resistance against colonial forces. In its variety and mutability, this theatre enacts 'complex archetypes of synthesis, which have emerged from cultural clash and conflict to accommodate all the cultural legacies involved' (McDougall 1987: 77). These principles were clearly recognised by Hill over twenty years ago when he wrote his first major critical work, *The Trinidad Carnival: Mandate for a National Theatre*. In what is something of a manifesto for his own dramatic work, Hill maintains that Carnival continues to operate counter to imported regimes of value, and that it therefore supplies the essential ingredients for an indigenous performative practice:

> Substantial material exists in the Trinidad Carnival, past and present, for the creation of a unique form of theatre – a theatre in which music, song, mime, dance, and speech are fully integrated and exploited; a theatre rooted in the culture of the country of its birth; a theatre of colourful spectacle; in short, a national theatre.
>
> (1972c: 110)

If some of Hill's claims for the subversiveness of Carnival must be modified in the light of its relatively recent takeover by big bands and commercial sponsors, his prescription for a theatre rooted in carnival traditions remains viable none the less and has been taken up enthusiastically by talented young directors such as the Barbadian, Earl Warner (now working in Jamaica), and his Trinidadian colleague, the playwright Rawle Gibbons.

Few critics would argue against assertions that the pre-independence Carnival in Trinidad was not only a repository of folk culture but also for many years the only vigorous form of indigenous theatre in a colony – or indeed in the wider Caribbean region – whose few purpose-built performance venues were governed by the hegemony of Shakespearian and other Anglo-European conventions (see W. Bennett 1974: 7; Omotoso 1982: 46–7). Opinion remains divided, however, over the efficacy of Carnival as a politically motivated art form once it became an institutionalised event approved by the government and the dominant classes. Walcott, for instance, has attempted to maintain a rigid distinction between festival enactments and 'serious art', arguing that Carnival is not adaptable for the stage (see Hamner 1993: 141), a curious position given that his works often borrow freely from its forms. In 1970, he wrote that contemporary Carnival was 'as meaningless as the art of the actor confined to mimicry' (1970b: 34). This criticism stemmed from a belief that figures such as the calypsonian, the steelbandsman, and the carnival masker were becoming reified tourist attractions, 'trapped in the State's concept of the folk form' and therefore 'preserving a colonial demeanour' (ibid.: 7). The opposing view, espoused by Gibbons, Hill, and other promoters of festival culture is that change is inherent to Carnival, and militates against any kind of stasis even in the face of commercial pressures. Gibbons argues that 'Carnival is not commemorative but a living, protean event, whose very validity depends on its capacity to absorb and express the current while containing the past' (1979: 100). A potent example of this precept has been the recent development of Talk Tent, a practice which has reinvigorated the oral traditions of such figures as the Pierrots and the Midnight Robber by setting up among the many carnival entertainments a new performance venue where the 'extempo talkers' reign supreme.[26] The success of Talk Tent and other adaptive practices designed to strengthen the non-commercial aspects of Carnival would seem to negate Walcott's argument that this particular festival has only limited relevance for the contemporary Caribbean stage.

CARNIVAL LOGICS

From a theoretical point of view, Carnival presupposes the possibility of social reform by activating the communal imagination. The Guyanese novelist/essayist, Wilson Harris, calls this the 'dream-logic' of Carnival, arguing that such logic enables us to conceptualise, through the masks and dances of the masqueraders, an 'absent' or ceaselessly unfinished body into which 'a present humanity descends' (1986: 41).[27] This view is compatible with Bakhtin's idea that carnival enacts a 'gay relativity' via regenerative laughter associated with images of bodily life presented through parody, caricature, and other comic gestures derived from the mask (1984: 39–40). Carnival is thus suitable as a model for post-colonial representations of the body politic that seek to dismantle the hierarchised corpus of imperial culture. Both Harris and Bakhtin also stress that carnival is a medium of the multivoiced or polyphonic spirit which effectively opposes monologic orders such as colonialism. Post-colonialism, which recognises the agency of the colonised as well as of the coloniser, enables polyphonic dialogue, an important part of the deconstructive project. In post-colonial contexts, Russell McDougall argues, carnival perspectives undermine 'the self-determining (im)postures of imperialism by activating that play of difference which is the principle of heterogeneous community' (1990a: 8). Along with dissent, difference is crucial if all possibilities for ontological change are not to be blocked. Hence heterogeneity 'sets carnival apart from the merely oppositional and reactive' so that it can operate as a 'site of insurgency, and not merely withdrawal' (Russo 1986: 218). In this respect, the conservative view of carnival as a licensed inversion has only limited usefulness for our analysis; more enabling is the idea of carnival as a subversion that undermines virtually all categories of social privilege and thus prevents their unproblematic reassemblage.

A theatre-specific criticism must do more than articulate theories concerning Carnival's potential as a metaphorical blueprint for reconceiving social hierarchies; it should also analyse how the performative patterns of festival enactments posit ways of translating those theories into action. In its emphasis on inclusiveness, Carnival is, above all, a popular theatre – a theatre of the streets and yards where urban populations congregate to do their daily business. Through particular uses of space/place, Carnival dissolves the usual demarcations between performer and audience, auditorium and outside street. It claims a right to all public space and creates a theatre wherever there is a confluence of people, thus giving the marginalised access to the privilege of self-representation.[28] Like ritual, Carnival favours the circle/arena rather than the proscenium in its spatial configurations, but whereas ritual generally demands a specially-prepared venue, the carnival 'stage' is a desacralised space that admits fluid and informal interface between all participants. Even in the tents and on the platforms and floats erected specially for festival enactments, theatrical space remains movable, mutable, and transient. And while the facts of 'real' place impose a certain character on street/yard theatre, the performers continuously present another 'place' through their enactments (Gibbons 1979: 41), destabilising the conventional set of relations designated by the site appropriated for performance. Relevant here is Michel Foucault's idea of theatre as a heterotopian site: a site 'capable of juxtaposing in a single real place several [incompatible] spaces' (1986: 25). If these spaces are never isolated but dynamic and interacting, where they meet and clash is of crucial significance for a post-colonial theatre inspired by Carnival because it is in the nexus of debated (and debatable) space that pluralism and difference emerge. The street, the oval, the marketplace, the arena, the crossroads, the yard – these are the places where the conflicting identities of Trinidad's multicultural society are negotiated.

Carnival foregrounds verbal/aural languages which are derived from yard culture. Music is paramount to the event and syncretic in composition. The ubiquitous steelband emphasises the Caribbean's links with the 'percussive cultures' of Africa while stringed instruments such as the cuatro point to the Latin-American elements of the Carnival. More recently, East Indian music has been added to the repertoire,[29] not to mention the pervasive influence of western (particularly American) popular forms. The continual hybridising of Carnival's musical base functions as yet another expression of the polyphonic spirit that makes Carnival a productive model for the theatre of marginalised cultures. What integrates disparate musical elements is a rhythmic sensibility that permeates all festival activity. Hill argues that 'speech patterns are also part of the polyrhythmic symphony of sound and movement' (1972c: 115). In this respect, it is the performative aspect more than the semantic content of language that accounts for its effects. The 'call and response' songs of the parading bands, for instance, follow the basic structure instituted by the shantwelle of old, emphasising strong group feeling. The solo calypso pays more attention to language itself but still depends on performative devices for its full impact. This is particularly evident in the art of 'picong' (from *piquant*), a traditional war of insults sung by rival calypsonians. Speech-based masquerades, only marginally less rhythmic in their linguistic conventions, also tend to stress sound over meaning. Overall, carnival language is marked by its insistent exploitation of all the resources developed by an oral culture. Despite the fact that much of it is highly structured, this language none the less maintains an uncanny ability to adapt to new pressures, to improvise. Based on satire and self-satire, it is continually open to the kinds of reformulation and change that achieve release from the normal social and linguistic order. This is partly due to the carnival emphasis on mimicry, which, as Walcott explains, is an act of 'imagination' and 'endemic cunning' (1992: 27).

The carnival body is similarly open, multiple, split, and transformative; it 'takes pleasure in the processes of exchange and is never closed off from its social or ecosystemic context' (Stallybrass and White 1986: 22). In this respect, it shares the ritual body's potential to disrupt what Veronica Kelly has called the 'closed and perfected bodily ego-ideal of Western civilisation' (1992b: 61). Through movement, costume, and mask, Carnival constantly reconstructs the docile (colonised) body as an unruly (resisting) body that threatens to loosen institutionalised authority's grasp on representation. The perpetual 'jumping up' (dancing) of the revellers emphasises the life-force, displaying at the same time a delight in transgressive sexuality and excessive corporeal states. Though such dance consolidates the idea of a collective body politic instead of expressing individualised identities, it does not demand uniformity. It integrates African and European elements into a theatricalised presentation of Creole culture[30] without attempting to change 'their habitual relationship [which] is one of tension and confrontation' (Gibbons 1979: iv). Even the patterned movements of the festival procession must be seen within this context as a form of communal choreography rather than an orderly routine designed to discipline the body. Overall, the performative 'force' that drives Carnival is similar in effect to that of ritual but different in shape; it depends less on a concentrated focus of spiritual and physical energy than on the exuberant kinesis of the unrestrained body.

The carnival 'mas'' brings into focus the theatrical functions of costume and mask as powerful signifiers not only in themselves but also in conjunction with the body. Here, the colloquial term mas' refers to both the face mask and the masquerade – that is, to the fully costumed character created by appearance and role-play. Until recently, the convention at *j'ouvert*,[31] the early-morning beginning of the Trinidad Carnival, was that all performers wore masks to preserve anonymity (see Gibbons 1979: 137). This was particularly important to speech mas' such as the Pierrot Grenade, whose verbal licence often depended on his not being recognised by the figures he lampooned. Today, anonymity serves mostly to refuse the markers of social classification; it is a sign of absence, a form of transgression. At the same time as the mask disguises the individual, it presents a strong visual focus for audience recognition; the masked character becomes archetypal in dimension, especially when large groups of masqueraders wear the same 'face' as part of their band identity. Hence, 'playing mas'' both effaces and effects character. Whereas the mask/costume of ritual, though often spectacular, is generally the vessel through which a god's presence/action can be manifested, Carnival celebrates the artificiality of the mas' itself. Carnival's emphasis on the mode of excess – actualised by the fantastic, often grotesque, larger-than-life figures which surge through the streets every year – foregrounds the gap between performer and role, preventing naturalistic characterisation's seamless application of costume to the body. This is particularly the case with transvestism – a popular feature of Carnival, here taken to include cross-cultural as well as cross-gender dressing – which can both invert and displace gender and racial binaries. Thus the carnival mas' provides a model of disruptive difference in its display of an 'alter-body' (in the Bakhtinian sense) that beguiles and reworks imperialist systems of representation.

In its insistent sense of metatheatre, Carnival offers an important framework through which to interrogate received models of performance. The self-conscious role-play of the performer demands a spectator whose scepticism as much as his/her participation is vital to the success of the masquerade. The semiotic codes of such a theatre are always under question, subject to revision through re-enactment and parody. Linda Hutcheon argues that parody 'signals how present representations come from past ones and what ideological consequences derive from both continuity and difference' (1989: 93). This is an important observation for a post-colonial theatre which draws inspiration from carnival forms. If, as Gibbons maintains, the task of Caribbean theatre is to 'traditionalise itself' by appropriating carnival and/or ritual modes (1979: 300), we must continue to ask what principles lie behind these systems of representation. Hill sets out an important starting point for this analysis in his call for a carnival theatre which integrates movement, music, language, and rhythm so that 'verbal metaphor [would] be matched by visual symbol' (1972c: 116). Such a theatre organises all the communicative resources of person, place, and object for an aesthetic presentation which presupposes an interpretive *and* interactive community, rather than an 'audience of disciplined applauders' (Tiffin 1993a: 915). It shuns realism to revel in the magic of artifice, always pushing against the limits of the imagination. Like ritual theatre, it aims to transform the ways in which 'reality' itself can be conceptualised.

CARNIVAL PLAYS

Our discussion thus far has treated Carnival as a distinctive form of theatre rather than solely as a theatricalised activity. Unlike ritual, which, as we have outlined, is distinguishable from theatre by its emphasis on the 'reality' of a performed presentation, Carnival is centred on fiction and fabrication. This is not to deny that it may also effect ritual catharsis and/or community renewal, but instead to suggest that Carnival positions itself deliberately and self-reflexively as art, even if Eurocentric modes of thinking would deny it that status. The idea that the formal Caribbean stage has appropriated Carnival as a way of 'transform[ing] the theatrical into theatre'[32] is surely misleading in this respect, since it depends on received notions of the genre and thus excludes certain varieties of theatre. While such hierarchies are clearly not acceptable to a post-colonial critique, it is nonetheless necessary for the purposes of this analysis to separate Carnival as a particularised annual event from the many other theatre events which use its forms and/or themes in self-contained performance pieces (usually) designed for a paying audience. These 'plays' tend to operate outside the commercial frameworks of Carnival itself, so they escape the materialism perceived as its current corruptive force and are ideally positioned to critique Carnival conventions even while attempting to emulate them.

An analysis of the ways in which Carnival tropes have been taken up and reworked on the 'formal' stages of the Caribbean and how they have in turn transformed those stages reveals as much about the ideological functions of theatre as a system of representation as it does about the significance of Carnival. Since the 1960s, a period which marked the last vestiges of colonial rule in much of the region, Carnival has emerged as one of the primary influences on Caribbean drama. Even if it is treated ambivalently, it still permeates a number of levels of theatre practice and criticism. Not only do Carnival motifs appear with great frequency in the work of well-known playwrights such as Errol Hill, Earl Lovelace, Mustapha Matura, and Derek Walcott, but they have also featured in Marina Maxwell's experimental Yard Theatre in Jamaica, in Trinidad's Village Theatre, and in other community-based projects. Carnival drama has been institutionalised in schools through the teaching of plays on the subject – Euton Jarvis and Ronald Amoroso's *Master of Carnival* (1974) is a case in point

– and presented abroad as one of the defining elements of Caribbean culture in, for instance, Helen Camps's highly successful *Jouvert*, which toured England and Europe in 1982.[33]

In some cases, the model for this kind of theatre has not been the Trinidad Carnival *per se* but other festivals closely related to it in form and style. In Guyana, people jump up at the annual 'tramp', which resembles the Carnival road-march of Trinidad. Ian McDonald's *The Tramping Man* (1969) uses this event as a symbol of unity in a country deeply divided by racial and social tensions. The St Lucian version of Carnival is the La Rose festival, aspects of which are recreated in Roderick Walcott's comedy, *The Banjo Man* (1971). Jamaica's tradition of carnival drama often draws from the Jonkonnu festival, which Sylvia Wynter celebrated in her 1973 play *Maskarade* and later in television programmes.[34] More recently, the Sistren Theatre Collective initiated a group-devised piece, *Ida Revolt Inna Jonkunnu Stylee* (1985), as part of the Caribbean Popular Theatre Exchange, an event which drew practitioners from Dominica, St Vincent, Trinidad, Cuba, and other countries of the region. This piece combines Trinidadian characters – Pierrot Grenade and Dame Lorraine – with Jonkonnu figures such as Set Girl and Bellywoman,[35] using Carnival as a theatre form common to the various countries represented. One of the play's distinctive features is its deployment of Carnival forms for feminist purposes; this represents something of an incursion into a style of performance that is often the terrain of male-oriented theatre.

The incorporation of carnival elements into a play necessarily impacts upon its form. This is clearly illustrated by Derek Walcott's *The Joker of Seville* (1974), an adaptation – or rather a reworking – of Tirso de Molina's *El Burlador de Sevilla*, the seventeenth-century Spanish play about Don Juan. In framing his version of the story with a prologue that 'resurrects' Juan as a champion stickman, Walcott seizes upon the legendary Spaniard as an apt figure through which to present the picaroon sexual exploits of his Caribbean counterpart, the jamet folk hero. This prologue sets the action in the stick fighting arena (or *gayelle*) and begins with a procession of villagers carrying candles, a scene that is reminiscent of canboulay in the late 1800s. When Rafael and his troupe of actors/dancers/singers stage a stick fight before introducing the play proper, their accompanying calypso with its refrain of 'sans humanité'[36] enhances the festival atmosphere. Dressed as the Jack, the Queen of Hearts, and the Ace of Death, these figures, along with Juan as the Joker, would be familiar to Caribbean audiences as carnival mas'.[37] That Rafael and his troupe periodically draw attention to their roles as actors (rather than characters) reminds us of the artifice of the performance, a manoeuvre which, like Walcott's call for the play to be staged in the round, is also in keeping with the conventions of Carnival. At the end of each act, in particular, the narrative action is brought back to Trinidad, to the gayelle of the jamets, to the theatre space where the audience participates in the collective recreation of the story. The final scene shows Juan's body borne off by stick fighters in a celebratory ritual designed to affirm his immortality. Through the re-enactment of Juan's deeds, the actors have ensured that this trickster/joker cheats death and gains freedom. Thus the seasonal renewal central to Carnival is complete.

Within this frame, Walcott uses a number of other carnival tropes. Calinda rhythms are evident not only in the numerous duels but also in the shout-and-response pattern of the songs which punctuate the action. Musically, the play borrows heavily from calypso, its verse steeped in the satire and innuendo that characterises this form. Whereas Tirso's version of the legend is shaped as a morality tale intended to warn against libertine behaviour, Walcott's joker/trickster stands as a critique of the social mores upheld by the jamets' colonial masters. The burlesque style of *The Joker of Seville*, foregrounded through techniques such as mimicry and metatheatre, constantly subverts any censure of its subject. Emphasis on the transformative functions of masquerade further strengthens the carnival theme since it is largely through disguise/role-play that Juan is able to stage the sexual conquests which threaten to disrupt the moral order of his society. Despite his misogyny, in the carnival context he emerges as a 'force and an amoral principle' (Juneja 1992a: 258) more than a fully realised character; he is, in many respects, the spirit of the flamboyant and rebellious jamet culture rekindled through performance. It is fitting, then, that Juan meets his death at the hand of his original *animateur*, Rafael, rather than that of his enemy, as in Tirso's text. As John Thieme notes, the 'bacchanal of the skeleton' performed by the actor troupe (with Rafael masquerading as death) 'provides a Trinidadian version of the play's *carpe diem* theme, which appears to be based on the devil bands of Carnival' (1984: 69). In combination, these carnival elements creolise the Spanish source text

Plate 3 Dancing Troupe, Derek Walcott's *The Joker of Seville*, Trinidad Theatre Workshop, 1993

Source: Photo: Helen Gilbert

on a number of levels, reworking Eurocentric forms to produce a distinctively West Indian play and turning an imported moral lesson into a celebration of local culture and history. As markers of a carnival kinetics expressive of Caribbean identity, movement forms such as folk dance and stickplay are quite common in a number of other plays. Whether 'written' into the action of a play as in much of Hill's work – *Man Better Man* (1985) and *Dance Bongo* (1971) are two of the more prominent examples – or used in the performative realisation of the script as, for example, in a United States production of Matura's *Playboy of the West Indies*,[38] these movement patterns often resist dominant cultural inscriptions on the performing body. In a parallel project, Earl Warner attempts to decolonise Caribbean theatre in his work as a teacher and director by instilling his productions with a 'carnival aesthetic' expressed primarily through the acting style.[39] He maintains that the percussive rhythms of carnival movement jog the black body's memory of its African roots, facilitating that connectedness with the earth that is often the goal of ritual enactment. For Warner, imbuing the formal theatre with carnival kinetics is not only a way of denaturalising (moving away from naturalistic styles *and* exposing the artifice of their seeming naturalness) received performance conventions, but also a means of preserving his own heritage.

In terms of dialogue, calypso remains one of the prime weapons of a carnival language often appropriated to reform the standard English of colonial theatre. While its metrical rhythms are used to produce a stylised and poetic language, calypso also maintains the lexicon of the yard, of the underprivileged classes. Its oratorical patterns, along with its emphasis on praise, criticism, and challenge, make it an ideal medium for social comment. Since in Caribbean culture, 'the orator speaks [or sings] in the face of at least implied adversaries' (Ong 1982: 111), calypso also sets up a particularly interactive relationship with the audience, intervening in the reception processes of naturalistic theatre. It is an effective vehicle for satire and, simultaneously, for the affirmation of folk traditions. The dialogue of *Man Better Man*, for example, is laced with picong, especially when the supporters of the rival stick fighters prepare for the duel by baiting each other verbally (Hill 1985a: 99–100). As well as augmenting the carnival atmosphere, this particular picong situation gives the actors the opportunity to present an improvised performance in keeping with the play's theme and form. Thus Hill celebrates the verbal traditions of Carnival at the same time as he exploits them to parody the posturing that is part of the jamet ethos. In a similar fashion, Matura's *Rum an' Coca Cola* (1976) matches language with subject, using calypso in a self-reflexive critique of the worlds of both his characters, Bird and Creator. As the younger calypsonian, Bird stands for contemporary Caribbean society with its dependence on the tourist dollar, while Creator is a hard-drinking misogynist who lives in the past. Although neither character can fully recuperate calypso from the margins of an increasingly commercialised entertainment culture, the play as a whole affirms it as a valid and vital performance style.

Earl Lovelace takes up the heroic aspect of the calypso tradition in his complex allegorical play, *Jestina's Calypso* (1984). Jestina embodies the spurned colonial subject; hers is the ugly black face constructed as western imperialism's other. In what could be seen as one long calypso poem or song, Jestina's dialogue expresses not only her own personal history but also the tragedy of her country, its exploitation and degradation by foreign powers. At the same time, however, this poem conveys her resilience and bravery as a figure who refuses to internalise the self-defeating identity ascribed to her. In response to insults about her ugliness – this kind of ridicule is called 'pappyshow' and is a common feature of calypso – Jestina declares her own inner beauty:

> They have made you the jailers of your own prison. So poison yourselves with your laughter. Watch me and envy me, for long after the last poor one of you suffocate in the vomit of your cowardice, long after the echo of your laughter dies, I shall be walking still, striding still, with my head up against the winds of the world, battling to become myself. So laugh on bretheren [*sic*], laugh.
>
> (1984a: 25)

Lovelace's use of calypso in this play is particularly interesting in so far as he applies a predominantly masculinist tradition to assert female identity. Through metaphor, Jestina articulates the legacy of Trinidad's colonial experience in terms of her own relations with men, bemoaning the 'rape' that has left her 'breasts dragged down by centuries of bearing cane and coffee and cocoa' (ibid.: 23), an image which encapsulates her country's exploitation by western powers. As a critique of both imperialism and patriarchy,

Jestina's dialogue resists cultural hegemony while intervening in the sexism that has been part of her local environment and a defining characteristic of traditional calypso. Simultaneously, her woman-centred verse claims access to the verbal bravado of the rebel calypsonian.[40]

The linguistic conventions of the various carnival speech mas' are also used, often in tandem with dance/movement, to signal and/or to produce post-colonial stage languages. Again, it is their satirical functions that make these mas' attractive to Caribbean dramatists as vehicles through which to deflate colonial pretensions and dismantle hierarchies of imperial language. Walcott capitalises on verbal parody in a number of his plays, often staging a battle of words/wits designed to disrupt the dominant linguistic order. Corporal Lestrade, the mulatto prison warden of *Dream on Monkey Mountain*, provides a notable example of a character (de)constructed through carnival language. Having internalised the values of his white masters, Lestrade functions as their mouthpiece, his speech replete with the scholarly verbosity of such figures as the English Pierrot. This disruption of linguistic order is most evident when he assumes the role of a judge presiding over his prisoners:

> When this crime has been categorically examined by due process of law, and when the motive of the hereby accused by whereas and ad hoc shall be established without dichotomy, and long after we have perambulated through the labyrinthine bewilderment of the defendant's ignorance, let us hope, that justice, whom we all serve, will not only be done, but will appear, my lords, to have itself, been done.
>
> (1970a: 221–2)

Here, as elsewhere in the play, Lestrade's rhetorical flourishes set him up as a figure of ridicule, a mimic man whose Anglo-ventriloquial speeches carnivalise[41] dominant language systems even while attempting to establish their authority.

Lovelace also draws on the various speechifying traditions of Carnival, often foregrounding specific mas' as a way of establishing political frameworks for what seem at first like domestic dramas. *The New Hardware Store* (1980) for example, presents the Midnight Robber as the alter ego of the neo-colonialist Ablack, a Trinidadian merchant who has adopted the values of western commercialism to the point of exploiting his workers and former friends. In an expressionist interlude, Ablack's transformation into his carnival double is effected primarily through 'robber talk', a series of long and boastful speeches in which he refers to himself as a notorious criminal (1984b: 70–2). He also adopts the movement and gestures of the Robber, punctuating his tales of banditry with a threatening 'dance'. This kind of verbal/kinetic display is a common feature of robber talk (see Wuest 1990: 43), which Lovelace uses not only to enliven the performance but also to give Ablack a degree of self-insight he has hitherto lacked. Rooso, Ablack's advertising man and night watchman, participates in the role-play as 'mockman' (antagonist), but, unlike his boss, Rooso is able to move beyond his carnival mas' rather than becoming reduced to it. In the context of *The New Hardware Store*, the Robber/Ablack is a figure guilty of the worst kind of betrayal because his rebellion against law and order has become an excuse to rob the poor to line the coffers of the rich. Thus Lovelace's play gives contemporary relevance to the Robber mas' while harnessing its rich theatricality to conduct a searing indictment of materialism. Allegorically, the 'new hardware store' stands for post-independent Trinidad, now run by a new capitalist class of 'thieves' who perpetuate the same old colonial relations.

Carnival tropes, then, are not always used to deliver a wholly-positive celebration of Caribbean culture. Perhaps one of the most enduring Carnival traditions is the tendency towards self-reflexive criticism. In this respect, plays which focus on Carnival itself provide important sites for the analysis of its customs, its relationship to other systems of representation, and its changing functions in the wider society. Lovelace's 1986 play, *The Dragon Can't Dance*, adapted from his earlier novel of the same name,[42] is notable for its thorough investigation of the carnival mythos in contemporary Trinidadian culture. In many ways, the play makes an epic attempt to stage the competing texts of Carnival as a form of national identity that urges people to rise above the class and race conflicts endemic to their society. On the other hand, it also critiques the masquerade of solidarity central to the annual 'jump up', the carnival myth that 'all ah we is one' (Lovelace 1989: 7). This ambivalence is less a function of any indecision on Lovelace's part than of his perception that carnival discourse is multivalent and sometimes contradictory. As Steve Harney notes, 'common participation [in Carnival] does not mean common readings, only common participation in the act of reading' (1990: 131).

For Aldrick, the nominal hero of *The Dragon Can't Dance*, Carnival is a serious and significant event and one which requires ritual preparation. Each year, he sews the scales on his dragon costume with 'ceremonial solemnity', reconstructing, through the mas', a personal and communal history of survival despite poverty and oppression. One scale is for his grandfather, working the stone mountain; the next for his mother, bringing up five children and waiting for her man. Each scale tells part of a complex story:

> Every year I do it again. Every threat[43] I sew, every scale I put on the body of the dragon is a thought, a name, a chant that celebrate how I get here and how I survive on this Hill. Every year I trace my life again.
>
> (1989: 11)

This ritual is Aldrick's way of pulling together the threads of the past. On a broader level, his dragon functions mnemonically in so far as it embodies a history of 'slavery, emancipation, deferred dreams and the constant struggle for cultural affirmation' (Reyes 1984: 111). By focusing on Aldrick's painstaking ritual in the play's opening image, Lovelace anticipates the possibility of transformation through 'playing mas''. The communal function of Carnival as a rite of purification is also established by the chorus as they 'dance to the hurt' of their daily existence, their song an incantation designed to ward off evil (Lovelace 1989: 6). In this context, Carnival continues to express the spirit of revolution, and to provide the disenfranchised with the opportunity to choose their own roles and to affirm their own worth. That Aldrick eventually discards his dragon mas' does not necessarily diminish the potential liberation of Carnival; in fact, it is only through his experience of becoming the dragon every year that he begins to recognise a point for moving forward beyond the temporary 'magic' that playing mas' offers. At the end of the play, he is proud of having been a 'good dragon' but also ready to assume greater responsibilities towards his people. Aldrick's recognition of the artifice of Carnival is central to his personal growth, a factor which distinguishes him from many other characters on the Hill.

The reverse side of the carnival masquerade is self-delusion and/or withdrawal. Lovelace represents this potential trap through such characters as Cleothilda, the aging mulatto woman who assumes the role of queen of the Hill, and Fisheye, who plays at being a revolutionary but learns little from his failed rebellion. In a slightly different category is Philo: he remains aware of the artificiality of his role as Calypso King even though he has capitulated to the lure of the fast buck. Even Aldrick is in danger of using Carnival as a form of retreat from involvement with the beautiful young Sylvia, the virgin/whore who is yet the Hill's unbroken spirit of beauty and resilience. On this level, carnival masquerade affects only the surface and image of the community; it does not lead to transformation or acceptance of difference, a point stressed by the black characters' failure to recognise the full humanity of the Indo-Trinidadian, Pariag, who settles in their midst.

While the narrative action of *The Dragon Can't Dance* reveals the need for a national myth that might synthesise the conflicting movements of Carnival into a more enabling expression of individual and communal identity, the performative text of the play shows no such reservations. As well as following the verbal rhythms of Carnival in the songs and even the everyday dialogue, Lovelace peoples his stage with masqueraders – the Robber, the Jab Molassi, the fancy Indian – whose impassioned dance is a form of revolt against the dominant social (and theatrical) order. A voice from the chorus gives a running metacommentary that makes the transgressive functions of Carnival abundantly clear: 'This is warriors going to battle. This is the self of the people that they scrimp and save and whore and work and thief to drag out of the hard rockstone and dirt to show the world they is people' (1989: 29). With the dragon as its centrepiece and ritual source of energy, the whole Hill/stage is a moving, chanting force[44] that refuses imperial authority over the body and over theatrical representation itself. Overall, Lovelace's criticism of Carnival is outweighed by his celebration of its performative traditions. Even though the changes in Aldrick's life mean that the dragon can no longer dance, the kinetic force of Carnival will continue, perhaps in some other form. As suggested by the play's closing song/dance, re-acting (to) Carnival is more than an empty ritualised act. In this sense, carnival's thematic and performative functions cannot easily be separated.

Rawle Gibbons's *I, Lawah* (1986) invests even more significance in Carnival as a regenerative act which revivifies both the community and its drama. This play, subtitled 'a folk fantasy', explores Carnival's ritual origins in the post-emancipation era by focusing on the 1881 canboulay riots. At the centre of the narrative are members of a jamet band, the Helles Enfants, whose lawlessness is expressed through stick fighting and periodic challenges to colonial authority. Their leader is Lawah (from the French *le roi*), the batonye whose skills at stick fighting, womanising, and dancing have won him the status of the 'warrior king' of his band. At the same time as it dramatises yard culture through a fragmented collage of images, the play tells the story of Lawah's former woman, Sophie Bella, who has escaped the squalor of the yard to work for the white gentry, only to be coerced into the bed of Monsieur Le Blanc, her employer. After Lawah is imprisoned by the British police for marching in the streets, Sophie, inspired by the self-immolating sacrifice of her young mistress, Therese, returns to the yard to galvanise the disempowered jamets into fresh resistance. As she dances, flambeau in hand, leading the canboulay parade in defiance of the British ban, those who choose to follow her are transformed by the experience. The carnival dance/procession revitalises the jamet culture as a whole while allowing each participant to recuperate his/her own 'warrior' self. As the shantwelle, Popo, declares in the play's final verse: 'The Lawah leading me, is me' (1986: 64), a statement which affirms solidarity with Sophie Bella, and, simultaneously, a new sense of personal subjectivity.

Although Gibbons celebrates folk culture, he does not shy away from criticising some of its components. In particular, *I, Lawah* shows that heroism does not derive from the batonye's *bois/* phallus;[45] rather, it is driven by memory and faith translated into subversive action – in this case, the song/movement of the canboulay parade. The play intervenes in the masculinist ethos of jamet culture by highlighting Lawah's impotence in contrast to Sophie Bella's strength, and by including such figures as the female batonye and the obeah woman, Nen. In so far as it presents the women characters as the 'restorers of a temporarily defeated culture' (Fido 1990a: 336), *I, Lawah* not only writes women back into the history of Carnival but also engages with current Caribbean gender struggles. Notwithstanding this significant aspect, Gibbons's primary concern is with the spiritual purification of the wider society, a process which he represents through the central motif of fire. Fire is the literal force that spurs Sophie Bella into action when Therese sets herself alight to protest against being compelled into a marriage she does not want. More importantly, fire is the energising spirit of the rebellion, the 'eternal flame' which 'burn[s] from yard to yard/Down the streets of time' (1986: 62) to remember – to recall *and* to make whole – the past of the *cannes brûlées* era, the fictional present of the riots against imperial rule, and the future which the audience of the play inhabits. In the context of Gibbons's 'folk fantasy', the ever-permeable boundaries between Carnival and ritual dissolve completely as the subversive elements of the riot take on spiritual, as well as political, significance.

In structure and style, *I, Lawah* follows the performative conventions of the jamet Carnival. Its action is set in the gayelle and is arranged according to the rhythms of the calinda, which, as Elaine Fido explains, 'is divided into three steps or "pas": Karray, the opening move of the stick fight, which is very confrontational; Lavway, meaning roughly roadmarch, "the song that moves the people"; and Pas, or step, as in dance, a display of self' (1990b: 255). Within this framework, a raggedy band of players re-enacts scenes out of their collective memory. The narrative is told elliptically, often through mask, dance, song, procession, and incantation, with players returning to the chorus circle when they are not presenting their particular character(s). Particularly noteworthy is Gibbons's use of the chorus, which is always central to the action rather than merely functioning as a vehicle for commentary and/or criticism or for filling in gaps in the narrative. In keeping with the tradition of the calinda, the shantwelle and the chorus constitute the force that propels the performance forward, their verse and refrain enacting a form of ritual 'magic' that makes things happen. Similarly, their rhythmic dance functions less as an illustration of the story than as a kind of alchemy. This sense of magic is enhanced by the ring of flambeaux that lights the gayelle, giving actual presence to the catalytic energies of fire and reinforcing its symbolism in the play.

As well as reinvigorating the black community, the various carnival forms in *I, Lawah* undermine imperial authority. When Inspector Baker ventures into jamet-town to view the 'bacchanal', he is met by the chorus who immediately deflate his status by parodying him in a Dame Lorraine routine. Then Jal, the prostitute, targets an important icon of British imperialism by playing mas' as Queen Victoria:

> Yes, my dear Inspector, those neg jade in that colony are a worrisome lot. In my bountiful generosity, I give them freedom. How do they say thanks? They run up and down the streets like naked savages. Naked, I tell you. What an

embarrassment to the crown! See, my dear Inspector, that
they stay off the streets. Or get them some decent clothes.
Too much public exposure.

(Gibbons 1986: 26)

Faced with the grotesque masks and mocking language of his
so-called charges, the Inspector is not only enraged but also
unnerved. The masqueraders' performance activates precisely that
movement which reveals the instability of colonial authority as
theorised by Bhabha: a turning 'from mimicry – a difference that
is almost nothing but not quite – to menace – a difference that is
almost total but not quite' (Bhabha, 1984: 132). At the same time,
Jal's dialogue takes up a common trope in colonial discourse: the
distinction between civilised and savage as a function of clothing.
Her speech, which can be seen as a cryptic metadiscourse on the
idea of masquerade itself, thus politicises costume as a signifier.
In a related strategy, the play draws attention to carnival language
as a site of resistance to imperialism when the Inspector reads
out a document condemning the canboulay procession while
each of his phrases is interrupted by the choric refrain of 'no
surrender' (Gibbons 1986: 38). Here, the dialogue follows the
chant-and-response structure for subversive purposes: to fracture
the coherence of the Inspector's speech and thus disperse its
power.

As *I, Lawah* demonstrates through its combination of ritual and
carnival tropes, the sacred is not always separable from the pro-
fane in many indigenous traditions. By reinvesting in Carnival that
sense of ritual purification that informed its earlier expression,
Gibbons follows the dramatic spirit of such African playwrights
as Soyinka, confirming, at the same time, that Carnival has not
necessarily lost its political agency. Nor is the carnivalesque, as a
subversive strategy, confined to Caribbean theatre, despite the fact
that its most concentrated practice is undoubtedly found there.
Apart from its historical suitability as an influential form for post-
colonial drama, Carnival, like ritual, provides an appropriate
model for a culture which does not always have access to the costly
theatre technology upon which many western conventions rely. In
this respect, the representation of ritual and carnival through
drama establishes the 'umbilical link between art and tradition'
that is necessary for decolonisation (Gibbons 1979: 300).

NOTES

1 Soyinka has also disparaged the ways in which western critics are exceedingly selective about what African cultural icons they deem to be significant: 'The persistent habit of dismissing festivals as belonging to a "spontaneous" inartistic expression of communities demands re-examination' (Soyinka 1988: 194).

2 Bishop gives the following account of the reception of one of Soyinka's plays. Gerald Fay reviewed *The Road* for *The Guardian*, commenting that 'when [Soyinka] knows, or perhaps more accurately when he can make us others know what he is trying to say, he will be going places'. Robert Serumaga's retort contextualises Fay's comments: 'but it may at least equally forcibly be argued that the shoe is on the other foot. When Mr. Fay can understand at once what a play set in a different culture is all about, he will be going places. On the evidence of the review he may not even be trying.' Serumaga preferred a *Daily Mail* critic whose response leaves open the opportunity for cross-cultural dialogue: 'I do not myself pretend to have understood half of Soyinka's play. I am sure for one thing that I have got the plot all wrong. But throughout the evening I was thrilled enough to want to understand' (the above example is quoted in Bishop 1988: 63). Soyinka's *Death and the King's Horseman* received similar press, particularly from Frank Rich, the drama critic for the *New York Times*, when the play was staged on Broadway in 1987. In his highly unfavourable review, Rich misreads Soyinka's play, even claiming it to have a 'classical [European] shape' (*New York Times* 2 March 1987: 13).

3 Asagba illuminatingly defines the ways in which critics' accounts of African drama since the 1960s have set up misleading paradigms of its history (1986).

4 It is important to note that the Judeo-Christian rituals common to western cultures do not, in most cases, still retain a high degree of intersection with the people's lived reality, as ritual usually does in many African contexts.

5 Indigenisation is not to be confused with creolisation; whereas the latter focuses on the synthesis of elements from dominant and dominated cultures, indigenisation is 'the more secretive process by which the dominated culture survives' to humanise the new landscape (see Wynter 1970: 39).

6 See Hussein (1980) who outlines several possible paths for the development of drama in Africa, and Asagba (1986) whose evolutionary scheme is slightly different.

7 Asagba discusses several festival theatres where ritual events take on theatrical dimensions (1986).

8 Drewal is speaking here specifically of Yoruba ritual, but this characteristic seems common to ritual generally.

9 More specific definitions of ritual may, of course, be required for particular communities.

10 Some possession rituals present an 'inner' mask created by the (usually involuntary) immobilisation of the facial muscles into a fixed

expression which signifies the presence of the spirit (see Gibbons 1979: 136).

11 This incident has also been described by an early Nigerian playwright, Duro Ladipo, in his play, *Oba Waja* (1964).

12 Ritual's location offstage in drama does not, of course, prevent initiates participating at the imaginative level.

13 The Nine Night ceremony (similar to the Haitian Ceremony of the Souls) is one of the standard death rituals observed in Afro-Caribbean religions, particularly in revivalist cults such as Pocomania. It derives from ancestor possession cults of the Ashanti and involves rigorous dancing, often called *Kumina*, which leads to the manifestation of the spirits. The term '*Kumina*' is sometimes used in the wider sense to refer to syncretic cult religions and/or rituals which maintain significant African influences, particularly rituals based on possession (see Wynter 1970: 46; Juneja 1992b: 98–9).

14 Some commentators make no distinctions between *Etu*, Nine Night, and a number of similar death rituals while others seem to present *Etu* as one of the many kinds of possession dances that might occur as part of the Nine Night ceremony (see Cobham 1990: 247; Wynter 1970: 47). Commenting on *QPH*, Sistren specifically refers to the use of *Etu* (which they also call *Kumina*) and describes the traditional features of this ritual in ways that do suggest it is a separate version of the standard dead-wake ceremony (see Allison 1986: 11).

15 Beverly Hanson of the Sistren Theatre Collective explains that actors were 'really scared of doing the play because it was about dead people and involved certain spiritual things that [they] would not normally practise outside of the church because people can get possessed' (Hanson and Matthie 1994).

16 While the ritual element in *Township Fever* is pertinent to our discussion, it is important to note that the play was a critical and box office failure. See Ngema (1992) for details of the video *Out of Africa: The Making of Township Fever*, which presents the play text in addition to problems in its construction.

17 The published play script notes that such sacred songs were used with permission only for the performances and could not be reproduced otherwise in any textual form (Diamond *et al.* 1991: 65).

18 We use the capitalised spelling, 'Carnival', to indicate the particular Caribbean event held each year in Trinidad; lower case spelling refers to more general forms of carnival and/or adjectival uses of the word.

19 Bakhtin (1984) demonstrates at length the thesis that popular festivals/carnivals invert conventional social hierarchies.

20 Folk historians point out that whereas the festivities of the white plantocracy had been largely confined to 'genteel' activities such as masquerade balls, house-to-house visits, and horse-driven carriage promenades, the black populace's version of Carnival became a boisterous street celebration much closer in spirit to the original Saturnalian revels of pre-Christian Europe. The catalyst for this change was the emancipation of the black slave class in 1834.

21 This procession, originally held in August on the anniversary of

emancipation, was derived from the slaves' experiences of being mustered into groups by the planters and then driven with whips to the cane fields to put out fires. According to Gibbons, the procession's transfer to Carnival 'indicates that the ex-slave projected in [*sic*] Carnival the sense of bold freedom' associated with canboulay (1979: 31).

22 The history of gumboot dancing in South Africa is similar: conceived by black miners as an alternative to the drumming that the authorities restricted, it used available objects such as gumboots, tin cans, and bottletops.

23 Also spelled 'jamette', from the French *diametre* – the outside, other half, or underworld. The jamets lived in barrack yards, cramped tenements situated behind the frontage of the city streets, which enforced communal life with all its associated tensions.

24 These figures were usually gendered male although female performers may have adopted such roles on rare occasions.

25 The robber masque synthesised old elements of the oral tradition with the lawlessness of the western cowboy figure. According to Wuest, a 'dual process of establishing "authority" and recognition through the display of scholarly verbosity and simultaneous mockery of the British educational system is the most conspicuous element of the robber's act' (1990: 51).

26 Talk Tent is modelled on the traditional calypso tents except that the roles of the main performers are reversed so that the calypsonians talk and the Emcees sing.

27 Harris's novel, *Carnival* (1985), attempts to demonstrate this principle in fictional form by using Carnival as a mode of refiguring and renouncing colonialism.

28 In his recent theatre work, Rawle Gibbons has attempted to reproduce the characteristics of carnival space by staging productions in various (often outdoor) non-dedicated venues.

29 Although post-independence Carnival has a history of being primarily an event for the black and Creole classes, there is increasing evidence of Indo-Trinidadian participation in the event and of the incorporation of carnival forms into traditional East Indian rituals such as Hosein.

30 The Creole cultural model is fairly standard for Trinidad and the Caribbean. It focuses on the ways in which the conflicting influences of African- and European-based practices/ideologies are constantly assimilated to produce a composite culture which remains mutable and open-ended. See Ashcroft *et al.* (1989: 44–51) for a concise summary of the principles behind creolisation and its linguistic effects. This topic will be dealt with in further detail in Chapter 4.

31 Derived from the French *jour overt* meaning daybreak and also called 'jouvay'. See Hill (1972c: 86) for a detailed description of j'ouvert conventions.

32 Originally Walcott's phrase (1970b: 34), this has been a common catch-cry of critics of Caribbean theatre – see Omotoso, who titled his 1982 book on Caribbean drama *The Theatrical into Theatre*, and also Fido (1992: 282).

33 Camps has been a major figure in the promotion of 'Carnival Theatre' which draws on traditional mas' to produce a new style of musical theatre. In 1980, she produced *Mas in Yuh Mas* (written by Paul Keens-Douglas), the first full-length stage play to consist entirely of carnival characters, and then later followed this example in *King Jab Jab* (1981) and *Jouvert* (1982). In particular, Camps made use of the highly dramatic dialogue of such figures as the Midnight Robber and the Pierrot Grenade.

34 Wynter has also written a very informative account of the Jonkonnu festival in Jamaica, tracing its history and function in relation to imperialism (1970).

35 Set girls formed an elegantly costumed chorus which sang, danced, and protected the set, while Bellywoman (pregnant woman) is, of course, a celebration of fertility. See Wynter (1970) for a full explanation of the various characters of the Jonkonnu, which is thought to have derived from African yam festivals.

36 Literally meaning 'without mercy', this phrase was the standard cry (a war invocation) used in nineteenth-century *Kaiso* – an early form of calypso. Gibbons explains that colonial authorities also made efforts to ban this refrain (1979: 204).

37 Walcott also draws on elements of the English mummers' play which he indigenises so that the traditional death and resurrection of the mumming hero acts as a symbol of the virility of jamet culture.

38 Pacquet notes that the Arena Stage production of this play in Washington DC (1988–9) foregrounded the rhythms of carnival in both the language and the movement of the characters (1992: 96).

39 Although as yet unable to fully articulate the specifics of this aesthetic, Warner explains that it is dependent upon a non-naturalistic style which physicalises emotion through the stance of the actor (1993).

40 Of course, there have been female calypsonians in the past and they are now becoming increasingly popular as Caribbean women demand greater public representation in the arts.

41 'Carnivalise' is used here and elsewhere in this book as a general term (derived from Bakhtin's work) meaning to subvert through parody or otherwise diminish the authority of a discourse or system. In this instance, Walcott also uses specific Carnival tropes in the subversive process.

42 This analysis deals solely with the dramatic version of *Dragon*. Apart from the change in genre with its necessary stripping down and concentration of the narrative action, the play ends more ambiguously than the novel. Lovelace omits the distinct suggestion that Sylvia will choose Aldrick/love over Guy/material comfort and leaves her standing undecided between the two as the lights go down.

43 The transcription of Trinidadian English renders 'threat' from 'thread'.

44 Earl Warner, who directed the Trinidadian production of *Dragon*, explains that his ideal design concept for the play would image the entire Hill as a dragon (perhaps a fibreglass structure) in order to encapsulate the mythic elements of Carnival. Aldrick lives in

the mouth of the dragon because he's dealing with the head; other characters live at various levels in the body. On j'ouvert morning at the beginning of the second act, the entire dragon would 'come alive' and move into the audience in carnival costume. Unfortunately, Warner was unable to realise this design because the playwright wanted a less stylised set (1993).

45 The term '*bois*' (or wood in the English) is used in many Caribbean societies to refer to the erect penis. *I, Lawah* uses this word for humour and innuendo at a number of points.

3

POST-COLONIAL
HISTORIES

History is not so much fact as a performance.

(Dening 1993: 292)

———————————

Today, history is generally accepted to be a discourse that is as
open to interpretation as any other narrative discourse (such as
fiction). In his history of the mutiny on the *Bounty*, Mr. *Bligh's Bad
Language*, Greg Dening attempts to demonstrate the ways in which
history entails an ongoing reassessment of the past that facilitates
a perception of the present and the future: 'History is not the
past: it is a consciousness of the past used for present purposes'
(1993: 170). Following the influential work of Hayden White,
Dening, like other contemporary historians, condemns conventional historiography (in which the present arises 'naturally' from
the trajectory of a constructed 'past') and argues for a praxis that
accounts for the political processes inherent in the selection,
organisation, and presentation of events as history. This comparatively recent development in historical methodology does not
generally coincide with the machinations of colonial history
which, under the guise of ideological neutrality, often replaced
local, indigenous histories with a Eurocentric account of the
past. In other words, a colony's history frequently 'began' when
the whites arrived: any events prior to contact with Europeans
were irrelevant to the official record which became *the* history, a
closed narrative designed to remove traces of alternative histories.
This displacement of indigenous histories was paralleled by the
substitution of imperial systems of government for local, culturally
specific ones. For instance, native Canadian peoples were
encouraged to swear allegiance to the 'Great White Mother', the
translation for Queen Victoria,[1] instead of to their own deities and
leaders. The veneration of the Queen thus fostered a paradigm

whereby natives were seduced into collapsing their own varied social organisations into one system, fixing a distant, disinterested Queen as their political, cultural, and economic leader.

History has been generally figured as true, immutable, and objective, as opposed to fiction which is defined as untrue, changeable, and subjective. While history validates a project – much the way that science does – fiction does not. Since much of the 'truth value' (in the Foucaultian sense) of orthodox history derives from the contingency of its closure in written form, such history characteristically privileges the texts of literate societies while discounting all other narratives by troping them as fiction. Hence, the binary oppositions of fact/fiction and literate/non-literate serve to authorise or make official certain versions of history, and to show others as lacking credibility. By reclassifying indigenous histories as myth or legend, or disclaiming them altogether because they are not written down, colonialist historians and officials dismissed as less significant all methods of 'story-telling' but their own. In a related strategy, European history applied its unequivocal concepts of linear time and segmented space to regions which had always calculated time and space differently. While these attempts to reorder the colonial world to suit European sensibilities may have been initiated for reasons of convenience, they were also intended to secure complete authority over colonised populations. Frequently, the conquered were prevented – either by the absence of primary tools and access to information or by loss of self-esteem or even by genocide – from providing an alternative to that official narrative.

This chapter assesses ways in which history is re-evaluated and redeployed in post-colonial drama. Rather than historicising theatre productions, we focus on how plays and playwrights construct discursive contexts for an artistic, social, and political present by enacting other versions of the pre-contact, imperial, and post-imperial past on stage. Aside from the basic reviewing of a fragment of history when new 'facts' come to light, post-colonial histories attempt to tell the other sides of a story and to accommodate not only the key events experienced by a community (or individual) but also the cultural context through which these events are interpreted and recorded. Reconstructing the past in this way usually heralds the emergence of new voices and new tools for understanding that past. The empirical historical method that explorers, missionaries, and settlers brought to colonial territories is thus rejected as inappropriate for recording events in time and space, and as inadequate for marking harvest seasons, weather patterns, and wildlife tracking. Such attention to the construction of history is vital to the post-colonial agenda since history has been seen to determine reality itself. As a result, the reassessment of history inevitably becomes a political endeavour since, as Stephen Slemon maintains, 'post-colonial *texts* [are central] in the sphere of cultural work and in the promulgation of anti-colonial resistance. . . . This social emplacement of the literary text thus affords post-colonial criticism a material reference in social struggle' (1989: 103). The political project of decolonising history can be just as complex an operation as the initial establishment and maintenance of imperial history, which fashioned into a narrative/story the exploration and naming of space, the conquest of cultures, the declaring of heroes and villains, and the perceptual arrangement of temporal consequences.

History's intersection with drama is, according to Dening, not merely coincidental. He quotes Roland Barthes to demonstrate that history and drama are both based on a conscious interpretation of events:

> The theater is precisely that practice which calculates the place of things as they are observed: if I set the spectacle here, the spectator will see this; if I put it elsewhere, he will not, and I can avail myself of this masterly effect and play on the illusion it provides.
>
> (Dening 1993: 295)

History inevitably manoeuvres a strategic presentation of certain views and a suppression of others. Post-colonial plays employ many similar strategies of (re)presentation in order to foreground other(ed) historical perspectives and so to disperse the authority inherent in official accounts. This broadly deconstructive project demands not only a rethinking of history's content but also a reworking of its axiomatic forms. As Ashcroft, Griffiths, and Tiffin argue:

> The myth of historical objectivity is embedded in a particular view of the sequential nature of narrative, and its capacity to reflect, isomorphically, the pattern of events it records. The post-colonial task, therefore, is not simply to contest the message of history, which has so often relegated individual

post-colonial societies to footnotes to the march of progress, but also to engage the medium of narrativity itself, to re-inscribe the 'rhetoric', the heterogeneity of historical representation as [Hayden] White describes it.

(1995: 356)

In performative genres, unlike in literary modes of representation, narratives unfold in space as well as through time. Whereas words on a page must be interpreted sequentially, theatre offers the possibility of a simultaneous reading of all the visual and aural signifiers embedded in the text as performance. It lends itself particularly well to the interrogation of spatial and temporal (teleological) aspects of imperialism and facilitates the telling/showing of oppositional versions of the past that propose not only different constitutive events but different ways of constructing that past in the present. This is a larger exercise than the project of reworking classical European texts discussed in Chapter 1: while canonical counter-discourse offers the opportunity to dismantle the tropes of textual and literary hierarchies, counter-discursive histories address the foundations of colonialism and the ways in which a continued colonial authority in a particular place has been sanctioned by official historical accounts.

If history has conventionally determined the parameters of a past, it has also determined the positioning of the colonised subject within that past. Hence, post-colonial reworkings of the European master historical narrative are not always concerned with constructions of history *per se* but with constructing the self *in* history. This process is both crucial and problematic for colonised peoples whose 'historical' role has generally been that of history's 'other'. The multiply-coded representational systems of theatre offer a variety of opportunities for the recuperation of a post-colonial subjectivity which is not simply inscribed in written discourse but embodied through performance. Most often, the post-colonial subject is figured as a split site defined by the remnants of a pre-contact history, the forces of the more official colonial record, and the contingencies of the current situation. Subjectivity can be further fragmented when characters exist within regimes (such as apartheid) which dictate the spatial and temporal limits to personal action, as well as to political and intellectual discourses. Questions of subjectivity are also implicit in national histories – a concept often conveyed allegorically – further complicating imperial history's claim to completeness, uniformity, and truth.

FRACTURING COLONIALIST HISTORY

Occupation histories

Dismantling imperial history is a complex process which requires more than merely filling gaps with untold stories, or substituting culturally specific narratives for Eurocentric ones. It is inevitable that history will present a productive site for hybridity in post-colonial drama when several narratives coexist in however uneasy a union. Most often, histories *compete* with each other to form a complex dialectic which is always subject to change as new players enter the field of representation. One of the first ways in which post-colonial cultures address the ideological biases of imperial history is by establishing a context for the articulation of counter-discursive versions of the past. To refute the misguided belief that colonised people do/did not have a history of their own, many plays stage aspects of the pre-contact past in order to re-establish traditions, to lay claim to a heritage or territory, and to recuperate various forms of cultural expression. While these works invest significant historical value in what western discourse has erroneously relegated to the category of pre-history, they do not necessarily present a static or rarefied vision of their subjects. Rather than perpetuating misconceptions about the past by positing a harmonious pre-contact period in contrast to the fraught post-contact past and present, a number of dramatists also foreground the battles and disagreements that inevitably characterised the time before European invasion. Tsegaye Gabre-Medhin's *Collision of Altars: A Conflict of the Ancient Red Sea Gods* (1977) presents a version of the history of Axumite Ethiopia in the sixth century. In this verse drama, the Royal Crier speaks the Axumite kingdom into the memory of its descendants, keeping its pride alive thirteen hundred years later in the wake of the destruction of other empires. The Royal Crier recalls the strength of the Axumites with a view to entrusting contemporary Ethiopians with the memory of their otherwise ill-documented pre-contact history.

In many countries, official accounts of the post-contact period are among the most common targets of counter-discourse, not only because imperialism precipitated a rupture in traditional ways of recording and relaying history but also because that epistemic rupture has often been presented as natural and un-controversial. In particular, colonialist history tends to suggest that there was little or no resistance to imperial conquest although post-colonial literatures reveal otherwise. By establishing counter-narratives and counter-contexts which refute, or at least decentre, orthodox versions of history, marginalised cultures insist on a more equitable and representative starting point from which to negotiate a post-colonial identity. Wálé Ògúnyemí's historical plays pit colonial agents against Nigerian peoples in order to fore-ground sides of history that are frequently forgotten or forbidden. *Kírìjì* (1970), for example, details various battles among the Yoruba in the latter part of the nineteenth century; these conflicts complicate binarist histories based on notions of a simple con-frontation between the coloniser and a united colonised group. In the play, the Ekitiparapo people attack the Ibadan people for selling them into slavery, and the presence of the colonial adminis-tration and the missionaries does nothing to assist the cause of peace. The Reverend Wood, not understanding the gravity of the war to the participants, belittles it by ineffectively pleading with Ore, the King of Otun, to 'stop this useless tribal feud' (1976: 44). Thus *Kírìjì* retells the history of early colonial Nigeria in a context which suggests that contemporary conflicts among the Yoruba (as well as between the Yoruba and the Ibadan peoples) had their own agency before the institution of imperial rule. Ògúnyemí's *Ijaye War* (1970) also details events that occurred in the nineteenth century and that would otherwise have been relegated to minor footnotes in colonial history books, if mentioned at all. While finding new contexts for colonialist history, these plays offer more than just alternative or subsidiary accounts of various wars: they also depict the market sellers, the festivals held in spite of the war, the ritual sacrifices, the praise and war songs, and other details of historical Nigeria that would only be marked in imperialism's master narrative as anthropological curiosities, not as essential aspects of living communities. By chronicling the strong vibrant cultures into which Europeans insinuated themselves, Ògúnyemí's theatre restores a sense of the many local histories which have been erased by a monolithic official record.

Presenting imperial wars within the context of a local social history ascribes renewed political agency to the colonised culture itself, not just to the war. Crucial to this recuperative project are the ways in which narratives of/about the past are conceived and circulated. The deployment of indigenous forms to enact a historical moment reinforces the validity of local histories and

111

distinguishes them from official, textual documents. Since non-western societies usually do not engage in the calculated, chronological, 'fact'-based mission of imperialist history, the reworking of the past in post-colonial theatre is also entwined with the re-establishment of pre-contact forms of history-making and history-keeping. For instance, Utpal Dutt's *The Great Rebellion 1857 (Mahavidroha)* (1973) uses the epic traditions of Indian oral narrative as it chronicles the experiences of several generations of an Indian family in their battles against the British. In style, the play also borrows from the Bengali *jatra*, a theatre tradition which relies on intensified action and poetic expression to mythologise its subject. By interweaving a family history with his exploration of the effects of the British industrial revolution on the handloom industry, Dutt constructs a narrative of resistance that is both specific and broadly representative. *The Great Rebellion* challenges the history and the literary forms of the imperial centre as it harnesses the power of culturally specific Indian traditions to re-enact this historical moment. The play also dispels the myth that British power was absolute in nineteenth-century India: the colonised subject is presented as more articulate and more authoritative than the coloniser/colonised binary presupposes, while the coloniser has less agency than is generally assumed. This breakdown in the binary further dismantles the colonial authority of the past, forces re-evaluations of contemporary Indian complicity in oppressive institutions, and provokes audience members to resist the lessons that imperial history is supposed to impart.

In many instances, dramatic representations of the past are further modified by the place, occasion, performance style, and metatheatrical frameworks of a particular production. This is in keeping with the post-colonial concept that history is a discourse which is 'culturally motivated and ideologically conditioned' in the present (Slemon 1988: 159). A notable case in point is the 1993 Trinidadian production of C.L.R. James's *The Black Jacobins* (1936),[2] which was directed by Rawle Gibbons and staged in a pan-yard at Curepe in Port of Spain. The play details the major events of the Haitian Revolution in 1791, exposing the French and English colonial wrangling over control of the colony and giving theatrical life to the principal players in the slave rebellion. By presenting an action-packed centre-stage always in contact with the collective body of a surrounding crowd of villagers, Gibbons emphasised the folk roots of a revolution which drew strength from the dances, songs, and vodun rituals of the general slave populace. His choice of venue and style also linked the play to Trinidad's own canboulay riots almost a century later than the play's historical setting. At the same time, an added frame and the use of direct audience address at several points in the action grounded the performance text firmly in the 1990s. The frame positioned James's historical drama as a village play re-enacted by modern-day descendants of the rebel slaves in a defiant protest against human rights abuses in contemporary Haiti. Unpredictable interruptions to the staging of the internal play occurred when the sinister Ton Ton Macoutes (representing the Haitian military) invaded the audience and the playing space in a chilling reminder of the extent to which everyday life is compromised under a corrupt political regime. Not simply a device for updating a compelling history, Gibbons's metatheatrical framework was designed to unsettle the audience, and to rebuke them for the general Caribbean indifference to the situation in Haiti, a country which had, until the twentieth century, been a symbol of hope and possibility for black people throughout the African diaspora. On another level, the refusal of a comfortable narrative order in this particular production of *The Black Jacobins* had an even more local resonance: as one critic remarked, it prompted Trinidadians to remember the 1990 attempted coup on their own island and to realise 'how precious a gift political stability can be' (Ali 1993: 5).

Settler histories

History is a particularly fraught issue for settler societies because of their ambivalent positioning in the imperial paradigm as both colonisers and colonised. By their very name, settlers are implicated in the dispossession of indigenous peoples from their homelands and in the (partial) destruction of their cultures. Nevertheless, settler histories do not simply replicate the master narrative's characteristic tropes; instead, they are often concerned with establishing authenticity for a society dislocated from the imperial centre and, simultaneously, alienated from the local land and indigenous culture. In this respect, many settler histories act counter-discursively to imperial accounts while being distinct from indigenous histories. These divergent claims on 'history' further compromise the viability of a discursively fixed and uniform past; they point to the diversity and complexity of post-colonial experience and demand that historical texts acknowledge the interests of colonialism's various protagonists. Canada's Sharon Pollock, New Zealand's Mervyn Thompson, and Australia's Louis Nowra have discussed how playwrights in their countries resist theatrical investigations of the past under the mistaken impression that their histories are boring or uneventful.[3] These countries have not, apparently, waged a bloody war which would, it seems, qualify as 'history'.

Of course, this false claim to a peaceable past ignores the massacres (even attempted genocide) of indigenous peoples, downplays the violence inherent in other so-called 'historical' events – the war between the French and English over control of Canadian colonies is a case in point – and denies tensions between imperialist and nationalist forces over issues such as independence. That unpleasant events and attitudes are conveniently dismissed or concealed foregrounds history's selectivity. Non-indigenous plays which do concern themselves with history often participate (albeit unwittingly) in the dominant mythologies of a society even while they attempt to articulate suppressed versions of the past. Such plays are thus marked by the contradictions particular to their position as texts constructed by and for settler subjects. These contradictions dislocate old hierarchies without proposing new orders of privilege.

Without recourse to pre-contact traditions or non-western systems of knowledge, settler texts are often compelled to interrogate imperial history through a direct deconstructive attack on its modes of narrative emplotment. Michael Gow's *1841* (1988) and Stephen Sewell's *Hate* (1988) both expose official Australian history as a complex web of lies designed to produce discourses of nationality that allay the anxieties of a dystopian settler culture. Commissioned especially for the Bicentenary of Australia's settlement (invasion) by Europeans, these two plays enact a particularly effective assault on imperial history, not only because they present dissident views of a country's perceived communal past, but also, and perhaps more crucially, because they dared to air those views on an occasion officially designated for the 'celebration of a nation'.[4] Using the expectations of both the public and the funding body as a context which might strengthen his political point, Gow deliberately wrote a 'pageant play gone wrong' (1992: 5) in order to critique the Bicentenary's specific drive towards historicity. He chooses a year when, according to the official record, nothing happened, and then presents a metahistorical and self-reflexive play which is much less about Australian society in 1841 than about how that past is currently constructed and for what purposes. History is thus revealed as an intentional text – in this case, one riven by the conflicting impulses to mythologise *and* to erase the iniquities of the convict system. The play shows how myth, usually positioned with fiction in the history/fiction binary, is ironically recuperated in the 1988 Australian celebrations: imperial history condemns myth while at the same time mythologising itself. Sewell also illustrates history's processes of selective filtering and strategic forgetting. Although set in the present, *Hate* is also a parable of settlement, but its post-coloniality is articulated more elliptically. Whereas Gow uses his epic, anti-historical 'pageant' to split open the fissures in the imperial textual record, Sewell undermines history's claim to impartiality by unveiling the workings of patriarchal power within the family as a correlative of the larger society's history. The allegorical modes of both plays are not incidental to their carefully targeted assault on the self-congratulatory histories endorsed by most white Australians during the Bicentenary. As Slemon argues, 'in saying one thing [allegory] also says some "other" thing'; allegory thus 'marks a bifurcation or division in the directionality of the interpretive process' which cuts across imperial tropes (1987: 4).

Rick Salutin's *Les Canadiens* (1977) uses allegory not as much to deconstruct imperial discourses as to explore tensions between Anglophone and Francophone settlers in Canada since the British conquest of the French at the Plains of Abraham in 1759.[5] The playwright's choice of hockey as a versatile metaphor through which to stage the history of Canada's most enduring cultural division is particularly appropriate since it stresses the idea that discourses of nationhood coalesce around conflict and competition. Act 1 of the play focuses on how the Montreal hockey team, les Canadiens, rose to ascendancy in Canada's premier sporting league. The spatial and conceptual overlaying of the staged hockey game with representations of what Salutin himself calls Québec's 'interrupted history of resistance' against British/ Anglophone imperialism (1977: 13) mythologises les Canadiens as the standard bearers of a frustrated and exploited people. Québec's political defeats in events such as the 1837 rebellion, the World War One conscription crisis, and the FLQ (Front Libération du Québec) riots of the 1960s are retroped as a series of sporting victories. Act 2, on the other hand, is primarily concerned with demythologising the team and relocating it within contemporary Canadian culture: as the provincial election of the Parti Québécois in 1976 detracts from hockey's importance as a surrogate battlefield, the real political action is resituated outside the sporting arena. Together, the play's two parts trace the 'birth, growth and maturation of a political process in Québec' (Miller 1980: 57), illustrating, at the same time, how myths of identity intersect with historical consciousness. Acclaimed as a play which captured the spirit of its time, *Les Canadiens* offered to audiences across Canada the opportunity to reflect on issues of national unity, in the wake of the political upheaval surrounding the victory of the Parti Québécois.

Reclaiming lost heroes

A specific strategy of revisionist histories in both settler and occupation colonies has been the reclamation of subversive figures to make them into heroes. The leader of a rebellion against colonial forces or someone generally historicised as villainous is often reconstructed in post-colonial theatre to play a highly prominent role in the struggle for freedom from imperial rule. Canada's exemplary Métis rebel, Louis Riel, has been reclaimed by several plays, including John Coulter's *Riel* (1967) and, in a more exciting way, Carol Bolt's *Gabe* (1973) in which Riel and Gabriel Dumont are not only rehistoricised but also reincarnated as contemporary, urban, disenchanted Métis characters. In a related endeavour, Ebrahim Hussein's *Kinjeketile* (1970) stages the battle waged by a Tanzanian prophet against invading German forces. Allegorising his own resistance to German imperialism, the 'outlaw', Kinjeketile, explains that his rebellion will be considered legendary by future generations. Militant activist Stephen Biko is resurrected in a number of South African plays, including *Woza Albert!* (Mtwa et al., 1983), which also 'raises' various other anti-apartheid 'revolutionaries'. In the Caribbean, Roger Mais's *George William Gordon* (1976) and Sistren's *Nana Yah* (1980) each celebrate specific figures among Jamaica's national freedom fighters, while Derek Walcott's *Henri Christophe* (1950) honours one of the leaders of the Haitian Revolution. In all these examples, the past is constructed according to the perspectives of the colonised whose 'stories', integrated by the focus on a local legendary figure,[6] loosen imperialism's stranglehold on historical representation.

One of the most spirited reclamations of a vilified figure occurs in *The Trial of Dedan Kimathi* (1976) by the Kenyan writers, Ngũgĩ wa Thiong'o and Micere Githae Mugo. The play revises historical accounts of the Mau Mau uprising in the 1950s when Kenyans resisted British control and exploitation. This first history of Mau Mau written from the Kenyan perspective thirteen years after independence offers an opportunity to praise leaders like Kimathi wa Wachiuri and Mary Nyanjiru. The trial itself is presented in a context that allows for the celebration of many of Kimathi's deeds since he is depicted not only as the 'criminal' that he was labelled by the colonial government but also in his roles as leader and teacher. In Kimathi's formal trial, conducted according to the British definition of justice and order, the white judge takes into account only the colonial government's treason laws when handing down his verdict. The audience is then given a chance to judge Kimathi in an extension of the trial metaphor. The power of the community and its response to Kimathi is made clear from the beginning: the large cast divides into the singers (of Kikuyu and Swahili songs) who look to the end of imperial rule and those who re-enact, behind the singers, the history of colonial exploitation, from the slave trade to plantation history to the rebellion against the white colonial government. Not just a hagiography or an excuse to celebrate the liberation movement, the play offers the community ways of working together after Mau Mau and after Kimathi's execution: other characters, such as the woman, the boy, and the girl, combine the past with the present and future. These nameless figures become emblematic of the country and stress the importance of its people reuniting to pursue Kimathi's philosophy of peace and equity. Kenya of the 1960s and 1970s was preoccupied with dissension between rival tribal groups and with the economic realities of neo-colonialism manifest in an influx of multinational companies which ensured a continuation of rule by a tiny, wealthy minority. *The Trial of Dedan Kimathi* acts as a warning against these various factors which threaten to undermine Kenya's establishment as a viable independent society.

The play uses parody to depict many white settlers who are 'unsettled' by Mau Mau, but they are not paid enough attention to develop fully as caricatures even though the trial devolves into a demonstration of the farcical nature of 'justice' in an attempt to disempower the colonial authority. That the British officers and settlers communicate their fear contributes to the revisionist history presented: Mau Mau's serious threat to the whites re-inforces the resistant control exerted by the Kenyans. While Christianity has succeeded in stalling some of the rebellion's sup-porters and in bringing them back into the colonial administrative fold, Kimathi will not capitulate to the Bible's teachings. To him, turning the other cheek represents a further acceptance of the oppression and exploitation endured by Kenyans since their contact with Europeans. His rejection of Christianity is common to many African plays and it represents a refusal to grant agency to one of imperial history's key events: the first western contact moment when missionaries opened the way for the settlers and colonial governments throughout Africa. As he becomes an icon of resistance, Kimathi provides a historical site from which to undermine presumptions of white superiority and so to galvanise contemporary Kenyans to resist white rule. This overall repo-sitioning of Dedan Kimathi's life and times creates a theatrical event by which to activate, teach, and entertain local audiences. At the same time, the play, like other post-colonial histories discussed here, displaces the singular authority of imperialism's master historiographic narrative.

WOMEN'S HISTORIES

Revisioning history also enables the reinstatement of interest groups who have been left out of the official records because they were victims of prejudice or punishment, or because they were denied an opportunity to speak. The recuperation of women's histories is particularly relevant here and has been a fundamental task for women all over the world. It is important to remember, however, that the ways in which women are 'written back' into history varies greatly from country to country, and that the inter-secting specificities of race, gender, and class necessarily complicate a concept/practice such as feminism. If American, British, and French feminisms all claim to be markedly different from each other, the disjunctions between western feminisms and 'third world' feminisms are even greater. Ama Ata Aidoo, the Ghanaian playwright and novelist, has criticised European feminists[7] for becoming a new wave of imperialists eager to invade the African continent brandishing a particular political doctrine while remaining blissfully ignorant of the culture, history, and needs of individual groups of African women. Western ideals of wage equity, access to the workplace, and sexual freedom are not necessarily what all women want. Moreover, the western tendency to group women from various so-called 'third world' cultures together (in a false opposition to the 'first world') collapses their differences and produces a false homogeneity that limits opportunities for self-determination. As Chandra Mohanty argues in reference to the over-determined phrase, 'women of Africa', such broadly collective identities assume:

> An ahistorical, universal unity between women based on a generalised notion of their subordination. Instead of analytically *demonstrating* the production of women as socio-economic political groups within particular local contexts, this analytical move limits the definition of the female subject to gender identity, completely bypassing social class and ethnic identities.
>
> (1991: 64)

Historically, western feminism's blindness concerning race in particular has compromised the movement's claim to representativeness and limited its usefulness as a broadly referential model of political action. Accordingly, Cheryl Johnson-Odim maintains that a globalised gender identity will be possible *only* when gender does not overshadow other classificatory factors:

> If the feminist movement does not address itself to issues of race, class, and imperialism, it cannot be relevant to alleviating the oppression of most of the women of the world. ... [Black women] are aware that in the late nineteenth and early twentieth centuries, racism was pervasive in the women's movement. ... They wonder, therefore, if white feminists will embrace the struggle against racism as vehemently as they exhort black women to join in the fight against sexism.
>
> (1991: 321–2)

Johnson-Odim anticipates a feminism which unites women without pre-ordaining their place.

Whereas these critics warn against the dangers of over-emphasising gender classifications, Rey Chow notes how quickly a Chinese woman's gender is subsumed by her race: 'the Chinese woman, who is forever caught between patriarchy and imperialism, disappears as a matter of course. Where she appears, she does not appear as "woman" but as "Chinese"' (1993: 88). Likewise, western discourse most often characterises Indian women according to race, not gender. As Rajeswari Sunder Rajan argues, 'The "monolithic 'Third World Woman'" as subject instantaneously becomes an overdetermined symbol, victim not only of universal patriarchy but also of specific third world religious fundamentalism' (1993: 15).[8] The multiple locations/subjectivities which women occupy must be critically repositioned to prevent the subsuming of one category of difference/identity by another. Similarly, their respective 'feminist' projects must be recognised and respected. To maintain, as some western critics do, that economic development is a priority for all 'third world' women is to ignore both the variety of women (mis)represented under the term and the varieties of their goals.

The historical links between imperialism and patriarchy suggest that gender complicates the positioning of a range of colonised subjects, albeit in very different ways. Settler women, for example, may be disadvantaged by the contingencies of imperialism but their situation cannot be unproblematically equated with that of, say, indigenous women. Hence, gender should be delineated as but one 'category of difference for designating the relation between colonizer and colonized' (Sharpe 1993: 12), rather than merged with race (and/or class) under the general concept of marginality. A number of post-colonial plays provide contexts for the specific refiguring of gender roles/identities and the articulation of a multiplicity of feminisms within restructured histories. This is accomplished in various (sometimes mutually exclusive) ways: by critiquing the gender-specific constructions endorsed by imperial history; by mapping out the areas of women's subjugation and invisibility in the colonial situation; by redressing gender-related gaps in the official record; by casting historical women as powerful, respected community leaders; by refusing existing gender-stereotypes (including 'positive' ones which can also restrict possibilities for self-definition); and, crucially, by staging self-reflexive interventions into theatrical representation itself. Such interventions commonly involve some kind of stylistic feature, narrative structure, and/or metatheatrical device designed to denaturalise the histories performed and to foreground their ideological functions.

Dramatising women as history's central figures can be particularly subversive in cultures which have always reserved for male elders both the power and prerogative of public action. Likewise, theatre that contests the myth of women's compliance with patriarchal authority focuses attention on reviewing and renewing debate about women's roles within post-colonial cultures. Two of Tess Onwueme's plays, *Parables for a Season* (1993) and *The Reign of Wazobia* (1993), envisage a restructured Igbo social order through their focus on influential women who replace the king and rule the kingdom as well as any man could. These allegorical texts dramatise what Eugene Redmond calls the 'clash of historical myth and revolutionary intellectual modernity' (1993: 17). By positioning women in power – they are even able to outwit the canniest of men – Onwueme's work restores a sense of autonomy and political agency to Nigerian women who are usually portrayed as either dutiful or disobedient wives, if at all. *Parables for a Season* concludes with Zo dancing and declaring:

> I am woman! I carve my
> Own path.
> Termites of Idu,
> A female leads you in
> The new dance step. Up!
> Lift your hands to the horizon.
> A woman leads.
> The future is in our hands.
>
> (1993: 121)

Zo's triumphant movement into the play's future performs a history for Igbo women located specifically in post-contact days of slave-trading; yet this history/parable is equally resonant for twentieth-century Nigerian women whom the play exhorts to 'carve [their] own path'. *The Reign of Wazobia*, which can be seen as a companion piece to *Parables for a Season*, also foregrounds well-defined and intelligent female characters who question the traditions held by the male elders. These dissidents are not superwomen who are above failure; nevertheless, the staged women who do succeed provide women in the audience with models for individual and collective action. At the play's closure Wazobia entreats her followers not to wage war against the men – patriarchal society's conventional method for solving disputes – but to find other ways of inducing social change:

> Women, peace! Peace! Spill no blood. Ours is to plant
> seed yams. Not blood to feed worms.

Sing, women! Stand firm on the soil! Sing! Sing!
Sing, women! Plant on firm soil. Sing, women!

(1993: 173)

Onwueme's plays recognise and respect the more traditional
roles of women as mothers and nurturers but do not confine
women to their reproductive functions. Her women's histories are,
then, broadly based documentations of an active and diverse
community. Centralising women is only part of the feminist project in South
African theatre. Fatima Dike identifies as a feminist, but her plays
may not immediately be classified in that mould, particularly
by western critics. Certainly *The Sacrifice of Kreli* and *The First South
African* (1977) highlight one strong female character who has
managed to maintain a community's health despite external
attempts to destroy its people's dignity, histories, and cultural
traditions (not to mention their liberty). These two plays do not,
however, focus on feminist 'issues' such as freedom or equality
for women. Rather, they are implicitly concerned with restoring
the pride and place of a larger community of women and men:
the black South Africans disenfranchised by imperialism and the
continued insult of apartheid. Spurred to write by her outrage at
the violent rape and murder of a seven-year-old girl in Guguletu,
a township near Cape Town, Dike says, 'I had something to say
to my people for that' (qtd in Gray 1990: 81). Her particular
brand of anti-apartheid theatre amalgamates in a complex way
the politics of a nascent Black Consciousness movement with those
of a feminist push to recognise the roles that women have played
for years in black South African culture.[9] While *The Sacrifice of Kreli*
marks a historical point in pre-apartheid South Africa, *The First
South African* provides a history (through one man and his family)
of the dispossession and alienation that apartheid has bred. By
establishing history as an important site of ideological struggle for
all marginalised blacks, Dike's highly successful work has opened
up a space for more overtly feminist recuperative projects. One
such example is Gcina Mhlope, Thembi Mtshali, and Maralin
Vanrenen's *Have You Seen Zandile?* (1986) which dramatises three
generations of women's stories, including the disagreements
between South African women. In performance, this play, staged by
two female actors, presents a multi-dimensional, multi-directional
metahistory in which women's lives intersect and influence each

other across space and time. The history of a people is thus explored through the stories of individual women. At the same time, the women gain status and authority by their story-telling, not only because it gives them access to self-representation but also because the story-teller holds a position of considerable historical power in many cultures.

Some women's histories attempt to bypass the entrenched 'factuality' of the past by deliberately mythologising events or characters in ways which draw attention to the 'fictions' thus constructed. Rather than masquerading as fact, however locally relevant, these fictions delight in fancy. They destabilise the epistemological category of history itself by suggesting that exaggeration and fabrication are inevitably functions of historicity. This deconstructive process informs Sistren's *Nana Yah*, which dramatises the story of a transported slave, Nanny, who escapes from a sugar plantation to join the Maroons in their guerilla war against the white plantocracy of eighteenth-century Jamaica. Although she is celebrated for her courage and her determination, it is ultimately Nanny's magic that sets her apart as a hero and gives her legendary status. Magic endows her with the physical and spiritual strength to disperse evil spirits, to overthrow, single-handedly, the male leaders of the Maroons, and, more crucially, to out-manoeuvre the white military by catching bullets with her backside. The historical 'truth' of Nanny's accomplishments is never in question; indeed, the play suggests that such implausible feats are precisely the events from which history is made. By presenting Nanny as a character with the extraordinary powers of the Ashanti trickster, the play recuperates a cultural tradition at the same time as it endorses particular 'fictions' as valid representations of the past. In this doubly politicised context, even Nanny's death does not reduce her historical agency. As the storyteller reminds the audience:

> Dem trap up de Maroon an destroy Nanny town. But no mine. Nanny a fe we hero, fah she do what plenty udda people never do, an me wan you fe know say, just like how Nanny dwit, you can dwit too.
>
> (1980: 21)

Overall, Nanny's story is presented as a historical 'fantasy' which is much less concerned with documenting a life than with dramatising a legend in ways which might inspire contemporary Jamaican women to reposition themselves in society and in history.

In performance, *Nana Yah* further dismantles axiomatic ways of conceiving and relaying historical narratives. The play opens with a wake for Nanny, and the audience are given hymn sheets (so they can participate in the singing) followed by cocoa and fish. Then, a member of Sistren introduces the tale to be enacted by informing the audience of its genealogy:

> So unoo lissen me good
> fe me no read dis inna no whiteman book
> Is me madda self learn me
> fe is me grandmadda madda tell me granny
> An she tell me madda
> An she pass it on to me.
>
> (ibid.: 91)

As she rejects the 'whiteman book' in favour of a folk history passed on through 'women's talk', the speaker validates the conceptual structure and content of the action to follow. Her monologue leads into a scene during which various gods appear, heralded by a drum roll, to discuss the slave trade and thus to contextualise Nanny's story within a broad historical moment. The actual capture of the slaves is figured by a stylised dance/mime sequence which uses the performing bodies of the all-woman cast to form abstract shapes and symbols – such as a circle broken by a triangular missile – that relay the disruption of African culture. Similarly, the slaves' limbo dance[10] tells a story of entrapment more poignantly than any language could. In the plantation scenes, which provide yet another context for the telling of Nanny's history, the performance returns to language-based narrative forms, juxtaposing several monologues to a work song. Here, the past is presented by a number of voices whose individual stories are punctuated by the collective refrain of the singers/workers. Cumulatively, the interactive and/or embodied histories outlined construct a theatrical event that attempts to dilute and disperse the power of a unitary system of historical knowledge.

The case of settler women exemplifies the multiple locations that the female subject can occupy within the discursive matrix of imperialism. Already complicit in the attempted containment – or even erasure – of indigenous peoples from the historical record, settler women are themselves frequently victims of patriarchal control. None the less, simply to position them as inferior to white men (who are themselves in an ambivalent location with respect

to imperial authority) yet superior to indigenous men and w(
sets up a false hierarchy that threatens to reinforce the divisive categories and classes that imperialism institutes. Some theorists have
argued that whereas the indigenous woman is doubly colonised,
the settler woman is only half-colonised (see Visel 1988: 39) but
such terminology is problematic – a bit like digging half a hole –
for it quantifies what should be qualified, and also considers
oppressions and privileges to be summative (hence one adds to or
takes away from the other) rather than dynamically interactive. A
more appropriate model for considering settler subjectivity (both
male and female) might follow Chris Prentice's assertion that 'any
individual is interpellated by multiple discourses and multiple
social formations' (1991: 64). This suggests that colonisation is not
a state but a process, a continually self-constituting hegemony
which is always under threat from competing discourses.

Feminist theatre in the settler cultures often aims to deconstruct
hierarchical structures by demonstrating the multiple histories
in which women can be implicated without further defending
imperialism's historical hegemony. Yet, as in Wendy Lill's play, *The
Occupation of Heather Rose* (1986), there often are no answers – just
more questions. Heather Rose, a naive young nurse determined
to do charitable works, takes a job on a native reservation in
northern Ontario but she soon discovers that the community will
not respond as she expected to her exercise classes and nutrition
lectures. Their 'recalcitrance' subverts her medical 'authority'
and leaves her bewildered and uncertain of herself. Experience
teaches Heather that people like her are, in fact, part of the
so-called 'Indian problem'. This uncomfortable realisation challenges her sense of personal identity and her understanding of
Canada as a country. Isolated by the physical environment and
estranged from both white and native communities, she becomes
acutely aware of her status as an invader, which compromises
her culture's settler claim to legitimacy. The resulting destabilisation of her location in Canadian culture also unsettles her hold
on sanity. By showing the settler woman's complicity in the ongoing colonisation of indigenous peoples, the play disproves the
common assumption that the bonds of gender between white and
native women will somehow diminish their differences. Overall,
Heather is the vehicle through which Lill criticises the wider
Canadian society's sanctimonious way of addressing issues of native
health and autonomy. Nonetheless, some sympathy is reserved for

this ill-equipped young nurse because she is ultimately a victim of the same paternalistic systems that have eroded native culture/ identity.

While the examples discussed have dealt largely with women who claim access to public and broadly referential spheres of action, texts that emphasise what is loosely termed 'female experience' can also act counter-discursively by challenging the notion that history is necessarily the record of signal events initiated by prominent men. The well-worn feminist slogan that 'the personal is political' is particularly relevant here since gender-related oppression, although often experienced in domestic spaces, is deeply inflected by the structural hierarchies of imperialism. A focus on women's experiences illustrates a different historical trajectory, and, in performative contexts, allows the presentation of an embodied subjectivity and the demarcation of a place/space from which women can speak. The insertion of their histories into the larger discourse of the past broadens the ambit of history to dismantle further the authoritarian and imperialist claims of a univocal historical record.

STORY-TELLING

One of the most significant manipulators of historical narrative in colonised societies is the story-teller. Telling stories on stage is an economical way in which to initiate theatre since it relies on imagination, recitation, improvisation, and not necessarily on many stage properties. Its place as a strategy for revisioning history in post-colonial theatre is, however, not based merely on economics. In most non-literate communities, history was preserved by the story-teller who held a privileged place central to the maintenance and sustenance of the group's culture. The story-teller relayed the community's history, often in verse form, as an entertainment and an educational device. Frequently, s/he would augment the narrative with dramatic action, audience interaction, dance, song, and/or music of some description. This story-telling tradition transfers easily to the stage since its codes and conventions as a mode of communication are already highly theatrical. The differences between story-telling and western historiography can be discussed in terms of Émile Benveniste's notions of *discours* and *histoire*[11] though these terms should not be set up as absolute binaries. According to Benveniste, written history (a form of *histoire*) avoids interpretative nuances, abstracts the narrative from any enunciative context, and attempts to suggest that meaning is fixed in language. In contrast, story-telling (which resembles *discours*) foregrounds the role of the interlocutor and the specific context of language utterance to create meanings that are changeable and unfixed. Aware of the audience and of his/her own position as entertainer, the story-teller revises history in/through every performance by making the past 'speak' to the present. Improvisational references to highly current incidents or to the reactions of audience members foster an intimacy that reinforces the lessons which the story-teller gleans from the past for his/her community.

Story-telling's presentational style and format challenge the naturalistic conventions by which western theatre usually stages its subject matter. Gay Morris documents the *Iinstomi* tradition of story-telling and performance art found in both the Zulu and Xhosa cultures in South Africa:

> It has no knowledge of the fourth wall: that metaphor for the separation of communication and art which renders art meaningless and useless. It has no knowledge of a playset, a script or a pre-ordained performance; rather it reminds us to recreate the theatrical act because we enjoy it and believe in it, and to re-create meaning afresh each time.
>
> (1989: 98)

This reconstruction of even the basics of western theatre – script, location, sense of space and time – makes story-telling a potentially powerful, and more culturally relevant, mode of performance through which to interrogate received discourses and received models for staging them. Adapted for theatre, story-telling can form the structural and – metaphorically – the epistemological framework of the whole performance event (which thus unfolds at the behest of the story-teller) or it can be incorporated into a more conventional play, often through one (or more) of the characters. The story-teller's dramatic function varies considerably: s/he can take on the role of master of ceremonies, impartial narrator, social commentator, antagonist, or adjudicator. Whatever the choice of mediating role, the story-teller eschews naturalistic dialogue in favour of a direct address that generally historicises the action, calling for an intellectual response rather than merely an aesthetic appreciation. That the story-teller's narrative is generally distinct from – but interactive with – the play's dialogue reinforces the point that the past is always mediated through the present. While propelling the story forward – and sometimes participating in its enactment – the story-teller gauges his/her performance by the reactions of the audience and elaborates and/or improvises accordingly. This licence to alter the story necessarily challenges the assumption that history is closed or immutable, suggesting instead that the 'truth', if any, is in the telling.

The relationship between the raconteur and his/her audience can vary widely, and this inevitably influences the performance event. For instance, a knowledgeable, local audience will understand cultural nuances, jokes, and specific allusions or references, while outsiders will not necessarily comprehend them. Generally, the reaction of a mixed race audience will differ from that of a homogeneous group because viewers respond, by means of a constant interactive process, not only to the story-teller but also to other audience members. Group dynamics notwithstanding, the responses of individual viewers will also be affected by factors such as race, class, gender, age, and social affiliation. These discrepancies impact upon the performance and the reception of the tale since story-telling's inbuilt feedback mechanisms work through multiple systems and in multiple sites, refusing the closure common to western narrative discourses such as history. In fact, in forum-style theatre, the story-teller can engineer events to make absolutely explicit the audience's role as maker of meaning and, by implication, of history. In a radical exploration of Augusto Boal's work on theatre's capacity to effect social change, Femi Osofisan's *Once upon Four Robbers* (1978) offers the audience the opportunity to determine the play's conclusion. After it appears that the central conflict between robbers and soldiers in contemporary Nigeria will conclude in a stalemate, Aafa, the story-teller, asks the *audience* who should win: the forces of lawlessness or the brutal representatives of law and order. After some public debate led by the story-teller, the audience must decide the victors and face the consequences of its decision. Siding in favour of the robbers leaves the audience vulnerable to being robbed themselves whereas choosing the soldiers as victors leads to the execution of the robbers by firing squad, an event for which the audience must take responsibility.[12] With the help of the story-teller, the play moves into the realm of political activism when the spectators become actors (in both senses of the word) empowered to discuss the social conditions which have led to the widespread phenomenon of armed robbery, and to decide upon a course of action. Hence, each performance of the play determines its own theatrical and social conclusions. By combining forms of political theatre with the art of story-telling, *Once upon Four Robbers* alters the frame by which audiences have watched (and not participated in) staged history.

The figure of the story-teller lends cultural weight to the histories presented and foregrounds the ways in which such narratives are (re)constructed: they are learned and retold, given added inflections, altered slightly, and packaged in a way that pleases and instructs the listeners. At the same time, the story-teller's presence on stage provides at least two focal points for the spectator, re-inforcing the ways in which the story, mediated by the teller, acts as a play to be mediated still further by the audience in the context of other forms of history. Usually a metatheatrical device which draws attention to the relationships between the narrative and its performative enunciation, story-telling creates two levels of audience: the onstage audience's responses invariably affect those of the paying viewers, whose communal reaction reinforces any socio-political response. Frequently, the story-teller creates the play's frame, interrupting the action and breaking structural patterns to highlight the different sites of dramatic *inter*action by dispersing the viewer's focus. When the story-teller also performs as a character (aside from as narrator) this dual role further compli-cates the spectator's point of view, creating a dramatic irony that splits the focus image/figure but ironically multiplies the levels of meaning.

Human origin plays, dramatising stories of the gods, provide an example of the ways in which history becomes refocused as, among other things, a community affair. Originally stories which have been transcribed or transformed into plays, these histories require a degree of allegorical mediation as the narrator recounts tales *to* a variety of people (both the on-stage audience and the production's patrons) *about* at least two groups of people (those in the fictional drama and those in the wider audience who can use the play as a means of comprehending contemporary events). In *The Exodus* (1968), by Tom Omara of Uganda, the narration of a story for children acts as an allegorical frame for the people of Acholiland. The play begins with the narrator sitting 'among a group of children, either in front of the curtain, or among the audience' (1968: 47). When the children are sufficiently captivated by the introduction to his story, the inset 'play' begins. It relates the tale of the three great-grandchildren of Lwo, the first man on the earth, detailing how these triplets quarrelled and separated, deciding to live at various points around and across the Nile River. This morality play expresses not only how the ancestors of the children listening to the story arrived at their home east of the Nile, but it also warns the contemporary audience to live peacefully with other people. Written eight years after Uganda's independence, *The Exodus* prefigured the continued disruptions that would result not only in Idi Amin's expulsion of African-Asians but also in several decades of political and economic instability. In explaining the origins of three groups of people in the area and the genesis of their warring background, the play's story-telling mode serves to reposition the history of long ago as an allegory for present-day events such as the recurring tensions between the country's Bantu, Nilotic, and Sudanic linguistic groups.

Indigenous plays from the settler-invader colonies employ the story-teller to position within and alongside imperial and settler narratives the stories (both 'traditional' and post-contact) that constitute indigenous history. Usually figured within a larger dramatic text (to mirror the ways in which indigenous cultures have often been subsumed by European settlement), these stories nevertheless compete with and unsettle empirical histories and their associated theatrical discourses. In Jack Davis's plays, the least literate characters are typically the ones endowed with the most cultural authority because they maintain and circulate tribal memory. *The Dreamers* (1982), in particular, establishes the story-teller as a repository of Aboriginal culture by foregrounding the figure of old Worru, whose tales remit to his extended family not only a communal history but also fragments of a language no longer familiar to the younger generations. Laced with Nyoongah words and phrases, Worru's stories range over three levels of history to recount personal experiences, broader social events, and versions of a mythical past/present known as the Dreaming. Featured are several tales of Worru's escapades with his long-dead friend, Milbart, as well as the story of Billy Kimberley – also known as *Warhdung* or 'Black Crow' – the black tracker who committed a number of crimes against his own people in the name of the colonising agents. In combination with Dreaming tales which explain, for example, the significance of the *moodgah* tree and the transmigration of Nyoongah *kunya* (souls), these stories are

Worru's – and his family's – history. Apart from providing the play's most entertaining theatrical moments, the story-telling episodes structure the overall drama as it unfolds around, between, and through Worru's tales which are, in turn, punctuated by another level of signification via the figure of the dancer who performs much of the narrated action. This structural intervention in an otherwise realist text strengthens the counter-discursivity of the oral histories recounted. In its specific emphasis on story-telling as a form of cultural retrieval, *The Dreamers* makes clear that the official narrative of Australia's 'settlement' must learn to accommodate both the forms and the versions of history it has hitherto suppressed. More recently, Aboriginal theatre has featured performers such as Ningali Lawford whose work, *Ningali* (1994), based primarily on story-telling, moves further away from the conventions of naturalistic theatre.

Many pre-contact story-tellers were women, and thus their authority as historians was doubly discounted by invading Europeans. That many women playwrights have returned to the story-telling tradition (using a narrator/raconteur of either gender) attests to its importance as a form of cultural historiography and as a potential mode of empowerment for (post-)colonial subjects. Two well-known Ghanaian dramatists, Ama Ata Aidoo and Efua Sutherland, have devised plays which foreground women themselves as well as recognising women's historical roles as story-tellers. In addition, these texts attempt to preserve pre-contact traditions in/through a contemporary form, producing hybridised theatrical discourses that can be used to comment on or critique contemporary society. Aidoo's plays, *The Dilemma of a Ghost* (1964) and *Anowa* (1970), present stories about women, slavery, and its personal and social effects, using several older members of the fictional community to act as choric story-tellers who relate current issues to traditional contexts. Often polemical in tone, Aidoo's work is concerned with morality and the ways in which people ought to operate within a social structure; hence, those who disobey the rules and/or threaten the survival of the community are punished. Equally significant, it is usually the women who maintain the plays' morality. The female elders who comment on and advance the action in *The Dilemma of a Ghost* reinforce the strength of the women and the ineffectiveness of the men whose access to western education has, if anything, diminished their useful archive of local knowledge/history. Ato, the young man who attended university in the United States, is left helpless at the end of the play because his education has not equipped him to know how to treat his African-American wife, Eulalie, nor how to conduct himself according to the community's customs. It is up to the story-tellers – who have, in effect, presented the social problem – to proffer a solution by taking care of Eulalie when Ato is incapable of responding appropriately to her culture-shock and grief for her mother. Ato's book-learned intelligence is entirely useless, while the women's oral history provides comfort, practical advice, and support. In *Anowa*, an old man and an old woman together form a 'character' known as 'the-mouth-that-eats-salt-and-pepper'. These two gossips set the scene and frame and explain the action, commenting at the end of the performance that 'This is the type of happening out of which we get stories and legends' (1970: 63). The play has itself become a legend of Anowa and her independence, of the perils of slave-trading, and of the ways in which story-telling can edify a community's art.

Efua Sutherland's three plays, *Edufa* (1962), *Foriwa* (1971), and *The Marriage of Anansewa* (1975), are each inspired by a traditional story which is altered, in some cases only slightly, for stage presentation. The rejuvenation of oral culture in Sutherland's drama functions partly to demonstrate the important place of women in Ghanaian society and partly to maintain the customs/ history of the community as a whole. Sutherland adapts the Ananse story-telling tradition to offer a resonating theatrical experience of the story of Anansewa's marriage. The Ananse stories and per- formances centre on an Everyman character, named Ananse, whose schemes for getting rich or becoming successful are always thwarted by his own overactive ambition or greed. When Ghanaian audiences laugh at Ananse, they recognise in him their own human foibles. The story-teller's *sisi* or hoaxing of the audience (Sutherland 1975: vii) blends entertainment with morality: while cautioning audiences to reject the stupidity of the farcical Ananse character, the story-teller tells the story, interacts with the audience and the players on stage, foregrounds points of interest for par- ticular audience attention, and even occasionally assists the actors in continuing the story:

AKWASI: [*to Storyteller*] Please sir, did a girl pass by, this way?
STORYTELLER: Do you mean that one standing over there?
AKWASI: Aha! Thank you, sir.

(ibid.: 17)

The story-teller coaches the players and makes clear the lesson which people should learn and the ways in which the overall performance event can apply to their own lives. Guiding the action, literally as well as metaphorically, he also directs the music of the play and motions to his assistant, the property manager, when to begin drumming. As a multi-purpose stage-hand-cum-musician, the property manager further facilitates the story's theatrical realisation, producing props as required and making no attempt to hide his attendance. At one point, he brings on a screen that is decorated with a spider, the symbol of Ananse. Together, through their particular emphasis on details of staging, the story-teller and his assistant stress that although the story itself is important, it is not the crucial event in its own right. Of equal consequence is the telling of the story and the maintenance of the Ananse tradition in theatre, or what Sutherland calls Anansegoro (ibid.: v). In *The Marriage of Anansewa*, a statement against the commodification of one's daughters, Ananse learns once again that trifling with his daughter's affections (and even her life) will inevitably not provide the riches, fame, and attention he desires, particularly if he attempts to achieve his goals by trickery rather than by hard work.

The Ananse tradition has travelled to the Caribbean with certain modifications. One of its earliest dramatic manifestations in the formal theatre occurred in Kingston, Jamaica, where the annual pantomime, initiated in 1941, originally centred around the performance of Ananse stories. Transported and indigenised according to the contingencies of a Caribbean culture historically rooted in slavery, such stories tended to de-emphasise moral lessons and to play up the inherent subversiveness of Ananse as trickster. In more recent times, Derek Walcott has explored the figure of the trickster in theatrical contexts, especially in *Ti-Jean and His Brothers* (1958) which dramatises a St Lucian folk tale. The play is presented as a children's story, told by a frog and a cricket, of a woman's three sons who are set the task of making the devil experience human emotions. Walcott explains how this kind of folktale can be used as a form of 'guerilla resistance' against cultural hegemony, not only because it is firmly grounded in the mythos of the local community but also because it deliberately eschews the values of the imperial centre:

> Our art, for the time being, because it emerges from and speaks to the poor, will find its antean renewal in folklore

and parable. We present to others a deceptive simplicity that they may dismiss as provincial, primitive, childish, but which is in truth a radical innocence.

(qtd in Hill 1985b: 8)

It is this 'radical innocence' that Walcott uses to full effect in *Ti-Jean and His Brothers*, both in the play's disarmingly simple style and in its characterisation of the seemingly artless Ti-Jean, who eventually succeeds where his brothers have failed. By presenting an animal fable in which the forces of good are pitted against those of evil, the text seems to be working mostly at the level of myth; however, the localising of that myth ironically subverts its conventional codes by insisting on the cultural specificity of so-called 'universal' archetypes. This transformative shift is achieved primarily by the devil's appearance as Papa Bois – the 'bogeyman' of the St Lucian forest – in one of those 'skin prickling'[13] images whose mnemonic power invests the communal past with a magical immediacy. Moreover, since the devil also doubles as the white plantation owner, the story of how he is outwitted by Ti-Jean becomes a historically grounded allegory. Within this context, it can be interpreted as a post-colonial narrative of resistance which is all the more effective for its use of a simple story-telling mode that beguiles the dominant discourses in order to rework them. The play's presentational style, formulaic structure, melodic language, and fairytale characters – not to mention its highly improbable story-tellers (frog and cricket) – are thus part of its 'trick'. Ananse's power permeates the entire performance even though his subversiveness is most obvious in the development of Ti-Jean himself as both innocent and radical trickster.

Story-tellers in post-colonial theatre sometimes help to maintain other traditional customs which assist in the redefinition of history as a form of cultural capital. In Graham Sheil's *Bali: Adat* (1987), which demonstrates the destruction wrought on the colony of Bali by the ruling Dutch, the narrator relies on Balinese dance, music, and shadow puppetry to assist in the telling of his story. His account of the final step in Dutch ownership of Indonesia early in the twentieth century becomes the main play within which he also recounts a portion of the Hanuman tale from *The Ramayana*. There are, of course, connections between the play's exploration of historical colonialism and more contemporary neo-colonial events in Indonesia. The emphatic presence of the story-teller

Plate 4 Papa Bois, Derek Walcott's *Ti-Jean and his Brothers,*
Trinidad Theatre Workshop, 1993
Source: Photo: Helen Gilbert

reinforces the point that while the Dutch were successful in their political takeover of Bali, the cultural continuity of the Balinese people remains relatively intact. Although the story-teller exits at the moment when the Dutch are victorious, his influence nonetheless pervades the rest of the dramatic action, which concludes with his gamelan music. Meanwhile, Goitois, one of the Dutch, reports that the story-teller is 'declaiming to the biggest audience he's had in years how his Raja inflicted an ignominious defeat upon [the] Dutch' (1991: 127). What Van Horring dismisses as 'Native nonsense!' (ibid.: 127) transpires to be of greater relevance than he realises: in the play's final moments, Goitois holds the *kris*, or ceremonial blade belonging to the Raja, but after his attempts to imitate a *baris* dance, the blackout engulfs him. Remaining on stage is the projection of *Sanhyang Widi* (the supreme god of the Balinese people) whose omniscient screen 'presence' subverts the colonisers' claims to authority. Ultimately, 'defeat' has not impeded the telling of the Balinese people's history.

Rendra also uses the *dalang* or puppet master from the *wayang kulit* tradition as his story-teller in *The Struggle of the Naga Tribe* (1975). This allegory of the destruction of Indonesia at the hands of multinational companies (and corrupt state officials) is carefully constructed to make clear the unfavourable impact of foreign industry on the country, without attracting government censorship.[14] Following convention, Rendra's *dalang* is a figure who interprets the action, links the scenes together, and exercises his accepted right to insert satirical material and to comment on events. He connects the present with the past as a means of reminding Indonesian audiences that their heritage is being eroded by foreign intervention, and he 'interferes' with the action throughout the play to reinforce its allegorical implications: no matter how he has structured his 'story' to avoid the censors, the *dalang* makes clear that the fictional Astinam *is* Indonesia and that the Japanese, American, Russian, Chinese, and German officials are destroying Indonesia's cultural integrity. This story-teller is clearly the 'controller' of the play, engineering events as he wishes.

In a number of countries, story-telling has become a common mode for the presentation of personal histories which have been gathered through interviews, transcribed, collated, edited, translated into theatrical images, and then delivered back to the community as a dramatised narrative. If, as practitioners such as

Boal argue, theatre's most effective political action can be located in its processual workings (1979: 122), the story-telling that occurs 'behind the scenes' is another site of intervention in western historiography. Sistren characteristically devise plays according to this story-telling model, which members of the collective call 'witnessing', a term that lends both legal and religious authority to the histories thus recounted. The theatrical end-product of their community work often combines personal stories with texts (tales and images) from a less specific past that circulate in the wider society as folklore. Integrated in the body/discourse of the story-teller, these different levels of history claim a performative space in the broader social narrative of the past.

By revealing the ways in which new narratives are formulated and how even very old and well-known tales are changed by their delivery, by the audience's response, and also by the circumstances of the performance, a theatre praxis based on story-telling conventions foregrounds history not as a pre-ordained and completed truth, but rather as a continually (re)constructed fiction which can only ever be partial (in both senses of the word), provisional, and subject to change. It follows that story-telling, like other traditional or folk forms, gives to post-colonial history plays a certain cultural specificity and a corresponding tenor of resistance. The story-teller, then, is a potential political agitator: as Fatima Dike puts it, 'we don't tell "bedtime" stories to put people to sleep; we want to scare the shit out of them and wake them up'.[15]

TIME SPAN

The complex time scapes instituted by story-telling in its various forms suggest that the concept of history is contingent upon an understanding of how time works in any particular region. This, in turn, is often inflected by a community's appreciation of the gods and their governing cosmologies, as well as by other specific cultural phenomena. In many cultures, concepts of temporality are centred on an acknowledgement of mythical time which occupies a discursive and spatial field characterised by timelessness. The Aboriginal Dreaming, for example, posits the existence of a continual present which also includes past and future, so that memory can consist of historical recall *plus* a psychic transmission of oneself into a spiritual time and place. Such conceptual frameworks, common to other indigenous cultures and to a number of

Plate 5 Beverly Hanson of Sistren Theatre telling stories.
Australian tour, 1994
Source: Photo: Helen Gilbert

non-western societies, categorically reject the view that history is merely contiguous with the present but not enacted in it. They assert, instead, a notion of 'ambiguous' time in which the boundaries between past and present, and ultimately future, are permeable. The dialectic created between different temporalities refuses the kind of historical consciousness by which, as Hayden White points out, 'the presumed superiority of modern, industrial society can be retroactively substantiated' (1973: 1–2).

Theatre lends itself particularly well to representations of temporal (and spatial) ambiguity because 'all performances create a here which is not "here", [and] a now which is not "now", restlessly slicing time and space into layers of "difference"' (D. George 1989–90: 74). Even though a performance is a linear event in real time, a movement – no matter how circular – from beginning to end, it allows for the representation of different temporal moments simultaneously, thus bringing into question the 'narratability' of the world, or at least opening up the possibility of synchronic histories that are not necessarily bound to any notion of telos. Unlike writing, which remains as residue in between readings and thus announces its own historicity, performance is characteristically ephemeral, forcing a recognition of the role of the present in constructions of the past. The span of time dramatised in post-colonial 'history' plays varies greatly and any number of temporal moments may be presented: the present, the post-independence past, the colonial era, the crucial moment of contact, the pre-contact period, and the even older and highly significant past of the pre-human world. All these historical markers determine, and are determined by, the ways in which the contemporary world is defined. Some plays depict the span of history by relating a series of events that have occurred over a long period of time while others situate one or more historical moments in a context that is directly relevant to current concerns.

Jack Davis's *Kullark* (1979) provides the paradigmatic example of a performance event that interrogates conventional European concepts of temporality and narrativity. The play is composed of scenes from different time periods, ranging from 1979 back to the moment of Western Australia's invasion by European peoples. As a cinematic montage, it collapses over 150 years of Nyoongah experience into a few hours of stage time but does not construct events as strictly chronological. Instead, history is presented as multivectored and interactive through a number of techniques:

the juxtaposition, elision, and overlaying of different time frames; the repetition of visual and aural images; the staging of Dreaming events; and the incorporation of documents from the official historical record into the enacted text. Moreover, characters often step outside theatrical time, in Brechtian fashion, to comment on the stage action, so that the play's metaphysics continually interrogates European epistemological systems. The overall result is a panoramic reframing of history that balances the decimation of Aboriginal culture in the past with a focus on its survival (in whatever form) in the contemporary moment.

Although Davis relies heavily on historical documents as source material for *Kullark*, the play's performative structures none the less articulate the incompleteness of such archival texts by presenting many different fragments of a possible past/present. There is no attempt to achieve 'historical verisimilitude' in the dramatised account of colonisation. Such a venture is doomed to failure anyway because the available documentary material is generally amassed by whites, controlled by whites, and housed in predominantly white institutions. Instead, Davis's work contextualises imperial versions of a monologic history within a wider concept of the past which conveys the historical, mythological, and political meaning of that past for the present Nyoongah community. This process, whereby the European textual record experiences a theatrical 'time warp' which undercuts its authority, has also been evident in performative approaches to other Aboriginal texts such as *Bran Nue Dae* (1990) by Jimmy Chi and Kuckles. The 1993 Australian touring production used theatre's capacity for simultaneous representation of different time frames to interrogate history as it has been officially documented. Slides depicting scenes from the past were projected behind the contemporary action to illustrate aspects of imperial history without necessarily affirming its agency. Despite the solemnity of this tableau, its visual and conceptual overlaying of time and space historicised the play's action in ways that confirmed the current vitality of Aboriginal culture (and theatre).

Combining separate time-scapes – and interpretations of them – reinforces the fluidity of the temporal past and makes possible synchronic and intertextual apprehensions of historical time. Indigenous theatre in particular avoids a fixed diachronic sequencing through its preference for dramatic structures which evoke some kind of temporal circularity. Mythical figures, such as

Plate 6 Archival slides projected behind the action in Jimmy Chi and Kuckles's *Bran Nue Dae*, 1993. Black Swan Theatre Company.

Source: Photo: Reprinted with the permission of Jeff Busby

the native Canadian trickster[16] or the Australian Aboriginal dreamer, collapse present, past, and mythic time and foreground points of overlap and contact between the spiritual world and the more mundane time/space of the 'ordinary' action. In many cases, their appearance signals a ritualised moment which represents timelessness, or the state of being outside the dominant society's temporalities, so that a ceremonial catharsis of colonial oppression is possible. Similarly, Maori spirits refuse temporal boundaries and are often part of the theatrical apparatus by which the past and present are made concurrent. Hone Tuwhare's *In the Wilderness Without a Hat* (1985), for instance, begins with several Maori characters cleaning and restoring the carved ancestral figures inside the marae which is, in itself, a spiritual place that protects and maintains the community's law/lore. This restoration demonstrates the importance of the ancestors whose place in the contemporary characters' lives is reinforced when they 'come alive' towards the end of the play. Hopu, one of the ancestors, tells Waimiria that the names of the 'lost' figures will be found: 'a time will come soon when you shall dream a dream. In this dream, the names of all the people in this house will be given to you' (1991: 110). Later, Hopu says, 'We leave now. We'll be back' (ibid.: 115), but they never quite 'leave'. Instead, these spirits maintain over the community a physical and metaphysical vigil in which the non-specific mythic time can interact with, and even control, chronological time.

These examples show that a cyclical notion of time can be reproduced in theatre provided that the discursive context in which temporal signifiers are presented and interpreted is itself non-linear: stage space rather than page space. Because they question the simple correlation between history and time, plays which reconstruct empirical time as multi-directional, elliptical, fragmented, and even unpredictable loosen imperialism's control over historical discourse. Equally effective is the dramatic rupture of time, a strategy that Daniel David Moses uses in *Almighty Voice and His Wife* (1991) to dramatise the 'shock' of colonisation to native culture in Canada. The play is divided into distinct halves: the first, set in the 1890s, depicts Almighty Voice and White Girl in their struggle to resist the colonial forces, while the second uses the same two actors in a contemporary stand-up comedy routine which parodies stereotypes of the 'Indian' as constructed in/ through imperial discourses. The temporal rupture in the middle of the play not only frustrates narrative expectations – and generic ones as well since the style of the play changes abruptly – but it also has the effect of foreshortening time. The overall performance thus incorporates a significant time warp, complicating the cause-and-effect logic implied by the play's thematics. A further refusal of causality is implied in the play's ending as the narrative comes full-circle when the comics, Interlocutor and Ghost, transform to their original character identities.

The idea of a journey through time (and space) is crucial to Alma De Groen's *The Rivers of China* which uses disrupted chronologies and intersecting narratives to problematise the linear histories which underpin imperialism.[17] Again, two distinct stories are presented: whereas one follows Katherine Mansfield's final few months of life in France, the other depicts the experiences of an unnamed man who wakes up in a Sydney hospital after a suicide attempt thinking he is Mansfield. Although these narratives are nominally separated by the space of some fifty years, they are tightly interwoven in the performative text. While constructing a present that looks backward to recuperate some aspects of the past, the play also creates a past that looks forward into the present/future so that events in different time frames affect each other. Unlike playwrights whose access to an indigenous metaphysics might posit the possibility of timelessness, De Groen must conceive a structure which, in its emphasis on double and split perspectives, confounds the logic of linear time while nevertheless accepting some notion of teleology.

Plays which experiment with the structural organisation of history suggest that theatrical form is inherently a political concept. At issue here is the coercive power of narrative, a central concern for feminist and post-colonial theorists alike. As Elin Diamond argues:

> To understand history as narrative is a crucial move for feminists, not only because it demystifies the idea of disinterested authorship, but because the traditionally subordinate role of women in history can be seen as the legacy of narrative itself. With its relentless teleology, its ordering of meaning, narrative accrues to itself the power to define and legislate; it is, as Mária Minich Brewer puts it, the 'discourse of authority and legitimation'.
>
> (1990: 95)

Although Diamond's point is made chiefly in relation to feminist texts, it applies equally well to post-colonial theatre. The dismantling of narrative and its underlying structures of 'authority and legitimation' proceeds through a reorganisation of relations between the basic content and the form of representation, as illustrated by the fragmenting and resequencing of events, the chronological looping, the overlaying of time frames, the refusal of closure, and the other narrative interventions identified across the categories of drama under discussion.

Other theatrical devices contribute to constructions of temporality: for instance, dual roles that span different times destabilise the sense of an unbroken historical record in much the same manner as story-tellers or narrators break the time frame of a play. In Tomson Highway's *The Rez Sisters*, the trickster is variously manifested as a white seagull, a black nighthawk, and a Bingo Master. The significance of the trickster as a traditional native Canadian force/spirit takes on a specific contemporary component when he appears as the dynamic, handsome man calling the bingo numbers. Similarly, costumes and sets of different eras, or visibly layered costumes that are intended to be removed for subsequent roles, draw attention to the dismantling of a uniform chronology. Ian Steadman describes a production of Matsemela Manaka's *Pula* (1982) from South Africa in which one actor deliberately staged the processes that effected his temporal transformation to:

a smooth-talking 'man-about-town'. He changed quite casually from his traditional 'tribal' costume and began to dress very deliberately, dabbing aftershave lotion on himself, carefully combing his hair, admiring himself in a mirror, and gradually becoming a smooth 'with-it' young rake of the township. The deliberate change of costume and character functioned in performance to signify the subsidiary theme of assimilation and incorporation: the young rural worker became the township playboy and the audience witnessed the nuances of 'character-change'.

(1990: 10)

Metatheatrically, this example illustrates not only the constructedness of character but also one of the many possible performative manipulations of history/time.

SPATIAL HISTORIES

In many post-colonial plays, the fracturing of time works in tandem with the historicising and remapping of space. This is a central project for colonised peoples whose lands were invaded, and in some cases permanently sequestered, by European powers. Even in the occupation colonies where local cultures regained control over their land after independence, the spatial inscriptions of imperialism have had an enduring legacy. For example, the political unit now known as Nigeria is determined by an arbitrary border – drawn along the coast and beside/through several other (European-determined) topographical features – which does not take account of the ancient boundaries which the Yoruba and Igbo established to keep peace between themselves. Similarly, the division of Ireland into two separate countries can be traced back to British imperialism. The political agency of imperialism's spatial history has been even more pronounced in the settler colonies where linguistic, economic, and cultural domination by Europeans depended on the conquest of the land as a site from which to articulate power over the indigenous inhabitants of the settler colonies. For the early explorers and settlers, space was a 'text that had to be written on before it could be interpreted' (Carter 1987: 41). In other words, colonial space was inscribed according to the imperatives of settlement, initially by European cartographers whose segmentation, classification, and hierarchisation of space transformed it into a *place* that could be known and inhabited. The surveys of areas of New Zealand and central Canada, for instance, show how so-called empirical methods of calibrating space were in fact deeply ideological since they established grids, acre lots, and boundaries that became the explicit determinants of white land ownership. In these two countries and also in Australia, indigenous peoples were written out of historical space by a map/history which ignored their spatial epistemologies and wrote over their traditional place names.[18]

Both settler and indigenous playwrights engage, albeit often in quite different ways, with the spatial aspects of imperialism. In many cases, dramatised images of the landscape reveal how space[19] has been constructed by imperial history and, concomitantly, how it might be deconstructed and reorganised according to the imperatives of various colonised groups. Since space is the grammar not only of the landscape but also of the *mise-en-scène*, theatre has the potential to reconstitute the structural basis of historical conception, to make space/place a performer rather than the medium on and through which the pageant of history seems to merely unfold. The more conservative view of theatrical space – that it 'colours' all relationships within its limits (see Suvin 1987: 322) – does not adequately account for the proxemic systems of much post-colonial theatre where space becomes a force that potentially *determines* such relationships rather than simply affecting them. This can be illustrated in reference to the positioning of settlers and/or indigenes within the landscape/stagescape – in this case, the land tends to be presented in concrete form rather than signified indexically by 'outdoor' costume or a few stage properties – or through an analysis of the 'territorial disputes' commonly staged in indigenous plays.

Space, as it is determined by the contours of the landscape and the vagaries of the weather, figures prominently in settler narratives where it often becomes a site of anxiety and struggle. More radical texts reject the Romantic impulse towards pathetic fallacy and present the landscape/stagescape not as a metaphor for human attitudes or psychological states but as a palpable force that shapes human experience. This is exemplified in Janis Balodis's *Too Young for Ghosts* (1985) which enacts a complex version of Australia's spatial history by staging both the processes of imperial cartography and, more sympathetically, the settler's encounter with alien space. In the play's contrapuntal narratives, Ludwig Leichhardt's exploration of north Queensland in the 1840s is paired, seemingly incongruously, with the experiences of a group of Latvian immigrants (formerly 'displaced persons') in the same place one hundred years later. While the Latvians are positioned as exiles in a landscape with which they must somehow learn to coexist, the explorers' expedition is shown quite clearly as a strategic exercise designed to erase Aboriginal history/space and to open up the land for European settlement. Leichhardt's cartographic gaze appropriates and totalises all that he surveys, allowing him to construct the country as *terra nullius* because, in his opinion, Aboriginal dreaming tracks – a form of travelled space – leave no significant mark of ownership on the landscape. Imperial space, here scripted by the map (as well as by Leichhardt's diary) is thus exposed as a palimpsest which obscures alternative spatial configurations. In this respect, Leichhardt's determination to make his map record what he expected to encounter illustrates J.B. Harley's point that the surveyor 'replicates not just the "environment" in some abstract sense but equally the territorial imperatives of a particular political system' (1988: 279).

While the play demonstrates, step by step, the inscription of colonial space, it also undercuts such endeavours. The fact that the explorers seem to be continually lost, going in circles, or even going backwards, ironises both the map and its instruments – the compass and the sextant – as well as the explorers themselves. However, Balodis is not content simply to identify and deconstruct the hegemonic tropes of imperial cartography; he also attempts to find a different spatial logic through which to interpret history/geography. This emerges most insistently through the performative structures of the text: role-doubling, used in conjunction with one multipurpose set, overlays narratives that are often geographically and temporally distant. That the Latvians and the explorers watch, and sometimes enter, each other's stories suggests the existence of an interactive historical space that records the inscriptions of past and present simultaneously rather than sequentially. The visual effect of these superimposed spaces is a dissolution of edges, frames, and boundaries so that distinctions between various landscapes and time periods become blurred. At the same time, empirical space metamorphoses into 'phenomenological space'[20] in so far as it is felt/experienced by the characters rather than simply seen. Balodis's expressionistic dramaturgy thus resists the closures of imperial cartography to construct, in opposition, a spatial history that is never finished or final. Within this schema, the Latvians can be inserted into historical space alongside the other 'ghosts' of Australia's collective past: the explorers, the Aborigines who were annihilated, and the landscape itself.

Aside from reworking the mapping process, theatre can present a map itself as a visible site of deconstructive attack. A case in point is the Melbourne Theatre Company's premiere production of Balodis's *No Going Back* (1992), a sequel to *Too Young for Ghosts*. The set consisted largely of a floor-to-ceiling colonial-style map of Queensland, which not only provided an apt image for the central action but also influenced its spatial configurations since the stage entrance and exit points were constructed as irregularly shaped holes in the backdrop, with the cut-out sections being used as a clump of trees. By showing gaps in the map and staging parts of it in relief at unconventional angles, this particular set design unsettled the authority of the imperial text – Leichhardt's diaries/ sketches – upon which it was based. In a more politicised interrogation of conventional cartography, Davis's *Kullark* calls for a backdrop painted with Warrgul the Rainbow Serpent in the shape of a map of the Swan River in Western Australia. As a different kind of spatial knowledge, this map situates the landscape within an Aboriginal cosmology and shows that it is not an empty space awaiting the settlers' inscriptions. Moreover, by foregrounding 'the inevitable discrepancy between the "natural" and the "imitated" object' (Huggan 1989a: 121), the stylised serpent image holds the supposed mimeticism of the western map up to question. Such ideological interventions are important to post-colonial discourse because they expose the processes through which subjective and contingent models of 'reality' were (and, in some cases, still are) passed off as objective and universal representations.

The mimetic fallacy which underlies the map is also common to naturalistic theatre which presents features of the set (itself a spatial map) as if they were real rather than representational. Non-naturalistic theatre, on the other hand, draws attention to its own signifying systems, thereby historicising the images presented. Altering the proportional logic of the landscape/stagescape is one method of foregrounding how space is constructed by both culture and power. For instance, in the Auckland production of Stuart Hoar's *Squatter* (1987), the Mercury Theatre Company staged the landscape in miniature, effectively deconstructing its iconisation in colonial history as an object of settlement and potential ownership, and making explicit the settlers' attempts to segment and hierarchise particular spaces.[21] Set in New Zealand when the Liberal government was forcibly breaking up many privately owned large Pakeha farm estates for subsequent purchase by the rising middle class, the play critiques as folly the historical claims on property made by *all* the characters: the wealthy and the indigent squatters and their families, the government, the would-be socialist revolutionaries, the 'carpet-baggers', and the representatives of the middle class. Significantly, there are no Maori claims on the land in *Squatter*, but New Zealand audiences would inevitably have made the connection to the dispossession of Maori lands and to the contemporary Land Rights Tribunal. Although the deliberate telescoping of the landscape functions in part to establish an immediate sense of geographical location, the spatial incongruity between the human figures and the landscape at once makes clear *and* undercuts the squatters' efforts to exert power over the land. As well as parodying the characters, such visual ironies also have the paradoxical effect of making humans look small because of the sheer expanse of land pictured. In this unconventional history of squattocracy, liberalism, and socialism, anarchy frequently 'reigns' as the spatial logic of a hierarchised colonial order breaks down.

Maurice Shadbolt's war play, *Once on Chunuk Bair* (1982), also from New Zealand, explicitly images territorial disputes in spatial terms, functioning primarily as a critique of the British Empire's historical stranglehold over the land, the people, and the political decisions of distant colonies. Set in Turkey during World War One, this play questions the wisdom of New Zealand's participation in a remote European conflict. It illustrates how great numbers of colonial troops were sacrificed in the name of Empire in order to gain only minimal stretches of land, and how colonial soldiers were abandoned by their British superiors at Gallipoli and Chunuk Bair (not to mention at the Somme and several other battle sites on the western front in World War One alone). At the same time, the play holds up to scrutiny New Zealand society's persistent mythologising of the 'Anzac' as a national hero.[22] The imperialist and nationalist opportunities offered by war – to serve one's King and country – are thus sharply separated *and* deconstructed. As Shadbolt suggests, the routine binary construction of ally versus enemy breaks down when allegiance to the 'motherland' leads to decimation of the colonial troops.[23] In terms of staging, the Mercury Theatre's production of *Once on Chunuk Bair* presented a potent image of the futility of such territorial wars. Since the play takes place in trenches, the set was built vertically, partly in order to provide a sightline for the audience. Thus the land which the New Zealand troops have captured and try to hold is geographically skewed – much like the skewing of history that has led to their presence in Turkey – and the difficult ascent to the summit represents only a dubious win: the soldiers have gained an insubstantial hill, but they have sustained monumental human losses. On another level, the stagescape recalls the mountainous landscape of New Zealand itself, thereby alluding to the white invasion of Maori land during the country's earlier imperial war.

Dramatised images of an outdoor landscape frequently reveal the ambivalent positioning of the settler *vis-à-vis* the land and its original inhabitants. Sharon Pollock's *Generations* (1980) endorses

Plate 7 Staging the land in miniature. Mercury Theatre production of
Stuart Hoar's *Squatter*. Bracken (top) and Olive
Source: Reprinted with the permission of Victoria University Press.
Photo: Michael Tubberty

Plate 8 The vertical set for Maurice Shadbolt's *Once on Chunuk Bair*
Source: Reprinted with the permission of Hodder Moa Beckett Publishers and the estate of Brian Brake

the (male) farmer's claim to a small section of the prairie that his father and grandfather have cultivated, but also acknowledges, somewhat tentatively, the spatial priority of indigenous Canadians. The play's one native character is Charlie Running Dog, described as an old man whose skin has been 'eroded' to resemble 'some outcropping of arid land' (1981: 141). Through this portrait, Pollock almost suggests that Charlie *represents* the land, but her dramaturgy ultimately saves him from such objectification by constructing the land itself as a final 'character' with many moods and 'many faces' (ibid.: 141). In fact, the central action revolves around the land, which is a compelling force in the lives of all members of the Nurlin family, whether they want to escape it, tame it, or simply learn to live with its intransigence. To suggest the interface of culture and nature, the specified set features a veranda – a commonly staged space in settler theatre[24] – which connects the house to the outdoors so that a portion of the kitchen is shown on one side and a semblance of the drought-parched prairie landscape on the other. Assisted by lighting which suggests that the prairie stretches almost to infinity, the play's spatial structures convey the precariousness of the settler position since the house is displaced from centre stage and grafted onto the edge of the landscape. The veranda, however, remains a site of negotiation and a corridor of possible dialogue, not only between the various characters but also between the settlers and the land. That the proxemic space of the veranda is not used as strategically as it might be reflects *Generations*'s overall ambivalence as a play that tries, rather unsuccessfully, to mediate between white desires and native land claims.

As these few examples depict, the land plays a powerful role in history despite (and because of) efforts by settlers to counteract its power with an assertive human presence. In Canadian and Australian history plays in particular, nature, in its various guises, often shapes the contours of the performance text, at times propelling the action towards some kind of apocalypse. Louis Nowra's plays characteristically feature fires, floods, and all manner of meteorological disasters which eventually engulf many of the characters. The more nightmarish scenes – as found in *Inside the Island* (1980) and *Sunrise* (1983) – chart in spectacular style the disintegration of colonial rule and the reinstatement of a spatial order which has nature as its controlling force. Instead of being construed as unrelentingly bleak, Nowra's apocalyptic

Plate 9 The veranda set in the Tarragon Theatre production of Sharon
Pollock's *Generations*, 1980. Old Ed, Alfred, and David
Source: Reprinted with the permission of Playwrights' Union of Canada, Toronto,
the actors (Ed McNamara, Colin Fox, and Stephen Ouimette), Tarragon
Theatre, and Ellis Bartkiewicz. Photo: Ellis Bartkiewicz

vision should be read in terms of a crisis of settlement rather than a temporal closure or conclusion. Implicit in crisis is a cycle of transition and renovation, enacted in a number of his texts through a ritual purgation of the landscape. In this context, fire, for instance, becomes a positive force which cauterises the colonial wound and regenerates the land.[25] Overall, Nowra's theatre tends to use the landscape/stagescape as a mnemonic device that records the repressed traumas and historical cataclysms of imperialism, and replays them as part of an ongoing rehearsal towards a more enabling future for all Australians (see Kelly 1992b: 55).

Imperialist history established the pioneer myth which set up spatial relationships between settlers and the land, often ignoring the possibility that indigenous peoples also moved in the same historical time/space as the settlers. A spatial history, on the other hand, may suggest a dimension in which disparate cultures interact, where the pioneer myth can be rewritten, or re-enacted, as a dialectic between invader and invaded. Almost without exception, Aboriginal, Maori, and First Nations Canadian playwrights stage, in some way, the historical displacement of their people as a consequence of imperialism. Many of their plays use proxemic signifiers to demonstrate how indigenous spaces have been invaded and desacralised by the expansion of an alien culture, how indigenes themselves have been confined spatially under colonisation, and how their relationships with whites continue to be negotiated through spatial structures. Even more radically, indigenous performances frequently remap stage space strategically in order to reclaim land or to subvert the dominant society's control over social space. While such gestures may be largely symbolic, they none the less speak to a wider political action.

Land rights are a dominant focus in indigenous theatre, which is not surprising in view of the tardiness that has characterised government responses to native land claims in Canada, Australia, and New Zealand over the last few decades. David Diamond's *No' Xya'* for instance, was specifically devised to protest against the government's handling of issues relating to land ownership/use in British Columbia. *Bran Nue Dae*, though put together in an entirely different way and for different purposes, none the less prefaces its closing song with a demand for land-rights: 'This fella song all about the Aboriginal people, coloured people, black people, longa Australia. Us people want our land back, we want em rights, we want em fair deal, all same longa white man' (Chi and Kuckles

1991: 84). Craig Harrison's *Tomorrow Will Be a Lovely Day* (1974) brings the symbol of Maori land loss directly to the stage in its narrative about a group of young Maori men who storm the National Library in Wellington in order to steal the 1840 Treaty of Waitangi, the first 'legal'[26] determinant of land ownership in post-contact New Zealand.[27] The treaty thus embeds in the stage space the signification and the memory of all the lost land (as well as the resentment it still fosters). In all of these plays, the stage is inscribed not only as a fictional space which 'acts' as part of the dramatic narrative but also as a site from which indigenous groups can chart a course for cultural and political protest.

Rore Hapipi's *Death of the Land* (1976) foregrounds debates over land ownership by detailing the somewhat farcical legal processes involved in the 'sale' of Maori land to a Pakeha, a move in which several Maori are implicated. Most of the action is set in the Maori Land Court of New Zealand in 1977,[28] where the (Pakeha) legal discourse is incomprehensible to some of the Maori characters who are militantly opposed to the land sale because it will sever them from yet another part of their history/heritage. The entire debate over the land sale and 'Te Tiriti' (the Treaty of Waitangi) is itself a debate over authenticity and/or authority, culminating in the conclusion that 'The Maori always gets the justice but the Pakeha always gets the land' (1991: 43). Yet the play reaches beyond such purely binary oppositions to explore a broad range of Maori attitudes towards the land. The events suggest that while the Maori argue among themselves, they lose their land and their history, a point underscored in the last moment of the play by the sounds of a *tangi* (wake) for the land, heard as the Judge continues his land transfer hearings in assembly-line fashion.

Jack Davis's theatre illustrates particularly well the recuperative power of spatial histories, even when it is not dealing specifically with land-rights issues. While often depicting the historical confinement of Aborigines within institutions – notably missions and gaols – designed to segregate them from white society, Davis none the less stresses the importance of subversion and resistance. In his plays, boundaries designed as markers of hermetically sealed worlds segregating racial groups frequently dissolve to become, instead, 'debatable places' that 'speak' through their violation. A prime example of this occurs in *No Sugar* as the Aborigines repeatedly break out of the mission compound and refuse to respect other restrictive enclosures created by representatives of white authority. The idea of contested space is emblematic of the play as a whole and, ironically, it is precisely the colonisers' continued efforts to construct and enforce spatial hierarchies that emphasise the Aborigines' insistent visibility, allowing them to define themselves spatially by resisting physical and/or cultural ghettoisation. Jimmy, for example, flaunts his non-compliance with the rules of the spaces assigned to him by venturing 'out of bounds' when confined to the mission and by disrupting legal proceedings when put in gaol. Through his amusing antics as performer and entertainer, he transforms the prison cell and the courtroom into a form of theatre where he asserts control over the spaces designed to segregate and punish him. Such subversions of 'white man's law' are widespread in Davis's plays and generally function to question the validity of that law and its historical repercussions.

Post-colonial spatial histories dramatise the 'dialectic of place and displacement' which has been identified as a key issue in societies affected by imperialism (Ashcroft *et al.* 1989: 9). Such histories work against models of theatre which subordinate spatial signifiers to other thematic and generic concerns, and/or which present the landscape merely as a scenic device, designed at best to heighten narrative emplotment and, at worst, to recede as a naturalised backdrop for signal events. In settler colonies, spatial histories can effectively dismantle the myth of *terra nullius* by revealing the land as an object of discursive and territorial contention, as well as an 'accumulative text' that records in multiple inscriptions the spatial forms and fantasies of both settler and indigenous cultures.

THEATRE SPACES

The architectural design of theatres, or spaces co-opted as theatres, significantly affects the performance event, especially as site is almost always a key aspect of narration. Hence, constructions of (the self in) history in post-colonial drama are in many ways related to theatre history itself. In the heyday of imperialism, most colonised countries boasted theatres, usually proscenium-arched, which were intended to replicate, both in proxemic design and associated performative style, the conventions of the metropolitan centre. Such theatres were, in many ways, anathema to any kind of strategic post-colonial drama, not only because they were elitist but also because they fostered performance paradigms that were often foreign to the local culture. In particular, the separation of the viewing subject and the distant object of his/her sight was alien to many non-western societies whose traditional theatre had been a more participatory event. In many countries, the development of a contemporary post-colonial theatre praxis has necessitated the rejection of formal western theatre spaces in favour of 'outside' alternatives, or at least the adaptation and appropriation of those proscribed spaces according to the political contingencies of the colonised society. In reference to Malaysia, Margaret Yong claims that much local theatre is dismal, principally because it remains inside English buildings where it cannot abandon European acting styles. Those plays that move out of the conventional theatre buildings become instantly more vibrant (1984: 238).

Moving away from the conventions of imperial theatre and its associated legacies is, however, not always easy. Ola Rotimi has tried – with only limited success – to wrest Nigerian drama away from proscenium-arch theatres but he has found that many of his colleagues remain bound to a historically anomalous form:

> Sadly, folk opera groups in Nigeria, in spite of their close link with the traditions of precolonial theater, have found it somehow difficult to free themselves from the shackles of the proscenium anomaly. I've tried to persuade some of these groups to make use of the arena setting, but they just won't touch it.
>
> (1974: 61)

Rotimi himself prefers a small, round, outdoor theatre that incorporates the audience into a communal event rather than dividing it from the actors with an invisible fourth wall. He claims that this is 'the only formation that approximates aboriginal theater arrangement, at least in Africa south of the Sahara' (ibid.: 60). When he is obliged to use the proscenium theatre, Rotimi refuses to be constrained by its spatial hierarchies or its stylistic norms. As he explains,

> We deliberately set out to affront the conventions of the proscenium style of production which interfere with our desire to feel the audience as being one with us. Our entrances and exits find access through the wings onstage as well as through aisles in the auditorium. . . . Our crowd scenes further defy the proscenium laws, overflowing, as

such scenes often do, the 'apron' of the stage, and sluicing
over when necessary right into the orchestra pit!

(ibid.: 60)

This kind of intervention in the conventions which govern
performance space usage is crucial because, until they are adapted
to the expressive and semantic intentions of colonised peoples,
such spaces exist primarily in the dominant society's history.

Rawle Gibbons makes the important point that theatre, as an
arrangement of people, 'can create its architecture anywhere'
(1979: 47). In the Caribbean, Marina Maxwell's Yard Theatre in
Jamaica was one of the most significant experiments in relocating
theatre performance to more culturally appropriate sites. Running
for several years in the late 1960s and early 1970s, the Yard Theatre
– literally a yard rather than a building – addressed itself to
the people of the street, the poorer classes who had no access to
a formal theatre often segregated along the lines of race and class.
Edward Kamau Brathwaite describes the anti-conventional aspects
of Maxwell's experiment as follows:

[There was] no 'fixity'; no audience for one thing in the
traditional sense; no gate, no entrance fee, no foyer, no box
office, no boxes; therefore no dress-up, no gossip between
acts; no drinks, no clinks, no place where the privilege of
those who could afford to pay could be displayed. . . . And
since there was no pay, no privilege, no fixed seats, there was
no social stratification; instead, there was this democracy
of witness . . . and a democracy of participation, since in the
small place available in the yard, actor=dancer=singer
was also often audience: watching with the 'audience' his
brothers and sisters 'perform'.

(1977–8: 181)

Brathwaite goes on to argue that the Yard Theatre was revolutionary not simply because it rejected the traditions of colonial
Euro-American theatre, but because it provided a viable and
creative alternative. This, in turn, fostered a performance style
that accommodated the folk forms and traditional enactments
of the common people. Sistren's community theatre work, along
with Rawle Gibbons' recent productions in Trinidadian panyards
and other functionally flexible public spaces, represents similar
attempts to refuse the historical inscriptions of purpose-built
theatres and their associated aesthetic and social conventions.

In some instances, the absence of spaces designed or easily adapted for performance purposes drives theatre underground, if it does not inhibit it altogether. Martin Orkin points to this as a crucial factor in the history of black South African drama under apartheid: 'The lack of theatrical space in the townships continued until the end of the 1980s and remained for the state a primary significant *de facto* means of limiting and containing theatrical growth' (1991: 150). The state's efforts were not, however, entirely successful. Orkin continues to outline how 'The influence of the Black Consciousness movement . . . contributed to the recognition particularly amongst other theatre practitioners, that theatre space might be recovered by the oppressed classes for their own use in political struggle' (ibid.: 158). The development of township theatre over the last decade and a half demonstrates precisely this recovery of social space, not just for the performers but for the audience as well, as explained in the published text of *Woza Albert!*:

> There are minimal facilities – few lights, no fixed seats, no carpets. High-heels sound. Cold-drink cans roll. Babies cry. Friends call to each other. Drunks heckle. People come and go. Performers must fend for themselves – and they do – in the broad, loud, triumphantly energetic 'township' style.
>
> (Mtwa, Ngema, and Simon 1983: v)

This introductory note makes clear that township theatre has necessarily adapted to the circumstances which are part of its social context. Actors modulate their voices and adapt their gestures to play over, and even to revel in, the constant interruptions which make township theatre a culturally situated theatrical form.

Tar Ahura insists that Nigerian theatre move from its elitist physical buildings to wherever the 'people' are (1985: 97). As Ross Kidd explains, this move has been effective in areas of rural India and Bangladesh where labourers have found theatre to be an effective tool in reducing exploitation and victimisation. When these tenant farmers prepare scenarios for presentation to other landless villagers, they make room towards the end of the performance for 'actors and audience [to] discuss real plans, to be carried out the following day, to pressure government to deepen their well. . . . Each drama not only shows the problems but gets the audience talking about them' (1983: 131). Such village level outdoor theatre can lead to further social action and generate solutions unlikely to be canvassed were it staged in a metropolitan building. The multiple and varied histories which circulate in post-colonial societies overlap, intersect, and compete with each other. They can be neither conflated into a singular national (or any other kind of) narrative nor completely separated from each other or from the particular contexts in which they are constructed. Rather, history remains a site of struggle and contention, a hybridised discourse fraught with conflicts and contradictions. In this respect, it may be easier to understand Dening's claim that 'history is something we make rather than something we learn' (1993: 366); solutions, then, are also to be made, not learned. Any history that claims to be representative must now 'fabricate' discourses that incorporate the desires, stories, and identities of the multitude of people who make up any one nation or region. This political and cultural pluralism must be fostered in a way that dismantles a univocal imperial history to establish equal voices that can remain in contention for authority and authenticity. Such an epistemological approach would usefully deconstruct notions of historical autonomy on the part of either the colonisers or the colonised.

NOTES

1 Sharon Pollock's play, *Walsh* (1980), depicts this practice as part of her critique of British colonialism (1993: 144).
2 The play itself has an interesting curriculum vitae: written in 1936 and staged in London (under the original title of *Toussaint L'Ouverture*) when Trinidad was still a British colony, it was undoubtedly conceived, at least in part, as a protest against imperial rule. Some thirty years later, the play was revised for production in Nigeria at a time when the country was ravaged by a bloody civil war. On this occasion, the audience found, in James's depiction of black leaders struggling for independence and then plunging into post-revolutionary bloodshed, parallels with their own situation (see Stone 1994: 20). *The Black Jacobins* was mounted for the first time in James's native Trinidad in the early 1980s.
3 Such claims now require modifying in the face of a large body of theatre in all three countries which seems obsessively centred on historical representation. Pollock, Thompson, and Nowra have themselves been leaders in this movement, both in their investigation of indigenous experience and in their critiques of settler society. In the wider canon of contemporary 'historical theatre', some plays are less

concerned with interrogating the 'truth value' of the imperial record than with mythologising various local characters, but this in itself can be seen as part of the imperative to establish post-colonial histories that carry as much cultural weight as do imperial ones.

4 This was one of the official bicentennial slogans, along with the phrase, 'Let's celebrate '88'.

5 Our discussion of *Les Canadiens* is based on the published version of the script which was reworked for a wider national audience shortly after the play's initial production in Montreal.

6 A slightly different tack is taken in Andrew Whaley's *The Rise and Shine of Comrade Fiasco* (1990) which is about the discovery of a man who has been hiding in Zimbabwe and who could be a freedom fighter from Zimbabwe or Mozambique, or merely a thief or a madman. The play explores the possibilities that such a discovery presents and argues that whatever the truth of the man's origin, his story deserves a hearing. By allowing this 'anonymous' character to claim legendary status, Whaley suggests that a self-created history is as valid as any other story.

7 Aidoo was a guest speaker at the Post-Colonial Women Conference, York University, Toronto, Canada, 12 October 1988.

8 Trinh T. Minh-ha's work (1989) is also crucial to this debate.

9 Stephen Gray claims that Dike's work 'established almost all the elements of the "black drama"' that would influence both men and women playwrights succeeding her (1990: 82).

10 See Harris (1970: 6–9) for an extended discussion of limbo dancing as a response to slavery. Harris maintains that the limbo reflects not only the slaves' dislocation from African tradition but also the possibility of a renascent 'body' that could accommodate African and other legacies within a new architecture of cultures.

11 Benveniste's *histoire* is, as Elam explains, 'dedicated to the narration of events in the past, which eliminates the speaking subject and his [*sic*] addressee, together with all deictic references, from the narration'. *Discours*, not directly translatable to 'discourse', is 'the "subjective mode" geared to the present, which indicates the interlocutors and their speaking situations' (1980: 144).

12 Tejumola Olaniyan notes that in a number of the play's performances which he attended, the 'hard choice' was palpable, and that even though the aesthetic logic of the play regularly induced the audience to vote for the robbers, no one appeared comfortable with the consequences (1996).

13 Walcott's term – see Hill (1985b: 5) for further discussion of Walcott's views on story-telling.

14 Despite Rendra's attempts at subterfuge, it is possible that the play contributed to his arrest in 1978 for allegedly 'spreading hatred' against the government.

15 From Dike's keynote address, International Women Playwright's Conference, Adelaide, Australia, 4 July 1994.

16 The African trickster, particularly in the Yoruba tradition, can connect the effects of the ritual past to the present, but is firstly a figure of fun.

17 Feminist theory also refuses the linear time/history imperative,

preferring the choice of a cyclical time frame. *The Rivers of China* enacts both a feminist and a post-colonial repudiation of patriarchal/ imperial assumptions of chronological time and space.

18 Indigenous informants no doubt assisted in this mapping, but ultimately, settlers and explorers refigured colonial space without regard for indigenes. Even when indigenous place names were kept, the colonising culture decided the merit and appropriateness of such names, setting down on paper (and therefore in history) their newly ascribed signification.

19 Space, in our terms, refers to geographical locations (and how they are translated into a theatrical context) as well as to theatrical buildings and stage locations in which the body is situated.

20 See Ferrier (1990: 45–6) for further discussion of this concept and of the intersections between postmodern, post-colonial, and feminist cartographies.

21 In the Melbourne Theatre Company's production of Louis Nowra's *Summer of the Aliens* (1992), the landscape was similarly miniaturised, though perhaps less as a deconstructive technique than as a nostalgic recognition of the passage of time and the functions of memory.

22 The Australian Anzac hero functions in much the same way.

23 In Shadbolt's play, as well as in John Broughton's World War One play, *ANZAC* (1992), and in Vincent O'Sullivan's *Shuriken* (1983) (World War Two), the New Zealand soldiers find that the empire and their duty to the empire put them in unwinnable situations; hence, their supposed ally is, in many ways, more dangerous than the 'official' enemy. In Broughton's *Michael James Manaia* (1991) (Vietnam War), the ally may have changed to the Americans, but the protagonist finds that his experiences are uncomfortably similar to those of his father in World War Two.

24 See, for instance, David Malouf's *Blood Relations*, Louis Nowra's *Inside the Island*, and John Kneubuhl's *Think of a Garden* (1991). It is also favoured by designers of many settler colony plays.

25 The trope of the bushfire as a regenerative force takes on particular resonance in Australia where some native flora depend on intense heat for germination.

26 The legality of the Treaty is doubtful, not least because it was never ratified.

27 Land forms the basis of many New Zealand plays, from Bruce Mason's *The Pohutukawa Tree* in 1957 to Mervyn Thompson's *Songs to the Judges* in 1980 to Bruce Stewart's *Broken Arse* in 1990. Approaches to land rights are of course widely varied among these examples: Mason's view can now be read as a patronising account of Maori identification with the land, written from a Pakeha point of view. Thompson's play, written with the assistance of Don Selwyn (who left before the production was mounted) and Hemi Rapata, is a more informed account of dispossession, again by a Pakeha. Stewart's play interrogates several strangely enduring misconceptions concerning the land rights debate, most memorably, Henry's naive claim that his Pakeha family were the original owners of his estate.

28 Our discussion of Hapipi's play is based on the published version which refers specifically to the Land Court trials of 1977 although the earlier stage version preceded this date.

4

THE LANGUAGES OF RESISTANCE

We make the mistake of thinking that language will
somehow clarify things between us and the native.

(Vincent O'Sullivan, *Billy* 1990: 13)

Language is one of the most basic markers of colonial authority.
In *The Tempest*, Caliban's claim, 'You taught me language and my
profit on't / Is, I know how to curse' (I.ii.363–4) confirms both
Prospero's role as teacher and Caliban's ability to subvert that
role. Part of imperialism's project has been to impose the English
language on colonised subjects in an endeavour to control them
more completely. Language, so used as a manipulative tool, is
rendered 'obscene when it proceeds from an imperium or power
base so secure that it can abandon even the pretence of referen-
tiality or the negotiation of truth' (Tiffin and Lawson 1994: 4). One
method of installing the overarching power of an imperial tongue
is to prohibit the 'old' language. Forbidding people to speak their
own tongues is the first step in the destruction of a culture: Granny
Doll, a character in Jack Davis's play, *Barungin (Smell the Wind)*
(1988), notes that the *wetjalas* (whites) 'killed [her] language'
(1989: 36), which, to her, is the most monumental crime that
the *wetjalas* could have committed. The loss of language (which,
in Australia, means the loss of hundreds of discrete Aboriginal
languages since contact) leads to the possibility of a loss of names,
of oral history, and of a connection to the land. Indigenous
children in Canada and Australia were frequently taken from their
parents to be educated in the coloniser's language and customs.
Prevented from speaking their own languages and severely
punished if they disobeyed, these children often refused to pass on
their languages to their own children in an attempt to prevent the
repetition of such punishments.

164

Integrally associated with language is the speaker's sense of autonomy and dignity, both of which are diminished when the coloniser denies the linguistic validity of indigenous languages. Language's 'system of values – its suppositions, its geography, its concept of history, of difference, its myriad gradations of distinction – becomes the system upon which social, economic and political discourses are grounded' (Ashcroft *et al.* 1995: 283). The authority that the imposed language commands is much the same as the authority of literate, official history over the unwritten, changeable histories of the colonised subject. The naming and interpellative functions of the imperial language exacerbate the disempowerment of indigenous peoples/cultures. To name people and places in English, replacing any earlier constructions of location and identity, is to establish at least partial control over reality, geography, history, and subjectivity. Interpellation, or ascribing a subjectivity to – here – the colonised subject, equally denies the existence of a previous subjectivity or selfhood. The interpellative process of European languages frequently resulted in a reductive and simplistic construction of colonised subjectivity as 'other', ignoring the necessary cultural and personal individuation that selfhood generally presumes.

The wide-ranging power of the imperial language has, however, not been entirely successful in its attempt to eradicate local, potentially resistant languages that threaten the borders of imperial authority. The Maori people, who now speak one language distilled from several varieties, have demonstrated how powerful a force language can be: in New Zealand/Aotearoa, even though the dominant language is English, most institutions boast Maori names in addition to their English counterparts. While the 'Queen's English' is still often maintained as the linguistic – and even moral – standard in most countries of the former British Empire, language inevitably changes as its surrounding culture changes. The addition of technological or colloquial words, the disuse of now archaic words, and the relaxing of once-rigid grammar rules are but a few examples. More colloquial Englishes also inevitably compete for attention with standard English. As well as being inherently mutable over time, an imperial language alters when its speakers are exposed to other languages. Indigenous words that are more descriptive or accurate than any imposed terms become 'adopted' into English and its grammatical structures are sometimes inserted into those of other languages. Some colonised subjects abrogate

– or refuse to privilege – the imposed language, at least in its more formal registers, in order to regain a speaking position that is not determined by the coloniser. Other colonised subjects appropriate words or forms of English and employ them to a different purpose in an indigenous or a creolised language, again to make the language articulate a different authority (see Ashcroft *et al.* 1989: 38). Still others highlight the mutability of language by creating and maintaining a syncretic language built on words, forms, and grammatical constructions from several languages which have a particular local history. In Tasmania, attempts have been made to piece together what remains of the seven local Aboriginal languages to construct one indigenous language which restores a modicum of the sense of place that language affords. These strategies are just a few of the methods by which colonised subjects decentre the European hegemonic powers embedded in an imposed imperial language.

Post-colonial stages are particularly resonant spaces from which to articulate linguistic resistance to imperialism. Such a location for post-colonial agency is ironic given that the imperial theatre assisted in the inculcation of the coloniser's language both through the training of actors and the conditioning of audiences. The mistaken assumption that the heightened language of, for instance, Shakespeare's plays was most suitable as a theatrical language frequently prevented colonised subjects, whose facility with the coloniser's language was never 'good enough', from being able to theatricalise anything but a 'pale' imitation of European classics. Now determined to interrupt the transmission of 'correct' English in favour of local languages, regional variants, shifting registers, and indigenous accents (among many other forms of linguistic communication), post-colonial playwrights have concentrated on speaking in voices less inflected by imperialism. Moves to recover pre-contact languages or to *re*-present English on stage have been highly successful. The staging of various extant indigenous languages, for instance, gives rise to renewed debate over the authenticity of the Queen's English – the ostensibly pure version of the highly impure and derivative language of English – helping to destabilise colonial authority and provide other means of communication. Yet as this chapter contends, alterity is not simply unlocked by 'translations' from standard to non-standard linguistic forms; language functions as a basic medium through which meaning is filtered, but it also acts as a cultural and political system that has meaning in itself. The post-colonial stage acts as a principal arena for the enunciation of such a system.

Theatre also assists in the maintenance of spoken languages that are essential to oral traditions and their transmission of history, culture, and social order. Oral cultures emphasise not only the sound and rhythm of language and its accompanying paralinguistic features, but also the site from which it is spoken. A dramatic focus on oral traditions opens up the possibility of challenging the tyranny of the written word through which many imperial languages claim their authenticity. By restoring to oral discourses their topology as performance pieces, theatre allows the orality of post-colonial languages to be fully realised, especially since each performance defers and deflects the authority of any written script. This descripted (performative) model of orality refers not to a language that has never been written, but to one which is *unwritable* at its moment of enunciation.

While orality's utterance is unable to be inscribed, the inscriptions/utterances prohibited by censorship can be inferred in performance. Expressing that which has been forbidden in a public forum like the theatre can be effective in challenging a repressive law or state. Many South African plays devised during the apartheid era used mime, movement, and gesture to articulate various protests against the system since the potential for subversive activity was, to the censors, only to be found in language.[1] Language's interruptions of the vestiges of colonial conquest are also apparent in attempts to eradicate censorship. In Rendra's *The Struggle of the Naga Tribe*, the Dalang playfully goes to great lengths to reassure the audience that the play is not about Indonesia, but rather the fictional kingdom of Astinam. Yet later, Abivara's uncle 'slips' into the 'wrong' language and inquires of his nephew's friend, 'Can he speak Indon . . . I mean, Astinamese?' which prompted conspiratorial laughter from the audience in the original 1975 production in Jakarta (Lane 1979: 19, note 24).[2] Less concerned with offending the government than with altering conservative social sensibilities, the Australian writer, Alex Buzo, used the vernacular language spoken by many Australians of the time. His play, *Norm and Ahmed*, included the word 'fuck' in its 1968 première, precipitating the arrest of several cast members. Whether or not this language was a serious attempt to address British control over Australian affairs, it was *interpreted* as a nationalist move by which Australia declared a metaphoric independence: the ensuing furore that the arrests created assisted in the easing of Australia's censorship rules. *Norm and Ahmed*, together with many other Australian plays of the 1960s and 1970s, established as 'legitimate' on local stages the Australian colloquial and metaphoric 'dialect' of English that incorporates particular idiomatic expressions and rhyming slang.

While language acts as one of the main loci of censorship battles, it is also politically charged in other ways: its agency in the post-colonial context is not confined to the substitution of another language for English, and those writers who use English are not necessarily endorsing British authority. Among the necessary diversity and linguistic freedom that South Africa's eleven official languages present, English's commonality (and its difference to Afrikaans, the imposed language of the creators of apartheid) ensures that it is likely to reach the widest audience. The degree to which other languages (including the important theatrical language of silence) combine with and/or subvert the dominant code is crucial to a discussion of post-colonial languages. Even in plays that 'only' employ English, political statements are articulated with the use of a variety of rhetorical devices that may originate in, for example, oral traditions. Song also affects the agency of language, altering the way that it 'means', while silence on stage can be a forceful and effective manner in/through which to express a post-colonial discourse of alterity, difference, and autonomy. The careful redeployment of lingistic signifiers – such as tone, rhythm, register, and lexicon – can generate as much political resistance as the rewriting of history or the introduction of politically embedded properties to a stage. The strategic use of languages in post-colonial plays helps to reinvest colonised peoples and their characteristic systems of communication with a sense of power and an active place on the stage.

INDIGENOUS LANGUAGES AND TRANSLATION

Choosing a language (or languages) in which to express one's dramatic art is, in itself, a political act that determines not only the linguistic medium of a play but, in many cases, its (implied) audience as well. Ngũgĩ wa Thiong'o, for example, now refuses to write in English, preferring to use Gĩkũyũ for his plays, novels, and criticism since they are written primarily for the Kenyan people. Similarly, the Natal Workers Theatre of South Africa performs in

Zulu, designed to mirror the colloquial discourse of the working-class black audience. Rather than writing speeches, this theatre collective 'put[s] the ideas simply in everyday language. . . . They do not speak from "above" in a foreign language but they show that Zulu can be a language on stage' (von Kotze 1987: 14). Such strategic choices can be exercised in the literary production of a play as well as in its initial scripting, as demonstrated by Michel Tremblay's refusal (until recently) to grant rights for English-language productions of his plays in Québec. He allowed his work to be translated for the stages of other Canadian provinces, but he insisted that it be presented *only* in French in his home province, which, at the time, was actively attempting to maintain the sometimes precarious autonomy of the French language by limiting the amount of English used in public. The printed text of Graham Sheil's *Bali: Adat* is an artefact of linguistic difference: the English text, studded with Balinese words and expressions, is printed on one side of the page, and the full Indonesian version (translated from Sheil's original by Indrawati Zifirdaus) is printed directly opposite so that in the published version, English is not privileged at the expense of the Indonesian language. The play has been performed twice in English, but the text enables the possibility of a subsequent Indonesian production.

When a playwright chooses an indigenous language over English, s/he refuses to submit to the dominance of the imposed standard language and to subscribe to the 'reality' it sustains. Indigenous languages can be broadly defined as those which were native to a culture prior to colonisation and which have since maintained their original grammatical structures and their basic lexicon. (Of course, such languages do not remain static: they undergo changes, mostly at the lexical level, as speakers adopt 'foreign' words and invent new ones to describe a changed order of experience.) Given that colonial authorities often banned the use of indigenous languages, especially in public places, their presentation on stage can represent an act of defiance and an attempt to retrieve cultural autonomy. While in semiotic terms, language resonates with every other theatrical signifier, it is often viewed by audiences as the fundamental and most important system through which a play 'means'. When colonised people hear dialogue spoken in their own tongue – and not in the 'correct' British English often erroneously assumed to be the only language worth staging – they understand it through literal, metaphorical, and political frames of reference which are specific to their own culture and experience. The use of an indigenous language on stage therefore 'localises and attracts value away from a British "norm" eventually displacing the hegemonic centrality of the idea of "norm" itself' (Ashcroft *et al.* 1989: 37).

While some post-colonial dramatists eschew the imperial language altogether, many more use it as a basic linguistic code which is necessarily modified, subverted, or decentred when indigenous languages are incorporated into the text. This is particularly common in the settler colonies where indigenous playwrights attempt to recuperate their own languages at the same time as they address a predominantly white audience. Because these languages are performed rather than inscribed in writing, they proclaim radical alterity in a context where non-indigenous viewers can neither 'look up' the meaning nor quite imagine how such words might be scripted. If, as Ong suggests, the literate mind's sense of control over language is closely tied to its visual transformations in writing (1982: 14), then theatre offers an important site of resistance for oral cultures against the hegemony of scribal ones because performance emphasises spoken rather than written discourse. Moreover, the use of unglossed indigenous languages establishes a gap between (white) viewers and (native) performers which disproves notions of the infinite transmissability of language (Ashcroft 1989a: 72).

One of the defining features of contemporary Maori drama in New Zealand is its increasing use of a local language which now has a visible political profile in the country's overall culture. John Broughton's *Te Hara (The Sin)* (1988) includes a number of isolated Maori words but confines its more sustained usage of the language to the mourning song at the end of the play. Similarly, in Rena Owen's *Te Awa i Tahuti* (1987), Maori is more often sung than spoken but its function is quite varied even within this form: Toni, the protagonist, breaks into song to avoid being questioned, to show her anger, and to perform, ironically, a traditional welcome for the unwelcome counsellor. Songs are an obvious and effective means through which to stage an indigenous language, particularly since their tunes, if not their words, are likely to survive colonisation; songs are also likely to be recognised by Maori members of the audience who may not be otherwise conversant with a repressed or forbidden language. Yet the use of the indigenous language in Maori theatre involves more than just recognising and maintaining songs from a pre-contact era. Toni also turns to Maori to reminisce about her childhood, and her grandfather's presence in her healing dream is communicated in Maori as well. In this context, language is closely linked to memory: it acts as a site of meaning in itself *and* as a conduit to the immediacy and plenitude[3] of the past, thereby foreshadowing a recuperated Maori culture. In Rore Hapipi's *Death of the Land* and Hone Tuwhare's *In the Wilderness Without a Hat*, Maori is the colloquial tongue used for endearments as well as the formal language used for reciting the *whakapapa* (or tribal genealogy). Although the ancestral figures in Tuwhare's play speak Maori almost exclusively, reinforcing its gravity, the more intimate forms of address remove any connotation that Maori might only have a place in historical or sacred contexts.

As these plays suggest, Maori functions on New Zealand stages as part of a cultural heritage and, simultaneously, as a living language, a medium through which contemporary indigenous characters express solidarity, reclaim the past, and establish a linguistic location that is closed to non-speakers. Yet, since even many Maori do not speak the language very well, it can signify only 'history' to some audiences, and a superseded past at that. In order to broaden the Maori language's possible significations, various theatrical methods have been devised to assist in its 'articulation'. Tuwhare's *In the Wilderness Without a Hat* uses offstage, almost simultaneous translation of the Maori dialogue as soon as it is spoken, while Broughton's plays explain virtually every Maori word in the context of the action. On one level, this kind of translation and/or contextualisation – which seems to acquiesce to the demands of Pakeha and non-Maori speaking audiences – risks denying Maori its agency as an autonomous language; however, it could be argued that the indigenous dialogue is none the less heard as a signifier of alterity and that translation itself often foregrounds the gaps between two languages. Other Maori plays avoid such overt contextualisation, simply letting proxemic, kinesic, and other theatrical codes 'speak' in a less obtrusive manner, while some texts even draw attention to their refusal to translate or explicate a passage. These reversals of the normal linguistic power structures are designed to valorise the indigenous language and to privilege a particular sector of the audience over the dominant English-speakers. Hone Kouka's *Mauri Tu* (1991), for instance, uses direct audience address to underline the linguistic subversions consciously embedded in the play as a performance piece. After a long speech in untranslated Maori, Matiu says to the Pakeha in the audience, 'So this is what it's like when a Maori speaks in his own tongue . . . or is it that you just switch off? . . . Listen here, listen well. This incomprehension is what it is like for many of us in this world' (1992: 21). This particular passage is not, like many scenes, capable of being translated through action, nor does the Maori speaker make any explanatory body movements or gestures to clarify the context for non-speakers. As Matiu implies, the linguistic authority arrogated by English for centuries no longer prevails automatically: English speakers/audiences will also be forced to endure misunderstandings which disrupt their linguistic (and naturalistic) expectations. By stressing that words can be used to block certain kinds of communication, such scenes also hold up to question the assumed transparency of language as a passive medium for the transmission of meaning.

In some cases, words and/or sections of dialogue may be glossed in ways which seem to make them accessible to non-speakers but which still refuse to provide all levels of meaning, often by the play's design. This careful layering of linguistic codes tends to be common in plays devised by indigenous writers/performers for a predominantly, but not exclusively, white audience. In their analysis of Jack Davis's *The Dreamers*, Bob Hodge and Vijay Mishra argue that there are hidden codes attached to the Nyoongah words which are interspersed throughout the play and sometimes translated by the dialogue and/or action. A case in point is the word *gnullarah* which, according to the glossary given in the published text, means variously 'we' and 'our'. This word, however, is not merely equivalent to the English pronoun; it is also 'the exclusive form, a "we" that links the speaker to others as a collective ego but specifically excludes the people spoken to from that identity' (Hodge and Mishra 1991: 207). In other words, the term *gnullarah* 'divide[s] the social world into two opposing groups, lumping the audience into the single category of "Other"' (ibid.: 207). Only those viewers who are fluent in the Nyoongah language will recognise that the non-indigenous audience is being constructed as different from the Nyoongah speakers. Similarly, humour frequently functions in precisely this manner since it is the cultural codes of language as much as its specific semantic content that allow some listeners, and not others, to access irony, *double entendre*, certain nuances, and other potentially ludic meanings.

Tomson Highway alludes to the exclusionary functions of the Cree language in this respect by claiming that it automatically endows his plays with a humorous subtext: 'When you speak Cree you laugh constantly' (1992a: 27). Non-Cree speakers are thus positioned outside the social as well as the cognitive world of the characters. The multivalent signification made possible by such indigenous languages not only disperses any particular discourse's claim to singular authority, but it also opens up new topics which are unsuitable to, or which cannot be translated into, the imperial language.

The influx of non-British migrants to the settler colonies in the nineteenth century has engendered the staging of other marginalised languages which further dismantle the hegemony of English. As a number of plays illustrate, migration commonly involves linguistic displacements as well as physical and cultural dislocations. By presenting dialogue and/or narration in languages that are foreign to the dominant society, playwrights such as Australia's Tes Lyssiotis or Canada's Guillermo Verdecchia express the 'double vision' which typically characterises migrant experience.[4] Lyssiotis's *The Forty Lounge Café* (1990), which chronicles the experiences of a Greek migrant in Australia, foregrounds language as a key site of struggle. On one level, the play seems to diminish the linguistic gap between the two cultures by staging its Greek words and phrases in ways that make them largely self-explanatory to an Anglo-Australian audience. For instance, Irini tells her sister that a prospective suitor is not appropriate for her: 'Forget him. Bad blood runs in that family. Ξέχασέ τον [*Forget him*]' (1990: 20). Despite this apparent concession to the dominant language, the performance text retains some signs of alterity, primarily in its numerous untranslated songs. These songs act as particular points of linguistic disruption for English-only speakers and as (perhaps unexpected) points of connection for Greek-speaking viewers. An additional focus on the *mis*translations which can arise when a person is learning a new language complicates the play's overall linguistic codes by foregrounding the possible differences between semantic and idiomatic meanings. Even Sonia, who adapts to her new environment quite rapidly, makes some fundamental errors when she attempts to speak English:

SONIA: You know what you say when you meet someone you're happy to see?

173

ELEFTERIA: Hello nice day.
SONIA: Hello. My glad is very big.

(ibid.: 24)

The English spoken by those Australians adept in only one language is also presented as a curious hybrid that must itself be learned; blended with cliché, Australian metaphors, rhyming slang, and shortened words, 'English' is presented as doubly alien to the would-be English speakers.

When plays written predominantly in English are infiltrated with both indigenous and so-called 'foreign' languages, the question of authenticity becomes even more vexed. Vincent O'Sullivan's *Shuriken* (1983), about Japanese prisoners of war who were interned in New Zealand in the early 1940s, stages its action in/through several linguistic layers so that the Maori character is differentiated from the other (white) New Zealand soldiers, who are, in turn, positioned as separate from the Japanese. This seemingly neat division of characters along the lines of language is deliberately blurred by the fact that some characters are bilingual and can therefore cross borders. As the play suggests, however, such crossings do not always lead to cultural tolerance or understanding, even though both the New Zealand troops and the Japanese POWs they guard assume that language is the biggest barrier between them. The point that language is often deployed to erect barriers rather than dismantle them is amply illustrated when Pom teaches the Japanese how to swear in English and then laughs when they repeat his words (not unlike a perverse Prospero). Throughout the play, members of each cultural group attempt to discover – usually by trying to understand 'language' – why the 'other' is so inscrutable. A scene in which the New Zealand officers endeavour to find out why a Japanese prisoner has killed himself clearly illustrates the misunderstandings that result from simplistic translations; the scene attempts to bridge complex cultural differences, but mere mediation between the respective languages is insufficient. The audience watches four men stand over the dead body, which is shadowed by the body's spirit, played by an actor in a Noh mask. Adachi's Japanese dialogue expresses the dead man's thoughts while the Noh spirit translates them into English for the audience. Meanwhile, Tiny, the Japanese-speaking New Zealander, translates the same dialogue for his superiors. While the gap between the different interpretations of the dead man's words becomes metonymic of the schism between the two cultures, this multilayered translation scene does not suggest that any particular rendition is completely authentic: the masked spirit seems to elaborate meaning for the benefit of the audience whereas Tiny summarises in order to transfer only the information relevant to his particular context. Similarly, there can be no 'perfect' translation of the play's other culturally inflected dialogues, including Tai's Maori lament. *Shuriken* demonstrates that discrete linguistic codes have their own political and theatrical agency and that they cannot be collapsed into one another. At the same time, their dialogic interactions produce a performative metalanguage that stages the provisionality of all meaning.

In order to represent 'foreign' languages to a predominantly monolingual audience, some plays rely on the viewer's participation in a paradoxical process of 'double hearing' which distinguishes between two planes of utterance. Janis Balodis's *Too Young for Ghosts* is written and performed entirely in English, but features Latvian characters who 'speak' their own language as well as that of their adopted country, Australia. Balodis calls for a specific performative technique to establish the linguistic disjunction between the two discourses: the actors use heavy accents when their characters converse in English but drop those accents when the same characters speak in their native Latvian tongue. Other characters who do not speak Latvian do not 'understand' them at these times. Ironically, the failure of characters who only speak English to 'understand' what the audience recognises as English (even if they actively construct it as something else) foregrounds the ways in which 'meaning' is only part of language's project. On another level, the presence/absence of the Latvian language alludes to the linguistic marginalisation of Aborigines who are evoked in the text but never actually seen or heard.

The oldest colony of the British Empire, Ireland, also faced the loss of linguistic autonomy when English was imposed on Gaelic speakers. Brian Friel's *Translations* (1980) details the insidious effects of the British military's attempts to anglicise Irish place names in accordance with the imperial standard. In an even less self-conscious manner than Balodis's Latvians, the Gaelic-speaking Irish in *Translations* converse freely in unaccented English, as do the British soldiers. The audience can therefore understand everyone, but the confusion that results on stage from the characters' inability to comprehend each other's speech makes the important point that understanding a language (here, the English used by all of the actors) is only the first step to understanding a different culture. The play exemplifies the slipperiness of language on a number of other levels, particularly in its numerous translation scenes. As shown by Owen's overtly skewed rendition of Captain Lancey's speech to the Irish villagers, language conceals and dissembles even as it conveys certain information, not always through semantic channels alone:

> LANCEY: His Majesty's government has ordered the first ever comprehensive survey of this entire country – a general triangulation which will embrace detailed hydrographic and topographic information and which will be executed to a scale of six inches to the English mile. . . .
>
> OWEN: [*translating*] A new map is being made of the whole country.
>
> (1984: 406)

As he condenses and simplifies Lancey's 'official-ese', Owen not only masks its more sinister implications but also subverts its rhetorical power with his succinctness. This scene clearly demonstrates that translation involves operations of power – usually of the translator over the translated material – and that language has the capacity to 'unsay the world' and to 'speak it otherwise' (Steiner 1975: 35). It is therefore important to query what translation allows to speak and what it silences. This question applies not only to Friel's play but also to the many others which stage, in some form, non-English languages that are designed to contest the authority of a hegemonic norm.

INDIGENISED LANGUAGES

Dramatists who choose to work in English and those who are forced to use it because they no longer have an alternative do not simply replicate the received imperial standard. As Soyinka argues, post-colonial writers are compelled to 'stress such a language, stretch it, impact and compact, fragment and reassemble it with no apology, as required to bear the burden' of their experiences, even if such experiences are not formulated within the conceptual idiom of that language (1988: 107). While this indigenising process may be more radical for 'occupation' cultures, settler societies also appropriate the imperial language and adapt it to the contingencies of a new context. In either case, the result is a production of various culturally marked Englishes which usually diverge from the Queen's English both lexically and semantically, as well as in pronunciation. These local languages can provide a particularised medium in/through which to stage a culture's stories and speak its concerns. At the same time, the use of variant Englishes offers one effective means of refusing to uphold the privilege of the imperial language as it has dominated both the theatre and the wider social realm.

Changing the social register of theatrical dialogue is one of the easiest ways to alter the overwhelming power of English. While there are abundant instances of British/American drama that does not adhere to a formal sociolect of English, many colonised cultures have been subject to the perception that the language of the stage is always heightened and 'proper', and is always English. Post-colonial theatre attempts to rebut this paradigm and there-fore to give voice to the many different narratives which circulate under the sign of a broadly common language. Performative aspects of speech such as tonality, diction, accent, inflection, and rhythm are clearly important tools here because they can be used to establish social registers that abrogate the privileged codes of the imperial standard. A particularly effective form of subversion occurs when one character moves between registers, showing that s/he is quite capable of using all manner of linguistic codes but chooses certain ones strategically. Robert Merritt's *The Cake Man* (1975) provides an excellent example of such linguistic versatility in a long introductory speech by Sweet William, a particularly loquacious Aboriginal narrator. After a monologue in which he alternately adopts the guises of story-teller, singer, Biblical inter-preter, drunken yarn-spinner, amateur philosopher, and cultural mediator, Sweet William addresses the (white) Australian audience with some antagonism:

> I suppose this shits you as much as it does me?
> [*He stands*]
> Look, actually I'm here to make an enquiry, to discover if possible what it is I have that you now want. [*Whining*] Please, boss, you bin tell 'im Jacky, then him plurry happy! What is it?
> [*Pause. He stands in appeal*]
> No? Well, there y'are. Me boomerang won't come back.
> (1983: 16)

In this speech, Sweet William's changes in register effect a multi-layered attack on the non-Aboriginal viewers by goading them with rhetorical questions, appealing to their liberalism, and parodying their stereotypes of Aborigines. Coupled with his earlier switches in persona, such dialogue illustrates Sweet William's command of a fully indigenised English at the same time as it creates a sense of continually shifting Aboriginal subjectivities.

When a language is indigenised, its lexicon changes to accommodate new words and/or new combinations of words which can be staged as part of a culturally inflected dialogue. In Davis's plays, for instance, Nyoongah characters use the term '*wetjala*' (singular and plural) to refer to whites; this is not an Aboriginal word as such but a new term created from the English: 'white' and 'fellow' (usually pronounced 'fella' in Australia) have been merged and given a different pronunciation, with a corresponding change in orthography. Likewise, the meaning of the original words has shifted, if only subtly, since *wetjala* usually carries a mildly derogatory connotation. Such changes in the lexicon illustrate the colonised subjects' ability to appropriate the language of the imperial centre and use it for their own expressive purposes. This indigenising process often has affective as well as referential functions; in other words, it produces languages which operate not only to convey new cognitive information but also to establish group identity. According to Mervyn Alleyne, an emphasis on affective functions is precisely what characterises Afro-Caribbean appropriations of imperial discourse:

> The mass languages of the Caribbean are constantly renewing themselves apparently both from a need to exclude the elite from gaining access (thus whenever new expressions are learnt by the elite, they are discarded or slightly altered in meaning and usage by the masses) and also from a creative impulse to renovate.
>
> (qtd in Gibbons 1979: 211)

The words which result from a politically motivated renovation of language frequently signal their politics in their new form. A good example here is the term 'downpression' which is a visually concretised derivation of 'oppression' designed to signify – far more potently than the original English word – the experience of many working-class Afro-Caribbean people.

Fully-indigenised versions of English can become the *lingua franca* of countries comprised of linguistically discrete groups. Singapore English is a case in point since it is used not only by speakers whose native tongue is English but also between different ethnic groups. Following the example of the Singaporean playwright, Robert Yeo, Jothie Rajah and Simon Tay explain that this language is not simply a version of English that deviates grammatically, lexically, and syntactically from the standard, but rather a speech continuum with upper and lower ends (1991: 406). The lower end or basolectal varieties of speech – often called Singlish – differ in accent, syntax, and structure from upper end varieties which more closely approximate the imperial standard. This speech continuum has been used to great effect by Stella Kon in *Emily of Emerald Hill* (1985). While Emily assumes a very 'proper' form of English when she encounters Mrs Schneider, a stalwart of her church, she uses Singlish to address her fishmonger:

> Hei, Botak! What are you doing ah! What kind of fish you sent to me yesterday? All rotten ones lah! Yes! How to eat ah? You want my family all go to hospital die ah? Mmh! You don't know ah, how can you don't know – all right. You give me good ones today. If not all right I bring back I throw at your head.
>
> (1989: 27)

Although the words of this passage are unmistakably English, its syntax and grammar show the influences of Malay, Mandarin, and Tamil, Singapore's other main languages. Along with the many other varieties of English used in the play, Emily's 'market' dialect affirms that Singapore English can communicate a broad range of local experience. Ironically, once designed to establish hierarchies, the imperial language has become the most enabling dramatic medium for Singaporean theatre because, in reflecting combinations of different languages, it now cuts across barriers of race and culture (Rajah and Tay 1991: 410).

Many other indigenised languages have been successfully staged, often within countries where they may reflect regional and/or political identities distinct from the national as well as from the imperial standard. Two Canadian examples occur in the plays of Michael Cook and Michel Tremblay. Cook's work articulates Newfoundland English – often ridiculed by other Canadians for its broad accent and its geographically particular lexicon – as a viable dramatic language. The old man in *Jacob's Wake* (1974) known as the Skipper uses the local vernacular which remains heavily influenced by the dominant local industry of seal hunting:

A man should be surrounded with ould friends in his dyin'. Ould shipmates. Not a bunch of harpies. . . . Over the side, lads. Over the side. Look lively, now. Gaff and sculp. Gaff and sculp[5]. . . . De yer worst, ye howling black devil. I'm not afraid o' ye, nor me boys neither. Out of my way. I'll git the men. Aye and the swiles [seals] too. I defy ye. I defy ye.

(1993: 224)

Similarly, Tremblay's *Les Belles Soeurs* captures the idiom of the characters it creates, in this case a group of East-end Montréal women. Tremblay was the first to establish *joual*, the local 'vulgar' dialect of French, as a language for Québec drama. *Joual* includes:

sacres [or 'swear' words], singly and strung together for fire-cracker effects (a serious problem for the translator, since the cultural frame of reference for the *sacres* is religious and sexual, whereas English equivalents must be found in the limited area of scatology); repetition, redundancy, vulgarity, humorous expressions; all combined through the syntax characteristic of the popular idiom.

(Usmiani 1979: 24)

Both writers' work demonstrates a movement away from the vehicular (which is used for communication across socio-cultural groups and, for example, in the media) to the vernacular, a form of language which functions to establish a 'communion' between peers. According to Sylvia Söderlind, such nationalist and/or regionalist movements in the literatures of colonised societies demonstrate an 'attempt to reintegrate the various functions of language under the sign of the vernacular' in an effort to (re)claim a degree of linguistic and cultural autonomy (1991: 10).

In conventional translation, the *joual* in *Les Belles Soeurs* loses much of its impact, but the indigenised discourse of the play has recently been transposed into another linguistically and culturally specific site, that of Glaswegian English. Bill Findlay and Martin Bowman translated *Les Belles Soeurs* into *The Guid Sisters* (1989), about Scottish women whose feelings of hopelessness (economical, political, and social) compare to those of their Québécois counter-parts. The adjustment of accent and expression in the new context matches the experiences of women in another part of the colonised world. In both locations, Lise's complaint about the lack of opportunity is comprehensible, despite the regional variants of its expression. In *The Guid Sisters,* she tells Linda:

> I want tae get somewhere. . . . But I'm damn sure I'm no gaunnae go on like this. I don't want tae be a naebody any more. I've had enough ae bein poor. I'm gaunnae make sure things gets better. I was mebbe born at the bottom ae the pile but I'm gaunnae climb tae the top. I came intae this world bi the back door but by Christ I'm gaunnae go oot bi the front. An ye can take it fae me that nothin's gaunnae get in ma way.
>
> (1991: 52)

Rather than attempting to repair a rupture between the Québécois or Glaswegian women and their surrounding political, social, and economic environments, these two plays offer the opportunity to encode the difference in linguistic terms and to engineer a linguistic – if not geographic – distance between the empire and the former colonies by severing the assumed connection that language is supposed to offer.

Altering the stylistic hierarchies of standard English expression is one of the most politically useful modes of subverting its authority. When playwrights interfere with received discursive codes (especially through parody) and/or introduce the rhetorical devices of other languages into English, they diminish the power invested in the colonisers' language and re-establish local/indigenous modes of expression for theatrical representation. Inflating or deflating rhetoric, exploiting grandiloquence, or incorporating aspects of the oral tradition – such as proverbs – into the dramatic text are just some of the more common ways of destabilising 'English' to ensure that other languages (and their correlative cultures and histories) are voiced.

Texts that play with inflated English rhetoric often critique the coloniser's legal or religious discourses and offer an ironic version that deflates the assumptions of privilege encoded by such language. The opening of Davis's *Barungin* depicts a fundamentalist preacher burying Eli to exaggerated and repetitive rhetoric that only succeeds in mystifying or angering the gathered mourners who try to comprehend how the language takes on an authority to which it does not necessarily have a claim. This language is designed to exclude the non-initiated – here, anyone who does not

181

subscribe to fundamentalist Christian beliefs – and to patrol certain boundaries since it positions those who understand the jargon in a closed linguistic circle separated from those who do not. In this instance, however, Davis ensures that English is not entitled to such privilege: the mourners' obvious incomprehension, discomfort, and annoyance in the face of the preacher's speech communicates his rhetoric's inappropriateness even before the audience hears the Nyoongah language which continues to destabilise the dominant society's discourses. More extensively, Rongo, the supernatural Maori ancestor in Hapipi's *Death of the Land*, continually deflates the Judge's legal jargon to illustrate both the nonsensical land acquisition laws and Maori complicity in destroying their heritage by selling land to the Pakeha. Rongo conducts what can be read as several mock trials in colloquial English in order to make clear the gravity of the situation to those who have not comprehended the Judge's rhetoric. While Rongo attempts to discover the vendors' motives, he suggests that the official linguistic 'crap' of the courtroom can give few answers for this Maori community. His cross-examinations ultimately say more about the land – the issue at stake – than the legal discourse ever could: they reveal what the land looks like, what happened there, and what the land means, rather than just recording the surveyors' marks and the land's supposed monetary worth.

Rongo's critique of English legal discourse is predicated on the words' failure to make sense to the Maori whose collective land is at the centre of the dispute. He also aims to find a substitute linguistic medium to communicate the devastation caused by the land transfers. Many African playwrights resort to indigenous discursive patterns and turns of phrase to communicate in English, and to bring to English something of their own language and oral traditions. Local proverbs, in particular, communicate a resonant, poetic meaning that standard English expression does not normally allow. Richard K. Priebe maintains that 'the proverb user tries to minimize conflict, to conspire with his audience to find a solution to a problem through a clear and direct appeal to tradition' (1988: 139). As short, easily-remembered, pithy statements that are passed on from generation to generation, proverbs are also attractive to indigenous communities because they recall oral forms of history and culture. Emmanuel Amali explains that proverbs 'add glamour, meaning, weight and beauty to elders' discussions, arguments and court proceedings' (1985: 31); in fact, to deny elders the use of proverbs is to render them silent. The translation of proverbs into English creates hybrid discourses that rely on the oral tradition to supply a voice and register appropriate to local populations. 'Zulu Sofola's *Wedlock of the Gods* (1972) chronicles the love between a young man and a young woman, Ogwoma, who has transgressed the laws of her community and the wishes of her Yoruba parents by entering into a sexual relationship when she should be still mourning the death of her hated first husband. The community's disapproval of the new couple's relationship is expressed through proverbs such as 'our people say that the man who ignores his family is the one who stands alone in the rain' (1972: 25). Such proverbs function not only to augment the characters' speech but also, in many cases, to shape the dialogue and action. Odibei, the young woman's mother-in-law, is warned that any retributive action for the apparent murder of her son will be counter-productive: 'This will not do. Anger leads nowhere. We cannot set fire to a whole house just to kill one rat because when the house is on fire the rat runs into the bush' (ibid.: 50). Despite this portent, Odibei refuses to listen to the logic of the proverb, taking up instead the metaphor of the rat to serve her own purposes: 'The rat will not run into the bush this time. I am ready. . . . Tell your rat that there is no bush she will run to that Odibei will not enter' (ibid.: 50). The proverb's subtext has some currency at the end of the play when she and her quarry, Ogwoma, are dead. While Ogwoma's refusal to listen to the earlier guiding proverb – that 'a man's daughter is a source of wealth to him' (ibid.: 9) – causes conflict, further breaches of proverbs, particularly by the vindictive Odibei, produce far more damaging consequences. The proverbs in Sofola's work are a repository of social laws and decorum, even in a changing world that *seems* to devalue the role of folklore. Proverbs invoke different kinds of authority that are heavily laden with cultural significance, although many colonialists would see them as outdated rhetorical devices which are of little importance.

In a similar vein, Matsemela Manaka's *Egoli: City of Gold* (1979), set among mine-workers in the Transvaal region of South Africa, uses local expressions, interjections, and many 'swear' words and phrases in the place of more formal English discourse. Manaka africanises English to suit his own purposes, providing a 'new' language for each new character; for instance, the black *baas* (or boss) imitates the Afrikaans *baas*, while the black workers parody both of their superiors in a move that draws attention to the hegemonic hierarchies encoded in/through language. The action focuses on two gaol-escapees who are living in Egoli, a gold-mining town whose pits are a site of hatred, misery, and enslavement. The traditional proverbs that they exchange at the beginning of the play, such as 'we must live within the skulls of our ancestors' (n.d.: 3), demonstrate ways of dealing with crises. Yet, just as the lexicon of any language changes over time, its rhetorical structures also change; hence, by the end of *Egoli*, such traditional sayings have been transformed into proverbs that are more useful to the men's struggle against apartheid: 'we shall all have to worship the spear and drink blood from the calabash until we all sing the same song, *Uhuru – Azania*' [Freedom for South Africa] (ibid.: 28). The old proverbs are not useless, but they must be mediated by the experience of apartheid, a situation which necessitates new laws and new methods for survival and resistance. The proverbs that life in Egoli has generated more accurately reflect the men's changed political circumstances. These proverbs also transmute into song which, anthem-like, further empowers the characters and, in turn, the audience:

Umkhulu, umkhulu lomsebenzi,	The work is great
Umsebenzi we nkululeko	The work of liberation
uMandela u funa amajoni	Mandela needs soldiers
amajoni we nkululeko	Soldiers of liberation.
	(ibid.: 21)

The use of song itself as an 'alternative' discourse and cultural signifier has acted as one of the few means of political resistance available to black South Africans.

CREOLE AND PIDGIN

The increasing use of Creole and Pidgin dialogues as part of a culturally matrixed theatrical language further dismantles the authority of standard English. Created from an amalgamation of different languages, Pidgin and Creole derive from trade and contact jargons which have expanded in referential functions and expressive resources to become first languages in some post-colonial cultures. The term 'Pidgin' tends to refer to linguistic forms which have arisen from the blending of one imperial language with an indigenous language, whereas 'Creole' often points to the input of several source languages. Many varieties of Pidgin and Creole are discrete languages with their own lexical features and grammatical structures; hence, they should not be regarded as 'bad' or inferior versions of particular imperial languages. Although their vocabulary commonly derives largely from appropriated and indigenised European words, Creole and Pidgin languages also maintain significant pre-contact elements, particularly in their phonology, syntax, and lexico-semantic structures.

Creole languages are prominent in regions where there has been a significant hybridising of disparate cultures. Mervyn Alleyne, among other linguists, uses the concept of the 'Creole continuum' to describe language usage in the Caribbean where dialects ranging from standard forms of English to basolectal varieties of Creole overlap to create a broadly comprehensible linguistic continuum (1985: 168). Depending on the context, most speakers will use forms belonging to a wide spectrum of the available linguistic levels. This variable use of language – referred to as 'code switching' – can be an effective means of abrogating the imperial standard in favour of a culturally significant discourse (Ashcroft *et al.* 1989: 46). Within the continuum, Creole languages are now becoming accepted not only as the mass vernacular but also as a more democratised language for art, commerce, and education. This movement represents a refusal to accept the imperialist judgement that Creole or dialect languages should be suppressed since they are 'corruptions' or 'bastardisations' of a pure model. As performance poet Louise Bennett points out, a serious attempt to stamp out dialect would have some far-reaching consequences:

> Yuh will haffi get de Oxford Book
> O' English Verse, an tear
> Out Chaucer, Burns, Lady Grizelle
> An plenty a Shakespeare!
>
> Wen yuh done kill 'wit' and 'humour'
> Wen yuh kill 'variety'
> Yuh will haffi fine a way fi kill
> Originality!
>
> (1983: 5)

Bennett's point is that English is itself a dialect language derived from many sources; it can claim no more authenticity than the linguistic forms it has helped to spawn.

Refusing the term 'dialect' altogether, Brathwaite refers to the English-based Creole of the Caribbean as 'nation language'. He maintains that nation language may be English in some of its lexical features but not 'in its contours, its rhythm and timbre, [and] its sound explosions' (1984: 13). Brathwaite's emphasis on the sound of nation language points to its origin in oral cultures and its inherent suitability for contemporary oral art forms such as theatre. Despite the seemingly natural fit between Creole languages and Caribbean theatre, however, the question of which linguistic medium to use is by no means clear-cut for many playwrights. Walcott, for example, argues quite forcefully for 'an electric fusion of old and new' forms (1970b: 17), yet he does not fully endorse Creole or Patois[6] as dramatic languages because of what he sees as their limited comprehensibility to people across the various islands of the region. While Walcott's solution has been to employ diluted Creole forms, other practitioners choose to exploit fully the rich resources of nation language, to make it 'speak' a powerful form of resistance to hegemonic norms.

Sistren perform almost exclusively in a Creole now often referred to simply as the Jamaican language. Their choice of linguistic media is consistent with their mandate to produce theatre for and about the working classes. At the same time, their use of Creole is a reclamation of sorts, a political strategy designed to give back to Jamaican women in particular the 'voice' that slavery denied them. This recuperation is clearly illustrated in *Nana Yah* during a series of monologues in which a character called Loss of Name demands that the colonisers who have 'thieved' her name and her language give it back:

> CUYAH! Look pon me, unoo look pon me de dat is me name. Cuyah. De fus ting dat happen is dat dem tak way me name, and de nex ting is dat dem doan wan we fe talk we language, an dem have we talking sinting dat doan mek no sense at all, at all. Me seh, me cyan get fe sey wha me want fe say. SARAH! is dat dem call me. SARAH de name deh pon me skin and it a itch me. De Backra man language deh pon me mout like a hebby padlock wha a bore thru me tongue and a hang hebby so till me cyan talk, me cyan seh wha inna me head, me cyan talk what me really know, and is so dem tink me fool, fool. Whaaai! Me spirit feel dead! But me sey Cuyah cyan dead, Cuyah nah dead. Me seh fe gimme back

misself yuh dam tief. Gimme back me talk and me drum.
Wha you gwine wid it? If you tek me name, you coulda never
be me. So gimme back me name.

(1980: 10)

Ironically, Cuyah communicates very clearly the frustrations of
having to use a language that 'doan mek no sense'. Part of her
speech's impact arises from the metaphorical force of images
which describe the imposed language as hanging heavily on her
mouth or as itching her skin. By using Creole as a means through
which to articulate her protest against the imperial language,
Cuyah does, in fact, reclaim her name/voice, albeit in a different
form.

The Pidgin languages of Africa perform a similar resistance to
the imperial language. 'Segun Oyekunle's play, *Katakata for
Sofahead* (1978), set in a Nigerian prison, is scripted almost entirely
in Pidgin. Validating a more commonly recognised and colloquial
language situated between English and Yoruba, this play establishes in language a site for anti-colonial activity in Nigeria.
The language that the warder uses in his infrequent checks on the
prisoners is the basic, functional English of a moderately educated
man. Lateef, the newcomer, who has achieved much more formal
education, speaks in a complex and measured English studded
with what Jangidi, the head prisoner, calls 'dogon turanchi' (1983:
39) or big English words that Jangidi doesn't understand and
which are therefore suspect. The Pidgin spoken by the other
prisoners is a combination of onomatopoeic words and a remade
English that is sometimes used to undercut Lateef's rhetoric.
Darudapo, for example, attempts to silence Lateef by saying 'Your
talk-talk too much' (ibid.: 9), the 'your' here meaning both 'you'
and 'your'. Okolo, in a role-play activity the prisoners share, tells
his friend, Buhari:

> You no sabi any ting, Yam Head! Which policeman fit aks for
> big man im particulars, hinside Mercedez, 'King of de Road',
> for dat matter? Dem nefer born dat police for dis we kontry.
> Na dat day water go pass im gari. Dem go commot im khaki
> for im neck one time!
>
> (ibid.: 26)

Okolo's Pidgin easily accommodates a range of topics – from
systems of law and order in Nigeria to more contemporary

commercialisation, to proverbs – in a form that subverts the primacy of English and its concomitant colonial/judicial authority. The Pidgin invests the prisoners with a power that their incarceration denies them: the ability to enforce their own linguistic freedom. At the same time, the street Pidgin establishes a different social hierarchy, just as the prison context sets up principles which differ from those of the 'outside'. English becomes further decentred in favour of the more culturally expressive and locally accessible Pidgin.

The potentially disruptive functions of Creole/Pidgin have led Louis Nowra to create such a language for the forest people (a 'lost' tribe of convicts) who feature in *The Golden Age*. Based on old ballads, nineteenth-century slang, and bawdy words, this invented language has an Irish lilting rhythm and non-standard syntax and grammar. It is deliberately designed to destabilise the authority of English and to decentre the dominant linguistic group – the Anglo-Australians who attempt to 'civilise' the forest people by reforming their language as well as their behaviour. One of the most subversive aspects of the play's arcane Creole is its sexual overtones. Through a process of joyful repetition and reassociation, this language retrieves words such as 'cunty' and 'spoonfuckin'' from negative/obscene contexts and valorises them as part of a local vernacular that celebrates sexuality. As well as carnivalising the socially approved language, the lost tribe's Creole forces a re-evaluation of cultural difference. Their initial moment of 'contact' with Francis and Peter problematises conventional notions of linguistic otherness since the forest people are as mystified by their 'discoverers' as the young men are by their own findings. As the two different groups attempt to find a common language through which to communicate, misunderstandings occur on both sides; however, it is Francis and Peter – and the audience – who are positioned as outsiders in relation to the adaptive culture and language which the forest people have developed. On a metaphorical level, the lost tribe represents not only a disenfranchised convict class but also Australia's indigenous people. The disappearance of the tribe's language when all of the group but Betsheb eventually die after they enter the 'civilised' world alludes to the loss of many Aboriginal languages as a result of colonisation. In Nowra's play, disjunctions between the two main languages, both forms of 'English', are often staged in ways that reveal the expressive gap between a fully indigenised Creole and an English that seems somewhat alien on Australian soil. This is illustrated by William's laborious translations which reduce Betsheb's dialogue to its functional equivalent, leaving it strangely devoid of beauty and power:

BETSHEB: I see car . . .
WILLIAM: 'I was in a car'.
BETSHEB: Windwhistlin.'
WILLIAM: 'It went quickly.'
BETSHEB: 'Ome, country groan 'n' moan 'n' run.
WILLIAM: 'Factories and houses make noises and the landscape from the car makes it look like it's running'.
BETSHEB: Voice in a stick.
WILLIAM: 'Telephone'. She loves hearing people speak on the telephone.

(1989: 38)

This passage, which reveals the sterility of English as compared to the figurative energy of Betsheb's visual language, suggests that the dominant society's reformation of the forest people's Creole is, in fact, a form of silencing.

SILENCE

In imperial history and theatre, the colonised subject has traditionally been figured as silent, in opposition to the linguistically adept coloniser in whose language is situated the key to authority and knowledge. The Caliban/Prospero narrative relies on precisely such (mis)constructions: prior to Prospero's tutelage, Caliban is apparently silent and passive, and even after acquiring his master's language he is left to imitate Prospero or grumble ineffectively. Yet the silence of the colonised subject is less clear and less total than the myth suggests. Moreover, Caliban's complaints are not as nugatory as they may seem since they undermine Prospero's role as teacher and as omnipotent ruler of the island. That Caliban is silenced – prevented from having a voice – at *The Tempest*'s conclusion reinforces the notion that silence has been *imposed* on the colonised subject rather than simply 'discovered' as his or her defining linguistic feature. This imposition does not necessarily condemn its victims to the impossibility of communication. As Rajeswari Sunder Rajan makes clear, there is 'silence that speaks, and . . . speech that fails as communication' (1993: 97). It follows that the natures of speech and silence are more complex than is often assumed and that the two linguistic states should not be understood in terms of a rigid binary. Michel Foucault observes that 'Silence itself . . . is less the absolute limit of discourse, the other side from which it is separated by a strict boundary, than an element that functions alongside the things said, with them and in relation to them within over-all strategies' (1981: 27). Silence can be more *active* than passive, especially on stage where a silent character still speaks the languages of the body and of space. Here, silence enacts more than a problematic absence of voice; rather, it is a discourse in its own right and a form of communication with its own enunciative effects. These effects emerge through the length and depth of the silence; through its tenor in relation to the volume, tone, and intent of the speech which circumscribes or interrupts it; and through the gestures and postures of the silent.

While language is commonly misperceived to be the loudest and clearest mode of theatrical communication, there are at least three 'silences' that are expressively deployed on the post-colonial stage: inaudibility, muteness, and refusals to speak. Elaine Showalter's concept of 'mutedness' (based on an analysis of women's speaking positions in patriarchal societies) can act as a type for the ways in which silence communicates in post-colonial drama. Mutedness transmits meaning in several ways: given that 'muted groups must mediate their beliefs through the allowable forms of dominant structures' (1985: 262), muted characters often communicate through normative discourses as well as 'speaking' more subversively. Showalter's feminist model easily transfers to post-colonial contexts, where the coloniser and colonised approximate her patriarchal dominant/muted groupings. The colonised subject, accustomed to the position whereby s/he is unheard, not listened to, or even prevented from speaking, has found ways to exploit this mutedness, transforming it into a language of resistance.

Post-colonial plays generally refuse to limit their characters to positions of linguistic marginality; instead, most dismantle such positions, even by means of the apparently non-communicative language of silence. The first silence, inaudibility, becomes obvious when the body's language or the proxemic signifiers are more expressive than his/her voiced utterance. A more specific instance of inaudibility occurs when a character cannot be heard by others on stage, but can be heard by the audience. Judith Thompson's plays frequently incorporate a Cassandra-like figure

whose inability to make herself heard mirrors many other characters' failure to express themselves. The main character in *Lion
in the Streets* (1990), a murdered mentally disabled Portuguese
girl in Toronto who is trying to discern where she is and what
has happened to her, represents marginalised peoples who face
particular difficulties in attaining a voice in society. Able to
communicate to some people, particularly children, Isobel fails
to warn others of the danger of the lion (her attacker) only partly
because of her elementary speech patterns and vocabulary. Her
'ascension' to peace and a form of heaven at the play's conclusion
represents a coming to terms with her murderer, while the other
characters who have not 'heard' her are still consumed by their
own 'lions'. The audience always hears and sees Isobel, whose
presence is magnified by proxemic signifiers (since she inhabits
a large portion of the stage). Through performance, this marginalised, silenced character is reinvested with a voice.

Silence in the form of physical muteness is also a common
trope in post-colonial drama. In Dennis Scott's *An Echo in the Bone*,
the mute drummer, Rattler, is emblematic of an Afro-Caribbean
community historically silenced by slavery. Apart from communicating through silence itself, Rattler is given several voices
with which to negotiate a 'speaking' position. As part of the ritual
invocation of the past, he enacts a speaking character whose voice
is silenced when the colonial master cuts out his tongue for in-
subordination. Shortly after this scene, Rattler plays a mute slave
who writes a note advising two black women to embrace slavery as
part of their Christian duty to God. This Anglo-ventriloquial
speech (read out by a fellow slave) suggests that learning another
'tongue' cuts off one's own (see Tiffin 1993a: 918). In the present-
day narrative, Rattler ignores such modes of communication,
choosing to express himself through his drum rather than through
the colonisers' language. By illustrating the ways in which muteness
can be both a result of colonialism and a strategic response to its
linguistic hierarchies, Scott dramatises Ross Chambers's argument
that very few colonial subjects are *incapable* of speech; most are
denied the *opportunity* to speak or choose silence in order to avoid
interpellation into the dominant discourse (Chambers 1991: 3). In
Leo Hannet's *The Ungrateful Daughter* (1971) a Papua New Guinean
girl is rendered metaphorically mute by her Australian 'protectors'
who presume to know what is best for her. She is taught the
'civilising' language of English but then denied permission to

speak when the Australians discover that she will not express the racist views which they expect her to parrot. Like Rattler's drumming in *An Echo in the Bone*, the drum beat and the New Guinean dance which conclude *The Ungrateful Daughter* symbolise a more culturally authentic discourse than the English that Ebonita is taught but prevented from using and manipulating.

Tomson Highway's *The Rez Sisters* and *Dry Lips Oughta Move to Kapuskasing* both include a mentally-handicapped character who has speech difficulties. Partly reflecting the realities of reservation life (where foetal alcohol syndrome and glue sniffing have affected the health of many indigenous Canadians), these characters also demonstrate the linguistic ruptures which have resulted from colonisation. In *Dry Lips*, Dickie Bird Halked's communications emphasise a gap in language transmission: he writes his speech acts, a habit which elongates their 'utterance' since Spooky Lacroix must wait until Dickie Bird finishes writing the notes before he reads them in his rather halting English and reacts to their content. Later, Dickie Bird's muteness is 'broken' by a vision of his mother: he speaks and chants, but in a childish form of Cree, most of which is not translated into English. Dickie Bird's arrested growth symbolises the effects that colonisation has had on many native peoples; nevertheless, his particular use of written English and spoken Cree hybridises written and oral traditions into a performative discourse that does communicate effectively.

One of the most complex muted figures in post-colonial drama is the title character of Vincent O'Sullivan's play, *Billy* (1989), which is set in Sydney in the 1820s. As a social experiment, Billy, an Aboriginal servant, has been trained to serve his colonial masters expertly, despite apparently being deafened and rendered mute in a childhood accident. The Anglo-Australian settlers treat Billy as a performing monkey and assume that he cannot speak. He does, however, choose to 'speak through' one of the women, Elizabeth, when her fiancé, Captain Forster, relates the story of how he led a brutal massacre of Billy's people. As Billy lays his hand on Elizabeth's shoulder, she begins to speak English with an Aboriginal inflection. S/he then tells a competing narrative of the massacre, alternating with the Captain's version. Finally, Billy speaks on his own, without mediation, but the assembled gathering assume that his 'voice' is merely another party trick. To his masters, Billy's apparent muteness casts him as a child or servant who is not heard. For most of the play, he does not communicate vocally because he is not given occasion to speak, and when he does take the opportunity, quite without 'permission', he is quickly relegated to a position of subservience, 'entertaining' the whites. His speech is circumscribed by his colonisers as Caliban's was by Prospero; hence, his sudden outburst is treated as a traitorous action that some guests deem best to ignore, while others choose to reinscribe it (and thus explain it away) as part of the party game scenario. Yet Billy's speech is not so easily silenced: he *is* heard since the audience registers his words as well as the colonisers' attempts to designify them. Once spoken, the words are released, and Billy both disrupts and escapes the confines of the whites' apparently perfect rendition of a little England in Sydney. His presence – and that of the rest of his people – must be acknowledged. In a play which explores the *silencing* of discourses which the settler does not want to hear, Billy's position is not that of the unspeakable but, to his on-stage audience, of the unhearable.

The ways in which Billy refuses the narrowly defined and class/race-based language of the colonisers only increases his agency. Rey Chow's comment that 'it is the native's silence which is the most important clue to her displacement' (1993: 38) is particularly appropriate to *Billy* and to other post-colonial plays in which the colonised subject refuses to speak. Ngũgĩ and Micere Githae Mugo's *The Trial of Dedan Kimathi* demonstrates this point provocatively: while Kimathi, the Kenyan Mau Mau rebel and outlaw, speaks very eloquently at times to his supporters, he is conspicuously silent during his treason trial, using silence as a tool against the colonial (in)justice system. He does not even attempt to answer the charges of treason, and his refusal to speak angers the court officers more than any plea could. The court is designed to deal with legally framed English words which are in themselves convoluted and double-meaninged, but it cannot deal with the silence that Kimathi presents. He is, then, able to contravene the colonial system more successfully in silence than in being co-opted by speech.

SONG AND MUSIC

Although sometimes used to convey, metaphorically, an idea and/or emotion, musical signification generates cultural meanings in its own right. A song's coding can be a discrete communicative system based on, among many other factors, pitch, accent, tune, musical arrangement, the kinesics and proxemics of the singer, and the historical layers of meaning to the lyrics. When music is combined with theatre, its signifying power inevitably multiplies: in addition to its own signification, music contributes to the *mise-en-scène* to, for instance, enhance a mood, or effect an atmosphere. Moreover, if post-colonial theatre provides an occasion for a vocal expression of solidarity, resistance, or even presence, song can intensify the reactions of both the actors and the audience. Its effects can be multiplied by the power of numerous voices of a chorus, reinforcing communal action/interaction by increasing both vocal numbers and volume. When song intersects with music in an otherwise non-musical play, it denaturalises the action and further increases the audience's attention, diverting it from one discourse to another to corroborate a point of view, or offer an alternative perspective. Post-colonial drama employs song and music in at least two ways that are more specific than music's general contribution to theatre: recuperating indigenous song and music, and hybridising new/old forms into specific types. The first obviously overlaps with issues discussed in the traditional enactments and history chapters. Indigenous song/music recalls pre-contact methods of communication, affirms the continued validity of oral traditions, and helps to break the bonds of conventional (western) representation. As part of a slightly different strategy, hybrid song/music often function to protest the domination of the coloniser's linguistic/musical tradition by liberally interspersing it with the words, forms, or musical structures of a less well-recognised and validated system of communication.[7] Among their other functions, song and music can also be 'detached' from the theatre event by the audience to live on after the performance's conclusion when the audience retells or resings parts of the theatrical presentation as an act of memory. The mnemonic functions of song and music amply demonstrate their positions as powerful 'linguistic' signifiers.

The folk opera[8] tradition of Nigeria is a popular form of dramatising events musically. Originally connected to the Christian church and its repetitive musical rhythms, folk opera experienced a critical shift with the prominence in the 1940s of Herbert Ogunde, who introduced Yoruba dance and music to the form. Bound up in reflecting political and social issues of the day, folk opera represents one of the first attempts to restore pre-contact traditions to Nigerian theatre, and a politicised theatre at that.

Borrowing also from the tradition of the populist itinerant concert party from Ghana, the Yoruba travelling folk opera groups played a variety of drums and wind instruments – including the *bata* drum, the *dundun*, the *sekere*, and the *igbin* (Ogunbiyi 1981b: 341) – incorporating indigenous and European musical styles. Folk opera has been popularised by Duro Ladipo, Kola Ogunmola, J.P. Clark-Bekederemo, and Wálé Ògúnyemí. Ladipo, attracted by the form when his Christian church refused to accommodate his 'talking drum' as an accompaniment to services (ibid.: 335), developed the model from Ogunde's lead, infusing it with more self-consciously traditional and historical material. Folk opera relies on spectacle, as well as atmosphere, establishing and shifting narrative action through music, drumming, and song, rather than using lighting to signify changes of location or mood. The drums are not, however, merely background; in fact, in the *Ikaki* masquerade, a traditional performance based on the popular tortoise and gods myths, the Drum Master's role is equal to the main protagonist's. The Drum Master is 'the only human principal who belongs to the same plane as the . . . spirit-actors. And his role is not only confrontational [musical language specifically juxtaposed to "spar with" verbally encoded language] but is equally vital to the timing and explanation of the sequences' (Nzewi 1981: 447). The Drum Master, who leads the action like a story-teller, is so integral to the dramatised narrative that an *Ikaki* play without him and his drum is impossible. Populist in appeal, the travelling theatre tradition 'is a contemporary expression of the collective identity of Yoruba society and as such should sustain and transmit the perceived traditional values of Yoruba people' (Jeyifo 1984: 5). Jeyifo explains the format of a typical folk opera:

> There is typically no big central climax; there is rather a series of climaxes corresponding to the charged moments of theatrical expressiveness or intensity . . . ; [it is] a celebration involving the entire community; an extended rendition of hypnotic poetic-chant; dance steps alternating between measured, stylised (and ritual) expression and fast, vigorous, mimetic jigs to the fulsome power of *Bata* music; a visual spectacle of swirling movement and extravagant colouration.
>
> (ibid.: 16)

A highly entertaining and usually moralistic/didactic form, folk opera takes the moral lessons embedded in the songs and the drumming to urban and rural communities where it can be performed inside or outside – in homes, restaurants, clubs. Folk opera's resistance to domination by western conventions lies in the music's maintenance of a variety of performance traditions that would otherwise be lost, as well as in its syncretic combination of traditional (and even European) forms. Various other factors can be present, including, in the context of Ògúnyemí's *Obalúayé* (1971), a call-and-response sequence that involves the audience implicitly in the action. Non-linguistic forms of dialogue, such as drumming, also 'speak' to Nigerian audiences, and are as vital as the human voice.

David Coplan argues in *In Township Tonight! South Africa's Black City Music and Theatre* (1985) that music has been paramount in the South African Black Consciousness movement and in the anti-apartheid struggle. Both the maintenance of the many indigenous musical traditions, and the strategic establishment of hybrid musical forms (including jazz which uses African rhythms, tunes, etc.) unite black artists against apartheid and/or exploit white forms to destabilise the authority of apartheid. Music's relative mobility ensures that it can be generated in townships and homelands, without, necessarily, the need for white assistance or white-owned technologies. Music's centrality to black South African drama, then, is not surprising. Generally used as part of a larger project of indigenising foreign theatre forms, music provides a means of expression that spoken dialogue cannot replace. Music involves the audience by inducing recognition; it provokes them to sing with the performers, and, on occasion, leads viewers to hum the tune once out of the auditorium. This Brechtian device unifies the community against the apartheid regime and stages a vibrant cultural face in the presence of an oppressive dominant paradigm. For Coplan, the performance of South African music 'is more than a reflection of socio-cultural dialectics; it embodies and actively participates in them' (1985: 246). Likewise, Gcina Mhlope, a South African playwright, maintains that:

> Music – if you're going to deal with political theatre – is unavoidable. It becomes people's strength. . . . People put their hearts [in] to the singing, and some of the songs are based on traditional dance songs, so they change the lyrics to suit whatever occasion. And it's really hard to stop people once they start singing, to carry on to the next speaker. So

it's unavoidable that political theatre will always have that thread of music.

(1990a: 124)

The uniting of the audience against apartheid – expressed by singing in unison – becomes music's resistant strategy. One recurrent way that music has achieved political and social agency in South Africa is through the singing of the powerful 'Nkosi sikelele iAfrika', the national anthem banned under apartheid but consistently deployed at the end of many theatrical performances to extend and reinforce the resistant discourses of the preceding play.

Music is similarly integral to contemporary theatre praxis in the Caribbean. Like the Creole and Patois languages of the area, many Caribbean musical forms owe their distinctiveness to the processes of cultural syncretism. Treating the Caribbean as an integrated musical region, Kenneth Bilby proposes that its characteristic forms/styles can be understood as part of an 'African–European musical spectrum' (1985: 184) which is analogous to the 'linguistic continuum' outlined by Alleyne and other theorists of creolisation. This model suggests that musicians frequently use a range of styles – even within a single work – sometimes stressing African-derived components (such as a syncopated drum-beat) and at other times using European metre and rhythm. Bilby calls this juxtaposition of forms 'polymusicality', arguing that 'it is possible to encounter virtually back to back the buoyant strains of string bands and the complex drumming of possession cults, the call-and-response of field gangs and the layered harmony of a Bach chorale' (ibid.: 202–3). Many Caribbean plays show evidence of such polymusicality, which can function as a celebration of the region's culture and/or as part of an overall strategy to appropriate and indigenise imperial forms of theatre. A case in point is Walcott's *The Joker of Seville*, which uses calypso, gospel, blues, and parang[9] music in its counter-discursive reworking of the Don Juan myth.

One of the features that cuts across many musical genres in the Caribbean is the use of song (laced with irony, *double entendre*, and veiled allusions) for social commentary (ibid.: 201). Along with the calypso tradition, already discussed as part of Carnival, reggae is one of the region's more political forms of music. Influenced by Jamaican *mento* (itself a mixture of European- and African-derived features), American rhythm-and-blues, and the

197

Rastafarian drumming tradition, reggae frequently addresses the latest local and political events. It is a form of music rooted in the experience of the underprivileged and hence often used as a vehicle of third world protests against imperialism. Sistren have experimented extensively with reggae music as part of their community theatre work which is specifically designed to address the problems of Jamaica's poorer social classes.[10] *Muffet Inna All a We* (1985), for instance, uses reggae songs/dance in a protest against the many levels of exploitation – social, sexual, and economic – endured by black women in post-imperial Caribbean societies.

Syncretic forms of music, particularly those derived from country-and-western styles, are common across a range of Aboriginal plays. Christopher Balme suggests that the country-and-western music in Jack Davis's plays signifies the Aborigines' enculturation (1990: 408–9); the assumption that musical forms are transported from one culture to another with their ideological apparatus intact is, however, problematic. Using the concept of 'ideotones', Mudrooroo argues that Aborigines frequently appropriate non-Aboriginal music, adapting it to their own purposes. Ideotones are audio-narrative units which suggest 'conjunctions that occur in the word/music nexus. They affirm or challenge the apparent unity of the dominant ideological discourses playing at any one time' (1990: 67). Chi and Kuckles's *Bran Nue Dae* displays precisely this kind of ideotonal subversion even while its music seems, on one level, to neutralise the oppositional tenor of the text. Using catchy tunes and pleasant rhythms in ironic apposition to lyrics which voice less than mellow protests against European colonisation, the play provides a sustained challenge to the hegemony of conventional forms of the Broadway musical. Singing is enacted in Aboriginal dialects, in English, and in a special blended language called 'Broome Kriol', while the musical score draws rhythmic inspiration from such disparate sources as country-and-western, calypso, reggae, gospel, blues, and tribal chant to articulate a syncretic mixture of song/sound/music that reflects the complex genealogies of the characters. In short, the play's music is used to carnivalise genre by appropriating borrowed forms, crossing cultural boundaries, and fissuring European notions of aural harmony. It also blurs the distinctions between performer and viewer functions when, consistent with forms of traditional oral narrative, the story-teller, Uncle Tadpole, begins a song in the course of narration and this is taken up antiphonally by the audience who eventually emerge from the theatre still humming its tune. Taking account of the characters' musical journey from Perth to Lombardina and the play's national tour, the dissemination of its music and lyrics among diverse audiences across Australia could be seen as a kind of 'song cycle' wherein a particular form of Aboriginal artistic expression progresses, song by song, along a given track in the country, creating a dialogue between spaces of cultural representation.

Several New Zealand dramatists, notably Vincent O'Sullivan, Renée, and Mervyn Thompson, have incorporated aspects of the Victorian and Edwardian music hall traditions into their plays to demonstrate not only their importance to New Zealand theatre history, but also their contemporary relevance as potentially political forms of theatre. Music hall's populist appeal is championed by playwrights who are keen to bring working-class experience to a stage that generally caters for 'higher' tastes. Because it can invest critical worth in a 'low-cultural' form, music hall is also an appropriate genre through which to critique the class hierarchies that colonialist discourse erected. Settler discomfort with both the colonisers and the indigenous populations in New Zealand thus placed considerable emphasis on music hall for those 'in-between' folk. Music hall does not just rely on nostalgia for old songs; rather, it stresses the popularity and topicality of such songs against the pomposity of more heightened forms of music that were associated with the British upper classes and the colonisers. These songs evoke a great deal quickly: many World War One songs, for instance, need only have the first line played/hummed/sung to recall both wartime deprivation and British exploitation of colonial forces. Vincent O'Sullivan's *Jones and Jones* uses music hall to evoke Katherine Mansfield's London, her New Zealand, and the disjunctions between the two geographical and musical locations. In Renée's *Jeannie Once* (1990) a metatheatrical music hall is the vehicle by which overly strict religious fundamentalism and righteous colonial authority are subverted.

Mervyn Thompson's *Songs to the Judges* (1980) shifts the emphasis from just music hall to exploit, as well, the parodic traditions of music theatre by employing Gilbert and Sullivanesque melodies and particular proxemic and kinesic designs to signify patronising and simplistic representations of Pakeha and Maori history. This musical discourse, which replaces more conventional, unsung dialogue, is part of an effort to discover ways of articulating and formulating a 'New Zealand' that does not resemble the existing smug versions. The play's songs generally introduce historical moments – for instance, 'The Law Song' highlights major political acts, such as the Native Land Act and the Maori Affairs Amendment Act – and frequently adopt an ironic tone to highlight the cultural insensitivity of the imperial system. Set in a style which targets the Pakeha in particular, another song, 'We Think You Ought to Die', concludes with the self-congratulatory Pakeha members of the chorus singing:

> For the Pakeha was Dutiful
> The Pakeha was Bountiful
> The Pakeha was Kind
> Dutiful
> Bountiful
> Magnanimous
> And Just!
>
> (1984b: 157)

Parodying the self-righteous discourse that Thompson found to characterise New Zealand self-representations as well as localising the more imperial Gilbert and Sullivan melodies, music in *Songs to the Judges* becomes culturally specific. Thompson's play concludes with a gospel-influenced tune that superficially appeals to harmony between Maori and Pakeha, while nevertheless recognising the unlikelihood of such an outcome. Localising such music rereads history comically and generates another form of communication for expressing difference from the imperial centre.

Whether they articulate their concerns through verbal or musical forms, or through silence, post-colonial plays reinforce language's heavy inflection with, and investment in, cultural specificity. *What* a culture communicates is inextricably bound up in *how* it communicates: the form, the style, the tone, the register, and the ways in which it structures its languages. As Deleuze and Guattari maintain, language is not a concrete and predetermined entity but a site of continual (re)construction:

> There is no language in itself, nor any universality of language, but a discourse of dialects, patois, slangs, special languages. There exists no ideal 'competent' speaker-hearer of language, any more than there exists a homogeneous

linguistic community. . . . There is no mother tongue, but a seizure of power by a dominant tongue within a political multiplicity.

(1987: 7)

It is this 'seizure of power' by a dominant language that post-colonial theatre seeks to address by abrogating the privilege of English in order to accommodate other 'tongues' as well.

NOTES

1 Orkin notes that, in an effort to side-step censorship, many scripts of this era were not written down (1991: 16). *The Island*, by Fugard, Kani, and Ntshona, provides another method of evading censorship: while the play *is* scripted, the metaphoric mime of the first scene is not inscribed on paper thus preventing the play's censoring for illegally discussing prisons (ibid.: 166). While the perpetrators of the South African apartheid regime clearly recognised the ways in which control of language amounted to political, social, and racial control, they apparently did not understand the other signifying and communicating functions that the stage – and particularly the body on stage – convey.

2 Rendra's work has been the subject of several censorship attempts. At the time of his writing, all plays required the approval of the Indonesian police before they could be produced. He was banned from performing in Yogyakarta from 1974 to 1977, and for some years after his 1978 arrest, the media was not allowed to report his activities (Lane 1979: 3, note 2).

3 This recalls Pierre Nora's concept of memory as a realm of presence (that is, it is constituted only by what is remembered in the present) as opposed to conventional history which attempts to construct a verifiable past (1989: 8).

4 Said argues that for an exile or migrant, 'habits of life, expression or activity in the new environment inevitably occur against the memory of these things in another environment. Thus both the new and old environments are vivid, actual, occurring together contrapuntally', leading to a double vision which can be not only disorienting but also pleasurable (1990: 366).

5 Gaff, known as 'Sealer's saviour', is now banned. It consisted of 'a stout stick, heavily bound, with a two-pronged iron hook at the end. It was used for clubbing the seal; for drawing pelts across the ice; for surviving when the sealers fell through' (Cook 1993: 224). A sculp is a skin.

6 'Patois' refers to French-based creoles, although it may also cover other syncretic languages.

7 While hybridity can in some cases indicate a rather less politically determined acculturation, it is also a highly useful strategy for decen-tring the agency of just one culture, language, or political system.

8 Christened 'folk opera' by Ulli Beier – a German academic and editor who travelled throughout Africa and Melanesia in the 1950s, 1960s, and 1970s – this term is a misnomer. Conventionally, folk opera refers to several types of musical drama based on traditional forms, containing little dialogue, and usually opposed to 'literary' drama.

9 Derived from Spanish music (usually for stringed instruments) originally associated with bullfighting.

10 See also Walcott's *O Babylon!* (1976) which incorporates a great deal of reggae music into a narrative specifically about a group of Rastafarians.

5

BODY POLITICS

> The body is the inscribed surface of events (traced by language and dissolved by ideas), the locus of a dissociated self (adopting the illusion of substantial unity), and a volume of disintegration.
>
> (Foucault 1977: 148)

Foucault's definition of the body omits a crucial performative fact: the body also *moves*. In the theatre, the actor's body is the major physical symbol; it is distinguished from other such symbols by its capacity to offer a multifarious complex of meanings. The body signifies through both its appearance and its actions. As well as indicating such categories as race and gender, the performing body can also express place and narrative through skilful mime and/or movement. Moreover, it interacts with all other stage signifiers – notably costume, set, and dialogue – and, crucially, with the audience. It is not surprising, then, that the body functions as one of the most charged sites of theatrical representation.

The colonised subject's body, as Elleke Boehmer explains, has been an object of the coloniser's fascination and repulsion (and, in effect, possession) in sexual, pseudo-scientific, and political terms:

> In colonial representation, exclusion or suppression can often literally be seen as 'embodied'. From the point of view of the colonizer specifically, fears and curiosities, sublimated fascinations with the strange or the 'primitive', are expressed in concrete physical and anatomical images. . . . [T]he Other is cast as corporeal, carnal, untamed, instinctual, raw, and therefore also open to mastery, available for use, for husbandry, for numbering, branding, cataloging, description or possession.
>
> (1993: 269)

203

Paying attention to the body can be a highly useful (and even essential) strategy for reconstructing post-colonial subjectivity because imperialist discourse has been both insidious and persuasive in its construction of the colonised subject as an inscribed object of knowledge. As Elizabeth Grosz argues, the body is never simply a passive object upon which regimes of power are played out:

> If the body is the strategic target of systems of codification, supervision and constraint, it is also because the body and its energies and capacities exert an uncontrollable, unpredictable threat to a regular, systematic mode of social organisation. As well as being the site of knowledge-power, the body is thus a site of *resistance*, for it exerts a recalcitrance, and always entails the possibility of a counter-strategic reinscription, for it is capable of being self-marked, self-represented in alternative ways.
>
> (1990: 64)

The ways in which the reinscription and self-representation of colonised bodies translate into performative strategies is obviously a key issue for post-colonial theatre. Hence, current movements towards cultural decolonisation involve not just a verbal/textual counter-discourse but a reviewing of the body and its signifying practices. Whereas narrative writing tends to erase the gender and race of its authors and protagonists through its production as an artefact of predominantly western cultures, performance centralises the physical and socio-cultural specificities of its participants. It follows that post-colonial theatre (much like feminist theatre[1]) finds in the body more than mere 'actor function' or 'actor vehicle'. The body's ability to move, cover up, reveal itself, and even 'fracture' on stage provides it with many possible sites for decolonisation.

In general, the post-colonial body disrupts the constrained space and signification left to it by the colonisers and becomes a site for resistant inscription. For instance, the Kathakali actor's stylised facial expressions signify the history of specific Indian acting traditions and communicate the carefully preserved systems of meaning through the actor's body. The colonial subject's body contests its stereotyping and representation by others to insist on self-representation by its physical presence on the stage. Corporeal signifiers quickly become politicised when a black actor appears in a traditionally 'white' role, or when a West Indian cast stages, say, a Shakespearian play; such choices, as well as colour-blind casting, contribute to the development of an identity independent from the imposed colonial one of inadequacy, subordination, and often barbarity. Because the body is open to multifarious inscriptions which produce it as a dialogic, ambivalent, and unstable signifier rather than a single, independent, and discrete entity, it is not surprising that the production of some sort of personal or cultural subjectivity via the body is complex indeed.

The post-colonial subject is often preoccupied with refusing colonially determined labels and definitions, especially those which operate in the name of race and gender. Part of the project of redefining staged identity is to affix the *colonised's* choice of signification to the body rather than to maintain the limited tropes traditionally assigned to it. This oppositional process of *embodiment* whereby the colonised creates his/her own subjectivity ascribes more flexible, culturally laden, and multivalent delineations to the body, rather than circumscribing it within an imposed, imperialist calculation of otherness. The post-colonial stage offers opportunities to recuperate the colonised subject's body – especially when it has been maimed or otherwise rendered 'incomplete' – and to transform its signification and its subjectivity. This chapter explores the process of recuperation by examining some of the basic performative elements of the post-colonial body: how it looks, what it does, how it is seen, and, most importantly, how it presents itself.

As *visual* markers of 'identity', race and gender are particularly significant in theatrical contexts even if their connotations are sometimes highly unstable. It is crucial to remember, however, that such markers are inscribed on the body through discourse – visual, verbal, or otherwise – rather than simply being unmediated or objectively given. In other words, the perceived (constructed) binary categories of male/female and white/black are never merely biologically determined but are also historically and ideologically conditioned. Moreover, as our earlier discussion of various feminisms indicates, race and gender are distinct, albeit sometimes intersecting and/or overlapping, factors which cannot be collapsed under the conceptual umbrella of marginalisation. It follows, then, that there can be neither an unproblematically essentialised 'black', 'female', or any other kind of body nor, conversely, can there be a universalised body which categorically avoids these markers of difference. If post-colonial theory has long rejected the idealised undifferentiated body of the other that is characteristic of imperialist discourse, representational practice – especially in largely iconic art-forms such as theatre – still faces the problem of how to avoid essentialist constructions of race and gender while recognising the irreducible specificity of their impact on subject formation. One possible solution is to conceptualise all markers of identity/difference as partial, provisional, and likely to change depending upon the context or the signifying system in which they operate at any particular time. This notion avoids a single (biological) origin for race or gender but leaves open the possibility of what Spivak calls 'strategic essentialism' (1988: 205) – the foregrounding of 'pure' difference[2] for particular political purposes.

RACE

Since one of the key features of colonialism has been the exertion of European authority over non-white peoples, it is not surprising that an emphasis on race is widespread in post-colonial drama, particularly when the projected audience includes a high proportion of white (or otherwise dominant) viewers.[3] Two parallel, if apparently contradictory, strategies are evident: to emphasise racial difference as part of a 'scrupulously visible political interest' (Spivak 1988: 205) designed to recuperate marginalised subjects, or, alternatively, to dismantle all racial categories by showing their constructedness. Some plays adopt both of these approaches simultaneously, a manoeuvre which often results in a dialectical tension that further destabilises 'race' as a signifying code. A case in point is Chi and Kuckles's *Bran Nue Dae*, which highlights the presence of a large cast of Australian Aboriginal characters/actors while at the same time insisting that race is less a colour than an attitude. In this context, it becomes artistically plausible that even several 'white' characters (played by non-Aborigines) eventually discover their Aboriginality. The play participates in current debates in Australia about the construction of Aboriginal identity and notions of authenticity based primarily on skin colour.

The physical stage presence of black, indigenous, or otherwise 'coloured' actors cannot be undervalued in discussing the counter-discursive possibilities of the body in performance, even if what constitutes race is neither fixed nor objectively measurable.

On one level, staging the visibility of imperialism's racial other is in itself a subversive act since Anglo-European theatre has a long history of excluding non-white actors while maintaining *representations* of racial difference, usually constructed through costume, make-up, and/or mask. The Othello of Shakespeare's day, for example, was played by a white actor who 'blacked up' and donned a curly-haired wig, a tradition which varied little for centuries. Not just a trope in popular entertainment (epitomised by Al Jolson's blackface performances in the early part of this century), blackface was used by Sir Laurence Olivier's version of *Othello* even as recently as the 1960s. When racially marked characters are played in this way, the resistance potential of the fictionalised black/coloured body is compromised by the 'wayward signification' of the actor's whiteness (Goldie 1989: 5). Matching the race (and/or gender) of the actor with that of the character does not mean, however, that the performing body completely escapes the web of imperial inscription. Rather, the body is inevitably 'read' through multiple codes and contexts and shaped not only by the narrative structures of a play itself but also by its audience. Historically, this has meant that when the non-white actor performed on western stages, his/her body generally carried a kind of mystique that both heightened and detracted from its significance. Another mode of *mis*representation consistent with colonial attempts to figure racial others as inferior and/or subordinate was thus conventionalised.[4]

Whereas much western culture constructs the female body on stage as a passive to-be-looked-at object rather than as an active subject, the racially distinct body is often designed to be *overlooked* (in two senses of the word: to be examined more fully than other signifiers as an object of curiosity *and* to be rendered invisible as an object of disregard). Until quite recently, many post-colonial plays devised by whites fell into this representational trap by depicting sentimentalised or exoticised versions of racial difference. Terry Goldie's study of settler drama in Canada, Australia, and New Zealand demonstrates the ways in which images of the indigene have been circumscribed by a semiotic field that is limited to seven signifiers: orality, mysticism, violence, nature, sexuality, historicity, and an imitation of indigenous 'forms' of communication (ibid.: 17). Often moved on or off stage to create a particular atmosphere and/or elicit laughter, indigenous characters have functioned as stage properties, as fragments of the setting, and, at times, as foils against which the normative values of white society can be defined.[5] Likewise, roles for blacks in the wider field of western drama have been constituted within racist discourses, with perhaps even more emphasis on their supposed violence and sexuality. In these prescribed spaces, imperialism's colonised subject is denied its full humanity; it performs an imposed representational function rather than being a focal point in its own right. And while some roles can be subverted in performance, there is little scope in such plays for significant interrogation of dominant assumptions about race.

When indigenous and black playwrights depict themselves on stage, the body is one of the first theatrical elements to take on new iconic possibilities. One text that manipulates the body's significa-tion for political purposes is Monique Mojica's *Princess Pocahontas and the Blue Spots*, which deconstructs the semiotic field of 'Indianness' – to use Daniel Francis's concept of the term (1992) – by staging its common inscriptions in juxtaposition to alternative (and generally more empowering) expressions of native North American subjectivity. Conflicting images/identities are held in tension through the performing body of Contemporary Woman #1, who plays (with) the white-defined stereotypes presented, as well as transforming herself into various native characters. In this way, Mojica provides a critical rereading of the ways in which indigenous women have characteristically been coded and constrained by North and South American history, culture, and lit-erature. The women's bodies contort to create images of imposed signifying codes; they also depict the scenery, including a volcano, thereby critiquing the conventional use of indigenous bodies to suggest the geographical landscape and/or to provide an appar-ently authentic atmosphere. The play employs an overabundance of clichéd Hollywood and explorer/pioneer depictions of the 'Indian' in order to demonstrate their emptiness as representa-tions: the sheer number of represented 'Indian' and 'native' bodies destabilises the power of the imposed depictions. Such fig-ures as the Cigar Store Squaw, the Storybook Princess, and Princess Buttered-on-Both-Sides are effectively meaningless, having been overdetermined by and within white discourse. More specifically, Pocahontas, Christianised and re-named Lady Rebecca, is 'stuck [and] girdled' in the costume of the 'good Indian' even if it is clearly an uncomfortable fit (1991: 29). These 'museum exhibits' contrast sharply with the two contemporary women and with others recuperated from the margins of imperial representation: Matoaka (the younger persona of Pocahontas), Malinche, and the three Métis women who demand that their stories be told. The Storybook Princess and the Cigar Store Squaw are predictably wooden in personality and in their movements on the stage, whereas Matoaka and Malinche, in particular, embody sexualities that cannot be contained within the virgin/whore paradigm imposed upon them by the British and the Spaniards.

Mojica's interest in countering the semiotic codes of cinema and television is shared by other native Canadian writers such as Margo Kane, Daniel David Moses, and Tomson Highway, all of whom have dramatised characters/events that rework the stereotype of the Hollywood Indian.[6] In Australia, the project of reconstructing an indigenous subjectivity is slightly different in so far as Aborigines have been less often mythologised in/through popular representation than simply ignored, especially in visual media. In some ways, then, the conventional Aboriginal body is underdetermined because of its systematic erasure, rather than overdetermined as a result of repeated exposure. This is not to suggest that Aborigines escape the designation of 'other', but to argue that this particular other is often less well-delineated in imperial discourse than is the 'Indian'. Nevertheless, Aboriginal inscriptions of corporeality – as opposed to European constructions of Aboriginality or a generic and even less specific otherness – function to embody in Aborigines on stage a different, more culturally accurate, subjectivity. Jack Davis's plays address the blind spots of settler history and literature on a number of levels, bringing the black body into acute visibility via individual characters (often dancers) and also through group interaction (especially across colour lines). *Kullark*, for example, inverts imperialism's racial norms in a comic depiction of first contact when Mitjitjiroo responds to Captain Stirling's proffered hand by rubbing its skin vigorously to see if the white stain can be removed. This gesture, along with the Aborigines' astonishment at the strange appearance of the Europeans, denaturalises the white body as the dominant sign of humanity. In a related manoeuvre, the play points to the *in*-humanity of the invaders when they decapitate Yagan and skin him in order to remove his tribal markings for a souvenir. Here, Davis suggests that the mutilated black body functions within the colonising culture as a fetishised object.[7] His overall project is to reinstate the corporeal presence of the Aborigines in history – and, on a metatheatrical level, in theatre – at the same time as he details the colonisers' attempts to annihilate all signs of difference. Reference to such atrocities does not mean, however, that *Kullark* simply stereotypes its characters according to race, reassigning the connotations of 'black' and 'white' in the process; rather, this play, like Davis's other works, carefully stages the misunderstandings brought about by discourses of racial otherness in a context where it is possible for conceptual gaps to be bridged.

Louis Nowra's *Capricornia* directly attacks the black/white binary, dismantling notions of 'pure' difference by foregrounding a number of racially 'impure' characters. While Norman, the part-Aboriginal protagonist, might bemoan being 'made out of bits' like 'the monster in Doctor Frankenstein' (1988: 91), the play ultimately celebrates the existence of such hybridity. Fat Anna, among others, impresses upon this confused youth the absurdity of fixed colour classifications:

NORMAN: I'm white, I'm black. I don't know what I am.
FAT ANNA: So what? Look at me, I'm half black, half Jap. Is this part Jap, is this part black? I don't like raw fish, does that mean my mouth isn't Jap?

(ibid.: 94)

By blurring distinctions between categories and by staging a number of visual ironies that widen the disjunctive gap between race and behaviour – Norman's initial appearance in a white safari suit is a case in point – *Capricornia* avoids the trap of situating Aborigines as the static objects of a plea for racial tolerance. The thematic and theatrical focus on miscegenation fortifies the disruptive potential of the body as an unstable signifier. Especially in performance, the play dramatises a multiracial society that inevitably displaces the ideally sanitised world of the white settlers. In this way, Nowra critiques racism by revealing that it is often based on differences which are discursively constructed rather than simply given.

Radically destabilising the 'otherness' of the black body is even more crucial in South African drama. As Martin Orkin argues, apartheid's ability to define race is located in the body: 'the state is unrelenting in its pressure to redefine, with its own discourse, [black and white] bodies, to demarcate, in ways that both entrench its authority and legitimate the actual conditions of domination and subordination within the social order' (1991:

106). In apartheid, the body – skin and hair in particular – is the
site of signification that overrides all subsidiary attachments (such
as clothing) or movements (such as dance). Race, the cornerstone
of apartheid, determines where people work and live, how they
are educated, and how they are treated by every level of authority
and bureaucracy. Given that apartheid's mandate was so wide,
one would expect its boundaries to be clearly established, but the
actual malleability of apartheid's laws points to methods for staging
the body's shifting significations. Hence, post-colonial resistance
focuses on subversions of apartheid's classified bodies with techniques such as the deliberately transparent bodily masquerades in
Zakes Mda's *The Road* (1982). In this play, a tired black farm
labourer meets a tired white farmer on the road. Their exchange
highlights the ways in which the dominant group can rewrite the
rules of apartheid – essentially the rules of skin/body – to suit
themselves:

> FARMER: My God, you are right! You are from there
> [Lesotho].
> LABOURER: How can you tell just by looking at me?
> FARMER: [*mysteriously*] We can always tell, you know. We have
> ways and means. We did it with the Japanese when we
> declared them honorary whites whilst the Chinese remained
> non-white. We are doing it again with the Chinese from
> Taiwan whom we have now declared honorary whites and
> those from the mainland who will always remain non-white
> because they are communists and we don't trade with them.
> We are very clever, you know.
> LABOURER: Very clever indeed. So what's the big deal?
> FARMER: Don't you understand man? It means that I can
> allow you to sit under my tree. You are a foreign Bantu. . . .
> It's all diplomacy, you see. Come now. You can sit under
> the tree, although you will have to sit on the other side of
> that trunk. We can't mix, you know. God wouldn't like that.
> That's why he made us different.
>
> (1990: 149)

Of course, the body in question remains unchanged: the colour
has not leached out of the labourer's skin when the farmer establishes the categories of race, and hence place/position in society.
The stage presence of the clearly black-bodied labourer (despite
what the white farmer decides to 'see' in him) defies the logic of

apartheid. More importantly, the white farmer is actually a black actor wearing a wig and false beard in the deliberately rudimentary disguise of a white man. The casting of this black actor illustrates the complexity of theatrical signification: the body works in conjunction with language and costume, but none of these semiotic codes is complete in itself. While the body appears to be one thing to the audience, the rhetoric of apartheid constructs it as another; the signifying systems of theatre are, however, able to reconvert this body into a sign of blackness so that it 'speaks' in an ironic register, thereby deconstructing apartheid's scrambled logic. Mbongeni Ngema and Percy Mtwa also subvert racial hierarchies in *Woza Albert!* (Mtwa et al 1983) by merely affixing half of a white ping-pong ball to their noses to 'reclassify' themselves as white. This small symbol of whiteness contrasts with the expanse of the actors' black skin, especially since many of the scenes in this technically spare play require the actors to be shirtless. The moving, dancing, acting, singing body in *Woza Albert!* performs multiple positions for black (and even some 'white') subjectivities in opposition to officially sanctioned images of binarised alterity. By foregrounding the possibilities of both parody and self-representation, these theatrical works reinvest the black South African body with a power and a presence that apartheid attempted to preclude.

GENDER

The South African plays discussed demonstrate the constructedness of racial categories at the same time as they attempt to (re)claim strategic, if negotiable, race-inflected identities. For many postcolonial dramatists, particularly women, a parallel project is to recuperate female subjectivities while showing that gender is an ideology mapped across the body in and through representation. It seems, however, that the imperative is less to deconstruct the category of female (or male) than to intervene in the discourses that naturalise gender hierarchies. This pattern is possibly related to the perceived fixity of the gender binary. White/black classifications are quickly broken down by racial hybridity – indeed the threat of miscegenation is precisely that it produces visible signs of the permeability of racial boundaries. Gender classifications, in contrast, most often admit androgyny as merely a hypothetical category which can be dissolved into male *or* female when the biological markers of sex are known. Some writers and practitioners do share Anglo-American feminism's interest in destabilising gender binaries, whether through 'sex-radical'[8] performance or through visually recoded (transvestite) bodies, but most are more concerned with demarcating areas of women's subjugation under imperialism. Accordingly, gender is less likely to function alone as a category of discrimination in post-colonial plays than in combination with other factors such as race, class, and/or cultural background. An additional factor complicating the delineation of a gender-specific body politics is the metaphorical link between woman and the land, a powerful trope in imperial discourse[9] and one which is reinforced, consciously or not, in much post-colonial drama, particularly by male writers. In some instances, women's bodies are not only exploited by the colonisers but also reappropriated by the colonised patriarchy as part of a political agenda which may not fully serve the interests of the women in question.

Rape is a prominent signifier in a number of plays, particularly in countries where settlers' annexation of so-called 'unoccupied territories' disrupted not only the culture but also the livelihoods of indigenous peoples. Both native and non-native dramatists have featured inter-racial rape as an analogue for the colonisers' violation of the land, and also for related forms of economic and political exploitation. Often such representations are designed to reveal less about the experiences of the oppressed than about the rape mentality of the oppressors. In the chilling final moments of Canadian George Ryga's *The Ecstasy of Rita Joe*, for example, the rape and murder of the central protagonist by three white men provides a graphic depiction of the widespread brutality of the colonial/judicial system. This play figures Rita Joe as the site on and through which the disciplinary inscriptions of imperial patriarchy are played out as her body is progressively marked by capture, assault, and sexual penetration. Politically, she functions less as an individual than as an emblem of native cultures in Canada; hence, her death signals the grim triumph of the imperial project. As Gary Boire argues, Ryga's text can be read as a 'Foucaultian allegory' which foregrounds the sexually fragmented body of Rita Joe in order to chart the systems of power that instigate and maintain the settler/invader society's dominance over indigenous groups (1991b: 15).

Depending on how they are staged, theatrical images of sexual violence can have more than merely illustrative functions; in some instances, they also challenge the voyeuristic gaze of the white spectator, inviting him/her to admit complicity in that violence. Janis Balodis's *Too Young for Ghosts* critiques white invasion of indigenous land/culture in Australia in a complex 'cross-over' scene in which the same actors play Aboriginal and Latvian women almost simultaneously. The scene collapses the rapes of two Aboriginal women with the sexual assault of their Latvian counterparts in a displaced persons camp after World War Two. This visual conflation – achieved through doubling roles and overlaying theatrical time and space – is a performative technique intended to elicit both empathy for the Aboriginal women and outrage against the colonial regime, here constructed as a more local 'war' for control over native land/bodies. Throughout the composite rape scene, the audience's perspective is further manipulated by the presence of Karl, whose position as a callous observer reminds the viewers of their own non-intervention. By collapsing chronological and spatial frameworks, Balodis is able to use the bodies of white characters/actors to stand in for black ones without appropriating Aboriginal figures in service of a narrative about migrant experience. Instead, by refusing to display the violation of the black women, the performance text frustrates the libidinal economy of inter-racial rape while still harnessing this trope's metaphorical power to express the colonisers' attitudes and actions. Using different strategies for a similar effect, Dorothy Hewett's *The Man From Mukinupin* (1979) stages the 'rape' of Aboriginal women through a savagely ironic song which details the settlers' attempts to conquer the recalcitrant landscape, a project explicitly figured as the male penetration of female space. Hewett's call for the doubling of her one Aboriginal character with the female heroine, presumably played by a white actor, effectively highlights the ways in which all women have been discursively merged with each other and with the landscape.

The treatment of rape in texts by native dramatists who recognise the significant intersections of race and gender[10] takes on slightly different inflections, especially when local mythologies inform the wider play. Tomson Highway's *The Rez Sisters*, for example, stages rape as a violation not only of the land but also of the very spirit of native culture. In a brief but visually haunting scene, the mentally disabled Zhaboonigan reveals that a gang of white boys penetrated her vagina with a screwdriver. While she details the event with the casual disinterest of a child who has only limited understanding of what has happened, the Ojibway trickster spirit, Nanabush, *embodies* her trauma by performing the 'agonising contortions' of the rape victim (1988: 47–8). Zhaboonigan's assault thus accrues wider significance, though her own body remains relatively unmarked because the trickster absorbs and transforms her experience. Moreover, the conventional gender paradigms of such a scene are somewhat complicated by the fact that Nanabush – a spirit who adopts the forms of either and both genders simultaneously – is played by a male dancer. In what is to some extent a mirror image of *The Rez Sisters*' rape scene, Highway's controversial companion play, *Dry Lips Oughta Move to Kapuskasing*, enacts a native youth's sexual assault of a young native woman, Patsy Pegahmagahbow. That the rape is performed with a crucifix by a victim of foetal alcohol syndrome suggests that Christian imperialism is at least partly responsible for the current schism between native men and women. On a performative level, this scene also points to the desecration of indigenous land/culture by the colonising forces, a resonance achieved in a series of stylised movements in which Dickie Bird Halked repeatedly stabs his crucifix into the earth while Nanabush, here played by a woman, lifts her skirt to reveal the blood which slowly spreads down her legs (1989: 100). In *Dry Lips*, Nanabush and Patsy are embodied by the same ever-transforming actor who variously functions as the *idea* of the 'real' women referred to in the play *and* as the female trickster who again absorbs Patsy's experience. Although Highway has been accused of displaying sexism and gratuitous violence, it could be argued that *Dry Lips*, like *The Rez Sisters*, actually refuses the power of rape by subsuming it within the mythological frameworks invoked, since Nanabush is, above all, the great survivor and healer. Once again, the trickster's body – operating in this text as a sign of native women/culture/land that refigures the imperial collapsing of these categories – absorbs and transforms the forces which would leave it vulnerable and degraded.[11] After the rape, Nanabush is visibly marked but still all-powerful as she reappears in various guises throughout the rest of the dream play, and then enters the 'real' action in a final triumphant moment with the baby that foreshadows a hopeful future for the Rez.

As all these images of sexual violence suggest, women's bodies often function in post-colonial theatre as the spaces on and through which larger territorial or cultural battles are being fought. In a similar fashion, representations of fertility, pregnancy, and motherhood frequently take on political inflections, a fact which is not surprising, given that imperialism's will to power over its (female) subjects also extended to the control of many aspects of reproduction. The slave trade, in which women were bought and sold for their 'breeding' capacities, is the most obvious example of a political economy based on the institutionalised commodification of the female body. Dennis Scott takes up this particular subject in one of the historical scenes of *An Echo in the Bone*, foregrounding the processes by which slavery reduced the female body to its sexual and reproductive functions. The setting is an early nineteenth-century auctioneer's office where three slaves are being inspected by a regular customer while the black middleman lists their attributes in turn, lingering over the two women:

> Now this – [*to* BRIGIT] please make note, the wide hips, the breasts just fulling out. No offspring yet. Do you wish to see proof of virginity – perhaps you'll wish to see for yourself – indeed, that's hardly necessary, we have a long association of trust, don't we, sir. Calves well muscled, exceedingly well turned, you will notice. . . . The other. . . . Here is the doctor's certificate, equally untouched. Notice the nipples. Fire in this one sir, you'll forgive my saying so. But the clear eyes show how easily she can be taught. All kinds of things.
>
> (1985: 99–100)

With their bodies anatomised by the imperial gaze, the women are positioned as merchandise and are thus denied all sense of subjectivity. At the same time, they are constructed as sex objects *and* as passive children ripe for the expert tutelage (read exploitation) of the white master. Further degradation follows when Stone puts on a glove to examine the 'goods', inspecting one of the women's teeth and then running his hand up between her thighs, as if at a livestock sale. While the male slave is also commodified, he is not described in corporeal terms; indeed, his best selling feature is that he 'can read, write and reckon like a schoolmaster' (ibid.: 100). This scene exemplifies gender's impact on slavery: women's bodies are marked for consumption within imperialism's particular brand of patriarchy. The added focus on the middleman's ingratiating 'sales talk' also gives weight to the theory that in patriarchal systems women function in a symbolic exchange which cements the relationships between men (see Rubin 1975) – in this

216

case between the white slave owner and the black agent who acts as proxy for the buyer.

Whereas the bodies of black women were commandeered in some colonies to breed a slave class to fulfil the demands of imperialism's labour market, white women's bodies were often appropriated to preserve the racial (and moral) integrity of the ruling class. In Africa and India, as well as in the Caribbean, the colonial woman/wife was expected, indeed compelled, to offer her sexual, social, and reproductive labours in the service of the Empire. Where the goal was settlement rather than rule, white women were even more crucial to the imperial project because of the imperative to (re)populate newly conquered lands. Jill Shearer's quasi-historical play, *Catherine* (1978), demonstrates how the body of the Australian settler woman functioned as part of the physical terrain upon which colonial expansion was mapped, both literally and symbolically. A large section of this metatheatrical text details the shipment of the first convict women to Botany Bay and makes abundantly clear the fact that such 'cargo' was designed to 'balance the imbalance' of the colony (1977: 30) – that is, to prevent the male settlers' deviant sexual behaviour (with indigenous women or other men) and to provide progeny for the successful peopling of the nation. The main character, Catherine, becomes pregnant by the ship's surgeon but will not be allowed to keep her child, who has been earmarked as the first of a new generation of Australians whose ignominious heritage must be suppressed. The proposed management of Catherine's pregnancy – she will be taken care of only until she can safely deliver the baby into its father's hands – highlights the transplanted society's complete disregard for women themselves. While much of the play's narrative content critiques the convict system by exposing the ways in which it facilitated institutional control over the female body, the performance text insists on staging women's subjectivity: its structure as a play-within-a-play enables the recuperation of Catherine's body as a group of contemporary actors continually rehearse and re-interpret the fragments of her history to provide a wider comment on gender oppression.

If the settler woman's reproductive labour was harnessed in the interests of expanding the Empire, the indigenous woman's fertility presented a threat to the colonisers and was often suppressed. Eva Johnson's *Murras* (1988) addresses this issue in Australia by referring to the deliberate and systematic sterilisation of pubescent

Aboriginal girls who are duped into taking medication that renders them infertile. *Murras* illustrates ways in which native women's bodies become sites of conquest in the imperial regime and how they are permanently marked by its various administrative systems, even those which purport to be benevolent. As Ruby says of her daughter in the closing scene, 'She carries the scars of the *wudjella's* [whitefellow's] medicine' (1989: 106). While generally much less harmful than the enforced sterilisation detailed in *Murras*, medical management of pregnancy and childbirth also has the effect, if not the intention, of bringing the bodies of indigenous women under control. Sistren Theatre Collective's *Bellywoman Bangarang* (1978) takes up the issue of western medicine as part of its focus on teenage pregnancy in Jamaica, and attempts to reclaim the birthing process through the use of African-based rituals which emphasise female power. The play's opening image features three masked inter-locking figures as the mother-woman, a healer and protector who mimes a traditional labour before transforming herself into a modern-day doctor in a movement which indicates the medical-isation of childbirth. After the stories of the four pregnant girls have been told, the mother-woman returns at the end of the play to oversee the births. She guides Marie through a difficult labour and also frees her from the ropes (symbols of fear and self-loathing) which have entangled her since her rape. Like the trickster in Highway's plays, the mother-woman is a regenerative force/spirit who disperses the effects of trauma, restoring the colonised body to physical and spiritual health.

Imperialism's attempt to exercise authority over the reproduc-tive processes of its female subjects is sometimes paralleled with more local tendencies to reduce women to functions of gender and/or fertility. Some post-colonial drama invests female fertility with great symbolic importance but none the less subordinates women to the interests of the colonised patriarchy. In India and Africa in particular, male writers are inclined to image the land as a mother and to present the truly-fecund woman as a signifier of nationhood. Giving birth thus becomes largely metaphorical, particularly in plays concerning independence from colonial rule, where the birth of a child mirrors the birth of the new nation. This trope, also common to Caribbean drama, occurs in Michael Gilkes's *Couvade* (1972) which invokes an Amerindian birthing ritual to articulate the play's complex dream-vision of a unified post-independent Guyana. The custom of *couvade* requires the father-to-be to undertake a trial or ordeal while his wife is in labour. This tradition is designed to affirm the connection between the unborn child and its father and to ensure a successful birth. *Couvade*, recently revised for Guyana's 1993 independence anniversary celebrations, uses the ritual to chart the psychological and spiritual 'rebirth' of the protagonist, Lionel, who, along with his new-born child, becomes emblematic of the nation. While the choice of ritual is apt for Gilkes's political vision, it shifts the focus of the birth from the woman (and the child) to the man and the community.[12] Such paradigms figure the paternal body as much more significant than the maternal counterpart; thus, possible representations of the female post-colonial subject are often limited to the merely practical.

The maternal body is also compromised by her child in several plays when, for instance, stalled or uncertain progress towards decolonisation is figured by some kind of failure in the reproductive process. The unborn, stillborn, or otherwise incomplete child has special significance in this respect and often features in several signifying capacities: as well as representing the specific and local community, this child also acts as a site of struggle between competing political groups, especially in cultures that acknowledge the presence of ancestral spirits. The *abiku* or Half-Child in Soyinka's *A Dance of the Forests* (1960), a play about and for Nigeria's independence, represents the contemporary Nigerian world of spiritual transition, matching the political and social transition of the country. *A Dance of the Forests* is a cautionary rather than a purely celebratory play in so far as it recognises the difficulties inherent in attempts to unite the variety of forces that would impact on an independent Nigeria. The uncertain location of the *abiku* in this text also points to some of the dilemmas Nigerians would face in the following decades. Just as the *abiku* is neither living nor dead, neither body nor spirit, neither recognised nor forgotten, Nigeria's independence augurs an ambivalent future. A more hopeful treatment of the spirit child occurs in Walcott's *Ti-Jean and His Brothers* where the *bolum*, a disfigured foetus who represents the Caribbean people under the tyranny of colonialism, is eventually wrested from the clutches of the devil/plantation owner and reborn into full human life. In both of these plays, the female body is once again completely removed from the (potential) birthing process: the *abiku*'s 'mother', the Dead Woman, has no say in the life or role of her half-child while the *bolum* is restored

219

to the human world as a result of Ti-Jean's victory over the devil. On a performative level, the incomplete child-figure simply transforms from the spirit state as if birthing itself independently of any mother figure. This process was imaged through costuming codes in one recent video production of *Ti-Jean* where the *bolum* was encased in a huge egg-shell which it broke upon 'hatching' (1979b).

Examples such as these suggest that male playwrights are primarily interested in childbirth as a symbolic, often unifying trope. Women, on the other hand, have a vested interest in refusing the gender-specific roles/images that circumscribe their representation. One of the most important achievements of recent women's post-colonial writing is its refusal to endorse the traditional signifiers of gender, particularly those linked to reproduction and mothering. When motherhood is invoked, it frequently becomes a very mixed 'blessing', much as it is in Buchi Emecheta's ironically titled novel, *The Joys of Motherhood*.[13] Interestingly, with a few exceptions, post-colonial plays by women tend not to centralise birth, perhaps in an attempt to fracture the concept of 'Mother Earth', an idealistic notion that denies women full humanity and compromises their ability to change, to choose, and to be individuated. The Canadian playwright, Judith Thompson, *does* frequently foreground pregnancies – in *The Crackwalker* (1980), *Tornado* (1987), and *I am Yours* (1987) – but these imminent births tend not to represent a bright hope for the future. Instead, they symbolise evil or a social cancer; regardless of the baby's health, pregnancy is a metaphor for dis-ease in Thompson's work. Likewise, Sistren's *Bellywoman Bangarang* and Shearer's *Catherine* construct the pregnant body in terms of disorder and/or pathology rather than invoking traditional images of fruition.

Our discussion of the gendered body supports Ketu Katrak's argument that 'the traditions most oppressive for women [in colonised societies] are specifically located within the arena of female sexuality: fertility/infertility, motherhood and the sexual division of labour' (1989: 168). While women as narrative subjects are characteristically erased in imperial and patriarchal discourses, their corporeal presence is often intensified through a focus on factors such as sexuality and reproduction. This habit can be just as limiting as the neglect of gender-specific issues. As Peggy Phelan argues, 'In excessively marking the boundaries of the woman's *body*, in order to make it thoroughly visible, patriarchal culture subjects it to legal, artistic, and psychic surveillance. This, in turn, reinforces the idea that she *is* her body' (1992: 30). The challenge for post-colonial dramatists – both male and female – is to refuse such body politics while re-inscribing all theatricalised bodies with more enabling markers of gender. Yet, as Monique Mojica makes clear in *Princess Pocahontas and the Blue Spots*, women as a group cannot claim a collective victim status when they have been – and continue to be – complicit in the colonisation, appropriation, and denigration of other women. In this play, Contemporary Woman #1 refuses the feminist label because its collectivity tries to override her individuality as a subject who happens to be native and who happens to be female. The contemporary characters (and actors) present to their audience transforming, individuated bodies that refuse collectivity of any type if it does not also recognise the rights of the singular subject. Contemporary Woman #1 rejects the International Women's Day march until 'feminist shoes' manage to accommodate her 'wide, square, brown feet' and so allow her to 'feel the earth through their soles' (1991: 58). Refusing to be both the token 'Indian' and to represent all natives, this woman demands, in Gloria Anzaldua's words, 'the freedom to carve and chisel [her] own face' (ibid.: 59), thus maintaining the individuality of her body *among* groups (mis)identified solely by race or gender.

DEROGATED BODIES

Imperialism not only attempts to determine corporeal inscriptions of race and gender, it also subjects the colonised body to various other disciplinary regimes designed to instigate and maintain the desired hierarchies of power. The body which has been violated, degraded, maimed, imprisoned, viewed with disgust, or otherwise compromised has particular relevance to post-colonial literatures and invariably functions within some kind of allegorical framework. Most often, the personal site of the body becomes a sign of the political fortunes of the collective culture, a sign which must be actively reassigned to a more productive representation through embodiments on the post-colonial stage. In the theatre, the derogated body is a potent site of representation since the constraints and oppressions it endures can be visually displayed rather than simply described. Moreover, this body plays out a performative contradiction which can be used subversively when the (presumably) powerful physicality of the actor is harnessed in order to convey the disempowered body of the fictional character as colonial subject.

Representations of the body in South African art, fiction, and certainly drama are deeply influenced by apartheid's violations of human rights and the human spirit. As if to physicalise the injustices of a system based on racial inequality, the country's theatre frequently foregrounds the degraded and/or maimed body as a protest against apartheid. As well as drawing attention to the black subject, derogation can suggest the dispersal of white authority, as figured through corporeal and/or psychological disintegration. *Diepe Grond* (1985), Reza de Wet's allegory of apartheid's self-destructive rhetoric and practice, illustrates imperial power's tendency to recoil on those who exercise it. Set in a derelict farmhouse, the play details the physical and mental regression of an Afrikaaner brother and sister, Frikkie and Soekie, who have killed their parents in order to prevent them from intervening in their incestuous relationship. Watched over by their old black housekeeper and nanny, Alina, this sibling 'couple' live in complete isolation and show physical signs of the general decrepitude that pervades their environment. Their bodies are dirty and flea-infested, while their infantile behaviour points simultaneously to arrested growth and premature senility. When the British-South African estate agent, Grove, visits to encourage Frikkie and Soekie to sell their disused land, he assumes that their frequent relapses into child-like language and actions signify madness. He, too, is soon murdered and the pair are left to perform their childish scenarios and violent tantrums that result from their seclusion. On a metaphorical level, Frikkie and Soekie represent the South African state: as apartheid's effect on their minds (to corroborate Grove's view) does manifest as madness, their psychological and physical degeneration becomes emblematic of a corrupt, crumbling regime. Alina, meanwhile, signifies the watchful black populace who only has to wait for the system's imminent and, in this case, unassisted demise.

Other South African plays are more inclined to stage black subjectivity in an obvious state of fracture. Zakes Mda's *We Shall Sing for the Fatherland* (1979), for example, exposes the derogation of blacks by parading bodies which are visibly 'broken' or otherwise mutilated. In addition to the ubiquitous crippled bodies supported by crutches, the play features literal voicelessness as a result of oppression. The two main characters are disenfranchised black men who live in a city park. Their past exploits as soldiers in what they call the 'Wars of Freedom' (likely various struggles against Angola or Namibia) instil in them a sense of patriotic pride which they try to express in a commemorative song:

SERGEANT: Come, Janabari, let us sing for the fatherland. The land we liberated with our sweat and blood. Our fatherland.
[*They stand together, and then open their mouths wide, trying to sing. But the voices won't come out. In frustration they stop trying and sit down.*]
It is of no use, Janabari.
JANABARI: Our voices are gone.

(1979: 23)

The men's inability to sing points to the literal disintegration of their bodies, marking the irony of their participation in a nationalist war which has not liberated them at all. After they die from exposure, however, they find that their bodies – still present on stage and still dressed in tattered military uniforms – have changed: Sergeant's missing leg is restored after his death, when, he comments, he doesn't need it; and, ironically, Janabari's health is also somewhat improved by death. The recuperation of Sergeant's dead body draws attention to the (sometimes playful) duality of the performing body: the presence of the able-bodied black actor complicates the metaphoric and literal mutilation of Sergeant's black body. That performative doubleness does not, however, image a renewed 'life' in death for the characters beyond their relatively minor, useless, and temporary health improvements. Janabari notes that, unlike their own pauper's burial and uncertain 'future', Mr Mafutha 'goes to heaven in style' (ibid.: 25). Generally 'written out' of history, these indigent, maimed men are forgotten in death and in life. Only the integrity of the theatricalised body on stage gives them a presence, but even that is unstable: fractured bodies exist (barely) in the apartheid regime.

As a powerful sign of brutality, the murdered or mutilated body features across a range of drama from various countries and generally operates as part of a strategic critique of imperialism's policies and practices. The decapitated Aborigine in Davis's *Kullark*, the raped native woman in Ryga's *The Ecstasy of Rita Joe*, and the muted slave (whose tongue has been cut out for spitting at his master) in Scott's *An Echo in the Bone* are but a few examples of disfigured bodies which physicalise the metaphor of imperial violation and so appeal to the audience on a visceral level. In some plays, the derogated body has not only an illustrative function but also a subversive one. Louis Nowra's theatre is thoroughly imbued with an insistent corporeality which is often used for satirical purposes even while it shows the denigration of colonised peoples. From his earliest anti-imperial plays to the more recent social satires, his work clearly illustrates Stallybrass and White's contention that 'the body cannot be thought separately from the social formation, symbolic topography and the constitution of the subject' (1986: 192). *Visions* (1978), for instance, presents a savagely parodic view of the ways in which imperialism produces dysfunctional societies where power is exercised *and* countered through corporeal inscription. *The Golden Age* reiterates this perspective through a similar repertoire of images in which the performing body is writ large, but in this play, Nowra attempts to balance dystopian forces with utopian energies so that the colonial subject/body is at least partly recuperated. Juxtapositions of classical and grotesque bodies usually function to expose and ridicule the colonising culture's representational motifs in each of these two plays. *The Golden Age* introduces the dominant ego-ideal through the statuesque (white) bodies of Elizabeth and William Archer, (arch-colonialists) whose affected gestures and manners indicate how completely they have internalised imperialism's constrictive norms. The audience is then rapidly transported to the bizarre and excessively corporeal world of the forest people who, although mostly mute and/or genetically deformed, none the less convey a tremendous vitality which carnivalises classical form with grotesque formlessness. As Kelly notes, these people represent the 'lost tribes' of modern Australia, the Aborigines and convicts expelled from imperial society and 'deformed physically and linguistically by the colonising ascriptions of alterity' (1992b: 63). Through such misfits, the play presents the unfinished protean and anarchic body/language extolled by Bakhtin, decentring imperial tropes to foreground a corporeal performativity that promotes unruliness. In this context, Stef's spasticity and Betsheb's epileptic attacks have a subversive function in so far as they bring images of disorder into acute visibility.

Nowra's *Visions* deploys the grotesque body in graphic depictions of both the colonisers and the colonised, suggesting that imperialism marks all who are enmeshed in its totalising systems. As the chief imperialists, Lynch and Lopez activate their bloody campaign to subdue the local populace, they find that it is literally impossible to keep their own hands clean. Instead, their bodies are progressively 'contaminated' by the violence they inflict upon others – as indicated on a number of occasions by the play's visual imagery – and eventually reduced to a state of total degradation during a series of surrealistic scenes that show the couple trapped in the festering swamps where they are eventually shot by their enemies. This focus on the corporeal effects of imperialism also encompasses more sympathetic figures such as Juana, who represents the indigenous subject profoundly and quite visibly marked by her contact with western values. Juana's interpellation into imperial discourse is strongly visualised during the play-within-the-play when, like the ventriloquist's doll, she functions as a literal mouthpiece for Lynch's propaganda. That her stomach pours out sand and her mouth spits diamonds as part of this 'magic act' illustrates her ingestion and processing of the dominant discourse, enacting in vivid detail the disembodiment of the colonial subject. These are, however, ambiguous images which also subvert Lynch's little play and thus deflate her claims to authority.

Frequently, Nowra's manipulation of the grotesque body as a particularly theatrical site of the abject[14] extends beyond an emphasis on physical pathology to incorporate those carnivalesque images which pertain to the 'lower bodily stratum', Bakhtin's collective term for the digestive and reproductive systems, including the orifices and protuberances through which the body maintains its connection to the outside world. Through motifs such as eating, *Visions* reveals the rapacious greed of empire and constructs imperialism as little better than an act of savage cannibalism. As well as providing a symbolic framework for the play's political narrative, eating as metaphor and dramatic action once again draws attention to the physical body and shows how even its most basic functions are inflected by discourses of power. In this respect, the staged tea parties serve as a performative technique designed to reveal the ways in which astonishingly trivial regulations of behaviour nonetheless territorialise the body, a process dramatised in sinister fashion when Lynch and Lopez invite the American Ambassador over to dinner, humiliate him about his manners, and then poison him. A more benign version of this trope occurs in *The Golden Age* as the Archers attempt to reform their charges' manners/bodies by initiating them into the dinner-party circuit, a project that backfires when the forest people's total ignorance of bourgeois etiquette turns the occasion into an elaborate farce which destabilises the established social hierarchy. Overall, both plays exploit the derogated body as a way of protesting against oppressive regimes, but only *The Golden Age* preserves, in Betsheb, a potential means to recovery. It is through this recuperation of the female body as emblematic of the Australian nation that Nowra most fully rehearses his version of an alternative and empowering post-colonial subjectivity.

As a variant – and sometimes more subtle – sign of derogation, the diseased body is another site on which regimes of power are played out. The links between disease, imperial medicine, and corporeal control of the sexual, cultural, or racial other have been the subject of much recent discussion, and it is by now a well-argued proposition that socio-medical constructions of infectious diseases in particular function ideologically to demonise a select group seen as responsible for 'defiling' the rest of (western) humanity.[15] Colonialist discourse has a long history of constructing such diseases – malaria is a good example – as natural when they are localised in the body of the 'savage' other, but unnatural when they cross the boundaries between coloniser and colonised to settle in the 'civilised' self. Post-colonial retroping of this motif interrogates the epidemiology of disease as something which invades cultures from without, and instead posits the possibility that disease arises from the circumstances of colonisation itself. Within this framework, the discursive agency of disease can be traced to history rather than physiology.

Although the diseased body figures most commonly in indigenous drama, where, like other manifest forms of derogation, it physicalises the oppressions endured by the subordinated group, it can also represent a dysfunctional dominant order. Alma De Groen's *The Rivers of China* uses illness to signal the social malaise of a settler society which is ambivalently aligned with both coloniser and colonised. As its central icon and most striking image, the play presents to the audience a body swathed from head to foot in bandages and confined to a hospital bed. This faceless, initially gender-indeterminate 'mummy' points to a generalised identity crisis. At the same time, it makes boldly visible not only Mansfield's physical illness – she is dying of tuberculosis – but also, and more importantly, her dis-ease as a colonial woman constrained by imperial and patriarchal authority. The bandaged figure, soon revealed as a man hypnotised to believe he is Mansfield, eventually dies of her tuberculosis, a disease that he does not have. His fate attests to the suggestive power of an imagination 'contaminated' by an alien history imposed initially upon the mind but subsequently manifest in the body with disastrous consequences. Overall, through a narrative focus on psychosomatic illness, aided by the theatrical translation of that illness into haunting visual images, *The Rivers of China* constructs disease as something expressed by, rather than rooted in, the physical body. Moreover, by questioning the belief that pathology is effectively addressed by the timely intervention of technology, the play points to a crisis of faith in the omnipotence of modern science. These are radical perspectives which have important implications for the colonised subject whose body has been, and in some cases still is, a site of intense interest to the knowing gaze of western medicine.

If the derogated body is maimed, degraded, infiltrated with disease, or figured as grotesque, it is also frequently denied freedom. Locked in prison (or, in some cases, an asylum), the colonised subject often appears to have a very limited scope for movement, self-expression, and liberation; however, as suggested by a number of post-colonial plays which dramatise prison life, performance offers one means by which some kind of agency might be recovered. Prisons perform, among other things, a situation of colonisation in miniature: the warden rules the prison just as the ultimate authority of the state manages the imperial enterprise. By replaying and reworking the disciplinary regimes upon which the penal system is based, prison theatre stages the possibility of liberation, if only metaphorically, even while it illustrates the physical capture and containment of the colonised body. Almost all prison plays demonstrate the adoption of roles and the establishment of a hierarchy among the internees. In post-colonial prison drama, a well-defined set of prisoners (usually a cell group)[16] characteristically becomes identified as a corporate body aligned with nationalist/post-colonial discourses.[17] Gary Boire's work on prison theatre (1990) demonstrates the specific ways in which this corporate, incarcerated body signifies. The structural organisation of the cell group and the interrelationships between prisoners and guards offer opportunities for microcosmic allegories of the 'outside' and for inversions of that outside authority through role play. As discussed in earlier references to the counter-discursivity of Fugard *et al*'s *The Island*, the use of metatheatrical devices enables the prisoners to enact their protest against the system in discourses that circumvent the rigid censorship which is usually a component of their punishment. In particular, parodies of the prison hierarchy – almost always found in the subversions enacted by a play-within-a-play – rehearse ways in which to resist the wider social and political structures underpinning the dominant society's construction and administration of (in)justice.

Prison drama is predictably widespread in South Africa where the physical brutality and psychological humiliation inflicted upon the incarcerated black South African (beyond the constraining effects of apartheid outside the prison) are legendary. Maishe Maponya's fragmented play, *Gangsters* (1984), about a death in custody which resembles the death of the now legendary Steve Biko, draws the physical/social boundaries that generally circumscribe the colonial subject even more restrictively as the authoritarian body of the state grows in potence and self-importance. The body of the dead prisoner, Rasechaba, however, claims the signifying space of the stage since the play begins and ends with the dead man in a parodic yet resonant pose recalling the crucifixion of Jesus. While Christian iconography is powerful in South Africa (among many other former colonies), it is too late for Rasechaba to be saved; thus the promise of Christian salvation is never fulfilled. Positioned above the white security police officer and his black counterpart, Rasechaba's body remains the central, 'unsaved' focus.

In Canada, Australia, and New Zealand, prison drama often centres on the colonised native subject, a trend which is not surprising since a disproportionate number of indigenous people have been, and still are, incarcerated in the settler colonies.[18] In focussing on the attempted takeover of the prison community by a Maori 'warrior', Bruce Stewart's *Broken Arse* (1990) illustrates the disastrous consequences that reactive militancy can elicit. Tu persuades the mostly Maori prisoners that they, like him, must attempt to overturn the entire Pakeha prison which has come to represent Maori loss of power in the country as a whole. Tu's half-real, partially dream-generated (and highly successful) warrior club encourages the prisoners to take control of their own bodies instead of relying on tranquillisers to cope with their situation.

Initially, this strategy provides the inmates with a Maori sense of self as they return to their Maori names and develop self-reliance through physical and spiritual strength. Tu's group, however, finally becomes too radical and too essentialist to consider discussion or compromise. The result is physically devastating for Henry, a Pakeha prisoner whose blundering kindness leads him to become a casualty in Tu's reconfigured world. The club fails, its impact destroyed by Tu's misguided insistence on the fixity of the Pakeha–Maori binary and his belief that race determines everything in New Zealand. While Henry's body is literally damaged, the collective Maori body is metaphorically derogated when it assumes that New Zealand history is predicated on an essentialist villain/victim basis.

In a more optimistic allegory of political liberation, Rena Owen's *Te Awa i Tahuti* stages the rehabilitation of a young drug-dependent Maori, Toni, whose incarceration reflects the alienation of her people. Set in a women's prison in England, the play traces several kinds of isolation that Toni experiences: from the self, from a dysfunctional family, from New Zealand, and from her Maori heritage. While the physical strictures of the prison setting – not to mention the psychological effects of confinement and constant surveillance – obviously construct Toni's body as an object of reform, she nonetheless exerts a degree of control over the space she occupies. Her vigorous exercises are not just a ploy to avoid talking to the counsellor but are also a way of marking out her own territory in corporeal terms. Similarly, her twirling *pois* (lightweight balls) and her performance of the Maori songs make a claim for personal space. Through recourse to a cultural heritage remembered partly through the body, Toni stages a newly-found, culturally specific subjectivity that reinvigorates her despite the degradations of prison life. Her recollection and re-enactment of a fragmented personal history facilitates healing so that she is eventually able to translate a dream about her Maori ancestors into practical knowledges that will help her shape a future on the 'outside'. Unlike the warrior, Tu, Toni resists overt violence in favour of a more measured approach to attaining spiritual autonomy and physical freedom.

As many of these prison plays demonstrate, a dramatic focus on incarceration can intensify a character's corporeal presence when the performing body is situated within a confined space. A more complex position from which to express subjectivity is the 'site' of absence. Already discussed as an aspect of race and gender representations, the absent body generates an ironic 'presence' in a wide cross-section of post-colonial drama[19] and has a powerful impact in performance situations. Whether signified through verbal reference, visual gesture, costume, props, or some feature of the set (such as an empty chair), the absent body occupies dramatic, if not always actual, space. It follows, then, that the audience experiences absence as a palpable, 'embodied' presence, a paradox which allows some scope for theatrical manipulations of the text. In other words, absence is a sign that can be coded within a range of semiotic systems. Depending upon how it is staged, absence can be extremely unsettling for the viewer. In political terms, the absent body is potentially subversive because, like the silent voice, it evades definition and, by implication, discursive capture. Saira Essa and Charles Pillai's *Steve Biko: The Inquest* (1985) stages the South African icon Steve Biko's dead body. As suggested by the absence of a performative body signifying the murdered man, this bilingual English/Afrikaans play, based on the actual transcripts of the inquest into Biko's death, presents an instance in which incarceration paradoxically produces a mythologised and intangible body which escapes the confines of the apartheid system. Biko's status as a cult and revolutionary leader in death became far more powerful as a tool for anti-apartheid activists than Biko himself could have been in life. To that end, no body is necessary on stage; Biko's presence is nevertheless almost palpably embodied by a highly metaphoric property: a set of leg irons he was wearing when he died. Representing the manacling of the South African people, this property remains lit on stage after the actors leave. Just before the play's conclusion, other absent presences are staged: a tape recording is played 'consisting of a comprehensive list of people who died during security police custody' (1985: 86) while the play's singers hum 'Nkosi sikelela iAfrika'. A similarly highly politicised recitation closes Jack Davis's *Barungin (Smell the Wind)*, a play which evokes the absent (collective) body of black Australians when Meena lists a vast number of Aborigines killed over the two hundred years of white settlement. The sheer length of the list is enough to shock the audience, and the cumulative 'presence' of the bodies invoked by the list creates a commanding image of imperialism's brutality. At the same time, these invisible bodies hover, like their South African counterparts, surrealistically about the stage space, eluding the imperial gaze and refusing to be marked by its disciplinary power. Here, the absent body/spirit penetrates the bodies of the 'real' characters who have gathered to mourn their dead. It is in this complex interplay of absence and presence that Davis stages one of his most compelling expressions of contemporary Aboriginality.

METAMORPHIC BODIES

The powerful presence of the theatricalised post-colonial body, despite (and sometimes even because of) its derogations, suggests that foregrounding corporeality can be a highly positive, active strategy for staging resistance to imperialism. Traditional enactments such as ritual and carnival demonstrate that the performing body can help to regenerate and unify communities despite the disabilities, disintegrations, and specific disconnections of the individual bodies involved. We maintain that a whole or completed sense of self is not characteristic of the colonised subject although it is sometimes the utopian goal of bodies/cultures inevitably fractured by western imperialism. Split or fragmentary subjectivity reflects the many and often competing elements that define post-colonial identity, whereas attempts to achieve a subjective 'wholeness' may merely replicate the limited significations of the coloniser/colonised binary through which imperialism maintains control over the apparently unruly and uncivilised 'masses'. Thus split subjectivity can be viewed, on a number of levels, as potentially enabling rather than as disempowering. If imperialism conventionally assigns the coloniser and the colonised to roles which determine how power is exercised, the splitting of the colonial subject's self into several varied entities enables him/her to split from the general site of disempowerment (see Bhabha 1984 and 1990). This separation removes both the coloniser and the colonised from their assigned positions of power and impotence; instead of being fixed and unitary, both subject positions are fragmented and dislocated. Crucially, both also have the capacity to fragment and dislocate. This means that their interrelationships can be re-evaluated in the light of a shifted power dynamic of negotiation rather than essentialism, opening up possibilities for new kinds of expression. Working in opposition to exclusionary identity politics, split subjectivity enables the recognition of several – even, potentially, all – of the factors and allegiances that determine the syncretic colonised subject.

Post-colonial theatre addresses this issue in various ways, one of the most interesting of which is the presentation of a narrator who is simultaneously staged in the shape of a different actor. This strategy ensures that the single character is embodied in several ways, and even in several sites. Louis Nowra's *Summer of the Aliens* (1992) positions the narrator, Lewis, on stage watching the activities of his younger, fourteen-year-old self. Occasionally the two actors interact, particularly when the older man forces his younger alter-ego to face unpleasant truths or to perform a task differently. These interruptions in the young Lewis's life are part of the process of self-realisation, as the two 'selves' grow closer to being a joint 'unit' – if an inharmonious one. In similar fashion, John Kneubuhl's *Think of a Garden* (1991) structures the memories of a forty-year-old man around the actions of his ten-year-old self in Western Samoa. By employing two actors as the same character, these plays divide roles/bodies in order to demonstrate the multiple entities that constitute a social subject, and the varied and various personae through which that subject is manifested. Rather than exemplifying schizophrenia, this split subjectivity reminds viewers that stereotypic portrayals of the static, uni-dimensional colonial subject are limiting. As the shifting, multivalent subject/body is brought into view, representation becomes more varied, more ambivalent, and, usefully, more difficult to categorise. In *The Belle of the Belfast City* (1988) by Christina Reid, the characters' past selves, activated by both memories and photographs, are played by adult actors. In other words, the enacted photographs function as flashbacks rather than as split personalities. The characters' bodies are, nevertheless, fractured, since their younger personae are invariably different, if only in performed age and energy, from the adult selves of the play's present. This is not an unusual strategy for suggesting the passage of time, but the constant replaying of subject positions serves to highlight the body's distinctions from stereotyped constructions of 'Irishness'. In Belle's case, the added inflection of race (her 'mixed blood' heritage) further emphasises the presence of the multiply identified body on stage.

These plays rely on multiple actors to challenge the viewer's gaze by articulating the body's fractures and shifting the action and/or point of visual focus. In contrast, the monodrama, a widely used form in post-colonial theatre, focuses solely on a single performing figure who expresses the 'splits' through at least two distinct methods of subject (de)construction. First, a single actor might play *one* character who usually adopts several different personae; or, second, the actor might perform *multiple* characters who, in turn, may or may not present different selves to the audience. The first kind of monodrama expresses the split subjectivity of one *character* – hence, the transformations of the performing body are relatively subtle – while in the second kind, the *actor* 'splits' into a number of subjects, a process which usually requires radical metamorphoses, especially when the body shifts across categories such as race and gender. In other words, the site of split subjectivity occurs at a different level of the performance text in each example, a factor which has implications for audience reception. In general, naturalistic models of reception can be applied more easily to one-character monodramas than to those which give dramatic presence to many characters, and which thereby make acutely visible the gaps between the performing body and the performed subject. Aside from reassessing the body's boundaries, the monodrama is a crucial vehicle for exploring post-colonial subjectivity because it is almost always biographical or autobiographical. Women in particular employ this form as it befits the expression of an identity often fractured by multiple discourses. The freedom of the empty stage and the prospect of solitude, audience notwithstanding, prompts the performer (who is frequently also the writer) to express parts of his/her self kept hidden in more public situations. The variety of subjects that the monodrama generates helps redefine self and identity as the body metamorphoses into new, more varied personae.

Stella Kon's *Emily of Emerald Hill* details the life of a wealthy Singaporean woman, in all the guises she adopted – mother, daughter, wife, employer, friend. This monodrama uses voice and situational kinesics as well as proxemics to indicate shifts in Emily's persona. Although naturalistic to some extent, the play refuses to allow a simple viewing position, foregrounding instead its own metatheatrical frameworks through the motif of role-playing. In summarising the different levels of performance/reception Jacqueline Lo observes that:

> *Emily* . . . revolves around the notion of 'seeing' and 'being seen'. The audience is reminded of the multiple levels of reflexivity at any one point in the performance. . . . [W]e are aware of the metacharacter Emily who is highly conscious of the surveying glance of the players in her life (and this

includes the audience), and who in turn scrutinises them in order to create various personae to match their individual and collective needs.

(1992: 126)

Overall, Kon's play decentres notions of the unitary subject by staging the ways in which the body is inscribed and transformed in the nexus of actor/character/audience interaction. George Seremba's *Come Good Rain* (1992) works in a similar way by using a single, constantly transforming body to present the various selves of George: the story-teller, the son, the student, George Bwanika, the political satirist, the exile in Kenya, the teacher, the erstwhile political protester, the prisoner marked for death, the escapee from the apparently inescapable graveyard of the executed in Namanve Forest in Uganda, and the exiled playwright living in Canada. In this case, however, George also plays the narrator and other characters; hence, the play combines both models of monodrama, and the performing body resists categorisation by re-enacting almost all possible representations of the Ugandan colonial subject.

Plays which use one actor to embody multiple characters usually aim for fluid action and role changes in order to emphasise the performativity of the body and thus to frustrate viewers' desire for a fixed and unitary subject. In Australia, Sarah Cathcart and Andrea Lemon's plays, *The Serpent's Fall* and *Walking on Sticks* (1991), both performed solely by Cathcart, rely on staging location, kinesics, linguistic modifications, and musical codings to signify shifts in character. These characters, however, are never entirely distinct because the actor's body always carries traces of other figures into her depictions of any one. Each play portrays about five different women, and as Cathcart demonstrates their varied personalities, she also plays out a multiplicity of representations of Australian women, particularly in *The Serpent's Fall* which gives more or less equal exposure to characters of different ages, including an Aboriginal woman, and a Greek migrant. Margo Kane's *Moonlodge* (1990) works in much the same way, but maintains a narrative focus on a young native Canadian woman who plays many other characters (male as well as female) as she recounts her travels and the growing social and cultural awareness they created in her. The play establishes a deliberate performative tension between the central character, Agnes, and the various

234

others that Kane manifests onstage. These plays use the stage extensively so that the lone actor's body occupies all proxemic locations at some point. The body takes on a much larger, more malleable form than that normally conveyed by the flesh and blood dimensions of an actor confined to one naturalistic role. This stretching of the borders of corporeality not only claims theatrical and, by implication, cultural space for the post-colonial subject, but also expresses his/her expansive and flexible identities. The strategic use of form emphasises the manipulations of the body on stage, as simultaneously split and multiple subjectivities develop into sites that disrupt the coloniser/colonised binary.

Other transformational figures that challenge the conventional body politics of western theatre include the trickster and the dreamer. While the Afro-Caribbean trickster, Ananse, (rooted in the Ghanaian Ananse tradition), usually *enacts* his/her subversiveness through language, the Amerindian trickster tends to *embody* subversive (and regenerative) power – at least in theatrical contexts.[20] This magical character maintains the spiritual energy of its native community, functioning as what Daniel David Moses calls a 'harmoniser', despite (and because of) its tendency to create chaos and/or engage in deliberate mischief (1994). The trickster evades and disrupts all conventional categories, including those corporeal hierarchies upon which various forms of discrimination are based. Neither specifically male nor female, the trickster's androgyny breaks down binary figurations of gender and thus *defers*, rather than *defers to*, gender-based authority systems. This figure also traverses the human/non-human divide by taking on the 'body' of animals[21] or other totems, or by metamorphosing into figures from the supernatural world. Shape-shifting, unbounded, timeless, and indestructible, the trickster is an ideal character through which to present the theatricalised body of the post-colonial subject. In performance, trickster transformations often structure the dramatic action as well as effecting and/or expressing the spiritual renewal of both the fictional community, and, potentially, the audience. Moreover, such transformations challenge conventional paradigms of spectatorship as the appearing and disappearing trickster traverses the stage, occupying all areas physically and psychically, in order to elude visual reification.

In Moses's re-working of the Orpheus and Eurydice legend, *Coyote City* (1988), the trickster takes the form of the dead man, Johnny, who functions as a bridge between the spirit and the human worlds. Invisible to the play's remaining characters, this trickster is thoroughly embodied for the audience as the culturally alienated 'Indian' who haunts (in both senses of the word) the bars of urban Toronto. Instead of merely representing the stereotype, Johnny functions as a figure whose paradoxical absence/presence directly challenges viewers to consider the ways in which native peoples are rendered in/visible in mainstream culture. In other plays by indigenous Canadians, the trickster continually transforms into figures from the narrative past, from mythology, or from the characters' fantasies. The most theatrically adventurous example to date occurs in Highway's *Dry Lips Oughta Move to Kapuskasing* in which Nanabush's transgressive agency derives largely from 'her' outrageous corporeality. Not only does the trickster body transform native experience, as discussed earlier in reference to the rape scene, but it also violates a number of social/performance taboos when, for example, Nanabush appears naked or sitting on the toilet, impervious to the audience's embarrassed gaze. Such gestures combine abjectivity with a predatory sexuality to unsettle the social order of both the dramatised community of men and the community of viewers watching the play. Maintaining her site (a huge balcony) above the rest of the action, the trickster overtly controls the overall performance just as a puppeteer manoeuvres his/her marionettes.

The Australian Aboriginal 'dreamer' is also a spirit with transformative powers. Usually accompanied by clapsticks and the music of the didgeridoo, the dreamer appears as a (male) dancer who is only visible to the audience and to certain chosen characters. He represents the pre-contact past (when traditions, laws, and taboos were observed without the interference of white society) and functions dramatically to highlight the destruction of Aboriginal culture that has ensued since European settlement. This emphasis on the past does not mean, however, that the dreamer is fixed in time and place; rather he is a timeless figure situated outside, and in opposition to, the bounded and quantifiable spaces of western empiricism. As a bridge to the ancestral world, the dreamer's tasks include 'dancing' the spirit of a dying person back to the land of his or her individual dreaming. Performatively, the dreamer embodies indigenous tradition since he is costumed, adorned, and otherwise marked (usually with ceremonial paint) as a cultural icon that signifies Aboriginality. Like the North American trickster, the Aboriginal dreamer performs subversively as he claims all areas of the stage, his dance reinforcing the tangible *presence* of the Aboriginal past in spite of western encroachment upon indigenous time and space. Davis's *The Dreamers* centralises its spirit character for precisely this purpose: while the derogated body of Uncle Worru is prominent at the level of realistic action, the metamorphic body of the dreamer supplies a surrealistic frame that stresses the persistence and resistance of Aboriginal culture. At times, the dreamer also temporarily imbues the ill, diseased, or frail human body with 'super-human' strength. Sally Morgan's *Sistergirl* (1992), for example, features a scene in which the dreamer enables a bedridden Aboriginal woman to dance through the hospital ward in a vigorous movement that transcends the limitations of her ailing body and thwarts attempts to regulate it within the western medical system.

Although Maori spirits are less well-defined into a character type, they also make their presences apparent on New Zealand's stages. The spirit, Rongo, who oversees the transfer of land from Maori hands to Pakeha title in Rore Hapipi's *Death of the Land* is seen only by the audience; he acts as a conscience, a story-teller, and a dissenting voice who communicates to the audience the significance of such land sales. Hone Tuwhare's *In the Wilderness Without a Hat* features several actors as Maori warrior statues/spirits who have lost their names through time and the influence of the Pakeha culture. Their presence enlivens the refurbishment of the marae (community network and meeting house), as well as intensifying the loss of the *whakapapa* (genealogy preserved through oral transmission). That these Maori 'statues' are fully embodied on the stage signifies more than just the entry of indigenous actors into the previously white dominated theatre: the Maori bodies are also invested with history and spirituality. Here, as elsewhere across a range of post-colonial performance texts, the metamorphic body transforms itself into numerous shapes that help to rework imperialist systems of representation and to develop more inclusive and culturally specific depictions of identity.

DANCING BODIES

In many cases, transformations of the post-colonial body are theatricalised through rhythmic movement such as dance, which brings into focus the performing body. We have already discussed ritual and carnival in this context, and indigenous theatre's various spirit figures provide further examples of highly physicalised

237

Plate 10 Michael Fuller performs as the dreamer in Jack Davis's
The Dreamers
Source: Reprinted with the permission of Currency Press, Geoffrey Lovell, and
Michael Fuller. Photo: Geoffrey Lovell

performances which are often shaped into some kind of dance. As a culturally coded activity, dance has a number of important functions in drama: not only does it concentrate the audience's gaze on the performing body/bodies, but it also draws attention to proxemic relations between characters, spectators, and features of the set. Splitting the focus from other sorts of proxemic and kinesic – and potentially, linguistic – codes, dance renegotiates dramatic action and dramatic activity, reinforcing the actor's corporeality, particularly when it is culturally laden. Dance is a form of spatial inscription and thus a productive way of illustrating – and counter-ing – the territorial aspects of western imperialism. Dance's patterned movement also offers the opportunity to establish cultural context, particularly when the dance executed challenges the norms of the coloniser. In this way, dance recuperates post-colonial subjectivity by centralising traditional, non-verbal forms of self-representation. Situated within a dramatic text, dance often denaturalises theatre's signifying practices by disrupting narrative sequence and/or genre. Dance thus draws attention to the con-structedness of all dramatic representation, suggesting that it can function as an alienating device in the Brechtian sense.[22] This argument calls for analysis of dance's ideological encoding, a project which is of considerable importance in the criticism of post-colonial texts. While dance can act as an immediate metaphor *for* certain cultures, dance – along with other kinds of movement – can be figured as more deeply significant for and in itself.

A number of plays centralise dance thematically as well as performatively. In a potent image of the diversity of Guyanese society, Ian McDonald's *The Tramping Man* opens with a crowd of dancers whose presence on stage imbues the performance with an energy that carries through the subsequent naturalistic scenes. Like other Caribbean Carnival plays, this text presents dance not only as an expression of individuality but also as an equaliser, a physical and social force which erodes hierarchies even as it foregrounds the specificity of the various participants. Despite their differences in race, class, occupation, gender, and age, the dancers enact a vision of unity, however utopian. It is therefore not surprising that they represent a threat to the governing authorities whose ability to maintain rule is dependent on social divisions and conflict. Discursively, those in power trope dance as a form of contagious possession: it invades the body, dislodging 'normal' behaviour patterns and overriding all sense of decorum. For the colonised subject, such anarchy can be both liberating and dangerous, as the closing moments of McDonald's play suggest when the dancing crowd becomes the site of a bloody massacre. This scene constructs dance as inseparable from life itself so that all energy is drained from both the fictional community and the performance text as the dance is brought to a dramatic halt. In his short but disturbing play, McDonald delivers a potent protest against an authoritarian system which cannot understand or accommodate overtly physical expression.

By encoding identity through movement, dance often functions as a mode of empowerment for oppressed characters, particularly when their attempts to articulate themselves verbally have been compromised by the imposition of an alien language. The widespread use of dance in indigenous drama testifies to its communicative power and subversive potential. It is important to remember, however, that movement, like language, never exists in a vacuum; it is always influenced by other theatrical sign-systems (such as costume) and interpreted according to ideological biases. Movement forms used for performance are also subject to change over time and as a result of experience, both at the broader level of culture and, more specifically, at the local level of theatre. In post-colonial contexts, traditional styles of movement are often hybridised with western form and fashion, so that the dance presented to the audience is less a reified 'traditional' art than a staged artistic process. This does not mean that such movement no longer functions as an act of cultural retrieval or that it becomes a sign of acculturation; instead these hybrid dance forms express a multi-faceted identity which takes account of tradition while refusing to be locked under the sign of 'authenticity'.

Bran Nue Dae is a valent example of a contemporary Aboriginal play that avoids privileging so-called pure forms of dance over more hybrid or syncretic ones. Not only does the performance text present modern disco, rap, and minstrel routines, along with corroboree dances and classical ballet,[23] but it also appropriates and parodies many of these dance forms while fusing styles in ways which multiply the coded articulations of the body. That all of the characters, even the white policemen, present themselves at some point in and through dance routines illustrates the importance of movement in constituting identity. The hybridising process ensures, however, that neither Aboriginal nor European forms of movement are constructed as closed systems. The tendency towards visual satire, particularly of western dances, reveals as well an oppositional current beneath apparently hegemonic forms. Even tribal dances are enacted with a degree of mockery but for quite different purposes: the corroboree, for example, is staged less as a sign of black identity than as a recognition, through self-conscious parody, of the ways in which the dancing black body has been looked at in the discourses of theatre, film, and especially tourism. Overall, the play uses dance to foreground the vitality of its characters who together form the collective 'body' of contemporary Aboriginality, a concept/identity that always remains negotiable within the framework of the performance text.

As a medium which easily accommodates adaptation and change, dance offers particular opportunities for staging the body in theatrically spectacular ways. The signification of many forms of dance in South Africa has changed considerably, as the gumboot dance – itself a hybrid creation that is an effect of apartheid – amply demonstrates. As Glasser explains in the stage directions for the gumboot dance in the play, *King Kong* (1959):

> Originally a Zulu tribal dance, it was practised in secret by pupils of a mission school near Durban during a time when local tribal dances were forbidden. Eventually it found its way into Durban and became a favourite among the dock labourers who performed it in the rubber boots supplied them as protection when handling chemical cargoes. The new effects obtained by the slapping and pounding of rubber boots made it a popular dance with labourers everywhere, especially on the Witwatersrand where it has been developed to a high degree of perfection in the compounds of the gold mines and the municipalities. The dance is divided into a number of separate routines, each with a name such as 'Salute', 'Horse Ride', 'Shoot'. It is accompanied by a loosely improvised guitar melody and the convention today is to use it as a means for all varieties of comic and satiric expression.
>
> (1960: 61)

One group of artists has reworked gumboot dancing to generate a form that is particularly appropriate for post-apartheid South Africa. Jazzart, a group of about twenty artists of varied racial and performance backgrounds, actively work to combine dance forms in their productions. Their 1994 trio of pieces was composed of performance styles that thematically and physically suggested ways of achieving social integration without erasing differences. A modern dance about a mixed-race romance followed a contemporary evocation of Cape Carnival Parades, popular entertainments in which gaily uniformed musicians parade their group's distinct music through the streets, particularly at New Year celebrations, competing against other Carnival groups for audience adulation. The main dance piece was a hybridised gumboot dance accompanied by Ravel's *Bolero*. The gumboot dance is a syncretic form – even the boots' embellishments are created from scrap metal, particularly soft drink cans and bottle caps. In this case, the use of *Bolero* broadened the musical range and, in combination with a dizzying array of dance and movement styles, removed the dance from its mining origins. Rather than an appropriation of miners' entertainment by more privileged performers, Jazzart's gumboot dancing represents the complexity and vitality of post-apartheid society. Such 'indigenised' syncretic forms – often combining jazz, classical, ballet, modern dance, traditional gumboot work, and Indonesian and Hindu dance, performed by racially diverse bodies whose choreography also allows for jazz-like 'riffs' in the movement – are a valuable performance tool in contemporary South Africa. Given the country's massive illiteracy and eleven competing languages, dance will likely become a crucial performance art that can partly bridge some of these gaps.[24] Gumboot dancing is already legendary on the stage, having been popularised by the highly successful 1959 musical, *King Kong*, which toured London as well as all South African centres. Maishe Maponya's more recent play, *The Hungry Earth* (1979), also stages gumboot dancing as a mode of protest against pass laws.

While the dancing body is by no means confined to the specific functions outlined here, these examples illustrate its importance to post-colonial theatre. Interpreting dance as a text in itself – and as part of a play's overall semiotics – provides an approach to drama that denaturalises notions of subjectivity as grounded primarily in dialogue. Dance thus emerges as a locus of struggle in producing and representing individual and cultural identity. As a site of competing ideologies, dance also offers potential liberation from imperialist representation through the construction of an active, moving body that 'speaks' its own forms of corporeality.

Plate 11 Jazzart performs the gumboot dance, Cape Town, 1994
Source: Reprinted with the permission of Alan Lawson. Photo Alan Lawson

FRAMED BODIES

How and what the performing body signifies are closely related to the ways in which it is framed for the viewer's consumption. The most obvious framing, costume, is particularly resonant since it can (mis)identify race, gender, class, and creed, and make visible the status associated with such markers of difference. The paradox of costume's simultaneous specificity *and* versatility makes it an unstable sign/site of power. In other words, items of clothing have quite specific connotations but these can be easily changed, extended, or inverted with a change in the wearer and/or the situation. Costume, then, occupies a complex position in the theatre's semiotic systems: while it acts as clothing for the actors and a means of setting the mood and/or period of the play, it also functions as a loaded and problematic signifier, an aspect of costume which is generally not acknowledged in western (naturalistic) drama. A deliberately politicised approach to costume recognises that its apparent neutrality in fact conceals a rhetorical power, both as a semiotic code and in its close relationship to the body. Perhaps more importantly in post-colonial theatre, costume enables subversions of colonial status. Like dance, costume can point to cultural *difference* without necessarily maintaining cultural *distance*: for example, the paint on the dreamer's body in Aboriginal drama quickly moves from being 'exotic' or 'other' to 'natural' in the context of the play and, perhaps, outside the theatre. In this case, the presentation of a 'traditional' costume performs a recuperative function, just as the use of ritual masks and clothing in African or Indian drama confirms the validity of pre-contact performance modes. Alternatively, clothing can be foregrounded as a representational sign with particular biases. This approach is equally important to post-colonial dramatists since imperial discourse often uses costume as a marker of difference to designate levels of 'humanity' whereby the 'civilised' can be distinguished from the 'savage' by the clothes they wear. Oppositional re-workings of this trope involve a specific focus on ritual/cultural aspects of costume as well as on its connotative functions.

Further subverting possibilities lie in cross-gender or cross-cultural dressing. In many post-colonial plays, dressing up in the other's clothing provides a central spectacular moment that can repoliticise costume, culture, and even bodies. When the coloniser wears the clothes of the colonised without cultural sensitivity, his/her body is marked by its continued appropriation of otherness. The destabilising force of costume is even more obvious when the colonised subject wears the costume of the coloniser, particularly when the former dresses 'up' or chooses a garment that exceeds his/her assigned status within the colonial hierarchy. Cultural cross-dressing and dressing 'up' enact the dressing down of sartorial and cultural limitations by fabricating self-conscious strategies for resisting the power inherent even in the coloniser's dress codes. Costume actively addresses the definition of colonised corporeality and can be used to resist hegemonic locations of the body.[25]

The old adage that 'clothes make the man' (or woman) is exploited to full effect in David Diamond's *No' Xya'* in order to demonstrate the ways in which the body is indelibly marked by what it wears. A further focus on how costume is interpreted by those who seek to exercise control over the colonisable body adds to this text's critique of imperial discourse. On a performative level, the ever-present ceremonial regalia of Chief Guu Hadixs is, in itself, a 'character' with considerable visual impact and the capacity to execute a range of theatrical functions. As the dialogue makes explicit, his Robe of Power is 'alive' with the strength of many previous chiefs and it must not be treated lightly (1991: 82). When the various actors take on the Chief's costume, they are invested with its spiritual and physical powers, both as performers of, and characters in, the play. Here, costume actually determines corporeal identity rather than serving as a secondary code or an adjunct to other embodied signs. Thematically, *No' Xya'* reiterates the close links between costume's literal and symbolic functions when the Christian missionaries demand that the natives burn their traditional 'heathen' clothes in order to enter into so-called 'civilisation' (ibid.: 62). The colonisers' assertion that the ceremonial regalia confirms an attachment to 'pre-historic' customs shows only too clearly how imperialist cultures use dress to signal certain categories, patrol the boundaries between them, and so verify orders of social privilege. For the indigenous community, on the other hand, these costumes act as a positive force, not least because they maintain vital links with tradition.

The 'civilising' intent of European-style clothing is an issue that is often taken up in a more overtly parodic form. To interrogate the ways in which costume is interpreted by those who seek to exercise control over the colonisable subject, Robert Merritt's *The Cake Man* makes an explicit point of showing how the Aboriginal body has been captured and contained by western dress. The protagonist, a tribal black who has been shot dead, 'awakens' and literally steps into the shoes of a stereotype after he discovers a pile of European clothes, and eventually, with some comic experimentation, puts them on to re-name himself 'The Australian Aborigine . . . made in England' (1983: 12). The subsequent narrative details what becomes of this culturally commodified 'artefact' in the contemporary era. A related form of the acculturated native – what Spivak has termed the 'domesticated other' (1985: 253) – is the colonised subject co-opted into imperialist systems of authority. In this respect, clothing such as military, police, or guard uniforms not only neutralises the threat of otherness but also signals categories of privilege which often intersect with and complicate other cultural classifications. In South African drama, for instance, wearing a police uniform does not make a black man white, but it does remove him from the same class as his fellow blacks. Percy Mtwa's *Bopha* (1985) clearly illustrates this through the figure of Njandini, who, by virtue of his uniform, finds himself ambivalently positioned between black and white antagonists. Relegated to a neither/nor category, he is thus open to abuse from both 'colour' groups.

Many African plays use western dress to signal acculturation with its concomitant dilution of traditional values. Such dress often indicates the wearer's obsession with fashion and wealth, and his/her scorning of Africanness. In *I will Marry when I Want* (1980) by Ngũgĩ wa Thiong'o and Ngũgĩ wa Mĩriĩ, the *nouveau riche* businessman (who makes his money by exploiting farmers) and his family are dressed in expensive, western clothes which initially signal hypocrisy to Kĩgũũnda, the farm labourer at the centre of the action. The play, which deals with economic and social manipulations effected by Kenyans in the wake of the British colonisers, establishes those Kenyans who have attempted to exploit others for their gain as untrustworthy and, ultimately, unpatriotic and imperialist. Eye-catching western clothing is one of the signifiers of such exploiters. In an effort to fit in with his friends' new-found wealth and importance, Kĩgũũnda, who has been dazzled by material goods, agrees to have a Christian wedding ceremony, complete with a white dress for his wife, Wangeci, even though they have been married for twenty years. Assuming that the wedding clothing will remake them into the suave, westernised couple they wish to be, they fail to recognise how ridiculous they look. More significantly, their new location between cultures (signified by clothing) is now deemed hypocritical to the independence of Kenya. Seduced by the European clothes her new wealthy boyfriend buys her (as well as the signifying power of his own expensive clothing), Gathoni, their unmarried daughter, becomes pregnant. The social scandal which ensues breaks the spell of European materialism on Kîgûûnda and Wangeci, and the western clothing becomes equated with a denial of local culture. The play's costuming 'transgressions' – reading western dress as 'wrong' – are determined by its distinctions between African modes of dress and a European or American fashion dictum.[26] They are also the result of conscious and constant change since the signification attached to a costume sign must be frequently established and re-established. That which signifies wealth and fashion in one play or year may be *passé* in the next; costume, as a signifier of the post-colonial body, therefore requires frequent updating, re-evaluation, and careful acknowledgment of cultural specificities.

When a colonised subject wears the dominant culture's costumes, s/he is never simply framed by and within imperial representation. Most often, some kind of appropriation is at work so that imposed or adopted dress codes, like hegemonic language(s), are changed or otherwise 'indigenised' in order to suit their new context. Even in situations which seem to present a simple case of acculturation, there is always a disjunctive gap between western clothes and their colonised wearers, especially when the usual race or gender significations are complicated rather than clarified by dress. Because it is in a position to manipulate costuming codes, theatre praxis can exploit this gap to foreground the ideological apparatus of representation itself. *Bran Nue Dae*, for instance, features a number of 'dominant' costumes – worn variously by Aboriginal and white characters – which allow for the effective subversion of imperial authority through the visual excesses of the carnivalesque. A case in point is the habit of Father Benedictus, who cuts a ridiculous, larger than life figure in his platform shoes, overall mitre, and cassock embroidered with the wrappers of a popular chocolate bar. The play concludes with the cast donning land-rights T-shirts, thus demonstrating the potential politicality of costume. A land-rights T-shirt signifies at least twice in performance: as a costume, it is part of the *mise-en-scène*, but as a political statement, it is a more potent and immediate reminder of the white theft of black land and of general Aboriginal disinheritance. A similar costuming strategy occurs in *Ktshaa, the Sound of the AK* (Zambuko and Izibuko 1988), a play which calls for freedom for blacks in South Africa. The simple costume worn by each cast member is either a T-shirt or a dashiki emblazoned with the continent of Africa over which is superimposed an AK–47 gun and the onomatopoeic word, Ktshaa. In this case, the political stance of a group of people who are determined to meet armed struggle with armed struggle is mirrored by the polemical costumes which stand in for military uniforms and signify just as potently.

Another crucial way in which the theatrical subject is framed is in/through the spectator's gaze which can hold and maintain the body in a position of subservience. The audience necessarily gazes at the spectacle on stage, but implicated in that action of watching theatre is an authoritarian gaze of watching *over* other(s). This kind of authoritarian gaze is precisely what characterises 'looking relations' between the coloniser and the colonised. As Bhabha maintains, the imperial gaze marks out the colonisable subject 'as a fixed reality which is at once an "other" and yet entirely knowable and visible' (1983: 23). Through networks of representation and surveillance, imperialism thus reproduces the other as an object of knowledge/power. How then can the theatre stage any kind of empowering subjectivity when the person who gazes tends to hold the power? This issue is problematic since it is through imperialism's scopic regimes as much as through its linguistic and physical domination that the colonised subject is denied power. The gaze therefore becomes a site for post-colonial resistance, and if theatrical representation means to undermine its authority, performance must somehow engage with the looking relations it establishes.

The gaze has been explored most notably in the context of feminist film theory/practice, not least because of Laura Mulvey's landmark analysis (1975) of the ways in which the camera constructs a specifically 'male' gaze in narrative cinema. The theatrical gaze, however, is not as regulated as a cinematic gaze, where the viewer is generally locked into the camera's viewing pattern. In live performance contexts, the gaze is immediately different, since, as Elin Diamond notes, 'Film semiotics posits a spectator who is given the illusion that he creates the film; theatre semiotics posits a spectator whose active reception constantly revises the spectacle's meaning' (1988: 88).[27] In post-colonial theatre, that revision of the spectacle's meaning materialises from, among other things, an attempt to subvert or escape – or at least to compromise – the usual patronising and objectifying gaze of the coloniser over the colonised. The ways in which the performance event focuses the gaze are, then, very important. Often it is the body itself, rather than the words, which works to maintain the attention of the audience. The active or decorative body in particular (that moving, dancing, and/or costumed body) generates immediate interest and engagement. The sightlines of the set and the configuration of the entire auditorium (as opposed to the more obvious camera lens in cinema) also subtly contribute to the direction of the audience's gaze.

Numerous feminist post-colonial plays interrogate the gaze of men (and women) at the staged female body in an attempt to prevent the (dominant) audience's unproblematic consumption of the theatrical spectacle. The issues of body, gaze, and power are productively combined with an exploration of race and gender in Djanet Sears's *Afrika Solo* (1987). In trying to establish a site in England and Canada for her own blackness, Djanet, the central figure, is constantly aware of the ways in which she is positioned as an object of scrutiny within predominantly white societies. Transformed by a journey to Africa which helps her to escape the imperial gaze and to situate herself outside that gaze, Djanet is able to reconstitute a fully embodied subjectivity: 'The base of my whole culture would be forever with me. And the funny thing is, it always had been. In my thighs, my behind, my hair, my lips. . . . Dorothy Dandridge, eat your heart out, I am beautiful' (1990: 91, 93). By directly engaging with the economy of power implicated in the gaze – as it is exercised through the discourses of both television and theatre – *Afrika Solo* establishes the black body as a focal point not of curiosity or of lecherous desire but for the deconstruction of white culture and looking relations. In doing so, it reconstructs histories and identities in the context of popular culture. As Djanet adds to her costume of jeans and a T-shirt the Boubou and head-dress that she has brought back from Africa, the audience watches this gradual accumulation of cultural objects which normalise (rather than exoticise) her Africanness, centralise popular cultures, and deconstruct colonialist history. The performance text presents a multiply positioned subject who insists on acknowledging all of the competing identities through which notions of the 'self' are constructed and articulated. The spectacle of such hybridity, as Bhabha argues, displays the necessary deformation and displacement of all sites of discrimination and domination. It unsettles the mimetic or narcissistic demands of colonial power, but re-implicates its identifications in strategies of subversion that turn the gaze of the discriminated back upon the eye of power.

(1985: 97)

The character, Djanet, also usefully explicates Elin Diamond's distinction between the looked-at-ness of the filmed female (Mulvey's construction) and the 'look*ing*-at-being-looked-at-ness' or the 'looking-ness' (1988: 89) of the staged female. By adding to her costume throughout the play, and by rehearsing and altering her identity and character, Djanet's performative presence refuses capture and containment by any one of the signifying codes through which she is constructed – in favour of the totality – while highlighting the importance of the female body in its changing context.

One of the most prevalent ways through which to subvert the gaze is by means of a play-within-a-play, a device which carefully focuses the audience's attention, while, paradoxically, fracturing assumed unitary sightlines. In this kind of metatheatre, the viewer watches several events at once (one within another), observing action and reaction in a process that not only shatters any illusion of the collectivity of the audience's responses, but also demonstrates the obvious political power involved in deconstructing assumptions of authority *on stage*. A play-within-a-play disperses the centre of visual focus to at least two locations so that the viewer's gaze is both split *and* multiplied. The ensuing double vision (a vision which is at least doubled) provides a way of re-visioning the entire spectacle as the audience watches the play *and* the play-within-a-play *at the same time* as it watches the actors watching the inner play. It follows that a play-within-a-play always creates a dialogical tension between the various levels of performance: it mimics and reflects the original (either the original action or the original text) and it refracts the entire text's meaning. As well as illustrating Bhabha's concept of the 'sign of double articulation' (1984: 126) in which the words of the colonised 'speak twice', plays-within-a-play demonstrate a split specularity that forms a location of difference: the two object sites of the gaze can never be identical. The refracted play-within-a-play thus has the potential to articulate a different interpretation of events, or to de-emphasise the power of axiomatic ways of seeing.

250

The split gaze also has the potential to activate a considerable resistant energy. In Athol Fugard's *The Island*, Winston and John use theatre – and thus metatheatre – on at least two levels as a survival tool in prison. Firstly, the pair play an improvisational game that not only keeps them sane in the notorious Robben Island prison but also allows them to rehearse alternative identities. This level of self-reflexive performance, which is intended only for John and Winston themselves (and of course the audience), enables the pair to escape – even if only for short periods – the surveillance of Hodoshe, the unseen guard. The second level of metatheatre arises from a more obvious source: the play-within-the-play. While his fellow prisoners perceive that complaining about the food is the only possible form of protest available to them, John teaches Winston to 'read' *Antigone* as a means of resisting the penal system. Whereas the improvisational game evades Hodoshe's gaze, the *Antigone* play subverts his gaze, while ironically being caught in it. The multi-layered performance text shifts the gaze from the unfamiliar (as Hodoshe laughs at Winston playing a prisoner in a dress) to the familiar when the theatre audience – but not Hodoshe – recognises the political significance of Antigone's speech in the South African context. Since John and Winston's *Antigone* also targets an unseen group of prisoners and guards as spectators, the *theatre* audience is uncomfortably co-opted to 'play' the absent *stage* audience. Hodoshe is a constant presence on the stage, surveying the audience which is also positioned within the prison panopticon. Hodoshe's specular gaze is, however, fractured by a complex system of intersecting gazes including those between guards and prisoners, between guards watching the play and watching the prisoners, and between prisoners (played by the audience) watching the base and inset plays. Hodoshe cannot, then, observe everything; instead, the split gaze subverts the surveying gaze. Hence, *The Island*'s metatheatre creates a location from which it *is* possible to escape the authoritative gaze of apartheid's representatives. The play presents the prison panopticon which ostensibly defines the prisoners as those who are always watched; yet these prisoners devise a way – by means of metatheatre – both to escape the confining gaze and to implicate the audience in the looking relations sanctioned by apartheid.

In Louis Nowra's *The Golden Age*, the audience also becomes party to various types of watching and voyeurism: the characters watch a wrestling match, several inset plays, the behaviour of others in a 'scientific' context, and also more private 'performances'. Usually, the actor/character who watches the on-stage action holds the power, although this voyeuristic activity also returns the gaze to the potentially invasive activities of medicine, anthropology, and various other sciences. The dominant society's surveillance of the forest people often takes on an anthropological guise as their as yet 'undocumented' history becomes useful to social science (and divorced from the people themselves). The play shows that such scientific approaches make 'observing' clinical and more empirical, an act of aggression and control, rather than an attempt to understand the workings of the forest family. Imperialist forms of observation are compared to more playful (theatrical) forms – the forest people watching their own play is a case in point – and deemed inadequate and appropriative. This emphasis on mediated voyeurism layers the various types of metatheatre enacted in order to reinforce the multiple ways of establishing specular and spectacular resistance to the empirical world, and indeed the empire.

Derek Walcott's *Pantomime* also uses metatheatre as a way of challenging imperialist looking relations. In the attempt to establish a working pantomime text, each of the play's two men is required to watch the other's performative tricks as well as his version of *Robinson Crusoe*, and the gaze of the lone spectator on the lone actor soon becomes a power struggle. Whenever Harry Trewe feels threatened, he adopts the role of a film director whose active editorial eye attempts to shape the action and regain control of the gaze by harnessing the agency of the 'camera' and its associated representational systems. Yet Trewe is not filming, and the cinematic gaze is not the same as the theatrical one. Nor is the audience constrained by Trewe's point of view; instead it registers both 'sets of action' – along with their interaction – as a complex process which continually shifts the metaphorical balance of power. In short, the play dramatises in a theatrically innovative way the interplay between viewer and spectacle, showing that 'reality' consists of not only what happens but also how it is seen.

The ways in which the body is framed by and within the gaze determines, to some extent at least, how and what it can 'mean'. The gaze establishes – and frequently redetermines – the *loci* of authority. By revising the gaze – and frequently fracturing it – post-colonial performance can invest the audience with more substantial and varied viewing frames through which to reinterpret the site of colonial authority. As Howard McNaughton explains, there is only ever 'this impossible possibility of escaping from the constructions of Empire' (1994: 218). While the abject desire to escape the constraints of imperial surveillance may remain only an impossible possibility, the staged post-colonial body is one of the most malleable and resonant vehicles for subverting and problematising the roles of identity, subjectivity, and corporeality that colonialism has assigned to the colonised subject.

NOTES

1 See, among many other texts, Phelan (1992) and Goodman (1993).

2 Of course 'pure difference' is largely theoretical: as post-structuralism reminds us, difference is always relative since any concept is inseparable from the apparatus against which it is defined.

3 To a certain extent, indigenous theatre in settler societies such as Australia, Canada, and New Zealand assumes a 'majority' audience and is often therefore in the position of having to validate its subject matter and approach (see Van Toorn 1990 on the politics of minority texts and majority audiences). In contrast, much African, Caribbean, and Asian theatre stages racial issues less overtly, presenting the non-white subject as already 'naturalised'. South African drama, inevitably inflected by apartheid, focuses most insistently on race, often regardless of expected audience composition.

4 This was not always the case in New Zealand, where some Maori actors in the nineteenth century were less implicated in such representations.

5 Examples include Henrietta Drake-Brockman's *Men without Wives* (1938), Katherine Susannah Prichard's *Brumby Innes* (1972), and Thomas Keneally's *Bullie's House* (1980) from Australia; George Ryga's *The Ecstasy of Rita Joe* and Gwen Pharis Ringwood's *Drum Song* (1982) from Canada; and Bruce Mason's *The Pohutukawa Tree* from New Zealand. Many of these plays are thought to be crucial texts for their time and some are even considered revolutionary in their 'treatment' of indigenes. Their representations, however, are clearly limited to the white-constructed semiotic field charted by Goldie.

6 See, for instance, Kane's *Moonlodge*, Moses's *Almighty Voice and his Wife*, and, as a less obvious example, Highway's *Dry Lips Oughta Move to Kapuskasing.*

7 Calling on Fanon, Homi Bhabha distinguishes the 'fetish of colonial discourse' from Freud's sexual fetish, explaining that:

> Skin, as the key signifier of cultural and racial difference in the stereotype [of race], is the most visible of fetishes [as opposed to the secrecy and hiddenness of a sexual fetish], recognised as 'common knowledge' in a range of cultural, political, historical discourses, and

plays a public part in the racial drama that is enacted every day in colonial societies. (1983: 30)

In this scene, Davis is playing with the possibilities that the black body on stage can present in both colonial and post-colonial contexts.

8 This term covers a variety of politically engaged 'deviant' sexualities. Sex-radical performance enables a critique of dominant or prescriptive regimes of gender/sexuality. Subjects explored include performance which figures lesbian, gay, and bisexual issues and/or other aspects of transgressive sexuality such as striptease, prostitution, and transvestism.

9 The women/land trope is variously figured as positive and negative. See, for instance, Kolodny (1975), Montrose (1991), Schaffer (1988), and Van Herk (1992).

10 See Sharpe (1991) for an analysis of the ways in which race problematises many western feminist assumptions regarding rape.

11 See Rabillard (1993) for an extensive discussion of the motif of 'absorption and elimination' in Highway's plays and its relationship to transformation.

12 This emphasis on masculine aspects of fertility is also evident in *Jokumaraswami* (1972), by the Indian writer, Chandrasekhar Kambar. To prepare for the *Jokumara Hunnive* fertility festival, women fashion clay phalluses and rub butter on the tips in order to increase their chances of successful pregnancy. The women themselves are of little consequence to the festival.

13 Boehmer also discusses how female (and some male) post-colonial writers have identified problems in equating the fecund woman with a united national image (1993: 271).

14 Existing, in Kristevan terms (1982), between the subject and the object, the abject expresses a desire to transcend the site of conflict by means of expulsion and/or corporeality. The body in post-colonial drama is a product of endeavours to fix varied expressions of the other's corporeality; the post-colonial abject exists in traces of what is unreconciled in the subject's object, or in coloniser/colonised depictions of self and other. The post-colonial abject can thus be described as that which is repudiated, expelled, and/or loathed (including the self). It remains at the borders of the new signification, threatening destabilisation. As the space between a newly constituted self and its threatening borders, the abject manifests itself in the body's staged presence. The grotesque body in Nowra's plays is one such site of representation.

15 See, for example, Watney (1990), Sontag (1978), and Tiffin (1993b). AIDS is a recent example of an infectious disease which has been constructed to demonise particular social groups (homosexuals) and various non-western regions (especially central Africa and Haiti).

16 Solitary confinement is usually only metaphoric in these dramas: rarely does prison theatre actually present a lone actor occupying the stage. Two exceptions, both from New Zealand, are John Broughton's *Michael James Manaia*, a prison drama of sorts, and Owen's *Te Awa i Tahuti*,

consisting of one prisoner and one counsellor. Some characters in other plays choose the solitary confinement of silence.

17 In some countries, the construction of nationalism has been so all-encompassing and so firmly entrenched that post-colonial discourse is perceived – erroneously – as contradicting the political agency of nationalism. New Zealand could be read as a country where nationalism (particularly a form that has absorbed Maori heritage for Pakeha consumption) is said to oppose post-colonialism even though both discourses employ similar tropes to strategically define the New Zealand self/identity in relation to New Zealand history, geography, and politics.

18 Australia's particular colonial history is also manifest in plays which foreground some kind of incarceration (sometimes in an asylum), often through allegorical narratives where imprisonment resonates with the unnamed/repressed trauma of convictism. See Kelly (1990) for further discussion of this issue.

19 Plays in which much of the narrative action centres on absent characters include Kevin Gilbert's *The Cherry Pickers* (1971), Dennis Scott's *An Echo in the Bone*, Judith Thompson's *Lion in the Streets*, and Patrick Yeoh's *The Need to Be* (1970).

20 This is not the case in other genres such as fiction and poetry, where the Amerindian trickster is often what Cox calls a 'word warrior against colonization' (1989: 17). See also Babcock (1985) and Vizenor (1989) on trickster discourse in the North American context.

21 Moses remarks that while non-native actors generally find it extremely difficult to become animals, this transformation is relatively easy for indigenous people who see the natural world as family (1994).

22 For an extended analysis of dance's signifying functions in drama, see H. Gilbert (1992b).

23 Classical ballet, complete with the usual costumes of that genre, was added to the 1993 production of the play.

24 Likewise in the Caribbean, dance integrates a linguistically divided population as evident in a number of regional theatre events which include performers from different islands.

25 See, for example, the ways in which cross-dressing is figured in Gaines and Herzog (1990), Garber (1992), and Ferris (1993). Brydon (1994), Low (1989), and Tompkins (1996) address the issue of post-colonial cross-dressing.

26 Make-up, an adjunct of costume signification, is also subject to post-colonial theatrical subversions. In *Otongolia* (1985) by Alakie-Akinyi Mboya, the use of western women's face make-up, which literally marks the body, however temporarily, is even more closely implicated with attempts to deny Africanness. The frequent re-application of lipstick identifies Oting as a woman who is seeking assimilation with the west at the expense of all Kenyan customs.

27 Diamond's use of the gendered pronoun is deliberate here, based on Mulvey's gendered gaze construction.

6

NEO-IMPERIALISMS

The power of our hands goes to feed three people:
Imperialists from Europe,
Imperialists from America,
Imperialists from Japan,
And of course their local watchmen.

(Ngũgĩ wa Thiong'o and
Ngũgĩ wa Mĩriĩ 1982: 35–6)

The insidious effects of post-enlightenment European imperialism are not only impossible to eradicate completely, as we have argued throughout our study, but they can also be complicated by other kinds of cultural domination which coexist with, result from, or are superimposed upon the original imperial order. In some cases, colonial relations between Europe and its periphery are now less central than those between relatively 'new' world powers (such as the United States) and other (particularly 'third world') nations. Certain forms of regional colonialism have also become significant, especially in areas where western nations are geographically proximate to non-western cultures – Australia's colonial activity in the Asian-Pacific area is a case in point. Internal manipulations of socio-economic power by different cultural groups within a nation can add to these more recent instances of colonisation. As a result, the centre-margin model for understanding imperialism can be problematic and, at times, inadequate, since many current forms of cultural domination intersect and interact. Post-colonialism as a theory and practice designed to include these various neo-imperialisms in its address must therefore become genuinely multi-discursive in order to deal with increasingly complex hierarchies of power.

While 'neo-imperialism' suggests new or current kinds of cultural domination, the term should not be understood merely in temporal frames of reference. In some instances, there is no clear

256

delineation between 'past' and 'present' forms of imperialism but rather a continuation of historical oppressions, or a legacy of connection between a colony and its former imperial power. Nevertheless, the ways in which cultural hegemony is exercised and the effects of its imposition often alter considerably over time. Further changes in the coloniser/colonised dialectic are inevitable when new imperial powers emerge, even if some of their practices replicate those of the recently dismantled European empires. In order to isolate such changes for discussion within the rubric of our overall approach to post-colonial drama, we use 'neo-imperialism' to cover situations in which the most significant coloniser is not Britain (or one of the former European powers) but some other nation or cultural group.[1]

In many respects, the emergence of modern neo-imperialism is directly related to European invasions of much of the world. The rise of the United States as a superpower was predicated on the colonisation of the north American continent, the decimation of its indigenous peoples, and the migration or transportation of a substitute population/culture. Similarly, European imperialism is at the root of other historical 'anachronisms' including the evolution of Canada as a nation comprised of mainly Anglophone and Francophone cultures, and the development of Australia and New Zealand as predominantly western countries. While some of these 'settler' cultures are now ideally positioned to exert power at a regional level – and, in the case of the US, at a global level as well – other ex-colonies (particularly in Africa and the Caribbean region) are often vulnerable to new forms of economic, political, and ideological domination precisely because they have endured centuries of European governance.

Although neo-imperialism also institutes unequal relations of power between cultures or groups, it tends to operate in less formalised and more covert ways than the imperialism which has spawned most of the drama and theatre discussed thus far. Whereas European empires maintained a stranglehold on their colonies through military force, many current forms of hegemony depend on economic and/or political pressure. In general, colonised countries no longer endure external control of their political regimes, but this does not guarantee autonomy. Many Caribbean, Central American, and South-East Asian countries have been (and in some cases still are) subject to the rule of puppet leaders installed and manipulated by major world powers such as the United States. Likewise, although educational systems in non-western regions are no longer controlled by distant administrators, they often remain geared towards perpetuating imperial culture while preparing students for university entrance in western countries. It could be argued, then, that neo-imperialism is even more insidious than overt domination because its hegemony often masquerades as a form of aid, advice, or non-partisan support. The notion of 'world responsibility'[2] is particularly relevant in this respect since it has been used to rationalise all manner of neo-imperial activity, including numerous US military interventions in 'third world' conflicts.

The intersection of various forms of cultural and political domination means that most hierarchies of power are now less stable and more complex than ever before. Nevertheless, neo-imperialism is marked by a number of features that have remained relatively constant over time and in different situations. In particular, race-based discourses are common to almost all forms of imperialism and continue to instigate or justify specific social and/or political orders. Since cultural power is largely concentrated in the west, such discourses have led to the consistent othering of non-western societies, a process greatly facilitated by the globalisation of the (western) media.

One of the most entrenched race-based discourses to affect contemporary neo-imperialist constructions of the non-western world is orientalism, which can be defined as the 'science' of studying, classifying, and speaking for the Oriental subject. In his landmark analysis of this ancient practice, *Orientalism* (1979), Edward Said exposes the ways in which Europe has historically constructed the Orient – sometimes termed the 'east' in opposition to the 'west' – as an other that is defined by European fears and desires. Depending on the particular context, the Oriental has been variously figured by the ostensibly neutral occidental observer as lazy, dirty, corrupt, lecherous, perverse, backward, and, most frequently, silent. This discursive means of control is not, however, merely historical: it is wide-ranging temporally and geographically so that the Orient can include all of Asia, parts of the Middle East and northern Africa, and some Pacific islands. The primary function of orientalism is to fortify European identity by setting up an other which operates as the west's 'contrasting image, idea, personality, [and] experience' (Said 1979: 1–2). The western subject can then be civilised, intelligent, sexually restrained, sophisticated, industrious, and moral. The east/west package of predetermined signifiers continues to be exploited in Hollywood cinema and other forms of popular culture, as well as in the news media. For example, during the 1990–1 US Desert Storm military offensive designed to 'protect' Kuwait from Iraq, then-president George Bush used orientalist rhetoric to sway public opinion to support his aggressive attack on a country which had previously been an ally of the United States. Even his unconventional pronunciation of 'Saddam' with the accent on the first syllable (instead of on the second) evoked the 'sadism' frequently linked to the Orient as a site of sexual degeneration and licentious behaviour. Equally problematic in such language usage is the implied construction of the occidental as 'normal', a moral benchmark.

Said's work on orientalism is useful to a post-colonial critique of contemporary cultural power, even though some theorists have expressed reservations about the implicit binarism of his model of east–west relations, and/or about his concept of orientalism as a monolithic discourse which allows little scope for subversion or contestation (see Porter 1983; Bhabha 1983; Parry 1987). In particular, Said's construction of a dichotomy between the European and the Oriental begins to break down when it is applied as a method for understanding relations between Asian countries and settler-invader societies such as Australia whose position as a new Asian-Pacific imperial centre is always compromised by its own history of colonisation.[3] Despite these limitations, Said's self-consciously political investigation of sites of otherness constitutes an important intervention into discursive forms of western power/ knowledge. Moreover, his discussion of the ways in which the Orient has been exoticised (and feminised) is pertinent to current debates about cultural authenticity. Like other race-inflected discourses, orientalism denies the colonised subject self-determined constructions of authenticity/authority by bestowing on him/her a reworked, European version of what authenticity *ought* to be. Once this is exposed for what it is (and is not), another – equally damaging – form of authentication can take place. As Rey Chow explains, contemporary criticism of imperialist discourse often reinscribes alterity even as it attempts to dismantle prejudice:

> Because the image, in which the other is often cast, is always distrusted as illusion, deception, and falsehood, attempts to

salvage the other often turn into attempts to uphold the
other as the non-duped – the site of authenticity and true
knowledge.

(1993: 52)

In other words, over-compensation does not solve the problem,
especially since it can amount to the same authoritarian gesture
which informs orientalism. Chow continues:

Our fascination with the native, the oppressed, the savage,
and all such figures is therefore a desire to hold on to an
unchanging certainty somewhere outside our own 'fake'
experience. It is a desire for being 'non-duped,' which is a
not-too-innocent desire to seize control.

(ibid.: 53)

This fascination with the 'native' is not focused exclusively on
so-called Oriental subjects; it continues to inform western
approaches to much of the third world, and is particularly prominent in the discourses of tourism, one of the more insidious forms
of contemporary neo-imperialism.

If various neo-imperialisms have redrawn socio-political boundaries and/or reinscribed certain privileges, they have also spawned
renewed resistance to hegemonic systems. Post-colonial plays
which respond to this situation use many of the narrative and
performative strategies we have already discussed, and share an
interest in history, language, and the body as sites of negotiation
and struggle. As part of their engagement with neo-imperial discourses, such plays frequently exhibit an acute cognisance of the
ways in which the western media produces transnational images
that define and delimit certain groups. This chapter surveys some
dramatised responses to contemporary cultural domination under
the intersecting categories of internal, regional, and global neo-
imperialism. A final brief focus on tourism as a special area of
investigation returns our discussion to the 'looking' relations
implied by theatre itself as a site of representation.

INTERNAL COLONIALISM

The vexed question of authenticity has special significance in
heterogeneous nations where varied cultural groups vie for recognition and political representation. In settler societies, a recent
generalised movement towards the recuperation of indigenous

cultures has often led to new forms of imperialist appropriation, if ones that lean towards political correctness. In New Zealand, for example, many Pakeha have embraced Maori history, iconography, and religion, not always in an attempt to understand Maori people, to make amends for past injustices, or to forge a new hybrid nation, but more often to claim an authenticity that Pakeha culture seems to lack (see Ruth Brown 1989). Chow's solution to this kind of neo-imperialism is a total reconstruction of images of the native: 'the agency of the native . . . needs to be rethought as that which bears witness to its own demolition – in a form which is at once image and gaze, but a gaze that exceeds the moment of colonization' (1993: 51). In this formula, the gaze 'makes the colonizer "conscious" of himself' as image maker (ibid.: 51), and so enables the dismantling of one-dimensional stereotypes. Like the staged versions of the gaze discussed in Chapter 5's analysis of body politics, Chow's concept is inherently theatrical. Its agency as a defence against imperial prescriptions of authenticity is evident, for example, in Margo Kane's *Moonlodge* which makes western viewers conscious of their position as potential members of the 'famous Wannabee tribe' of white North Americans who attempt to appropriate native spirituality (1992: 290).

In settler cultures, ongoing negotiations of identity are not exclusively the precinct of indigenous peoples. Various groups of migrants (including original European settlers) are also engaged in cultural struggles inflected by past and present forms of imperialism. Sneja Gunew calls for a thorough examination of such struggles, arguing that the burgeoning of academic discourses which deal (belatedly) with native issues absolves Anglo-Australians (and to a lesser extent, Anglo-Canadians[4]) from having to analyse the various internal colonisations specific to their nation (1993: 449). Gunew's observation seems particularly relevant in relation to non-indigenous, non-western minority groups which represent small percentages of national populations and which therefore find it difficult to access political power. When these minorities do demand attention, their protests are often muted by an imperialist system which reads all manner of opposition through racist stereotyping.

Sharon Pollock's *The Komagata Maru Incident* (1976) replays one historical instance of internal colonialism in Canadian society and uses this to comment on contemporary race relations. The play dramatises, in agit-prop style, an incident in which East Indian

British subjects with their immigration papers in order were denied their legal right to disembark in Vancouver. As a result of a bureaucratic standoff with Canadian officials, the potential emigrés were stranded aboard a freighter in Vancouver harbour, and denied food and fresh water until they agreed to return to their homeland. Although set just before the outbreak of World War One, the play is clearly informed by more recent debates about ethnicity in Canada, and, quite probably, by the anti-Sikh demonstrations in Vancouver in the 1970s. In her deliberately politicised treatment of the incident, Pollock exposes the racist attitudes of a white society bent on maintaining cultural homogeneity; she thus debunks the myth of Canada as a democratic nation that has always encouraged cultural diversity. The play also reveals the dominant society's attempts to construct the East Indians as objects of both fascination and repulsion. While they are seen as diseased and immoral, they nevertheless provide a compelling form of public entertainment, as suggested by the narrator's ironic spiel: 'Hurry! Hurry! Hurry! Absolutely the last and final chance to view the Komagata Maru! . . . Ladies and gentlemen, can you truly afford to bypass this splendid spectacle?' (1978: 41). By positioning the audience as uncomfortable voyeurs in a carnival side-show, Pollock's play critiques contemporary neo-imperialism at the same time as it stages the orientalist tropes through which the East Indians were historically constructed. According to Robert Nunn, this strategy forces a recognition that Canada's cultural composition has been *chosen* rather than constituted by fate: 'As an audience, we are alienated from our automatic acceptance of the predominance of "the White Race" in our country: it didn't just happen; choices were made and continue to be made to maintain it' (1984: 57).

Canada's most prominent internally colonised group is, of course, the French-speaking minority which is located primarily in Québec. Economically disadvantaged and constantly facing the threat of cultural and political domination by Anglophone Canadians, many Québécois have become vocal advocates of regional autonomy as the only solution to a protracted and often bitter debate about their position within Canada.[5] While the long-running conflict between Anglophone and Francophone communities has its historical roots in the political wrangling between France and Britain in the heyday of European empires, it has evolved into a specifically Canadian problem which can be analysed under the rubric of neo-imperialism. A number of playwrights have taken up the issue of Anglophone–Francophone relations in Canada, often in the form of some kind of debate about linguistic and cultural identity. During the 1970s in particular, Québec theatre was passionately engaged in a search for appropriate stage languages/images through which to express the experiences of French Canadians.[6] Much of this theatre responded not only to Anglo-Canadian hegemonies but also to French and American influences on Québec culture. Along with Michel Tremblay, dramatists such as Jean Barbeau and Jean-Claude Germain rejected classical French models of theatre (and standard versions of the French language) in favour of a culturally specific tradition fully adapted to the contingencies of Québec's positioning within Canada.

Barbeau's *Le chemin de lacroix* (1970) focuses explicitly on the political and cultural implications of language usage in Québec. Written in response to police suppression of protests against a government bill allowing Québec Anglophones to send their children to English schools, the play criticises the cultural elitism that deprives many Québécois of a secure identity. Here, and in later works such as *Ben-Ur* (1971) and *Le chant du sink* (1973), Barbeau illustrates the adverse effects of foreign cultural influences on Québec society. Likewise, Germain's historical plays – particularly *Un pays dont la devise est je m'oublie* (1976) and *A Canadian Play/Une plaie canadienne* (1979) – attempt to recuperate Québec culture from the margins of dominant myths of nationhood. Both playwrights use *joual* extensively in their work, which is characterised by an emphasis on non-naturalistic theatrical techniques. Their preference for Brechtian styles of performance suggests an attempt to politicise representations of internal colonialism in Canada. Tremblay's drama is also thoroughly imbued with a post-colonial consciousness, even when it appears to focus on other issues. Tremblay himself alludes to this in a discussion of his 1974 play, *Hosanna*, about a transvestite hairdresser:

> [Hosanna] always wanted to be a woman who always wanted to be an English actress in an American movie about an Egyptian myth in a movie shot in Spain. In a way, that is a typically Québécois problem. For the past 300 years we were not taught that we were a people, so we were dreaming about being somebody else instead of ourselves.
>
> (qtd in Benson 1985: 95)

Other Tremblay plays – *A toi pour toujours, ta Marie-Lou* (1971) is a case in point[7] – have also been read as allegories of Québec's struggle to assert political and cultural autonomy.

David Fennario, an Anglophone Montréal playwright, provides a different perspective on marginality through his class-oriented analyses of Québec society. In *Balconville* (1979), often hailed as Canada's first truly bilingual play, he stages the parallel stories of an English-speaking family and their French-speaking neighbours in a working-class suburb of Montréal. The performance text's emphasis on bilingualism breaks down linguistic hierarchies by presenting French and English as theatrical languages with equal agency.[8] On a thematic level, however, the play stresses that language is a site of difference which is itself the cause of cultural distance between various characters despite their common socio-economic circumstances. Whereas *Balconville* suggests that the linguistic gap between Anglophone and Francophone society is the root cause of their conflict, a more recent bilingual play, Marianne Ackerman's *L'Affaire Tartuffe, or, The Garrison Officers Rehearse Molière* (1993), deconstructs binary oppositions between French and English speakers. Set largely in 1774 when the Québec Act[9] was about to be passed, the play presents the story of a group of would-be actors who are preparing to stage Molière's *Tartuffe* at a garrison town in Lower Canada. This level of action is framed by a modern-day narrative which introduces the characters who will replay their historical counterparts in a projected movie about the 'business' of rehearsing *Tartuffe* during a period of political upheaval. All characters at both levels of action speak in French and English, often within the one sentence. While the specificity of each language is recognised, sometimes through debates about the pros and cons of using either one, there is no attempt to set up any kind of linguistic or cultural schism. In fact, Ackerman states in her introduction to the play that she specifically aims to break down the myth of a society divided along one simple axis:

> The reality of Quebec is and always has been much more dynamic and symbiotic than the internalized, polarized snap-shot of two solitudes, backs turned, guns pointed. As a ruling metaphor, two solitudes is not only too simple for the way things are, but useless as a guide through the chaos of life.
>
> (1993: 12)

Ackerman's vision of the 'dynamic' and 'symbiotic' nature of Québec society is fully realised in *L'Affaire Tartuffe*, both theatrically and thematically. Instead of making a simple call for peaceful co-existence between Anglophone and Francophone Canadians, the play suggests that the two cultures are neither discrete nor separable. For the bilingual, bicultural Canadian, identity then becomes a matter of strategic choice.

Choice (or rather the lack of choice) is precisely the issue fore-grounded in a number of Malaysian and Singaporean plays which are designed to protest against the authoritarian national governments which have replaced British administrators in the post-independence period. In Malaysia, despite paying lip-service to the idea of cultural heterogeneity, the ruling Malay elite have enshrined the Malay language, culture, and (Islamic) religion as the valorised norm through government policies that systemati-cally disadvantage all other racial groups not considered to be authentic or *bumiputera*.[10] Singapore, in contrast, has attempted to forge a single, multi-ethnic society but this strenuously pursued agenda is sometimes just as constricting since it is predicated on inflexible, state-defined notions of national identity which tend to subsume cultural differences. Both countries have rigid censor-ship laws which in turn often lead to self-censorship as playwrights cut and tailor their work in order for it to be produced in its intended medium.

Kee Thuan Chye's *1984 Here and Now* (1985) deals with the issues of racial hegemony and police brutality in Malaysia. Loosely based on George Orwell's novel, the play transposes its model's class-based critique into an agit-prop theatre piece that implicitly equates Orwell's party of oligarchs with the privileged Malay elite and his proletarians with the non-Malay underclasses. Less emphasis is placed on the need for individual freedom than on the rights of disadvantaged groups – basically all non-Malays – within the society. There is, however, a nominal 'hero', Wiran (modelled on both Orwell's Winston Smith character and on the traditional Malay hero, or *wirawan*), who begins to question his privileged position as a Malay intellectual after he becomes involved with a subterranean resistance movement. As well as dramatising Wiran's struggle to move beyond the limits of race-based discourses, the play presents scenes which take up issues such as Islamic fundamentalism, the marginalisation of non-Malay cultures, discriminatory legislation, and censorship.[11] In performance, cross-gender and cross-race casting were used to disrupt essentialist representations of difference, while shadow puppetry and gamelan music were combined with various Brechtian techniques to produce a highly politicised text rooted in local experience. In its appropriation of Orwell's work, Kee's play can be seen as counter-discursive to both British imperialism and to the internal colonialism which was partly intended as a corrective to the cultural denigration that was a legacy of British rule. This double articulation of resistant discourses is evident, for instance, in the play's linguistic structures, as Jacqueline Lo notes:

> The discourse of linguistic containment [in *1984 Here and Now*] points to a historical interstice. As a post/neo-colonial juncture, the irony of Standard English representing the present dominant position of Bahasia Malaysia is unmistakable to a local audience. Both languages signify discourses of domination based on myths of racial essentialism and cultural hegemony. Seen in this light, the use of 'pidgin' English by the Proles . . . can be read as a strategy of displacement and subversion of the official language by means of abrogation and appropriation.
>
> (1995: 234)

At the performative as well as at the thematic level, Kee's play thus disrupts dominant discourses to call for a conceptual restructuring of national identity.

Theatrical responses to internal manipulations of cultural power are widespread in other former colonies[12] but the examples given here will suffice to illustrate some of the more notable features of this particular form of neo-imperialism. Perhaps more importantly, these examples suggest ways of undermining both subtle and overt manipulations of power that are often exercised during the post-imperial period in the very name of decolonisation and nation building. As Bhabha asserts, 'Counter-narratives of nation that continually evoke and erase its totalizing boundaries – both actual and conceptual – disturb those ideological manoeuvres through which "imagined communities" are given essentialist identities' (1990: 300). While a genuinely multicultural approach to the ongoing process of decolonisation seems to offer the only viable step forward, it may be wise to maintain some reservations about such approaches, at least in their official versions. In reference to Canada and Australia, Alan Filewod argues that although

Plate 12 1984 *Here and Now* by Kee Thuan Chye. Director: Krishen Jit
Source: Reprinted with the permission of Kee Thuan Chye

government policies on multiculturalism are partly 'intended as the final stage of repudiating the imperial tradition', they none the less function as a way of 'defining the conditions of national distinctiveness and imbuing the state with a national mission' (1992b: 11). It is therefore important to remember that all post-colonial societies have their own internal centres and peripheries, and that discourses of nationhood are sometimes continuous with the epistemologies of imperialism.

REGIONAL NEO-IMPERIALISM

A country's geographical position often affects its potential to exert power over other cultures, or, alternatively, to resist the effects of neo-imperialism. Many of the Québécois plays discussed in reference to internal colonialism also express an urgent imperative to reject the influence of American culture and, more specifically, certain forms of American theatre. Québec's proximity to the United States has meant that its (desired) cultural identity often conflicts with its economic reality. As Jacques Godbout argued in 1980, 'our ideas might come from France but our myths, our credit cards, our comfort, come from the United States' (qtd in Weiss 1983: 68). Indeed, the economics and politics of Canada as a whole have long been inextricably bound up with those of the United States, a situation likely to become even more complex as a result of the North American Free Trade Agreement ratified in 1993.[13]

Regional factors have played a significant part in Australia's participation in various neo-imperial activities. Although a relatively minor player in world events, Australia has been able to exercise cultural, economic, and military power over some of its Asian-Pacific neighbours because of its positioning as a western country in a predominantly non-western region. In many cases, British and/or United States governments have authorised (or at least implicitly supported) the exercising of such power. These colonial and neo-colonial 'allies' have not only strengthened Australia's military ability to colonise other cultures, they have also given it a convenient alibi for its actions.[14] At the same time, the fact that Australia is a resource-rich country with a comparatively small population has led many inhabitants to fear invasion by Asian countries. This attitude, partly a function of racism and xenophobia, has led to an extremely complex political situation in which the positions of coloniser and colonised are often highly unstable. Current interactions between Australia and Japan (and similarly New Zealand and Japan), for instance, are influenced by a number of factors and cannot be described simply in terms of an occidental/oriental binary. In particular, Japan's economy and its position as one of Australia's most important trading partners subverts the paternalistic notion of an underdeveloped 'east' and a developed 'west'. In fact, recent Japanese investment in Australia (viewed by some people as economic imperialism) has played a significant role in Australia's development, particularly in the manufacturing and tourism sectors. Despite, and because of, its economic success, Japan has become a site of ambivalence for most Australians who must admit a grudging respect for the Japanese even while they consistently construct them within orientalist discourses. This situation would seem to modify Said's contention that 'Orientalism depends for its strategy on [a] flexible *positional* superiority, which puts the Westerner in a whole series of possible relationships with the Orient without ever losing him the relative upper hand' (1979: 7).

Australia's participation in the Vietnam War is one instance of its neo-imperial activity in Asia. Of the plays which deal with this subject,[15] Rob George's *Sandy Lee Live at Nui Dat* (1981) provides the most thorough-going indictment of Australian (and American) attitudes towards the Vietnamese. The play's narrative action focuses largely on the anti-war protest movement but also includes a number of scenes set in a soldiers' camp at the battlefront. No Vietnamese characters actually appear on stage; the emphasis is on how these 'others' are constructed and positioned by the Australian soldiers and the western media. In this respect, the play invokes orientalist discourses in order to deconstruct them. Consistent with orientalism's attempt to feminise the other and so render him/her conceptually colonisable, both the protesters and the soldiers figure Vietnam in feminine terms: 'she' is passive, weak, largely silent, and available for sexual exploitation. In an agit-prop performance put on by student radicals to protest against American imperialism in Asia, Uncle Sam leans over Vietnam (played by a woman) and aims a revolver at her head. The gender codes of this sketch are abundantly clear: male America stands poised to rape and/or murder a female Vietnam. Similarly, the soldiers' responses to Vietnam are expressed in terms of race and gender stereotypes, but with more emphasis on the sexual allure of the Asian other who is exoticised, fetishised, and denied

269

subjectivity. The fact that one soldier does not even know the name of his Vietnamese lover, whom he plans to take back to Australia, suggests that he regards her as a commodity to be imported at will. A slightly different kind of commodification is exposed by the mercenary's 'business' dealings which involve, among other things, a drug-smuggling racket. Through such characters, the play positions the Australian soldiers as anti-heroes whose invasion of Asia is the predictable outcome of a wider desire for self-authentication through conquest of the passive Oriental other. That this orientalist fantasy devolves into a 'bad trip' is one of the major ironies of the Vietnam experience.

Australia's dominance over nearby Pacific islands, a number of which have been under its governance at some point, has been much more 'successful' – at least from the colonisers' point of view. Papua New Guinea, originally comprised of territories annexed by Britain and Germany, came fully under Australia's administration in 1949, a situation reluctantly sanctioned by the United Nations.[16] Prior to this, white Australians had regularly recruited (or 'blackbirded'[17]) labour from the island, and had also secured various property interests there. In many ways, Australia's neo-imperialism in Papua New Guinea duplicated the main features of British imperialism in the occupation colonies: the local populations were inevitably constructed as heathen savages who were simultaneously child-like and dangerous, and, above all, in need of paternal guidance in order to enter into the modern, 'civilised' world. In combination, teachers, missionaries, government agents, and multinational companies promulgated western value systems while frequently exploiting Papua New Guinea's natural wealth. This situation, along with the country's geographic proximity to its former coloniser (unlike Britain's *distance* from most of its former dominions) has led to an especially difficult process of decolonisation in the post-independence period since 1973.

One of the most significant effects of neo-imperialism in Papua New Guinea and other Pacific islands has been the cargo cult[18] which can be loosely described as an expectation that ancestral spirits will return in ships or aircraft carrying goods which will provide for the needs of cult followers. Many cult religions in the region had traditionally fostered a belief in the imminent distribution of food and other riches by the ancestors. This belief becomes a point of confusion and disappointment at the moment of contact with the west when trade goods are proffered to indigenous peoples and, in particular, when Christianity entices them with heavenly riches. Not surprisingly, the promise of these metaphoric riches, combined with the introduction of manufactured items which would have been entirely unfamiliar to local populations, led many people to have unrealistic expectations of a cargo delivery of western goods and appliances that would alleviate their relative poverty. Anger and disillusionment were the understandable responses when the cargo failed to materialise.

Several Papua New Guinea plays explore the origins and effects of cargo cults in an effort to realign local expectations while exposing the damage caused by western interventions in local religions, economies, and culture. Turuk Wabei's *Kulubob* (1969) stages the story of a traditional cult centred on Kulubob the Creator, who returns to his people periodically to bestow on them fruit, vegetables, fair weather, and the promise of plenty. On his second visit, he is expelled from the village for having violated the incest taboo by marrying his sister, but this does not necessarily diminish his power or importance as a cult figure. In fact, he is expected to return one day bringing gifts that will make up for his transgressions and reward the villagers for their suffering. The play thus resituates the cargo cult in a specific tribal history while delivering to its audience a moral lesson about appropriate forms of marriage. Moreover, it concludes with a scene which shows how traditional cult practices have been realigned according to the contingencies of western imperialism: a missionary arrives in the village, stands in Kulubob's place, and begins to distribute trade goods before opening up his Bible to preach to the amazed and excited villages who clearly mistake him for their great ancestor. The final chant, 'Cargo for all', also contemporises the play with a call for more equitable distribution of wealth.

Whereas *Kulubob* ends at the moment of contact between Christianity and local cult religions, Arthur Jawodimbari's *Cargo* (1971) illustrates the ways in which the subsequent meshing of two sets of similar (yet also highly dissimilar) beliefs is destined to create chaos, disappointment, and feelings of exploitation. This short play takes place in the Northern District of Papua in the early twentieth century, after a Christian mission station had been established in a village of the Pure people. Two members of the tribe who have a limited capacity to read English find cargo boxes labelled 'Pure Soap' and deduce that the missionary, Albert

Maclaren (whom they trusted) has been stealing the goods which their ancestors have sent to them. Devastated and angry, the villagers meet to determine a plan of action for dealing with what they perceive to be exploitation. Dubo, whose son was recently killed by a volcano, presents her dream about him as a solution to their problem:

> [My son] said that we must not work for the white man. He said we must build big canoes of our own, and sail to where the sun rises. He said we will come to a place where sky and sea meet, and there we will climb up a ladder to Heaven. In Heaven are all the things we want. We'll carry them down the ladder, we'll load them into our big canoes, and sail home.
>
> (1971: 16)

To this traditional reading of the tribe's spirituality is added Dubo's own interpretation in light of the recent events: 'Only white men's ships go there; but when our relatives send our goods with them, the white men steal them. Our son promised they will make many more goods for us, by magic rituals' (ibid.: 16). Already introduced to Christian beliefs, this misperception of the white men's motives/actions is intensified by Maclaren's departing prayer for the villagers when he abandons the mission because his safety is compromised: 'Almighty God, giver of all good gifts and lover of all mankind, fill these thy people with heavenly grace, so they may live peacefully' (ibid.: 19). The cargo cult exists here as a problem of language and translation: heavenly grace and good gifts become translated as heavenly goods on earth. As well as failing to appreciate the linguistic *and* cultural misinterpretations that have occurred, Maclaren does not recognise the ways in which the Christian religion has been interpolated into local belief systems: instead of whole-heartedly accepting Christianity, the Pure people inevitably understand it and practise it in the context of their own spirituality. To clearly indicate the chronology, Dubo's dream and the village's decision to accept it as a solution is situated before Maclaren's prayer. This cult does not suggest the stupidity or naiveté of the Pure people; rather, it indicates the insensitivity of the whites who neither understand local traditions nor appreciate the unsurprising assumption among the Papuan people that wealth will be shared equally. The action concludes with the villagers taking up arms (spears against the whites' 'magic sticks') to defend themselves, regain their dignity, and liberate the 'cargo' they perceive the whites to be hiding from them. The play's setting – almost one hundred years ago – suggests that this conclusion can only be read ironically: the colonisers are never going to release the cargo. By implicating the missionaries in the cargo cult, however, Jawodimbari's text exposes the detrimental effects of western culture both in the past and, by analogy, in the contemporary period.

Tony Strachan's *Eyes of the Whites* (1981) uses the cargo cult as a potent metaphor through which to enact a more extensive critique of Australian neo-imperialism in Papua New Guinea.[19] The play opens with the sound of an aircraft and a brief spotlight on Juna, a native woman who awaits trucks and electrical appliances for her people as her just reward for years of service to an Australian family during their protracted stay in her country. The closing image shows Juna enraged and disillusioned when it becomes clear that all her sacrifices have led to nothing. These framing scenes create an allegorical context for the central action which focuses on the exploitative activities of Tom Lashwood, an Australian doctor-cum-politician. The idea of the cargo cult is woven into the main narrative from its beginning when Tom appears for his campaign speech dressed as Santa Claus, and then proceeds to distribute gifts in a clear bid to buy votes. In performance, Tom's costume functions as a visual hook reminding the audience of Tom's masquerade and heightening the sense of political satire. Even though her own son is campaigning with the opposing Pangu Party for political self-determination, Juna persuades the crowd to vote for Tom (who is her boss) because she has internalised his prejudices and so maintains that her people are not ready for self-government. Her firm belief in the cargo cult has also led her to surmise that Tom's daughter, Sera, whom she has practically raised from childhood, is her own murdered daughter reincarnated to help her secure cargo. Juna's version of a campaign speech clarifies what she expects Tom to provide once he is elected: 'Vote for me, Masta Tom, and I will give you white man's magic. I will bring trucks, iceboxes, record machines, na olgeda masin long wasim laplap. . . . Line up, line up for your nice Australian money' (1983: 38). Ironically, 'cargo' is being systematically stripped from the country through Tom's side-line export business which deals in valuable sacred artefacts. That a supposedly benevolent doctor is responsible for denigrating the indigenous culture and appropriating Sepik tribal land exposes the more insidious face of Australian neo-imperialism.

As well as presenting a trenchant criticism of the paternalistic relations instituted and perpetuated by the myth of 'development', *Eyes of the Whites* stages various overtly subversive scenes in which that myth is held up to question. For instance, two 'plays' are inserted into the overall action: the first, an appallingly amateur home video, shows the Lashwood family at leisure. The crass behaviour of the men in particular prompts Yulli, the visiting Nigerian World Health Organisation consultant, to ask, wryly, 'Is this typical of all Australian picnics?' (ibid.: 28). Yulli's ironic question situates the Australians as anthropological curiosities, neatly inverting the imperialist paradigm set up by the video, which includes some footage of native villagers. Susan Sontag's argument that photographic 'images transfix and anaesthetise' so that the camera becomes a kind of passport which annihilates moral responsibility (1973: 20, 41) is certainly evident in Tom's filming; but the play diminishes the authority of his scopophilia by turning the gaze of the camera back on the coloniser. In the second mini-play, Juna and Sera present a short dialogue, partly in Pidgin, that parodies a missionary's attempts to convert a young native girl to Christianity. The conventional racial roles are subverted by the fact that Juna plays the white missionary and Sera the native girl. Here, as elsewhere throughout the dramatic action, their relationship does not align with the approved imperial hierarchy since Juna is consistently positioned in the parental role when she teaches Sera Pidgin and tells her stories from the folk culture. Sera's failure to bring her 'mother' cargo when she returns from Australia after a long absence is thus seen as a callous betrayal. The play's ending stages the disintegration of colonial rule and, tragically, the psychological destruction of Juna, whose representative role as Papua New Guinea itself extends the significance of her breakdown, to further critique Australia's (sometimes well-intentioned) interference in the country. Strachan's use of performative devices such as local language and dance, along with his emphasis on the determined resistance of Juna's son, Peter, presages a possible resurgence of the indigenous culture but only without the patronising or appropriative 'help' of the Australians.

Papua New Guinean playwrights have also targeted Australian-imposed education systems as a divisive force which draws indigenous children away from their homelands to be seduced by western culture. At the high school level especially, children from remote villages often receive their education at boarding schools – in places such as Lae and Port Moresby, or in Australia itself – returning to their homes only for long vacations. The neo-colonial élitism that this arrangement can engender is based on a hierarchy of values which stipulates that village culture is outdated and that western education represents the only worthwhile repository of knowledge. John Wills Kaniku takes up this issue in *Cry of the Cassowary* (1969), which focuses on the return of three children to their village in Milne Bay. The play articulates its critique of the boarding-school system indirectly through the children's thought-less behaviour and, more explicitly, through the dialogue of one of the women, Sela: 'Every holidays when [the children] come home, they tell us how good and educated they are. And tell us how primitive we are. They talk to us as if we mean nothing to them' (1970: 16). At one point her daughter, Mebo, defends her education by explaining that she learns not only how to read and write the whiteman's language but also how to make baskets, mind infants, and care for sick people. The domestic nature of these lessons implies that the students are not being trained for a government or professional role, or – to Sela's disgust – even for village farming life. Sela emphasises that the colonial educators and administrators teach dependence, partly by breaking down family structures and traditional beliefs and practices. Her eldest son, Diko, attempts to hybridise the two cultures by claiming that the current generation of young students will eventually shape the schooling system; however, this foreshadowed inversion seems too distant to be credible and the play does not leave its audience reassured by Diko's optimism. Instead, the cry of the cassowary means death, a fate actualised by the death of the crippled boy, Pima, who refers metonymically to the indigenous culture at large.

In recent times, Papua New Guinea has developed a syncretic theatre practice which places more emphasis on local cultural forms than do any of the plays discussed above. Spearheaded by the Port Moresby National Theatre Company and the Raun Raun Theatre in Goroka, this movement towards cultural decolonisa-tion displays many of the characteristics discussed in reference to drama based on the traditional enactments of Africa and the Caribbean. Typically, plays are performed out of doors in market places, villages, school yards, and other venues not purpose-built for theatre. Dance, mime, music, costume, and language rhythms are rooted in Papua New Guinea's indigenous cultures, but are also often hybridised to produce new syncretic forms. An emphasis on collective collaboration as a basis for creativity situates this theatre firmly within a community model influenced by the theories of Grotowski and Brecht, and, more recently, by the folk opera tradition in Nigeria. One recent production, *Sana Sana* (1992) was devised by the National Theatre Company as a folk opera based on the legendary stories of the Milne Bay province.[20] Although its narrative derived from one particular area of Papua New Guinea, *Sana Sana* was designed as a cross-cultural event: it combined some western technology with performers and performance forms from a variety of the country's numerous and distinct indigenous cultures. According to Linda Schulz, this opera's 'synthesis of style and form works towards dissolving artificially imposed regional boundaries, through its recognition of both difference between and common concerns within diverse cultures' (1994: 48). Such theatre also inevitably works towards a cultural retrieval which counteracts the effects of Australia's neo-imperial activities in the region.

GLOBAL NEO-IMPERIALISM

The effects of regional neo-imperialism are magnified when a country has the means to assert cultural power at a wider level. Economic and military superiority are undoubtedly important in this respect, but it is largely the persuasive power of the media which effects and/or legitimates contemporary forms of global neo-imperialism. Said is not the first to argue that the emergence of the United States as the major imperial power in the twentieth century owes much to the globalisation of the media:

> This twinning of power and legitimacy, one force obtaining in the world of direct domination, the other in the cultural sphere, is a characteristic of classical imperial hegemony. Where it differs in the American century is the quantum leap in the reach of cultural authority, thanks in large measure to the unprecedented growth in the apparatus for the diffusion and control of information. . . . Whereas a century ago, European culture was associated with a white man's presence, indeed with his directly domineering (and hence

resistable) physical presence, we now have in addition an international media presence that insinuates itself, frequently at a level below consciousness, over a fantastically wide range.

(1994: 352)

This new discursive imperialism sets up relationships that are generally less formal than those established by the British Empire but no less profound in their capacity to determine the material and cultural parameters by which much of the world now lives. The largely US-controlled world media system has a tendency to produce discourses and images that reinforce hierarchies based on race, gender, ethnicity, religion, sexual preference, and class. The ongoing project of dismantling these hierarchies while maintaining cultural specificity is made all the more difficult by what Said calls 'the startling realities of human interdependence on a world scale' (ibid.: 401).

American neo-imperialism has been so widespread that it has spawned a body of post-colonial drama which itself could be the focus of an independent study. The examples chronicled here are merely intended to give some idea of recurrent tropes across some of the diverse regions affected. In Australia, the political, economic, and cultural influence of the United States has been an issue of concern to some sectors of the society for much of the twentieth century. Heated debates about the importation of American films in the 1920s suggests that the early impact of American hegemony was not confined to the political arena although various military alliances between Australia and the United States have undoubtedly had a profound effect on Australian culture. Towards the end of World War Two, for example, Australia's very small population was host to over a million American GIs whose 'invasion' was often regarded as both necessary to Australia's defence against the Japanese and detrimental to its moral and cultural integrity. This characteristic ambivalence towards the United States was subsequently exacerbated by the Vietnam War, which seemed to crystallise the dilemmas that Australia faced in aligning itself with a neo-imperial power whose influence was wide-ranging but always intended to serve the interests of Americans rather than Australians. In more recent times, American hegemony has been manifest most often in Australia's economic and cultural spheres and, in particular, in the arena of popular culture. As a result, a number of Australian plays rework and interrogate the conventions of Hollywood cinema, of Broadway theatre, and, more generally, of the US media in its various forms.[21]

Some of Australian theatre's more overt protests against US neo-imperialism occur in texts which combine an attack on American militarism (particularly in Vietnam) with a counter-discursive reworking of American models of popular culture. Barry Lowe's *Tokyo Rose* (1989), for example, uses the Broadway musical tradition to present a critique of American intervention in the Asian-Pacific region. Although set during World War Two and ostensibly about the trial of a Japanese-American woman suspected of treason, *Tokyo Rose* has the ambience of a Vietnam protest play. Its quasi-documentary structure and burlesque musical style invite a comparison with the agit-prop performance pieces that were common during the period of Australia's involvement in Vietnam. Moreover the play's portrait of a feminine Japan/Asia victimised by the menacing Uncle Sam replicates the iconography of the Vietnam protest movement. Lowe's inclusion of an Australian soldier as the adventitious 'innocent abroad', combined with costume and scene designs which emphasise the contrasts between the Aussie war uniform and the Yankee red, white, and blue, completes the picture of a refracted and displaced Vietnam narrative. Within this framework, the play criticises the Americans' treatment of Iva Toguri, the woman framed as Tokyo Rose, at the same time as it parodies American popular entertainment traditions, particularly through the figure of Carroll who wants to create a Broadway smash hit out of Iva's life. Carroll's dramatic vision, which expresses the western male fantasy of the fragile Oriental 'butterfly' at the mercy of her American captors, is clearly designed to expose his own racism/sexism. Constructed as the quintessential American con-man/entrepreneur, Carroll also contrasts with the naive Australian soldier who is thus excused for his complicity in Tokyo Rose's trial. Similarly, the presentation of Uncle Sam as Iva's corrupt and malicious prosecutor distances Australian audiences from the American-style (in)justice meted out by the judges, bureaucrats, and politicians whose prejudices deny her a fair trial. Always appearing in full stars-and-stripes regalia, Uncle Sam is both a grotesque parody of American culture and a potential threat to Australian autonomy. He therefore functions as a theatrical device which reassures Australians of their difference

278

from the neo-imperial centre. This emphasis on parody is a common feature in plays which respond to the Americanisation of culture, not only in Australia but also in other post-colonial countries.

Many Caribbean countries are particularly vulnerable to US neo-imperialism because of their small populations, their undiversified economies, and their reliance on US aid for development. Their proximity to the United States is also a key factor, especially when the available media is dominated by American programmes. In St Lucia, for example, only about 5 per cent of the television content is local (mostly regional news, weather, and current affairs), yet there are seventeen television stations available (mostly by satellite from the US) for a population of approximately 150,000.[22] Such situations, common throughout much of the Caribbean, result in the constant circulation of images and narratives that cannot represent the lived reality of most Caribbean people but which none the less affect that reality profoundly, often by making viewers acutely aware of what they 'lack' – in terms of material goods, technical expertise, cultural sophistication, and authenticity itself.

Set during World War Two, Sam Selvon's *Highway in the Sun* (1967) illustrates the initial impact of the US 'invasion' of the Caribbean. In the play, several market gardeners in rural Trinidad are compelled to relinquish their land so that American troops can build a road through the village to link their military bases. Although the villagers are compensated for their loss, the changes wrought by direct contact with US money/culture are clearly detrimental to the community, which is left with 'American dreams' of material wealth long after the troops have passed through. The Americans' presence exacerbates tensions among various members of the racially mixed community and deepens the rift between those who have some access to 'Yankee' money and those who have not. This rift is imaged quite clearly in the play's set by the partition which Tall Boy builds in his rumshop to screen his foreign customers from the local riff-raff. While it is a powerful sign of Tall Boy's capitulation to western capitalism, the building of the partition does not go unchallenged; instead, it initiates a debate on contemporary race relations, not just in Trinidad but in England and the United States as well. Such debates, expressed in the local vernacular and woven into the dialogue of a deceptively simple naturalistic text, subtly critique both western culture and its unspoken assumption that complex political analyses are only the precinct of the 'sophisticated' elite.

The American characters in Selvon's text are only rarely presented on stage; their relative absence undercuts the singular authority of the dominant culture even while demonstrating its effects on the local community. Likewise, the cheap baseball caps brought home by the villagers are both a metonym for the colonisers and a parodic comment on their crass commercialism. Except on a material level, the Americans' attempts to access the local culture are thwarted, especially when Tiger invites them to his earthen hut for an 'authentic' Indo-Trinidadian meal only to find that his wife, Urmilla, has borrowed the necessary utensils and furniture to make her guests feel more comfortable. Hence the play refuses to deliver to the Americans their version of the authentic/exotic. Despite the obvious negative impact of the Americans' brief stay, the community thus maintains some degree of autonomy. Even though old Sookdeo's death in a bulldozer accident functions as a potent reminder of the (sometimes unintentional) dangers of US imperialism, the play's ending implies that Tiger, unlike some of his friends, has learned enough of his elder's wisdom to recognise that the road/rhetoric of 'progress' leads to its own problems.

The often-invoked road is also a double-edged metaphor of progress in Walcott's hard-hitting farce, *Beef, No Chicken* (1981), a satire about the Americanisation of the Caribbean. In this case, 'development' is the prerogative of a local corporate giant, Mongroo, which is clearly intended as a parodic imitation of US multinational construction companies. Set in the small town of Couva in Trinidad, the highly improbable plot focuses on Otto and his family, whose Auto Repair and Authentic Roti shop is the last barrier to a new road planned by Mongroo and endorsed by Otto's fellow council members. Like most farces, *Beef, No Chicken* depends on stereotyping to set up sharply defined and immediately recognisable characters which critique certain aspects of society. As part of its protest against neo-imperialism, the play includes a number of figures seduced by the glamour, commercialism, technical expertise, and apparent authenticity of American culture: Otto's stage-struck niece, Drusilla; the smooth-talking, American-accented news-broadcaster, Cedric; a bribe-taking mayor who wants to run a community in which there are 'real'

(American-style) problems such as crime and industrial pollution; and Mongroo himself. While these characters are *framed* – brought into focus, contextualised, *and* regarded as suspect – by their own dialogue, other figures function as *framing devices* that provide a running metacommentary and/or an ironic perspective on the dramatic action. A case in point is the Limer[23] who shows absolutely no interest in taking a job or accumulating material wealth. Although he does not align himself explicitly with either the pro- or the anti-development group, the Limer's attitude is a direct affront to the promulgators of progress, as are his calypso and rap songs about the graft and corruption associated with Mongroo's project. Otto, one of the few who voice an open protest against so-called progress, is a more fully developed character although he is certainly not exempt from parody. At one point, in a somewhat farcical attempt to stop the project, he dresses up in women's clothes as the Mysterious Stranger – a figure which borrows from both the Midnight Robber and the Dame Lorraine mas' of Carnival – to haunt the construction site and thereby to convince the council that the project is jinxed. This futile gesture does not completely diminish his credibility; if anything, it foregrounds the tragedy of the 'little man' pitted against the corporate mogul. As director Earl Warner argues, 'The story is true for any developing society where choices are made in the name of progress and development at the cost of human life, leaving the pain of loss, the broken circle' (qtd in Stone 1994: 132).

By presenting the forces of neo-colonialism as not entirely external, Walcott is able to condemn mindless imitations of American culture at the same time as he illustrates the inappropriateness of that culture in a Caribbean context. The dialogue of *Beef, No Chicken* is liberally sprinkled with hackneyed catch-phrases – such as 'Building the nation' and 'You can't stop progress' – which are designed to parody local government policies and to draw attention to the incorporating universalism of the development ethos. Such phrases are also part of an overall linguistic structure which deliberately pits the clichéd expressions of the westernised characters against the rich speechifying traditions of the Caribbean in order to suggest that 'progress' leads to cultural impoverishment. As well as working against the inanity of imported rhetoric, local language forms often augment the play's direct attack on American culture as illustrated by the Deacon's declamation against the mad rush for malls, plazas, and expressways:

It's about McDonaldizing everything, it's Kentucky Frying
everything, it's about going modern with a vengeance and
televising everything, it's hamming up everything, traffic-
jamming up everything, it's about neon lighting everything,
urban-blighting everything. I'm warning you. I seen it with
my own two feet.

(1986: 204)

While similar warnings about the detrimental effects of industrialisation are reiterated at a number of points throughout the
text, Walcott reserves his most vehement criticism for the media.
Again, it is the Deacon as *raisonneur* who outlines most clearly the
imperialist functions of television:

> From reality to shadow, from the substantial
> to the insubstantial, we believe in our images
> instead of ourselves until everything that lives
> ain't holy no longer but fully photographed,
> and the test of our creed is: 'I saw it on T.V.'.
>
> (ibid.: 199)

Part of a farcical wedding scene, the Deacon's speech articulates
precisely that disjunctive gap which imperialism constructs
between local experience and imposed image. In this case, the
exemplary scope of the media exacerbates the colonised subjects'
sense of unreality and inauthenticity to the point at which all
representation becomes a simulacrum, a constant play of surface
images. This idea is reproduced performatively in the closing
scene which is composed as a TV news update featuring brief
reports from some of the characters who, having sold out to
capitalism, are reduced to media images of themselves. A final
focus on a television which 'glows like a bomb' in the darkness
of the stage (ibid.: 207) portends an ominous future for 'old
Trinidad'. Overall, while *Beef, No Chicken* seems to suggest that
many Caribbean people have little alternative but to imitate the
systems which are offered to or imposed on them,[24] the play enacts
not only a critique of American culture but also a subversion of its
authority. In particular, Walcott's emphasis on mimicry turns the
gaze of the colonising media back on itself in a movement which
undermines all claims to representation.

In many respects, the pervasive influence of American culture
has been felt just as strongly in Canada as it has been in the

Caribbean, albeit in slightly different ways. Canada shares not only a common border with the United States but also a closely related history and a continuous geography. The political, economic, and cultural ties between the two countries have long positioned Canada as a nation which must constantly struggle to avoid being subsumed by its more powerful neighbour. At the level of literary/ artistic expression, this struggle for autonomy leads to what Robert Kroetsch calls 'a writing *of* the border' (1990: 338), a process which endlessly attempts (without ever completely succeeding) to establish the specificity and authenticity of Canada as a discrete nation. Lacking a clear paradigm of cultural difference which might be used strategically to define themselves against Americans, Canadians have frequently sought to establish their difference in other ways. Again, a particularly effective method is through parody, which, as Hutcheon argues, can be used to signal 'ironic difference at the heart of similarity' (1988: x). In the drama which deals specifically with American–Canadian relationships,[25] such parody is frequently comparable to that of Walcott's farce, if sometimes divergent in purpose. *The Noam Chomsky Lectures: A Play* (1990) by Daniel Brooks and Guillermo Verdecchia parodies the lecture format, complete with the projection of complicated graphs and diagrams, to detail US invasions of and interference with countries in Latin America, the Middle East, and South-East Asia since the 1950s. More importantly, the play exposes Canada's official response to these historical events, concluding that the complex web of US presence in Canadian media and business institutions (a presence supported by numerous 'tycoons') has made Canada complicit – if guardedly so – in US military actions. Brooks and Verdecchia's subversion of the lecture format facilitates the presentation of material (facts, figures, newspaper articles, and pertinent quotations) in a manner which confronts the common assumption that Canadians are peaceful and non-interventionary – indeed instrumental to institutions such as the United Nations peace-keeping forces. The play concludes with a deliberately disturbing image: a projected quotation from the philosopher and linguist, Noam Chomsky, which reads '"The question for Canadians is whether they feel comfortable being accomplices to mass murder. In the past the answer has been yes, they do feel comfortable." – Noam Chomsky, *Language and Politics*' (1991: 65).

Parodies of American culture sometimes figure in accounts of Canada's colonial past where they function both as a marker of historical difference between the two countries and as a critique of contemporary forms of American hegemony. Rick Salutin and Theatre Passe Muraille's *1837: The Farmers Revolt* (1974) stages as part of its anti-imperial protest (mostly targeted at the British) a sequence in which a Canadian farmer travels in the USA in an effort to find solutions to the dilemmas facing his community. While the sequence does condemn the perceived Canadian apathy as opposed to American enterprise, the farmer's admiration for everything he finds in the United States is clearly designed to satirise American culture as well as those who aspire to emulate it. Moreover, although the sequence plays as high farce – complete with overtly amateur simulations of wheat fields, apple orchards, large herds of cattle, and six-storey buildings – there is a menacing edge to the Americans' benevolence, especially when one of them invites the Canadian farmer to bring his whole country down to the USA. At this point, the historical threat of American annexation of Canadian land becomes an analogue for the modern 'invasion' of American goods, capital, culture, and ideas. Through such scenes, the play suggests that Canada must find its own solutions to economic and political problems and that colonial subservience to either the British or the Americans is not only mindless but also damaging.

Even though its anti-imperial message is expressed in more elliptical terms, George Walker's *Bagdad Saloon* (1973), which maintains a sustained focus on American culture, can likewise be interpreted as a warning against Canadian acceptance of an imported mythos/ethos. Like Lowe's *Tokyo Rose*, this mordant satire uses the available forms of the dominant society – this time mostly movie texts – to intervene in its hegemony. Subtitled 'A Cartoon', *Bagdad Saloon* presents a cinematic collage of images based on American folklore/popular culture. The plot centres on the kidnapping of a number of American 'legends' – notably Gertrude Stein, Doc Halliday, and Henry Miller – by an Arab, Ahrun, who wants to learn the secrets of immortality. In the first part of the play, the American saloon with all its crass decorations and its grotesque characters is grafted onto Bagdad as Ahrun attempts to build a structure to house his 'heroes'. As the subsequent action makes abundantly clear, however, these cult figures are both pathetically flawed and culturally inappropriate; hence they can provide their kidnapper with neither immortality nor authenticity. Instead, a generalised chaos erupts and the legends take over Ahrun's palace leaving him finally as a motionless living corpse while they themselves, ageing and rotted, sit down to their bizarre banquet. Read as a metaphor for how not to build a 'new society', Walker's iconoclastic play discredits the American myths and dismantles their cultural power to suggest that Canada must create its own enduring mythologies.

Whereas many of the texts discussed in reference to US neo-imperialism attempt to distance their source culture from that of the United States, Guillermo Verdecchia's *Fronteras Americanas (American Borders)* (1993) dismantles all such oppositions between the new 'centre' and its margins. Written and performed by an Argentinian Canadian, this monodrama about cultural displacement creates a space/speaking position for the colonised subject by redrawing the imperial map – in this case the conceptual map of 'America' – in ways which break down binary epistemologies. The play does not attempt to deny the agency of racial, social, geographical, and political divisions, but to suggest that such divisions are artificially constructed and therefore ripe for *de*construction. Taking up the metaphor of the border in order to subvert its authority, Verdecchia (one of the characters, played by the author) firstly addresses the issue of geography. His claim, 'We are all Americans' (1993: 20), immediately intervenes in the conceptual paradigm through which the United States has arrogated the term/identity 'America', thereby marginalising all other inhabitants of the two continents known as the Americas. Within this huge continuous land mass, the mutability of borders between countries also problematises attempts to delineate an empirical map, as Verdecchia points out: 'Where does the U.S. end and Canada begin? Does the U.S. end at the 49th parallel or does the U.S. only end at your living room when you switch on the CBC [Canadian Broadcasting Corporation]?' (ibid.: 21). As well as continually redrawing geographical maps, the play presents an 'Idiosyncratic History of America' which is designed to decentre conventional accounts. Presented as a slide-show with narrative commentary, this history includes references to Aztec culture, Joan of Arc, a 680-pound giant sea bass, Christopher Columbus, Peter Rabbit, Fidel Castro, Ernest Hemingway, the Montréal Canadiens hockey team, and, finally, Verdecchia's first day at school. This collage of historical moments, each of which is given equal billing, further dismantles categories of privilege.

As Verdecchia discovers, personal and social borders are more difficult to break down because racial and cultural stereotyping confines the 'Latino' to North America's 'backyard'. However, with the aid of his other persona, Wideload, Verdecchia eventually reaches a point at which he can begin to forge an identity that exceeds and subverts the self/other binary. Wideload, a comic to Verdecchia's straightman, deliberately embodies the figure of the Latino stereotype in order to demonstrate its constructedness. As a character who inhabits the borders – the *barrios* – between self and other, Wideload is ideally suited to helping Verdecchia with his quest. On a performative level, the split subjectivity imaged by the actor's two separate personae reinforces the productive instability of the colonised subject. Verdecchia says towards the end of the play, 'I am learning to live the border. I have called off the Border Patrol. I am a hyphenated person but I am not falling apart, I am putting together. I am building a house on the border' (ibid.: 77). In its writing *on* the border rather than *of* the border, *Fronteras Americanas* dismantles the binary oppositions of centre/ margin and coloniser/colonised to relocate both in a continually negotiated dialectic. The play confirms this deconstructive move- ment as its explicit agenda by quoting Guillermo Gómez-Pena (a leading theorist of Latin American culture) in one of the slides which provide a constant metacommentary on the narrative:

> The west is no longer west. The old binary models have been replaced by a border dialectic of ongoing flux. We now inhabit a social universe in constant motion, a moving cartography with a floating culture and a fluctuating sense of self.
>
> (ibid.: 70)

As a blueprint for addressing global neo-imperialism, this caption – and the overall play – begins to address Said's concern with 'human interdependence' as a marker of the late twentieth century. If identity is never fixed but always fluid, it is conceivable that post-coloniality can be constructed even in the face of the increasing Americanisation of world culture.

TOURISM

The development of the so-called 'global village' over the last few decades in particular has contributed to a marked expansion in tourism which now occurs on an unprecedented scale world wide.

This in turn has resulted in increased opportunities for the west-erner (who can usually afford to travel) to develop a commodified relation to the non-western other. As John Frow argues, 'The logic of tourism is that of a relentless extension of commodity relations and the consequent inequalities of power between center and periphery, First and Third Worlds, developed and under-developed regions, metropolis and countryside' (1991: 151). For those who cannot or choose not to travel, the media provides ample occasion for a vicarious tour which the armchair traveller can enjoy in comfort by simply turning on his/her television. In many cases, such travelogues (often masquerading under the name of documentaries) present highly selective representations of various countries or cultures which are carefully constructed for the western viewer's specular consumption. News media are not exempt from this practice; in fact, their objectification of the other is sometimes all the more insidious because they present their stories as the 'here and now' facts of a situation or event.

As part of its border dialectic, *Fronteras Americanas* features a direct attack on the media for establishing and maintaining a repertoire of images that perpetuate notions of marginality. Wideload describes his vision for a 'third-world theme park' which he would like to build on a 'chunk of toxic wasteland' along the Trans-Canada highway:

> You know, you drive up to like big barbed wire gates with guards carrying sub-machine-guns and you park you car and den a broken-down Mercedes Benz bus comes along and takes you in under guard, of course. And you buy an International Monetary Fund Credit Card for fifty bucks and it gets you on all de rides.
>
> And as soon as you're inside somebody steals your purse and a policeman shows up but he's totally incompetent and you have to bribe him in order to get any action. Den you walk through a slum with poor people selling tortillas. And maybe a disappearing rainforest section that you can actually walk through. . . . I figure it would be great – you people love dat kinda *shit*.

(1993: 25)

While the parodic style of this scene distances its audience from any possible association with such a theme park, Wideload's final comment – 'you people love dat kinda *shit*' – is an uncomfortable reminder to the 'Saxonians' (his term for white North Americans) of their complicity in the media's representational systems. Later, Wideload presents a drug cartel movie, turning off the volume so he himself can editorialise. In this case, his tone is less overtly satirical as he draws the audience's attention to those details which the film does not show, before warning them to treat such propaganda with scepticism. The commodification of the 'Latin lover' stereotype in movies and in popular magazines also becomes a focus for Wideload's deconstructive attack. Examining *Elle* magazine, he cautions his audience to pay heed to the ways in which the Latin lover is simultaneously exoticised and dehumanised as a sex object. In each of these staged lessons on how to read the media's characteristic texts, Wideload's sustained use of irony and his deliberate narrative intrusions encourage an active 'double vision' as an alternative model of media spectatorship.

The discursive power of images circulated by the media has undoubtedly affected the construction of some holiday destinations as places which offer 'safe' access to an exotic and sexually available other. The commodification of non-western subjects becomes even more apparent when the cultural voyeurism facilitated by the popular media translates into an actual encounter with that other. Apart from setting up material relations with the culture, the hospitality, and the environment of the 'host' society, tourism also commodifies that society's people, especially when 'romance' is implicitly or explicitly the elusive goal of foreign travel. The Caribbean, for instance, is very much a 'playground' where the western (usually American) tourist can indulge his/her fetish for interracial sex without ever having to face the social consequences. Jamaica and Barbados, among other countries, have very well-established 'sex tourist' industries based on white men's *and* women's willingness to pay in money or in kind (meals, hotel rooms, expensive gifts) for the body of the black other. Trevor Rhone's *Smile Orange* (1971) takes up this issue in a biting satire of the economies of tourism in Jamaica's seaside resorts. The play focuses on the staff of the Mocho Beach Hotel, a third-rate establishment which caters mostly for Americans. Although the tourists never appear on stage, the play provides enough detail to suggest their sordid motivations and some of their more 'deviant' activities. Its criticism of the Americans notwithstanding, *Smile Orange* is perhaps less interested in exposing the tourists' commodification of Afro-Caribbean peoples (which is more or less assumed) than in illustrating how locals subvert that commodity relation to 'exploit di exploiter' (1981: 176). One of the waiters, Ringo, who is the play's trickster figure, demonstrates quite clearly the ways in which the hotel's tourist 'racket' operates as he gives a new busboy step-by-step instructions on how to manipulate white customers, and, most importantly, how to profit from rich American women. A crucial part of the game is playing (up to) the tourists' version of the 'authentic' by adopting the expected sexual and social roles. Play-acting thus becomes a central action and a key metaphor in the text which reveals the 'sly civility' of the ever-smiling 'natives' who act the part of the colonial stereotype without becoming reduced to it. Underneath its raunchy dialogue and slapstick comedy, the play also alludes to the tragic aspects of an economy which provides locals with few alternatives for making a living. The disillusionment that the tourist racket can bring is highlighted by the figure of Miss Brandon, who compromises her body to secure a work visa for the United States but is jilted by her 'consort'. More elliptically, tourism's figurative emasculation of the men – and, by implication, of the Jamaican society – is suggested through allusions to a folktale which maintains that eating oranges will make a man impotent. The play's closing image shows the young busboy reaching out for an orange, which indicates that a new generation of Jamaicans must capitulate to the realities of their location within the (sexual) fantasies of the western market economy.

In a different context, Michael Gurr's *Sex Diary of an Infidel* (1992) takes up the issue of Australian sex tours to the Philippines, using the sex trade as a metaphor of the congress between western and third world nations. Coercive sex thus becomes a trope for other kinds of imperialism: economic, cultural, and even military. In the play, a journalist and a photographer travel to the Philippines in order to complete an investigative current affairs report which will draw attention to the cultural and sexual exploitation perpetuated by the sex tourist industry. It soon becomes apparent, however, that the media's 'words and pictures' team are themselves deeply implicated in the neo-imperial process; hence, their purported exposé merely reinscribes western privilege and reinforces well-worn mythologies. As Susan Sontag argues, to take a picture (or write a story) is not passive observation but active participation which affirms 'complicity with whatever makes the subject interesting, worth photographing' (1973: 12). Gurr's construction of the

media as the prime sex tourist also points to the audience's participation in the cultural/sexual voyeurism promulgated by such
news reports. This particular point is emphasised by the ways in
which the play's opening scene – a direct address to the audience
– positions its viewers as party to, rather than simple observers of,
the ensuing action.

By featuring numerous instances of photo-taking, many of
which obviously reify the Oriental subject, *Sex Diary* thematises
(and implicitly condemns) what Sontag has termed the 'insati-
ability of the photographic eye' (ibid.: 3). The play's attack on the
conventions of photography also operates at the level of structure
and form, since the performance text actively engages with the
looking relations it wishes to subvert. The rapid shifts in locale,
combined with short, sharp, and imagistic scenes, presents the
narrative action as a collage of 'snapshots' interspersed with filmic
sequences. While the logic of the camera collocates disparate
images into a dramatic album/video, the performative presence of
fully embodied characters resists the closure of the cinematic gaze.
Moreover, the play's metatheatrical framework ensures that the
audience's gaze is always split between the focus/action and
the other characters watching that action. Further subversions of
the camera's eye/power are evident in the colonised subject's
parodically languid, B-grade movie poses. Fully aware that he
is being 'framed' as an Oriental stereotype, Toni (a transvestite
prostitute) presents back to the camera its own limited constructions. The play thus attempts to dismantle the axiomatic looking
relations sanctioned by the tourist gaze, a type of 'foreplay' to
sexual exploitation. In this respect, Gurr's text goes further
towards undermining the libidinal ecomomy of the tourist industry
than does *Smile Orange*. If, as John Urry contends, the photographic
image constitutes the grammar of tourism (1990), its deconstruction is crucial to the play's larger agenda of unsettling the west's
exoticised vision of Asia.

While tourism is undoubtedly one of the most insidious forms of
neo-colonialism, it can only continue to function as a stable site of
power if it successfully masks its vested interest in maintaining
the alterity of non-western peoples. As Frow maintains, 'The otherness of traditional or exotic cultures has to do with their . . . being
unaware of their own relativity, avoiding absorption into the
embrace of touristic self-consciousness' (1991: 130). Once the
other recognises his/her alterity as a function of western discourse,

the conditions of potential resistance are created. In this respect, the globalisation of the media may have the unintended effect of helping colonised peoples to achieve the 'condition of information' (ibid.: 130) which is a prerequisite of empowerment. And while various forms of neo-imperialism will continue to operate at local, regional, and global levels, so too will the decolonising process. Said's argument about the necessary provisionality of contemporary cultural imperialism reinforces this point: '[history] teaches us that domination breeds resistance, and that the violence inherent in the imperial contest – for all its occasional profit or pleasure – is an impoverishment of both sides' (1994: 348).

NOTES

1 In some instances, European countries exert a 'new' or different kind of power – which can be analysed as a form of neo-imperialism – over their former colonies. However, the distinctions between the two are by no means rigid.

2 See Said (1994: 345) for a discussion of the ways in which the USA has developed this notion from earlier national myths which postulated global leadership as the nation's 'manifest destiny'.

3 See Kelly (1994), Tompkins (1994c), and Dale and Gilbert (1993) for a fuller discussion of Australia's positioning within Said's Orientalist paradigm. Hodge and Mishra (1991) also explore Orientalism in an Australian context but adapt Said's work as a model for understanding internal race relations between settlers and Aborigines.

4 Gunew's distinction between Australian and Canadian treatments of internal colonialism is based on the fact that Aborigines, unlike native Canadians, are not officially categorised as part of the multicultural community. Whereas Australian 'multiculturalism' tends to deal with migration issues, Canadian versions focus more squarely on cultural difference (1993: 452–3).

5 Limitations of space do not permit a detailed analysis of Québec's position vis-à-vis Anglophone Canada. See McRoberts (1979) for a historical perspective on the issue, and Chanady (1994) for a discussion of the ways in which the post-colonial paradigms have been applied to Canadian literature dealing with Québec.

6 Our discussion of recent trends in Québec theatre is indebted to Jane Moss's account of the subject. Moss points out that the 1970s 'revolution' in Québec theatre was closely linked to the nationalist and regionalist movements of the time (1990: 256–7). Nationalist sentiment is also common in Anglo-Canadian and Australian drama of the same era. Although such sentiment is articulated differently in each culture's theatre, it performs a common function as part of the decolonising process.

7 Robert Nunn, for instance, interprets this play as a study of different

Québécois responses to cultural hegemony. In his schema, the character Carmen is a model of post-colonial hybridity while her parents maintain a position of marginalised powerlessness (1992: 222–3).

8 When it was revived in 1992, *Balconville* was produced more as a farce than a piece of serious social commentary since its topicality had diminished over the years of debate about language issues in Québec.

9 With this Act, the British colonisers of Québec legalised the Catholic church and guaranteed the protection of the French language and Civil Code in Canada.

10 Literally meaning 'son of the soil', *bumiputera* came into official use in 1970 and has since been used as a category of privilege. As Lo notes, however, *bumiputera* categorisations are themselves contentious and contradictory since they sometimes include (for census purposes) Straits Chinese who have lived in the area for centuries, while at other times they exclude such groups (1995: 64–5).

11 Interestingly, the play escaped censorship when it was initially performed, perhaps because Kee was a relatively unknown playwright at the time and/or because the censors did not understand the allusions to Orwell's work. Since then, Kee has spent time in detention for expressing anti-government sentiments (see Lo 1995: 217–18).

12 See, for instance, Kuo Pao Kun's *The Coffin Is Too Big For the Hole* (1985) which addresses the issue of Singapore's oppressive state ideologies, and Ngũgĩ wa Thiong'o's *Mother, Sing for Me* (1982) which was banned by the Kenyan government before its opening night because it attacked neo-colonial land appropriations. Its rehearsals were, however, extremely popular, as documented by Bjorkman (1989) who reports that busloads of people travelled from distant towns to witness the event.

13 Canadian theatre's response to American economic and cultural hegemony will be discussed below in conjunction with global imperialism.

14 For example, many Australians believe that their government was duped by the United States into sending troops to Vietnam. While racism, cultural xenophobia, and fears about the spread of communism undoubtedly contributed to Australia's political decisions on the war, there have been few analyses of these factors.

15 Although the Vietnam War figures in a number of contemporary Australian plays, it is frequently not the centre of focus but rather a site of repressed trauma. See Gilbert (1996) for an extended discussion on dramatic representations of Australian and American imperialism in Vietnam.

16 At various points, Australia has governed or significantly affected the politics and economies of other nearby territories and South Seas islands, including Fiji, the location of Alexander Buzo's anti-colonial play, *The Marginal Farm* (1983). New Zealand's administration, until recently, of Western Samoa and the Cook Islands can also be considered within the neo-colonial paradigm. John Kneubuhl's *Think of a Garden* is set in Western Samoa when it was governed by New Zealand.

17 Kidnapping someone with the intent of selling him/her into slavery.

18 The cargo cult also exists in a less spiritual form in Malaysia; see Patrick Yeoh's *The Need to Be* (1970). Also a common trope is the African experience of a 'been-to' (either the United States or England) who is expected to produce riches on (usually) his return.

19 David Lan's *Sergeant Ola and His Followers* (1980) enacts a similar critique.

20 Schulz notes that there is no script for this play: 'in keeping with the spirit of oral histories, it is still being "written" before and during each performance' (1994: 49).

21 See for instance Chi and Kuckles's *Bran Nue Dae*, which reworks both the Broadway musical and the picaresque road movie; Stephen Sewell's *The Blind Giant is Dancing* (1983) which invokes B-grade movie conventions in its critique of US economic imperialism in Australia; and Michael Gow's *The Kid* (1983), which satirises television evangelism as part of its narrative about modern urban alienation.

22 These figures are based on a television documentary, *And the Dish Ran Away with the Spoon*, co-produced by Banyan Studio, Trinidad, 1991. The documentary compares the St Lucian situation with that of Cuba which has 70 per cent local programming and four stations for over ten million people.

23 In Trinidad, 'liming' which involves 'hanging about' or loafing, usually with friends, is not just a recreational activity but something akin to an art. Mostly a male activity, liming often includes verbal repartee which has much in common with Carnival speech traditions.

24 Walcott discusses this issue at length in his essay, 'The Caribbean: Culture or Mimicry', arguing that a possible solution to the Caribbean's dependence on US cultural models is to remember that many of those models are significantly influenced by black culture (1992: 26–7).

25 The following discussion deals only with representations of Canadian–American relations as they are represented in a selected few playtexts. See Filewod (1992b) for an extended discussion of the ways in which Canadian theatre as a cultural practice has sought to define itself against the hegemony of American forms and the influx of American capital.

A PROVISIONAL
CONCLUSION

This study has pursued the relationship between some post-colonial and performance theories as they relate to drama from a range of countries. We have explored many ways in which theatre acts as a resonant site for resistance strategies employed by colonised subjects. The reclamation of, for example, pre-contact forms of performance, ritual, song, music, language, history, and story-telling facilitates the foregrounding of indigenous cultures in spite of imperial attempts to eradicate that which was not European and ostensibly civilised and controllable. The revisioning or reproducing of 'classical' texts deconstructs the hegemonic authority embedded in the original text. The syncretic combination of indigenous and colonial forms in the post-colonial world also contributes to the decentring of the European 'norm'. Hybrid theatrical forms recognise that colonialism can never be erased entirely to restore a pre-contact 'purity'; rather, hybridity reinforces the fact that hegemonic processes require continual deconstruction. The often uneasy amalgamation of colonial and pre-contact traditions in post-colonial drama admits the uses of a variety of forms in the construction of relevant, politically astute theatre that privileges a multiplicity of views and power structures to avoid the entrenchment of any one approach or authority. Examples of neo-colonialism on the post-colonial stage stress the need for further decolonising activities.

Our study cannot be exhaustive in terms of methodology and countries/plays discussed, partly because of the breadth of the topic, and partly because we are anxious not to subscribe to any prescriptive readings of a vastly diverse body of drama. Among the theatre traditions that have not been discussed to any great depth are those in the Indian subcontinent, South-East Asia, Melanesia,

Indonesia, and Polynesia. The developments of national theatre movements (which often coincide with independence) in many countries are deliberately not detailed here partly because most national theatrical histories can be found in libraries, and more importantly, because we prefer to read the drama from former colonies of the British Empire in the larger context of resistance to and reaction against imperial control. Further exploration of, for instance, the Ghanaian concert party or the Igbo *mmonwu* poetic masquerade play (and the many other festival-based plays and rituals in Africa) will yield a fuller understanding of the innumerable ways in which resistance to colonialism continues to be staged.

Our project has also been designed less to give an exhaustive coverage of the field than to promote the reader's own investigations into many areas that we have merely touched upon, including:

- The ways in which Indian theatre forms have, in many cases, maintained an extremely strong sense of diversity and autonomy of space, form, language, spirituality, and ancient historicity in the face of extensive bureaucratic and educational control, both by colonial and internal powers.
- The ways in which imperialism's authority extends from the physical and cultural spheres to include the more metaphoric space of the mind. These psychic effects of colonialism are obvious in most post-colonial states, but more particularly in the settler-invader cultures like Canada, Australia, New Zealand (and, with reservations, South Africa), where most non-indigenous colonial subjects continue to be implicated in some existing imperial ministrations. Figured on the stage in terms of yet another location that must be actively *de*colonised, the psychic space of the mind can become a potentially productive site for releasing – through theatrical experimentation – imperialism's hold on the colonised subject.
- The ways in which New Zealand's bicultural society signifies differently from the other, more 'multicultural' settler societies.
- The many other ways in which the body can signify on stage. These can include ritual scarification or tattooing, which, if rendered in paint, signify differently than permanent cultural markings of an actor's body. Another body coding is torture, a not uncommon mechanism of control in colonial *and* post-independent countries. Depictions of torture can communicate

very strongly to an audience, particularly if viewers are aware of the local, politically coded referents. An actor whose body (or mind) has actually suffered torture immediately signifies even more powerfully than an actor who enacts a tortured body.

- The ways in which postmodernist and radical feminist theatrical practices impact on post-colonial performative theories.

- The ways in which global political realignments – such as the North American Free Trade Association (NAFTA) and the Association of South East Asian Nations (ASEAN) – will alter the traditional trade and political alliances which countries (specifically here Canada, Australia, and New Zealand) of the former British Empire have forged.

- The ways in which South Africa's 1994 elections and the introduction of a democratic state there will affect the country's drama. For at least the two or three decades leading up to Nelson Mandela's 1990 release from prison, a vast majority of the country's plays were structured by a binary opposition of apartheid and 'freedom'. The shifts in the nature of the metaphoric, literal, and theatrical struggles in South African drama will be particularly worth following.

- The ways in which government-imposed censorship of art, and persecution of artists and other citizens alike continues in countries such as Burma (Myanmar) and 'colonies' like East Timor.

- The ways in which post-colonialism still faces – perhaps ineffectively or helplessly – crises of post-imperialism like the attempted genocide in Rwanda.

Post-colonial theatre is, of course, not static. The transformations, refinements, and even the eliminations of certain aspects of post-colonial performance are highly revealing. The Kwagh-Hir puppet theatre practised by the Tiv people in eastern Nigeria provides a chronicle of social and technological changes the community has witnessed: the introduction of new puppets to the existing locally known collection of familiar figures marks various significant moments 'such as when the first motor bike was ridden in Gboko or the first policewoman emerged or modern dress styles of European design gained local acceptance' (Enem 1976: 41).

Decolonisation is an ongoing process since, as Alan Lawson and Chris Tiffin argue:

[colonised subjects] continue to be interpellated by a range of imperial mechanisms just as effectively as they were previously coerced by the more overt and formal institutions of Empire. This too must be historicized: it is necessary to reaffirm that imperialism and its practices continue, but equally necessary to notice that they do not continue to take the same form and to register the historical, cultural, and geographical specificities of both their deployment and its effects.

(1994: 230–1)

Decolonisation and persistent attempts to deal with struggles in the post- and/or neo-colonial world remain issues that will be played out on the stages of Australia, India, Africa, Canada, the Caribbean, New Zealand, and other former colonies, in increasingly innovative and conflicting styles, languages, and forms. And, undoubtedly, post-colonial drama will continue to find new means of reacting to the containing and constraining borders which attempt to delimit the empire and its constructions of gender, race, and class.

BIBLIOGRAPHY

Achebe, C. (1993) 'The African writer and the English language', in P. Williams and L. Chrisman (eds) *Colonial Discourse and Post-Colonial Theory: A Reader*, New York: Harvester Wheatsheaf, 428–34.

Acholonu, C.O. (1985) 'Role of Nigerian dancers in drama', *Nigeria Magazine* 53, 1: 33–9.

Ackerman, M. (1993) *L'Affaire Tartuffe, or, The Garrison Officers Rehearse Molière*, Montréal: NuAge.

Adedeji, J.A. (1966) 'The place of drama in Yoruba religious observance', *Odu* 3, 1: 88–94.

—— (1979) 'Theatre forms: the Nigerian dilemma', *Nigeria Magazine* 128/9: 15–25.

Agbeyegbe, F. (1990) *The King Must Dance Naked*, Lagos: Malthouse.

Agovi, K. (1985) 'Is there an African vision of tragedy in contemporary African theatre?', *Présence Africaine* 133/4: 55–74.

—— (1991) 'Towards an authentic African theatre', *Ufahamu* 19, 2/3: 67–79.

Ahmed, U.B. (1985) 'A taxonomy of Hausa drama', *Nigeria Magazine* 53, 1: 19–32.

Ahura, T. (1985) 'The playwright, the play and the revolutionary African aesthetics', *Ufahamu* 14, 3: 93–104.

Aidoo, A.A. (1965) *The Dilemma of a Ghost*, Accra, Ghana: Longman.

—— (1970) *Anowa*, Harlow, Essex: Longman.

Akerman, A. (1989) 'The last bastion of freedom under siege: a reflection in theatre', in W. Campschreur and J. Divendal (eds) *Culture in Another South Africa*, London: Zed, 50–7.

Alekar, S. (1989) *The Dread Departure (Mahanirvan)*, trans. G. Deshpande, Calcutta: Seagull.

Ali, S. (1993) Review of *The Black Jacobins* by C.L.R. James, *Sunday Guardian Magazine*, 16 May: 5.

Alleyne, M. (1985) 'A linguistic perspective on the Caribbean', in S.W. Mintz and S. Price (eds) *Caribbean Contours*, Baltimore, Maryland: Johns Hopkins University Press, 155–77.

—— (1988) *Roots of Jamaican Culture*, London: Pluto.

Allison, H. (1986) *Sistren Song: Popular Theatre in Jamaica*, London: War On Want.

Alston, J.B. (1989) *Yoruba Drama in English: Interpretation and Production*, Lewiston, New York: Mellen.

Amali, E.D. (1985) 'Proverbs as concept of Idoma performing arts', *Nigeria Magazine* 53, 3: 30–7.

Amali, S.O.O. (1983) *The Nigerian Dreams and Realities*, Jos, Nigeria: University of Jos Press.

—— (1985) *An Ancient Nigerian Drama: The Idoma Inquest: A Bilingual Presentation in Idoma and English together with 'Odegwudegwu' an Original Bilingual Play in Idoma and English*, Stuttgart: Steiner.

Amankulor, J.N. (1980) 'Dance as an element of artistic synthesis in traditional Igbo Festival Theatre', *Okike* 17: 84–95.

Amankulor, J.N. and Okafor, C.G. (1988) 'Continuity and change in traditional Nigerian theatre among the Igbo in the era of colonial politics', *Ufahamu* 16, 3: 35–50.

Amanuddin, S. (1978) *The King Who Sold His Wife*, Calcutta: Prayer.

Amosu, T. (1985) 'The Nigerian dramatist and his audience: the question of language and culture', *Odu* 28: 34–45.

Angmor, C. (1988) 'Drama in Ghana', in R.K. Priebe (ed.) *Ghanaian Literatures*, New York: Greenwood.

Appiah, K.A. (1991) 'Is the post- in postmodernism the post- in post-colonial?', *Critical Inquiry* 17: 336–57.

—— (1992) *In My Father's House: Africa in the Philosophy of Culture*, London: Methuen.

Aremu, P.S.O. (1983) 'Spiritual and physical identity of Yoruba Egungun costumes: a general survey', *Nigeria Magazine* 147: 47–54.

Asagba, A.O. (1986) 'Roots of African drama: critical approaches and elements of continuity', *Kunapipi* 8, 3: 84–99.

Ashcroft, B. [W.D.] (1987) 'Language issues facing Commonwealth writers: a reply to D'Costa', *Journal of Commonwealth Literature* 22, 1: 99–118.

—— (1989a) 'Constitutive graphonomy: a post-colonial theory of literary writing', *Kunapipi* 11, 1: 58–73.

—— (1989b) 'Intersecting marginalities: post-colonialism and feminism', *Kunapipi* 11, 2: 23–35.

—— (1990) 'Choosing English/choosing an audience', *SPAN* 30: 18–26.

Ashcroft, B., Griffiths, G., and Tiffin, H. (1989) *The Empire Writes Back: Theory and Practice in Post-Colonial Literatures*, London: Routledge.

—— (1995) (eds) *The Post-Colonial Studies Reader*, London: Routledge.

Attwood, B. and Arnold, J. (eds) (1992) *Power, Knowledge and Aborigines*, Melbourne: La Trobe University Press.

Awoonor, K. (1981) 'Caliban answers Prospero: the dialogue between Western and African literature', *Obsidian* 7, 2/3: 75–98.

Babcock, B. (1985) ' "A tolerated margin of mess": the trickster and his tales reconsidered', in A. Wiget (ed.) *Critical Essays on Native American Literature*, Boston, Massachusetts: G.K. Hall, 153–85.

Badejo, D.L. (1987) 'Unmasking the gods: of Egungun and demagogues in three works by Wole Soyinka', *Theatre Journal* 39, 2: 204–14.

—— (1988) 'The Yoruba and Afro-American trickster: a contextual comparison', *Présence Africaine* 147: 3–17.

Baker, M.A. (1991a) 'An old Indian trick is to laugh', *Canadian Theatre Review* 68: 48–9.

—— (1991b) 'Angry enough to spit but with *Dry Lips* it hurts more than you know', *Canadian Theatre Review* 68: 88–9.

Bakhtin, M. (1984) *Rabelais and his World*, trans. H. Iswolsky, Bloomington, Indiana: Indiana University Press.

Balme, C. (1990) 'The Aboriginal theatre of Jack Davis: prolegomena to a theory of syncretic theatre', in G. Davis and H. Maes-Jelinek (eds) *Crisis and Creativity in the New Literatures in English*, Amsterdam: Rodopi, 401–17.

—— (1992) 'The Caribbean theatre of ritual: Derek Walcott's *Dream on Monkey Mountain*, Michael Gilkes's *Couvade: A Dream Play of Guyana*, and Dennis Scott's *An Echo in the Bone*', in A. Rutherford (ed.) *From Commonwealth to Post-Colonial*, Sydney: Dangaroo, 181–96.

Balodis, J. (1985) *Too Young for Ghosts*, Sydney: Currency.

—— (1992) *No Going Back*, Dir. R. Hodgman, Melbourne Theatre Company, Russell St Theatre, Melbourne, 16 July.

Balogun, O. (1981) 'The contemporary stage in the development of African aesthetic', *Okike* 19: 15–24.

Bame, K.N. (1985) *Come to Laugh: African Traditional Theatre in Ghana*, New York: Lilian Barber.

Barba, E. (1986) *Beyond the Floating Islands*, J. Barba (trans), New York: PAJ.

Barbeau, J. (1971a) *Le chemin de lacroix*, Montréal: Leméac.

—— (1971b) *Ben-Ur*, Montréal: Leméac.

—— (1973) *Le chant du sink*, Montréal: Leméac.

Barker, F. and Hulme, P. (1985) 'Nymphs and reapers heavily vanish: the discursive contexts of *The Tempest*', in J. Drakakis (ed.) *Alternative Shakespeares*, London: Methuen, 191–205.

Barratt, H. (1984) 'Metaphor and symbol in *The Dragon Can't Dance*', *World Literature Written in English* 23, 2: 405–13.

Baxter, J.K. (1982) 'Mr. O'Dwyer's Dancing Party', in H. McNaughton (ed.) *James K. Baxter: Collected Plays*, Auckland: Oxford University Press, 261–91.

Beckman, S.A. (1980) 'The mulatto of style: language in Derek Walcott's drama', *Canadian Drama* 6, 1: 71–89.

Beik, J. (1987) *Hausa Theatre in Niger: A Contemporary Oral Art*, New York: Garland.

ben Abdallah, M. (1987) *The Trial of Mallam Ilya and Other Plays*, Accra: Woeli.

Benitez-Rojo, A. (1992) *The Repeating Island: The Caribbean and the Post-modern Perspective*, trans. J. Maraniss, Durham, North Carolina: Duke University Press.

Bennett, L. (1983) *Selected Poems*, Kingston, Jamaica: Sangster's.

Bennett, S. (1990) *Theatre Audiences: A Theory of Production and Reception*, London: Routledge.

—— (1991) 'Who speaks? representations of native women in some Canadian plays', *The Canadian Journal of Drama and Theatre* 1, 2: 13–25.

Bennett, T. (1982) 'Text and history', in P. Widdowson (ed.) *Re-reading English*, London: Methuen, 223–36.

Bennett, W. (1974) 'The Jamaican theatre: a preliminary overview', *Jamaica Journal* 8, 2/3: 3–9.

Benson, E. (1985) 'Regionalism and national identity: the dramatic image', in R. Berry and J. Acheson (eds) *Regionalism and National Identity: Multidisciplinary Essays on Canada, Australia and New Zealand*, Christchurch, New Zealand: Association for Canadian Studies in Australia and New Zealand, 89–96.

Benveniste, É. (1970) *Problems of General Linguistics*, trans. M.E. Meek, Coral Gables, Florida: University of Miami Press.

Besong, B. (1986) *The Most Cruel Death of the Talkative Zombie*, Yaoundé, Cameroon: Nooremac.

Bessai, D. (1980) 'The regionalism of Canadian drama', *Canadian Literature* 85: 7–20.

—— (1989) 'Collective theatre and the playwright: *Jessica*, by Linda Griffiths and Maria Campbell', in K.G. Probert (ed.) *Writing Saskatchewan: 20 Critical Essays*, Regina: Canadian Plains Research Centre, 100–10.

—— (1992) *Playwrights of Collective Creation*, Toronto: Simon & Pierre.

Bhabha, H. (1983) 'The other question . . . ', *Screen* 24, 6: 18–36.

—— (1984) 'Of mimicry and man: the ambivalence of colonial discourse', *October* 28: 125–33.

—— (1985) 'Signs taken for wonders: questions of ambivalence and authority under a tree outside Delhi, May 1817', in F. Barker *et al.* (eds) *Europe and its Others: Proceedings of the Essex Conference on the Sociology of Literature, July 1984*, vol. 1, Colchester, Essex: University of Essex Press, 89–106.

—— (1990) 'DissemiNation: time, narrative, and the margins of the modern nation', in H. Bhabha (ed.) *Nation and Narration*, London: Routledge, 291–322.

Bharucha, R. (1983) *Rehearsals of Revolution: The Political Theater of Bengal*, Honolulu, Hawaii: University of Hawaii Press.

—— (1993) *Theatre and the World: Performance and the Politics of Culture*, London: Routledge.

Bhatta, S.K. (1987) *Indian English Drama: A Critical Study*, New Delhi: Sterling.

Bilby, K.M. (1985) 'The Caribbean as a musical region', in S.W. Mintz and S. Price (eds) *Caribbean Contours*, Baltimore, Maryland: Johns Hopkins University Press, 181–216.

Bird, K. (1989) 'The company of Sirens: popular feminist theatre in Canada', *Canadian Theatre Review* 59: 35–7.

Birringer, J. (1993) *Theatre, Theory, Postmodernism*, Bloomington, Indiana: University of Indiana Press.

Bishop, R. (1988) *African Literature, African Critics: The Forming of Critical Standards 1947–1966*, New York: Greenwood.

Bjorkman, I. (1989) '*Mother, Sing for Me': People's Theatre in Kenya*, London: Zed.

Black, S. (1984) '"What kind of society can develop under corrugated iron?": Glimpses of New Zealand history in New Zealand plays', *Australasian Drama Studies* 3, 1: 31–52.

Bloom, H. (1961) *King Kong: An African Jazz Opera*, London: Fontana.

BIBLIOGRAPHY

Boal, A. (1979) *Theatre of the Oppressed*, trans. C.A. and M.L. McBride, New York: Theatre Communications Group.

Boardman, K.A. (1994) 'Autobiography as collaboration: *The Book of Jessica*', *Textual Studies in Canada* 4: 28–39.

Boehmer, E. (1993) 'Transfiguring: colonial body into postcolonial narrative', *Novel* 27, 2: 268–77.

Boire, G. (1987a) 'Canadian (tw)ink: surviving the whiteouts', *Essays on Canadian Writing* 35: 1–16.

—— (1987b) 'Wheels on fire: the train of thought in George Ryga's *The Ecstasy of Rita Joe*', *Canadian Literature* 113/14: 62–74.

—— (1990) 'Inside out: prison theatre from Australia, Canada, and New Zealand', *Australian–Canadian Studies* 8, 1: 21–34.

—— (1991a) 'Resistance moves: Mervyn Thompson's *Songs to the Judges*', *Australian and New Zealand Studies in Canada* 6: 15–26.

—— (1991b) 'Tribunalations: George Ryga's post-colonial trial play', *ARIEL* 22, 2: 5–20.

Bolt, C. (1976) *Gabe*, in *Buffalo Jump and Other Plays*, Toronto: Playwrights Co-op, 81–127.

Booth, J. (1992) 'Human sacrifice in literature: the case of Wole Soyinka', *ARIEL* 23, 1: 7–24.

Bostock, G. (1985) 'Black theatre', in J. Davis and B. Hodge (eds) *Aboriginal Writing Today*, Canberra: Australian Institute of Aboriginal Studies, 63–73.

Botheroyd, P.F. (1991) 'Ireland and the Caribbean: two Caribbean versions of J.M. Synge's dramas', in J. Genet and R.A. Cave (eds) *Perspectives of Irish Drama and Theatre*, Gerards Cross, Buckinghamshire: Colin Smythe, 83–92.

Brask, P. and Morgan, W. (eds) (1992) *Aboriginal Voices: Amerindian, Inuit and Sami Theater*, Baltimore, Maryland: Johns Hopkins University Press.

Brassard, M. and Lepage, R. (1993) *Polygraph*, trans. G. Raby, in A. Filewod (ed.) *The CTR Anthology: Fifteen Plays from Canadian Theatre Review*, Toronto: University of Toronto Press, 647–83.

Brathwaite, E.K. (1967) *Odale's Choice*, London: Evans.

—— (1977/8) 'The love axe/l (developing a Caribbean aesthetic 1962–1974)', *Bim* 16, 63: 181–92.

—— (1984) *History of the Voice: The Development of Nation Language in Anglophone Caribbean Poetry*, London: New Beacon.

Bray, H. (1990) *Tomasi: For Islands Far Away*, Palmerston North, New Zealand: Nagare Press.

Breslow, S. (1989) 'Trinidadian heteroglossia: a Bakhtinian view of Derek Walcott's play *A Branch of the Blue Nile*', *World Literature Today* 63: 36–9.

Brisset, A. (1989) 'In search of a target language: the politics of theatre translation in Québec', *Target* 1, 1: 9–27.

Broinowski, A. (1992) *The Yellow Lady: Australian Impressions of Asia*, Melbourne: Oxford University Press.

Brook, P. (1968) *The Empty Space*, Harmondsworth: Penguin.

Brooks, D. and Verdecchia, G. (1991) *The Noam Chomsky Lectures: A Play*, Toronto: Coach House.

Broughton, J. (1990) *Michael James Manaia*, Wellington: Playmarket.

—— (1991) *Te Hara (The Sin)*, in S. Garrett (ed.) *He Reo Hou*, Wellington: Playmarket, 222–39.

—— (1992) *ANZAC*, Wellington: Playmarket.

Brown, L.W. (1978) 'The revolutionary dream of Walcott's Makak', in E. Baugh (ed.) *Critics on Caribbean Literature*, Boston, Massachusetts: Allen & Unwin, 58–62.

Brown, P. (1985) '"This thing of darkness I acknowledge mine": *The Tempest* and the discourse of colonialism', in J. Dollimore and A. Sinfield (eds) *Political Shakespeare: New Essays in Cultural Materialism*, Manchester: Manchester University Press, 48–71.

Brown, R[iwia]. (1991) *Roimata*, in S. Garrett (ed.) *He Reo Hou*, Wellington: Playmarket, 164–218.

Brown, R[uth]. (1989) 'Maori spirituality as Pakeha construct', *Meanjin* 48, 2: 252–8.

Brown, S. (ed.) (1991) *The Art of Derek Walcott*, Bridgend, Wales: Seren Books.

Bruner, C. (1976) 'The meaning of Caliban in black literature today', *Comparative Literature Studies* 13, 3: 240–53.

Brydon, D. (1984) 'Re-writing *The Tempest*', *World Literature Written in English* 23, 1: 75–88.

—— (1990) 'The white Inuit speaks: contamination as literary strategy', in I. Adam and H. Tiffin (eds) *Past the Last Post: Theorising Post-Colonialism and Post-Modernism*, Calgary: University of Calgary Press, 191–203.

—— (1994) 'The empire's bloomers: cross-dressing's double cross', *Essays in Canadian Writing* 54: 23–45.

Bukenya, A. (1987) *The Bride*, Nairobi: Heinemann.

Butler, G. (1990) *Demea*, Cape Town: David Philip.

Butler, J. (1990) 'Performative acts and gender constitution: an essay in phenomenology and feminist theory', in S. Case (ed.) *Performing Feminisms: Feminist Critical Theory and Theatre*, Baltimore, Maryland: Johns Hopkins University Press, 270–82.

Buzo, A. (1973) *Norm and Ahmed*, in *Three Plays*, Sydney: Currency, 1–26.

—— (1985) *Big River* and *The Marginal Farm*, Sydney: Currency.

Campbell, M. (1993) 'Introduction', in P. Mead and M. Campbell (eds) *Shakespeare's Books: Contemporary Cultural Politics and the Persistence of Empire*, Melbourne: Department of English, University of Melbourne, 1–5.

Carlin, M. (1969) *Not Now, Sweet Desdemona*, Nairobi: Oxford University Press.

Carlson, M. (1990) *Theatre Semiotics: Signs of Life*, Bloomington, Indiana: University of Indiana Press.

Carrière, J. (1991) 'What is not in *The Mahabharata* is nowhere', in D. Williams (ed.) *Peter Brook and* The Mahabharata, London: Routledge, 59–64.

Cartelli, T. (1987) 'Prospero in Africa: *The Tempest* as colonialist text and pretext', in J. Howard and M. O'Connor (eds) *Shakespeare Reproduced: The Text in History and Ideology*, New York: Methuen, 99–115.

Carter, P. (1987) *The Road to Botany Bay: An Essay in Spatial History*, London: Faber.

BIBLIOGRAPHY

Cary, N.R. (1988) 'Salvation, self, and solidarity in the work of Earl Lovelace', *World Literature Written in English* 28, 1: 103–14.

Cathcart, S. and Lemon, A. (1988) *The Serpent's Fall*, Sydney: Currency.

—— (1991) *Walking on Sticks*, La Mama Theatre, Melbourne, 12 October.

Césaire, A. (1969) *Une tempête: adaptation de "La Tempête" de Shakespeare pour un théâtre nègre*, Paris: Éditions de Seul.

—— (1976) 'Discourse on colonialism', in J. Hearne (ed.) *Carifesta Forum: An Anthology of 20 Caribbean Voices*, n.p.: n.p., 25–34.

Chambers, R. (1991) *Room for Maneuver: Reading (the) Oppositional (in) Narrative*, Chicago, Illinois: University of Chicago Press.

Chanady, A. (1994) 'Canadian literature and the postcolonial paradigm', *Textual Studies in Canada* 5: 15–21.

Chapple, E. and Davis, M. (1988) 'Expressive movement and performance: toward a unifying theory', *The Drama Review* 32, 4: 53–79.

Cheechoo, S. (1991) *Path With No Moccasins*, Toronto: Playwrights Canada.

Chester, B. (1993) 'Text and context: form and meaning in native narratives', *Canadian Folklore Canadien* 13, 1: 69–81.

Chester, B. and Dudoward, V. (1991) 'Journeys and transformations', *Textual Studies in Canada* 1: 156–77.

Chi, J. and Kuckles. (1991) *Bran Nue Dae*, Sydney: Currency; Broome: Magabala Books.

Chifunyise, S. (1990) 'Trends in Zimbabwean theatre since 1980', *Journal of South African Studies* 16, 2: 276–89.

Chimombo, S. (1975) *The Rainmaker*, Limbe, Malawi: Popular Publications; Lilongwe, Malawi: Likuni Press.

Chinweizu, Jemie, O., and Madubuike, I. (1983) *Toward the Decolonization of African Literature*, vol. 1, Washington, DC: Howard University Press.

Chislett, A. (1992) *Yankee Notions*, Toronto: Playwrights Canada.

Chow, R. (1993) *Writing Diaspora: Tactics of Intervention in Contemporary Cultural Studies*, Bloomington, Indiana: University of Indiana Press.

Chrisman, L. (1990) 'The imperial unconscious?: representations of imperial discourse', *Critical Quarterly* 32, 3: 38–58.

Churchill, C. and Lan, D. (1986) *A Mouthful of Birds*, London: Methuen.

Clark, E. (1979) *Hubert Ogunde: The Making of Nigerian Theatre*, Oxford: Oxford University Press.

Clark [-Bekederemo], J.P. (1964) *Three Plays* [*Song of a Goat, The Masquerade, The Raft*], London: Oxford University Press.

—— (1966) *Ozidi: A Play*, London: Oxford University Press.

—— (1981) 'Aspects of Nigerian drama', in Y. Ogunbiyi (ed.) *Drama and Theatre in Nigeria: A Critical Source Book*, Lagos: Nigeria Magazine, 57–74.

Cobham, R. (1990) ' "A wha kind a pen dis?": the function of ritual frameworks in Sistren's *Bellywoman Bangarang*', *Theatre Research International* 15, 3: 233–49.

Conradie, P.J. (1990) 'Syncretism in Wole Soyinka's play *The Bacchae of Euripides*', *South African Theatre Journal* 4, 1: 61–74.

Cook, M. (1993) *Jacob's Wake*, in J. Wasserman (ed.) *Modern Canadian Plays Volume 1*, 3rd edn, Vancouver: Talonbooks, 215–47.

BIBLIOGRAPHY

Cooper, C. (1989) 'Writing oral history: Sistren Theatre Collective's *Lionheart Gal*, *Kunapipi* 11, 1: 49–57.

Coplan, D.B. (1985) *In Township Tonight! South Africa's Black City Music and Theatre*, Johannesburg: Ravan.

Coulter, J. (1984) *Riel*, in R. Perkyns (ed.) *Major Plays of the Canadian Theatre 1934–1984*, Toronto: Irwin, 125–210.

Courtney, R. (1985) 'Indigenous theatre: Indian and Eskimo ritual drama', in A. Wagner (ed.) *Contemporary Canadian Theatre: New World Visions*, Toronto: Simon & Pierre, 206–15.

Cox, J. (1989) 'Dangerous definitions: female tricksters in contemporary native American literature', *Wicazo SA Review* 5, 2: 17–21.

Creighton, A. (1985) 'Commoner and king: contrasting linguistic performances in the dialogue of the dispossessed', in M. McWatt (ed.) *West Indian Literature and its Social Context: Proceedings of the Fourth Annual Conference on West Indian Literature*, Cave Hill, Barbados: University of the West Indies, 55–68.

Dale, L. (1993) '"Red plague rampant?": Shakespeare's *Tempest* in Australia', in P. Mead and M. Campbell (eds) *Shakespeare's Books: Contemporary Cultural Politics and the Persistence of Empire*, Melbourne: University of Melbourne English Department, 98–112.

Dale, L. and Gilbert, H. (1993) 'Looking the same: a preliminary (postcolonial) discussion of orientalism and occidentalism in Australia and Japan', *Yearbook of Comparative and General Literature Studies* 41: 35–50.

Dalrymple, L. (1992) *Drama to the People: The Challenge of the 1990s*, Zululand: University of Zululand Press.

Daly, A. (1988) 'Movement analysis: piecing together the puzzle', *The Drama Review* 32, 4: 40–52.

Dasgupta, G. (1991a) 'Interculturalism: a lettrist sampler', in B. Marranca and G. Dasgupta (eds) *Interculturalism and Performance*, New York: PAJ, 319–32.

—— (1991b) 'Peter Brook's orientalism', in D. Williams (ed.) *Peter Brook and The Mahabharata*, London: Routledge, 262–7.

Dash, M. (1973) 'Marvellous realism: the way out of negritude', *Caribbean Studies* 13, 4: 57–70.

—— (1989) 'In search of the lost body: redefining the subject in Caribbean literature', *Kunapipi* 11, 1: 17–26.

Davey, F. (1994) 'Mapping Anglophone–Canadian literary conflict: multiculturalism and after', *Textual Studies in Canada* 5: 124–34.

Davis, A.B. (1980) 'Dramatic theory of Wole Soyinka', in J. Gibbs (ed.) *Critical Perspectives on Wole Soyinka*, Washington, DC: Three Continents, 147–57.

Davis, G.V. (1991) '"Repainting the damaged canvas": the theatre of Matsemela Manaka', *Commonwealth Essays and Studies* 14, 1: 84–96.

Davis, J. (1982) *Kullark* and *The Dreamers*, Sydney: Currency.

—— (1986) *No Sugar*, Sydney: Currency.

—— (1989) *Barungin (Smell the Wind)*, Sydney: Currency.

—— (1992) *In Our Town*, Sydney: Currency.

Davis, J. and Hodge, B. (eds) (1985) *Aboriginal Writing Today*, Canberra: Australian Institute of Aboriginal Studies.

305

D'Cruz, G. (1993) 'A "Dark" Ariel?: Shakespeare and Australian theatre criticism', in P. Mead and M. Campbell (eds) *Shakespeare's Books: Contemporary Cultural Politics and the Persistence of Empire*, Melbourne: University of Melbourne English Department, 165–74.

Debenham, D. (1988) 'Native people in contemporary Canadian drama', *Canadian Drama* 14, 2: 137–58.

de Graft, J.C. (1970) *Through a Film Darkly*, London: Oxford University Press.

—— (1976) 'Roots in African drama and literature', *African Literature Today*, London: Heinemann, 1–25.

De Groen, A. (1988) *The Rivers of China*, Sydney: Currency.

Deleuze, F. and Guattari, G. (1987) *A Thousand Plateaus: Capitalism and Schizophrenia*, trans. B. Massumi, Minneapolis, Minnesota: University of Minnesota Press.

De Mel, N. (1990) 'Responses to history: the re-articulation of post-colonial identity in the plays of Wole Soyinka and Derek Walcott', Ph.D. thesis, University of Kent.

Dening, G. (1993) *Mr Bligh's Bad Language*, Cambridge: Cambridge University Press.

de Wet, R. (1985) *Diepe Grond*, unpublished playscript.

Diamond, D. with Blackwater, B., Shannon, L., and Wilson, M. (1991) *No' Xya' (Our Footprints)*, in A. Filewod (ed.) *New Canadian Drama 5*, Ottawa: Borealis, 42–87.

Diamond, E. (1988) 'Brechtian theory/feminist theory: toward a gestic feminist criticism', *The Drama Review* 32, 1: 82–94.

—— (1990) 'Refusing the romanticism of identity: narrative interventions in Churchill, Benmussa, Duras', in S.E. Case (ed.) *Performing Feminisms: Feminist Critical Theory and Theatre*, Baltimore, Maryland: Johns Hopkins University Press, 92–105.

Dibble, B., and Macintyre, M. (1992) 'Hybridity in Jack Davis' *No Sugar*', *Westerly* 37, 4: 93–7.

Di Cenzo, M. and Bennett, S. (1992) 'Women, popular theatre, and social action: interviews with Cynthia Grant and the Sistren Theatre Collective', *ARIEL* 23, 1: 73–94.

Dike, F. (1978) *The Sacrifice of Kreli*, in S. Gray (ed.) *Theatre One: New South African Drama*, Johannesburg: Donker, 33–80.

—— (1979) *The First South African*, Johannesburg: Ravan.

Dolan, J. (1992) 'Gender impersonation onstage: destroying or maintaining the mirror of gender roles?', in L. Senelick (ed.) *Gender in Performance: The Presentation of Difference in the Performing Arts*, Hanover, Massachusetts: New England University Press, 3–13.

Dorall, E. (1972) *The Hour of the Dog*, in L. Fernando (ed.) *New Drama Two*, Kuala Lumpur: Oxford University Press, 117–49.

Dorsinville, M. (1974) *Caliban Without Prospero*, Erin, Ontario: Press Porcépic.

Drake-Brockman, H. (1955) *Men Without Wives and Other Plays*, Sydney: Angus and Robertson.

Drewal, M.T. (1992) *Yoruba Ritual: Performers, Play, Agency*, Bloomington, Indiana: Indiana University Press.

Duffy, M. (1983) *Rites*, in M. Wandor (ed.) *Plays by Women*, London: Methuen, 12–25.

Dunstone, B. (1985) 'Another planet: landscape as metaphor in Western Australian theatre', in B. Bennett and J. Hay (eds) *European Relations: Essays for Helen Watson-Williams*, Perth: Centre for Studies in Australian Literature, University of Western Australia, 67–79.

Dunton, C. (1992) *'Make Man Talk True': Nigerian Drama in English Since 1970*, London: Hans Zell.

During, S. (1987) 'Postmodernism or post-colonialism today', *Textual Practice* 1, 1: 32–47.

Dutt, U. (1986) *The Great Rebellion 1857 (Mahavidroha)*, Calcutta: Seagull.

Echeruo, M.J.O. (1981) 'The dramatic limits of Igbo ritual', in Y. Ogunbiyi (ed.) *Drama and Theatre in Nigeria: A Critical Source Book*, Lagos: Nigeria Magazine, 136–48.

Edmond, M. (1988) *'Squatter* and the making of New Zealand theatre', *Untold* 9/10: 16–24.

Edwards, B. (1992) 'Australian literature and post-colonial comparisons', *Australian–Canadian Studies* 10, 2: 142–6.

Elam, K. (1980) *The Semiotics of Theatre and Drama*, London: Methuen.

Ellis, P. (ed.) (1986) *Women of the Caribbean*, London: Zed Books.

Emberley, J.V. (1993) *Thresholds of Difference: Feminist Critique, Native Women's Writing, Postcolonial Theory*, Toronto: University of Toronto Press.

Emecheta, B. (1980) *The Joys of Motherhood*, London: Heinemann.

Enekwe, O.O. (1981) 'Myth, ritual and drama in Igbo-land', in Y. Ogunbiyi (ed.) *Drama and Theatre in Nigeria: A Critical Source Book*, Lagos: Nigeria Magazine, 149–63.

Enem, E.U. (1976) 'The Kwagh-Hir theatre', *Nigeria Magazine* 120: 29–42.

Essa, S. and Pillai, C. (1985) *Steve Biko: The Inquest*, Durban: Art Printers.

Etherton, M. (1982) *The Development of African Drama*, London: Hutchinson.

—— (1990) 'African theatre and political action', in C. Nwamuo (ed.) *The Faces of Nigerian Theatre*, Calabar, Nigeria: Centaur, 42–54.

Fanon, F. (1967) *Black Skin, White Masks*, trans. C.L. Markmann, New York: Grove.

Fatunde, T. (1986) *Oga Na Tief Man*, Benin City: Adena.

Fennario, D. (1980) *Balconville*, Vancouver: Talon.

Fernando, L. (1972) Introduction, in L. Fernando (ed.) *New Drama Two*, Kuala Lumpur: Oxford University Press, vii–xix.

Ferrier, E. (1990) 'Mapping power: cartography and contemporary cultural theory', *Antithesis* 4, 1: 35–49.

Ferris, L. (ed.) (1993) *Crossing the Stage: Controversies on Cross-Dressing*, London: Routledge.

Fido, E.S. (1984) 'Radical woman: woman and theatre in the Anglophone Caribbean', in E.S. Smilowitz and R.Q. Knowles (eds) *Critical Issues in West Indian Literature*, Petersburg, Iowa: Caribbean Books, 33–45.

—— (1990a) 'Finding a way to tell it: methodology and commitment in theatre about women in Barbados and Jamaica', in C.B. Davies and E.S. Fido (eds) *Out of the Kumbla: Caribbean Women and Literature*, Trenton, New Jersey: Africa World Press, 331–43.

—— (1990b) 'Finding a truer form: Rawle Gibbons's carnival play *I, Lawah'*, *Theatre Research International* 15, 3: 249–59.

BIBLIOGRAPHY

—— (1992) 'Freeing up: politics, gender, and theatrical form in the Anglophone Caribbean', in L. Senelick (ed.) *Gender in Performance: The Presentation of Difference in the Performing Arts*, Hanover, Massachusetts: New England University Press, 281–98.

Fiet, L. (1991) 'Mapping a new Nile: Derek Walcott's later plays', in S. Brown (ed.) *The Art of Derek Walcott*, Bridgend, Wales: Seren Books, 139–53.

Filewod, A. (1992a) 'Averting the colonizing gaze: notes on watching native theater', in P. Brask and W. Morgan (eds) *Aboriginal Voices: Amerindian, Inuit and Sami Theater*, Baltimore, Maryland: Johns Hopkins University Press, 17–28.

—— (1992b) 'Between empires: post-imperialism and Canadian theatre', *Essays in Theatre* 11, 1: 3–15.

Fitzpatrick, P. (1979) *After the Doll: Australian Drama Since 1955*, Melbourne: Edward Arnold.

—— (1985) 'Asian stereotypes in recent Australian plays', *Australian Literary Studies* 12, 1: 35–46.

—— (1990) 'Staging Australia: models of cultural identity in the theatre', *Australian Studies* 13: 53–62.

Fitzpatrick, P. and Thomson, H. (1993) 'Developments in recent Australian drama', *World Literature Today* 67, 3: 489–93.

Flockemann, M. (1991) 'Gcina Mhlophe's *Have You Seen Zandile?*: English or english? the situation of drama in literature and language departments in the emergent post-apartheid South Africa', *South African Theatre Journal* 5, 2: 40–54.

Ford-Smith, H. (1986a) 'Sistren women's theatre, organizing and conscientization', in P. Ellis (ed.) *Women of the Caribbean*, London: Zed Books, 123–8.

—— (1986b) 'Sistren: exploring women's problems through drama', *Jamaica Journal* 19, 1: 2–12.

Foster, S.L. (1986) *Reading Dancing: Bodies and Subjects in Contemporary American Dance*, Berkeley, California: University of California Press.

Foucault, M. (1977) 'Nietzsche, genealogy, history', trans. D. Bouchard and S. Simon, in D. Bouchard (ed.) *Language, Counter-memory, Practice*, Ithaca, New York: Cornell University Press, 139–64.

—— (1980) 'Questions on geography', in C. Gordon (ed. and trans.) *Power/Knowledge: Selected Interviews and Other Writings*, Brighton: Harvester, 63–77.

—— (1981) *The History of Sexuality: Vol. 1, An Introduction*, trans. R. Hurley. Harmondsworth: Penguin.

—— (1986) 'Of other spaces', trans. J. Miskowiec, *Diacritics* 16, 1: 22–7.

Fox, R.E. (1982) 'Big night music: Derek Walcott's *Dream on Monkey Mountain* and the "splendours of imagination"', *Journal of Commonwealth Literature* 17, 1: 16–27.

Francis, D. (1992) *The Imaginary Indian: The Image of the Indian in Canadian Culture*, Vancouver: Arsenal Pulp.

Freedman, B. (1991) *Staging the Gaze: Postmodernism, Psychoanalysis and Shakespearean Comedy*, Ithaca, New York: Cornell University Press.

Friedrich, R. (1983) 'Drama and ritual', in J. Redmond (ed.) *Drama and Religion*, Cambridge: Cambridge University Press, 67–76.

Friel, B. (1984) *Translations*, in *Selected Plays of Brian Friel*, London: Faber, 377–447.

Frow, J. (1991) 'Tourism and the semiotics of nostalgia', *October* 57: 123–51.

Fugard, A. (1982) *'Master Harold' . . . and the Boys*, New York: Penguin.

Fugard, A., Kani, J., and Ntshona, W. (1986) *The Island*, in *Statements: Three Plays*, New York: Theatre Communications Group, 45–77.

Gabre-Medhin, T. (1977) *Collision of Altars: Conflict of the Ancient Red Sea Gods*, London: Rex Collings.

Gaines, J. (1988) 'White privilege and looking relations: race and gender in feminist film theory', *Screen* 29, 4: 12–27.

Gaines, J. and Herzog, C. (1990) (eds) *Fabrications: Costume and the Female Body*, New York: Routledge.

Gandhi, L. (1993) 'Unmasking Shakespeare: the uses of English in colonial and postcolonial India', in P. Mead and M. Campbell (eds) *Shakespeare's Books: Contemporary Cultural Politics and the Persistence of Empire*, Melbourne: Department of English, University of Melbourne, 81–97.

Garber, M. (1992) *Vested Interests: Cross-Dressing and Cultural Anxiety*, London: Routledge.

Gargi, B. (1991) *Folk Theater of India*, Calcutta: Rupa.

Gaston, R. (1985) *Another Cinema for Another Society*, Calcutta: Seagull.

Gay, P. (1992) 'Michael Gow's *Away*: the Shakespeare connection', in M. Harris and E. Webby (eds) *Reconnoitres: Essays in Australian Literature in Honour of G.A. Wilkes*, Sydney: Oxford University Press, 204–13.

Gendzier, I.L. (1973) *Frantz Fanon: A Critical Study*, New York: Pantheon.

George, D. (1988) '*The Tempest* in Bali: where should this music be?', *New Theatre: Australia* 3: 22–3.

—— (1989–90) 'Casebook: *The Tempest* in Bali – a director's log', *Australasian Drama Studies* 15/16: 21–46.

George, R. (1983) *Sandy Lee Live at Nui Dat*, Sydney: Currency.

Germain, J.-C. (1976) *Un pays dont la devise est je m'oublie*, Montréal: VLB.

—— (1983) *A Canadian Play/Une plaie canadienne*, Montréal: VLB.

Gerster, R. (1991) 'Occidental tourists: the "ugly Australian" in Vietnam war narrative', in P. Pierce (ed.) *Vietnam Days: Australia and the Impact of Vietnam*, Ringwood, Victoria: Penguin, 191–235.

Gibbons, R. (1979) 'Traditional enactments of Trinidad: towards a third theatre', M. Phil. thesis, University of the West Indies.

—— (1986) *I, Lawah, (A Folk Fantasy)*, unpublished playscript.

Gibbs, J. (ed.) (1976) *Nine Malawian Plays*, Limbe, Malawi: Popular; Lilongwe, Malawi: Likuni.

—— (1986) *Wole Soyinka*, London: Methuen.

Gilbert, H. (1990) 'Historical re-presentation: performance and counter-discourse in Jack Davis' drama', *New Literatures Review* 19: 91–101.

—— (1991) 'The boomerang effect: David Malouf's *Blood Relations* as an oppositional re-working of *The Tempest*', *World Literature Written in English* 31, 2: 50–64.

—— (1992a) 'Fish or fowl: post-colonialism and Australian drama', *Australian–Canadian Studies* 10, 2: 131–5.

—— (1992b) 'The dance as text in contemporary Australian drama: movement and resistance politics', *ARIEL* 23, 1: 133–48.

—— (1993a) 'The Catherine wheel: travel, exile and the (post) colonial woman', *Southerly* 53, 2: 58–77.

—— (1993b) 'The serpent's gaze: re-working myths for a feminist Australian drama', *Australian and New Zealand Studies in Canada* 10: 30–40.

—— (1993c) 'Post-colonial grotesques: re-membering the body in Louis Nowra's *Visions* and *The Golden Age*', *SPAN* 36, 2: 618–33.

—— (1994a) 'De-scribing orality: performance and the recuperation of voice', in C. Tiffin and A. Lawson (eds) *De-Scribing Empire: Colonialism and Textuality*, London: Routledge, 98–111.

—— (1994b) 'Monumental moments: Michael Gow's *1841*, Stephen Sewell's *Hate*, Louis Nowra's *Capricornia* and Australia's bicentenary', *Australasian Drama Studies* 24: 29–45.

—— (1994c) '"Talking country": place and displacement in Jack Davis's theatre', in G. Turcotte (ed.) *Jack Davis: A Critical Study*, Sydney: Collins-Angus & Robertson, 60–71.

—— (1994d) 'Occidental (sex) tourists: Michael Gurr's *Sex Diary of an Infidel*', *Australasian Drama Studies* 25: 177–88.

—— (1994e) 'Ghosts in a landscape: Louis Nowra's *Inside the Island* and Janis Balodis's *Too Young for Ghosts*', *Southern Review* 27: 432–47.

—— (1994f) 'Historical re-play: post-colonial approaches to contemporary Australian drama', Ph.D. thesis, University of Queensland.

—— (1995) 'Dressed to kill: a post-colonial reading of costume and the body in contemporary Australian drama', in J.E. Gainor (ed.) *Imperalism and Theatre*, London: Routledge, 104–31.

—— (1996) 'GI Joe versus Digger Dave: contemporary Australian drama and the Vietnam war', in A. Rutherford and J. Wieland (eds) *War: Australia's Creative Response*, Sydney: Allen & Unwin.

Gilbert, K. (1988) *The Cherry Pickers*, Canberra: Burrambinga.

Gilkes, M. (1974) *Couvade: A Dream Play of Guyana*, Sydney: Dangaroo.

Giresh, K. (1990) *Nāga-Mandala: Play with a Cobra*, Delhi: Oxford University Press.

Glasser, M. (1960) *King Kong: A Venture in the Theatre*, Cape Town: Norman Howell.

Glissant, E. (1989) *Caribbean Discourse: Selected Essays*, Charlottesville, Virginia: Virginia University Press.

Godard, B. (1981) 'The oral tradition and national literatures', *Comparison* 12: 15–31.

Goldie, T. (1989) *Fear and Temptation: The Image of the Indigene in Canadian, Australian and New Zealand Literatures*, Kingston, Ontario: McGill-Queen's University Press.

Goodman, L. (1993) *Contemporary Feminist Theatres: To Each Her Own*, London: Routledge.

Gorak, J. (1989) 'Nothing to root for: Zakes Mda and South African resistance theatre', *Theatre Journal* 41, 4: 479–91.

Götrick, K. (1984) *Apidan Theatre and Modern Drama*, Stockholm: Almqvist and Wiksell.

Gow, M. (1983) *The Kid*, Sydney: Currency.

—— (1986) *Away*, Sydney: Currency.

—— (1988) *1841*, Sydney: Currency.

—— (1992) Interview with J. Pearson, *Southerly* 52, 2: 116–31.

Gradussov, A. (1981) 'Thoughts about the theatre in Jamaica', *Jamaica Journal* 4, 1: 46–52.

Graham-White, A. (1974) *The Drama of Black Africa*, New York: Samuel French.

Grant, A. (1992) 'Canadian native literature: the drama of George Ryga and Tomson Highway', *Australian–Canadian Studies* 10, 2: 37–56.

Graver, D. and Kruger, L. (1989) 'South Africa's national theatre: the Market or the street?', *New Theatre Quarterly* 5, 19: 272–81.

Gray, C. (1968) 'Folk themes in West Indian drama', *Caribbean Quarterly* 14, 1/2: 102–9.

Gray, J. with Peterson, E. (1994) *Billy Bishop Goes to War*, in J. Wasserman (ed.) *Modern Canadian Plays: Volume II*, 3rd edn, Vancouver: Talonbooks, 51–78.

Gray, S. (1984) 'The theatre of Fatima Dike', *The English Academy Review* 2: 55–60.

—— (1990) 'Women in South African theatre', *South African Theatre Journal* 4, 1: 75–87.

Greenblatt, S. (1976) 'Learning to curse: aspects of linguistic colonialism in the sixteenth century', in F. Chiapelli (ed.) *First Images of America: The Impact of the New World on the Old*, Berkeley, California: University of California Press, 561–80.

—— (1991) *Marvelous Possessions: The Wonder of the New World*, Oxford: Clarendon.

Griffiths, G. (1984) 'Australian subjects and Australian style: the plays of Louis Nowra', *Commonwealth: Essays and Studies* 6, 2: 42–8.

—— (1987) 'Imitation, abrogation and appropriation: the production of the post-colonial text', *Kunapipi* 9, 1: 13–20.

—— (1992a) 'The dark side of the dreaming: Aboriginality and Australian culture', *Australian Literary Studies* 15, 4: 328–33.

—— (1992b) '"Unhappy the land that has a need of heroes": John Romeril's "Asian" plays', in B. Bennett and D. Haskell (eds) *Myths, Heroes and Anti-Heroes: Essays on the Literature and Culture of the Asia-Pacific Region*, Perth: Centre for Studies in Australian Literature, University of Western Australia, 142–54.

Griffiths, G. and Moody, D. (1989) 'Of Marx and missionaries: Soyinka and the survival of universalism in post-colonial literary theory', *Kunapipi* 11, 1: 74–86.

Griffiths, L. and Campbell, M. (1989) *The Book of Jessica: A Theatrical Transformation*, Toronto: Coach House.

Griffiths, T. (1983) '"This island's mine": Caliban and colonialism', *Yearbook of English Studies* 13: 159–80.

Grimes, R.L. (1982) 'Defining nascent ritual', *The Journal of the American Academy of Religion* 50, 4: 539–55.

Grosz, E. (1990) 'Inscriptions and body-maps: representations of the corporeal', in T. Threadgold and A. Cranny-Francis (eds) *Feminine/Masculine and Representation*, Sydney: Allen & Unwin, 62–74.

Gunew, S. (1993) 'Multicultural multiplicities: U.S., Canada, Australia', *Meanjin* 52, 3: 447–61.

Gupta, C.B. (1991) *The Indian Theatre*, rev. edn, New Delhi: Munsbiram Manoharlal.

Gurr, A. (1980) 'Third-world drama: Soyinka and tragedy', in J. Gibbs (ed.) *Critical Perspectives on Wole Soyinka*, Washington, DC: Three Continents, 139–46.

Gurr, M. (1993) *Sex Diary of an Infidel*, 2nd edn, Sydney: Currency.

Hagan, J.C. (1988) 'Influence of folktale on *The Marriage of Anansewa*: a folkloristic approach', *Okike* 27/28: 19–30.

Hagher, I.H. (1980–1) 'The aesthetic problem in the criticism of African drama', *Ufahamu* 10, 1/2: 156–65.

—— (ed.) (1990) *The Practice of Community Theatre in Nigeria*, Lagos: Society of Nigerian Theatre Artists.

Hamer, M. (1989) 'Putting Ireland on the map', *Textual Practice* 3, 2: 184–201.

Hamilton, A. (1990) 'Fear and desire: Aborigines, Asians and the national imaginary', *Australian Cultural History* 9: 14–35.

Hamner, R.D. (1981) *Derek Walcott*, Boston: Twayne.

—— (1985) 'Exorcising the planter-devil in the plays of Derek Walcott', *Commonwealth: Essays and Studies* 7, 2: 95–102.

—— (ed.) (1993) *Critical Perspectives on Derek Walcott*, Washington, DC: Three Continents.

Hannet, L. (1971) *The Ungrateful Daughter*, in U. Beier (ed.) *Five New Guinean Plays*, Brisbane: Jacaranda, 33–46.

Hanson, B. and Matthie, P. (1994) Interview with H. Gilbert, Melbourne, 19 July.

Hapipi, R. (1991) *Death of the Land*, in S. Garrett (ed.) *He Reo Hou*, Wellington: Playmarket, 16–51.

Harley, J.B. (1988) 'Maps, knowledge and power', in D. Cosgrove and S. Daniels (eds) *The Iconography of Landscape: Essays on the Symbolic Representation, Design and Use of Past Environments*, Cambridge: Cambridge University Press, 227–312.

Harney, S. (1990) 'Willi Chen and carnival nationalism in Trinidad', *Journal of Commonwealth Literature* 15, 1: 120–31.

Harris, W. (1970) 'History, fable and myth in the Caribbean and Guianas', *Caribbean Quarterly* 16, 2: 1–32.

—— (1985) *Carnival*, London: Faber and Faber.

—— (1986) 'Carnival theatre: a personal view', in *Masquerading: The Art of the Notting Hill Carnival*, London: Arts Council of Great Britain, 38–43.

—— (1988) *The Infinite Rehearsal*, London: Faber.

Harrison, C. (1975) *Tomorrow Will Be A Lovely Day*, Auckland: Longman Paul.

Hartel, R. (1991) *Clutching at Straws*, Cape Town: Buchu.

Hauptfleisch, T. (1988) 'From the Savoy to Soweto: the shifting paradigms in South African theatre', *South African Theatre Journal* 2, 1: 35–63.

He Ara Hou (1990) *Whatungarongaro*, unpublished playscript.

Hewett, D. (1979) *The Man From Mukinupin*, Sydney: Currency.

Highway, T. (1987) 'On native mythology', *Theatrum* 6: 29–31.

—— (1988) *The Rez Sisters*, Saskatoon: Fifth House.

—— (1989) *Dry Lips Oughta Move to Kapuskasing*, Saskatoon: Fifth House.

—— (1992a) 'Let us now combine mythologies: the theatrical art of Tomson Highway', interview with R. Enright, *Border Crossings* 11, 4: 22–7.

—— (1992b) 'The trickster and native theater: an interview with Tomson Highway', by W. Morgan, in P. Brask and W. Morgan (eds) *Aboriginal Voices: Amerindian, Inuit and Sami Theater*, Baltimore, Maryland: Johns Hopkins University Press, 130–8.

—— (1994) 'Twenty-one native women on motorcycles: an interview with Tomson Highway', by J. Tompkins and L. Male, *Australasian Drama Studies* 24: 13–28.

Hill, E. (1972a) *Dance Bongo: A Fantasy in One Act*, Trinidad: University of West Indies, Extramural Studies Unit.

—— (1972b) 'The emergence of a national drama in the West Indies', *Caribbean Quarterly* 18, 4: 9–40.

—— (1972c) *The Trinidad Carnival: Mandate for a National Theatre*, Austin, Texas: Texas University Press.

—— (1984) 'Caliban and Ariel: a study in black and white in American productions of *The Tempest* from 1945–1981', *Theatre History Studies* 4: 1–10.

—— (1985a) *Man Better Man*, in E. Hill (ed.) *Plays for Today*, Harlow, Essex: Longman, 139–233.

—— (1985b) Introduction, in E. Hill (ed.) *Plays for Today*, Harlow, Essex: Longman, 1–20.

—— (1992) *The Jamaican Stage, 1655–1900: Profile of a Colonial Theatre*, Amherst, Massachusetts: Massachusetts University Press.

Hlongwane, A.K. (1990) 'Soyikwa Institute of African Theatre – *SIZA*, the play's rural roots and its role in South Africa today', in G.V. Davis (ed.) *Crisis and Conflict: Essays on Southern African Literature*, Essen: Blaue Eule, 229–33.

Hoar, S. (1988) *Squatter*, Wellington: Victoria University Press.

Hodge, B. and Mishra, V. (1991) *Dark Side of the Dream: Literature and the Postcolonial Mind*, Sydney: Allen & Unwin.

Hollingsworth, M. (1985) *War Babies*, in *Wilful Acts: Five Plays*, Toronto: Coach House, 147–223.

Holloway, P. (ed.) (1987) *Contemporary Australian Drama*, Sydney: Currency.

Honegger, G. (1992) 'Native playwright: Tomson Highway', *Theater* 13, 1: 88–92.

Hopkins, L. (1987) 'Language, culture and landscape in *The Man from Mukinupin*', *Australasian Drama Studies* 10: 91–106.

Hopkinson, S. (1977) '*Dream on Monkey Mountain* and the popular response', *Caribbean Quarterly* 23, 2/3: 77–9.

Horn, A. (1981) 'Ritual drama and the theatrical: the case of Bori spirit mediumship', in Y. Ogunbiyi (ed.) *Drama and Theatre in Nigeria: A Critical Source Book*, Lagos: Nigeria Magazine, 181–202.

Hoy, H. (1993) '"When you admit you're a thief, then you can be honourable": native/non-native collaboration in *The Book of Jessica*', *Canadian Literature* 136: 24–39.

Huggan, G. (1989a) 'Decolonizing the map: post-colonialism, post-structuralism and the cartographic connection', *ARIEL* 20, 4: 115–31.
—— (1989b) 'Opting out of the (critical) common market: creolization and the post-colonial text', *Kunapipi* 11, 1: 27–40.
Hulme, P. (1986) *Colonial Encounters: Europe and the Native Caribbean 1492–1797*, London: Routledge.
Hunwick, U. (1986) 'Conjunctive drama – a ritual offshoot', *Nigeria Magazine* 54, 2: 36–41.
Hussein, E. (1970) *Kinjeketile*, Dar es Salaam: Oxford University Press.
—— (1980) 'Traditional African theatre', in U. Schild (ed.) *The East African Experience: Essays on English and Swahili Literature*, Mainz: Reimer, 35–54.
Hutcheon, L. (1986) 'Subject in/of/to history and his story', *Diacritics* 16: 78–91.
—— (1988) *A Poetics of Postmodernism: History, Theory, Fiction*, London: Routledge.
—— (1989) *The Politics of Postmodernism*, London: Routledge.
—— (1990) 'Circling the downspout of empire', in I. Adam and H. Tiffin (eds) *Past the Last Post: Theorizing Post-Colonialism and Post-Modernism*, Calgary: University of Calgary Press, 167–89.
Ijimere, O. (1966) *Everyman*, in *The Imprisonment of Obatala and Other Plays*, English adapt. U. Beier, London: Heinemann, 45–78.
Imbuga, F. (1976) *Betrayal in the City*, Nairobi: East African Publishing House.
Irele, A. (1981) *The African Experience in Literature and Ideology*, London: Heinemann.
Ismond, P. (1985) 'Walcott's later drama: from *Joker* to *Remembrance*', *ARIEL* 16, 3: 89–101.
Ivanov, V.V. (1984) 'The semiotic theory of carnival as the inversion of bipolar opposites', in T.A. Sebeok (ed.) *Carnival*, Berlin: Gruyter, 11–35.
James, A. (ed.) (1990) *In Their Own Voices: African Women Writers Talk*, London: Currey.
James, C.L.R. (1976) *The Black Jacobins*, in E. Hill (ed.) *A Time . . . and a Season: 8 Caribbean Plays*, Trinidad: University of the West Indies, Extramural Studies Unit, 355–420.
JanMohamed, A. (1984) 'Humanism and minority literature: toward a definition of counter-hegemonic discourse', *Boundary 2* 12/13, 3/1: 281–99.
—— (1985) 'The economy of manichean allegory: the function of racial difference in colonialist literature', *Critical Inquiry* 12, 1: 59–87.
JanMohamed, A. and Lloyd, D. (1990) 'Introduction: toward a theory of minority discourse: what is to be done?', in A. JanMohamed and D. Lloyd (eds) *The Nature and Context of Minority Discourse*, Oxford: Oxford University Press, 1–16.
Jarvis, E. and Amoroso, R. (1979) *The Master of Carnival*, in E. Hill (ed.) *Three Caribbean Plays*, Trinidad: Longman Caribbean, 68–99.
Jawodimbari, A. (1971) *Cargo*, in U. Beier (ed.) *Five New Guinea Plays*, Brisbane: Jacaranda, 11–19.

Jazzart (1994) Untitled Performance, Waterfront Auditorium, Cape Town, South Africa, 18 January.

Jeyifo, 'B. (1979) 'Literary drama and the search for a popular theatre in Nigeria', *Nigeria Magazine* 128/9: 62–7.

—— (1984) *The Yoruba Popular Travelling Theatre of Nigeria*, Lagos: Nigeria Magazine.

—— (1985a) 'Realism, naturalism, supernaturalism in contemporary African drama: dramaturgic and philosophic observations', *The Truthful Lie: Essays in a Sociology of African Drama*, London: New Beacon.

—— (1985b) 'Tragedy, history and ideology', in G.M. Gugelberger (ed.) *Marxism and African Literature*, London: Currey, 94–109.

—— (1989) 'On Eurocentric critical theory: some paradigms from the texts and sub-texts of post-colonial writing', *Kunapipi* 11, 1: 107–18.

Johnson, E. (1989) *Murras*, in *Plays from Black Australia*, Sydney: Currency, 79–107.

Johnson-Odim, C. (1991) 'Common themes, different contexts: third world women and feminism', in C.T. Mohanty, A. Russo, and L. Torres (eds) *Third World Women and the Politics of Feminism*, Bloomington, Indiana: Indiana University Press, 314–27.

Johnston, B.H. (1990) 'One generation from extinction', *Canadian Literature* 124/5: 10–15.

Johnston, D.W. (1990) 'Lines and circles: the "rez" plays of Tomson Highway', *Canadian Literature* 124/5: 254–64.

Joseph, M.P. (1992) *Caliban in Exile*, Westport, Connecticut: Greenwood.

Junction Avenue Theatre Company (1986) *Sophiatown*, Johannesburg: Junction Avenue Press.

Juneja, R. (1988) 'The Trinidad carnival: ritual, performance, spectacle, and symbol', *Journal of Popular Culture* 21, 4: 87–99.

—— (1992a) 'Derek Walcott', in B. King (ed.) *Post-Colonial English Plays: Commonwealth Drama Since 1960*, London: Macmillan, 236–65.

—— (1992b) 'Recalling the dead in Dennis Scott's *An Echo in the Bone*', *ARIEL* 23, 1: 97–114.

Kaine-Jones, K. (1988) 'Contemporary Aboriginal drama', *Southerly* 48, 4: 432–44.

Kambar, C. (1989) *Jokumaraswami*, Calcutta: Seagull.

Kane, M. (1992) *Moonlodge*, in D.D. Moses and T. Goldie (eds) *An Anthology of Canadian Native Literature in English*, Toronto: Oxford University Press, 278–91.

Kaniku, J.W. (1970) *The Cry of the Cassowary*, Melbourne: Heinemann.

Kaplan, C. (1987) 'Deterritorializations: the rewriting of home and exile in western feminist discourse', *Cultural Critique* 6: 187–98.

Kapur, A. (1990) *Actors, Pilgrims, Kings and Gods: the Ramlila at Ramnagar*, Calcutta: Seagull.

Katrak, K. (1986) *Wole Soyinka and Modern Tragedy: A Study of Dramatic Theory and Practice*, New York: Greenwood.

—— (1989) 'Decolonizing culture: toward a theory for postcolonial women's texts', *Modern Fiction Studies* 35, 1: 157–79.

Kee, T.C. (1987) *1984 Here and Now*, Selangor, Malaysia: K. Das Ink.

BIBLIOGRAPHY

Keens-Douglas, P. and Edinborough, F. (1980) *Mas in Yuh Mas*, unpublished manuscript.

Keens-Douglas, R. (1991) *Once upon an Island*, in D. Carley (ed.) *Take Five: The Morningside Dramas*, Winnipeg: Blizzard, 97–126.

Kelly, V. (1987a) 'Apocalypse and after: historical visions in some recent Australian drama', *Kunapipi* 9, 3: 68–78.

—— (ed.) (1987b) *Louis Nowra*, Amsterdam: Rodopi.

—— (1988) '"Nowt more outcastin": utopian myth in Louis Nowra's *The Golden Age*', in B. Bennett (ed.) *A Sense of Exile: Essays in the Literatures of the Asia-Pacific*, Perth: Centre for Studies in Australian Literature, University of Western Australia, 101–10.

—— (1990) 'The melodrama of defeat: political patterns in some colonial and contemporary Australian plays', *Southerly* 50, 2: 131–43.

—— (1992a) 'Falling between stools: the theatre of Janis Balodis', *ARIEL* 23, 1: 115–32.

—— (1992b) 'Louis Nowra', in B. King (ed.) *Post-Colonial English Plays: Commonwealth Drama Since 1960*, London: Macmillan, 50–66.

—— (1994) 'Orientalism in early Australian theatre', *New Literatures Review* 26: 32–45.

Keneally, T. (1981) *Bullie's House*, Sydney: Currency.

Kente, G. (1981) *Too Late*, in R. Kavanagh (ed.) *South African People's Plays*, London: Heinemann, 85–124.

Kidd, R. (1983) 'Stages of the struggle', *Commonwealth* 25, 4: 130–1.

King, B. (ed.) (1992) *Post-Colonial English Plays: Commonwealth Drama Since 1960*, London: Macmillan.

Kneubuhl, J.A. (1991) *Think of A Garden*, unpublished playscript.

Knowles, R.P. (1991) 'Voices (off): deconstructing the modern English-Canadian dramatic canon', in R. Lecker (ed.) *Canadian Canons: Essays in Literary Value*, Toronto: University of Toronto Press, 91–111.

Kolodny, A. (1975) *The Lay of the Land*, Chapel Hill, North Carolina: University of North Carolina Press.

Kon, S. (1981) *The Bridge*, in R. Yeo (ed.) *Prize Winning Plays 3*, Singapore: Federal Publications, 2–82.

—— (1989) *Emily of Emerald Hill*, London: Macmillan.

—— (1994) *Trial*, Singapore: Constellation Books.

Kouka, H. (1992) *Mauri Tu*, Auckland: Aoraki Press.

Kristeva, J. (1992) *The Powers of Horror: An Essay on Abjection*, trans. L. Roudiez, New York: Columbia University Press.

Kroetsch, R. (1990) 'Reading across the border', in A.E. Davidson (ed.) *Studies on Canadian Literature: Introductory and Critical Essays*, New York: MLA, 338–43.

Kruger, L. (1991) 'Apartheid on display: South African performance for New York', *Diaspora: A Journal of Transnational Studies* 2: 191–208.

Krupat, A. (1987) 'Post-structuralism and oral literature', in B. Swann and A. Krupat (eds) *Recovering the Word: Essays on Native American Literature*, Berkeley, California: University of California Press, 113–28.

Kumar, K. (1984) *Madhosingh is Dead*, trans. S. Jagmohan, Delhi: Unique.

Kuo, Pao Kun (1990) *The Coffin is too Big for the Hole . . . and Other Plays*, Singapore: Times Books International.

—— (1993) 'Theatre in Singapore: an interview with Kuo Pao Kun', by J. Lo, *Australasian Drama Studies* 23: 136–46.

Lachmann, R. (1988–89) 'Bakhtin and carnival: culture as counter-culture', *Cultural Critique* 11: 115–52.

Ladipo, D. (1964) *Three Yoruba Plays*, adapt. U. Beier, Ibadan: Mbari.

Laframboise, L. (1991) '"Maiden and monster": the female Caliban in Canadian *Tempests*', *World Literature Written in English* 31, 2: 36–49.

Lamb, J. (1986) 'Problems of originality: or beware of Pakeha baring guilts', *Landfall* 40, 3: 352–8.

Lamming, G. (1971) *The Pleasures of Exile*, London: Michael Joseph.

Lan, D. (1980) *Sergeant Ola and his Followers*, London: Methuen.

Lane, M. (1979) Translator's introduction, in Rendra, *The Struggle of the Naga Tribe*, St Lucia: University of Queensland Press, xvii–xl.

Larlham, P. (1985) *Black Theater: Dance and Ritual in South Africa*, Ann Arbor, Michigan: UMI Research.

Larsen, S. (1983) *A Writer and His Gods: A Study of the Importance of Yoruba Myths and Religious Ideas to the Writing of Wole Soyinka*, Stockholm: University of Stockholm Press.

Lawford, N. (1995) *Ningali*, Dir. A. Chaplin, Playbox Theatre, Melbourne, 27 May.

Lawson, A. (1992) 'Comparative studies and post-colonial "settler" cultures', *Australian–Canadian Studies* 10, 2: 153–9.

—— (1994) 'Un/settling colonies: the ambivalent place of colonial discourse', in C. Worth, P. Nestor, and M. Pavlyshyn (eds) *Literature and Opposition*, Clayton, Victoria: Centre for General and Comparative Literature, Monash University, 67–82.

Lawson, A. and Tiffin, C. (1994) 'Conclusion: reading difference', in C. Tiffin and A. Lawson (eds) *De-Scribing Empire: Post-Colonialism and Textuality*, London: Routledge, 230–5.

Leshoai, B.L. (1972) *Wrath of the Ancestors and Other Plays*, Nairobi: East African Publishing House.

Lill, W. (1987) *The Occupation of Heather Rose*, in D. Bessai and D. Kerr (eds) *NeWest Plays for Women*, Edmonton: NeWest, 63–94.

—— (1991) *Sisters*, Vancouver: Talonbooks.

Livingston, R.E. (1995) 'Decolonising the theatre: Aimé Césaire, Jean-Marie Serreau and the drama of negritude', in J.E. Gainor (ed.) *Imperialism and Theatre*, London: Routledge, 182–98.

Lo, J. (1992) 'Tracing Emily of Emerald Hill: subject positioning in performance', in B. Bennett and D. Haskell (eds) *Myths, Heroes and Anti-Heroes: Essays on the Literature and Culture of the Asia-Pacific Region*, Perth: Centre for Studies in Australian Literature, University of Western Australia, 120–31.

—— (1993) 'Political theatre in Malaysia: *1984 Here and Now*', *Australasian Drama Studies* 22: 54–61.

—— (1995) 'The politics and practice of opposition and resistance in Singaporean and Malaysian drama in English', Ph.D. thesis, University of Western Australia.

Loomba, A. (1991a) *Gender, Race, Renaissance Drama*, Manchester: Manchester University Press.

—— (1991b) 'Overworlding the "third world"', *The Oxford Literary Review* 13, 1/2: 164–91.

Lovelace, E. (1984a) *Jestina's Calypso and Other Plays*, London: Heinemann.

—— (1984b) *The New Hardware Store* in *Jestina's Calypso and Other Plays*, London: Heinemann, 43–88.

—— (1989) *The Dragon Can't Dance*, in Y. Brewster (ed.) *Black Plays Two*, London: Methuen, 1–44.

Low, G.C.-L. (1989) 'White skins/black masks: the pleasures and politics of imperialism', *New Formations* 9: 83–103.

Lowe, B. (1989) *Tokyo Rose*, unpublished playscript.

Lyn, D. (1980) 'The concept of the mulatto in some works of Derek Walcott', *Caribbean Quarterly* 26, 1/2: 49–68.

Lyssiotis, T. (1990) *The Forty Lounge Café*, Sydney: Currency.

MacAloon, J.J. (ed.) (1984) *Rite, Drama, Festival, Spectacle: Rehearsals towards a Theory of Cultural Performance*, Philadelphia, Pennsylvania: Institute for the Study of Human Issues.

McCallum, J. (1987) 'The development of a sense of history in contemporary Australian drama', in P. Holloway (ed.) *Contemporary Australian Drama*, Sydney: Currency, 148–60.

MacDonald, A. (1990) *Goodnight Desdemona (Good Morning Juliet)*, Toronto: Coach House.

McDonald, I. (1976) *The Tramping Man*, in E. Hill (ed.) *A Time . . . and a Season: 8 Caribbean Plays*, Trinidad: University of the West Indies, Extramural Studies Unit, 153–75.

McDougall, R. (1987) 'Wilson Harris and the art of carnival revolution', *Commonwealth: Essays and Studies* 10, 1: 77–90.

—— (1990a) 'Music in the body of the book of carnival', *Journal of West Indian Literature* 4, 2: 1–24.

—— (1990b) 'The snapshot image and the body of tradition: stage imagery in *The Lion and the Jewel*', *New Literatures Review* 19: 102–18.

—— (1993) 'Mask, music and the semiotics of *The Road*', *Kunapipi* 15, 3: 133–45.

McGrath, F.C. (1989) 'Language, myth, and history in the later plays of Brian Friel', *Contemporary Literature* 30, 4: 534–45.

McLeod, J. (1990) *Diary of a Crazy Boy*, in *Theatrum*, 19: S1–S11.

McNarn, M. (1979–80) 'From imperial appendage to American satellite: Australian involvement in Vietnam', *Australian National University Historical Journal* 14: 73–86.

McNaughton, H. (1994) 'The speaking abject: the impossible possible world of realized empire', in C. Tiffin and A. Lawson (eds) *De-Scribing Empire: Post-Colonialism and Textuality*, London: Routledge, 218–29.

McRoberts, K. (1979) 'Internal colonialism: the case of Québec', *Ethnic and Racial Studies* 2, 3: 293–318.

Maddy, P.A. (1971) *Obasai and Other Plays*, London: Heinemann.

Mais, R. (1976) *George William Gordon*, in E. Hill (ed.) *A Time . . . and a Season: 8 Caribbean Plays*, Trinidad: University of the West Indies, Extramural Studies Unit, 1–92.

Makotsi, J. (1988) *She Ate the Female Cassava*, Nairobi: Heinemann.

Makun, S. (1984) 'Ritual drama and satire: the case of Opelu song-poetry among the Owe-Kaba', *Nigeria Magazine* 148: 52–6.

Malgonkar, M. (1978) *Line of Mars*, Delhi: Hind Pocket.

Malouf, D. (1988) *Blood Relations*, Sydney: Currency.

Manaka, M. (1984) 'Some thoughts on black theatre', *The English Academy Review* 2: 33–40.

—— (1990) *Pula*, Braamfontein, South Africa: Skotaville.

—— (n.d.) *Egoli: City of Gold*, Johannesburg: Soyikwa-Ravan.

Mandiela, A.Z. (1991) *Dark Diaspora . . . in Dub: a Dub Theatre Piece*, Toronto: Sister Vision.

Manim, M. (1989) 'Journeys of discovery: thoughts on theatre in South Africa', *South African Theatre Journal* 3, 1: 69–80.

Mann, P. (1990) 'Confronting history: the abandonment of Mother England in contemporary New Zealand theatre', *New Literatures Review* 19: 4–13.

Mannoni, O. (1964) *Prospero and Caliban: The Psychology of Colonization*, 2nd edn, trans. P. Powesland, New York: Praeger.

Maponya, M. (1981) *The Hungry Earth*, London: Polyptoton.

—— (1986) *Gangsters*, in D. Ndlovu (ed.) *Woza Afrika! An Anthology of South African Plays*, New York: Braziller, 55–88.

Marchessault, J. (1992) *The Magnificent Voyage of Emily Carr*, trans. L. Gaboriau, Vancouver: Talonbooks.

Marranca, B. and Dasgupta, G. (eds) (1991) *Interculturalism and Performance: Writings from PAJ*, New York: PAJ.

Marshall, B. (1988) *The Crows and Other Plays*, Accra: Educational Press.

Masiye, A.S. (1973) *The Lands of Kazembe*, Lusaka, Zambia: National Educational.

Mason, B. (1975) *The Pohutukawa Tree*, Hong Kong: New Zealand University Press.

Massey, R. (1992) 'From Bharata to the cinema: a study in unity and continuity', *ARIEL* 23, 1: 59–72.

Mathur, J.C. (1964) *Drama in Rural India*, Bombay: Asia and Indian Council for Cultural Relations.

Matura, M. (1980) *Rum an' Coca Cola*, in *Three Plays by Mustapha Matura*, London: Eyre Methuen, 13–31.

—— (1989) *Playboy of the West Indies*, New York: Broadway Play Publishing.

Maxwell, A. (1994) 'Rewriting the nation', *Meanjin* 53, 2: 315–26.

Maza, B. (1989) *The Keepers*, in *Plays from Black Australia*, Sydney: Currency, 168–229.

Mboya, A.-A. (1986) *Otongolia*, Nairobi: Oxford University Press.

Mda, Z. (1979) *We Shall Sing for the Fatherland and Other Plays*, Johannesburg: Ravan.

—— (1990) *The Plays of Zakes Mda*, Johannesburg: Ravan.

—— (1993) *When People Play People*, London: Zed Books.

Mead, P. and Campbell, M. (eds) (1993) *Shakespeare's Books: Contemporary Cultural Politics and the Persistence of Empire*, Melbourne: University of Melbourne English Department.

Merritt, R. (1983) *The Cake Man*, rev. edn, Sydney: Currency.

Mhlope, G. (1990a) 'The Zandile project: a collaboration between UT,

Carpetbag Theatre, and South African playwright Gcina Mhlope', interview with P. Kagan-Moore, *The Drama Review* 34, 1: 115–30.
—— (1990b) Interview with T. August, *Journal of South African Studies* 16, 2: 36–47.
Mhlope, G., Mtshali, T., and Vanrenen, M. (1988) *Have You Seen Zandile?*, Braamfontein, South Africa: Skotaville.
Milgate, R. (1968) *A Refined Look at Existence*, Sydney: Methuen.
Miller, M.J. (1980) 'Two versions of Rick Salutin's *Les Canadians*', *Theatre History in Canada* 1, 1: 57–69.
Mishra, V. (1991) 'The great Indian epic and Peter Brook', in D. Williams (ed.) *Peter Brook and* The Mahabharata, London: Routledge, 195–205.
Mishra, V. and Hodge, B. (1991) 'What is post(-)colonialism?', *Textual Practice* 5, 3: 399–414.
Mlama, P.M. (1991) *Culture and Development: The Popular Theatre Approach in Africa*, Uppsala: Scandinavian Institute of African Studies.
Mohanty, C.T. (1991) 'Under western eyes: feminist scholarship and colonial discourses', in C.T. Mohanty, A. Russo, and L. Torres (eds) *Third World Women and the Politics of Feminism*, Bloomington, Indiana: Indiana University Press, 51–80.
Mohanty, C.T., Russo, A., and Torres, L. (eds) (1991) *Third World Women and the Politics of Feminism*, Bloomington, Indiana: Indiana University Press.
Mojica, M. (1991) *Princess Pocahontas and the Blue Spots: Two Plays*, Toronto: Women's Press.
Monkman, L. (1987) 'A native heritage', in T. King, C. Calver, and H. Hoy (eds) *The Native in Literature*, Toronto: ECW Press, 80–98.
Montrose, L. (1991) 'The work of gender in the discourse of discovery', *Representations* 33: 1–41.
Moody, D. (1989) 'The steeple and the palm-wine shack: Wole Soyinka and crossing the inter-cultural fence', *Kunapipi* 11, 3: 98–107.
—— (1991) 'Marx meets Masque: the play of history in African theatre', *World Literature Written in English* 31, 1: 93–102.
—— (1992) 'The prodigal father: discursive rupture in the plays of Wole Soyinka', *ARIEL* 23, 1: 25–38.
Morgan, S. (1992) *Sistergirl*, Dir. A. Ross, Marli Biyol Company, Arts Theatre, Adelaide, 17 March.
Morris, G. (1989) 'Theatrical possibilities of the traditional Xhosa Iintsomi: what do they offer here and now?', *South African Theatre Journal* 3, 2: 91–100.
Moses, D.D. (1987) 'The trickster theatre of Tomson Highway', *Canadian Fiction Magazine* 60: 83–8.
—— (1988) *The Dreaming Beauty*, Toronto: Playwrights Canada.
—— (1990) *Coyote City*, Stratford, Ontario: Williams-Wallace.
—— (1992) *Almighty Voice and his Wife*, Stratford, Ontario: Williams-Wallace.
—— (1994) Interview with H. Gilbert, Toronto, 8 January.
Moss, J. (1990) 'Drama in Québec', in A.E. Davidson (ed.) *Studies on Canadian Literature: Introductory and Critical Essays*, New York: MLA, 248–70.

Mtwa, P. (1986) *Bopha!*, in D. Ndlovu (ed.) *Woza Africa! An Anthology of South African Plays*, New York: Braziller, 225–58.

Mtwa, P., Ngema, M., and Simon, B. (1983) *Woza Albert!*, London: Methuen.

Much, R. (ed.) (1992) *Women on the Canadian Stage: The Legacy of Hrotsvit*, Winnipeg: Blizzard.

Mudrooroo (1990) *Writing from the Fringe: A Study of Modern Aboriginal Literature*, Melbourne: Hyland House.

Muecke, S. (1992) *Textual Spaces: Aboriginality and Cultural Studies*, Kensington, New South Wales: New South Wales University Press.

Mukherjee, A. (1990) 'Whose post-colonialism and whose post-modernism?', *World Literature Written in English* 30, 2: 1–9.

Mukherjee, S. (1982) *The Story of the Calcutta Theatre 1753–1980*, Calcutta: Bagchi.

Mukhopadhyay, D. (1989) *Culture, Performance, Communication*, Delhi: BR Publishing.

Mulvey, L. (1975) 'Visual pleasure and narrative cinema', *Screen* 16, 3: 6–18.

Murray, C. (1991) 'Three Irish Antigones', in J. Genet and R.A. Cave (eds) *Perspectives of Irish Theatre*, Gerards Cross, Buckinghamshire: Colin Smythe, 115–29.

Murrell, J. (1985) *New World: a comedy*, in *Farther West/New World: Two Plays*, Toronto: Coach House, 95–172.

Mutibwa, P.M. (1992) *Uganda Since Independence: A Story of Unfulfilled Hopes*, London: Hurst.

Mutwa, C.V. (1981) *uNosilimela*, in R. Kavanagh (ed.) *South African People's Plays*, London: Heinemann, 1–62.

Naik, M.K. (1977) 'The achievement of Indian drama in English', in M.K. Naik and S. Mokashi-Punekar (eds) *Perspectives on Indian Drama in English*, Madras: Oxford University Press, 180–94.

Naipaul, S. (1971) 'The writer without a society', in A. Rutherford (ed.) *Commonwealth*, Aarhus, Denmark: University of Aarhus Press, 114–23.

Narayana, B. (1981) *Hindi Drama and Stage*, Delhi: Bansal.

Nardocchio, E. (1986) *Theatre and Politics in Modern Québec*, Edmonton: University of Alberta Press.

Ndlovu, T.P. (1990) *The Return*, Gweru, Zimbabwe: Mambo Press.

Nelson, E.S. (ed.) (1992) *Reworlding: The Literature of the Indian Diaspora*, Westport, Connecticut: Greenwood.

Ngema, M. (1992) *Out of Africa: The Making of Township Fever*, Special Broadcasting System: 27 April 1992.

Ngũgĩ wa Thiong'o (1971) *This Time Tomorrow*, Nairobi: East African Literature Bureau.

—— (1982) *Mother, Sing for me*, (see Bjorkman, 1989).

Ngũgĩ wa Thiong'o and Mugo, M.G. (1977) *The Trial of Dedan Kimathi*, London: Heinemann.

Ngũgĩ wa Thiong'o and Ngũgĩ wa Mĩriĩ (1982) *I Will Marry When I Want*, London: Heinemann.

Nixon, R. (1987) 'Caribbean and African appropriations of *The Tempest*', *Critical Inquiry* 13, 3: 557–78.

Nkosi, L. (1981) *Tasks and Masks: Themes and Styles of African Literature*, Harlow, Essex: Longman.

BIBLIOGRAPHY

Nolan, Y. (1992a) *Blade, Theatrum* 31: 1–5.
—— (1992b) *Job's Wife, Theatrum* 31: 7–11.
Nora, P. (1989) 'Between memory and history: *Les Lieux de Mémoire*', *Representations* 26: 7–25.
Nowra, L. (1979) *Visions*, Sydney: Currency.
—— (1980) *Inside the Island* and *The Precious Woman*, Sydney: Currency.
—— (1983) *Sunrise*, Sydney: Currency.
—— (1988) *Capricornia*, Sydney: Currency.
—— (1989) *The Golden Age*, 2nd edn, Sydney: Currency.
—— (1992a) *Così*, Sydney: Currency.
—— (1992b) *Summer of the Aliens*, Sydney: Currency.
Nunn, R. (1984) 'Performing fact: Canadian documentary theatre', *Canadian Literature* 103: 51–62.
—— (1992) 'Marginality and English-Canadian theatre', in *Theatre Research International* 17, 3: 217–25.
Nwamuo, C. (1990) 'Which way Nigerian theatre?', in C. Nwamuo (ed.) *The Faces of Nigerian Theatre*, Calabar, Nigeria: Centaur, 62–6.
Nwankwo, C. (1985) 'Women in Ngũgĩ's plays: from passivity to social responsibility', *Ufahamu* 14, 3: 85–92.
Nwoga, D.I. (1976) 'The limitations of universal critical criteria', in R. Smith (ed.) *Exile and Tradition: Studies in African and Caribbean Literature*, New York: Africana, 8–30.
Nzewi, M. (1981) 'Music, dance, drama and the stage in Nigeria', in Y. Ogunbiyi (ed.) *Drama and Theatre in Nigeria: A Critical Sourcebook*, Lagos: Nigeria Magazine, 433–56.
Obafemi, O. (1986) *Nights of a Mythical Beast* and *The New Dawn*, Benin City: Adena.
Ochieng', W.R. (1989) *A Modern History of Kenya 1895–1980*, London: Evans.
Ogunba, O. and Irele, A. (eds) (1978) *Theatre in Africa*, Ibadan: University of Ibadan Press.
Ogunbiyi, Y. (1979) 'Opèrá Wónyòsi: a study of Soyinka's *Opèrá Wónyòsi*', *Nigeria Magazine* 128/9: 3–14.
—— (1981a) 'Nigerian theatre and drama: a critical perspective', in Y. Ogunbiyi (ed.) *Drama and Theatre in Nigeria: A Critical Source Book*, Lagos: Nigeria Magazine, 3–53.
—— (1981b) 'The popular theatre: a tribute to Duro Ladipo', in Y. Ogunbiyi (ed.) *Drama and Theatre in Nigeria: A Critical Source Book*, Lagos: Nigeria Magazine, 333–53.
Ògúnyemí, W. (1970) *Ijaye War (in the Nineteenth Century): A Historical Drama*, Ibadan: Orisun Acting Editions.
—— (1972) *Obalúayé: A Music-Drama*, Ibadan: Institute of African Studies, University of Ibadan.
—— (1976) *Kírìjì: an Historic Drama on Ekiti Parapo War in the Nineteenth Century*, Lagos: African Universities Press.
Olaniyan, T. (1988) 'Zulu Sofola and her sisters: the example of *The Sweet Trap*', in H. Wylie, D. Brutus, and J. Silenieks (eds) *African Literature 1988: New Masks*, Washington, DC: Three Continents, 39–49.
—— (1992) 'Dramatizing postcoloniality: Wole Soyinka and Derek Walcott', *Theatre Journal* 44, 4: 485–99.

—— (1993) ' "On post-colonial discourse": an introduction', *Callaloo* 16, 4: 743–9.

—— (1996) 'Femi Osofisan: provisional notes on the postcolonial incredible' *Kunapipi* (forthcoming 1997).

Omara, T. (1968) *The Exodus*, in D. Cook and M. Lee (eds) *Short East African Plays in English*, London: Heinemann, 47–66.

Omotoso, K. (1982) *The Theatrical into Theatre: A Study of the Drama and Theatre of the English-speaking Caribbean*, London: New Beacon.

Ong, W.J. (1982) *Orality and Literacy: The Technologising of the Word*, London: Methuen.

Onwueme, T.A. (1993) *Three Plays [The Broken Calabash, Parables for a Season, The Reign of Wazobia]*, Detroit, Michigan: Wayne State University Press.

Orkin, M. (1988) 'Body and state in *Blood Knot/The Blood Knot*', *South African Theatre Journal* 2, 1: 17–34.

—— (1991) *Drama and the South African State*, Manchester: Manchester Unversity Press.

Osborne, J. (1990) 'The gumboot dance: an historical, socio-economic and cultural perspective', *South African Theatre Journal* 4, 2: 50–79.

Osofisan, F. (1982a) 'Ritual and the revolutionary ethos: the humanist dilemma in contemporary Nigerian theatre', *Okike* 22: 72–81.

—— (1982b) *Once Upon Four Robbers*, Nigeria: BIO Educational Services.

—— (1988) *Another Raft*, Lagos: Malthouse.

—— (1990) *Birthdays are not for Dying and Other Plays*, Lagos: Malthouse.

O'Sullivan, V. (1987) *Shuriken*, Wellington: Victoria University Press.

—— (1989) *Jones and Jones*, Wellington: Victoria University Press.

—— (1990) *Billy*, Wellington: Victoria University Press.

Oti, S. (1977) *The Old Masters*, Ibadan: Oxford University Press.

—— (1985) 'Nigerian theatre today', *Nigeria Magazine* 53, 2: 30–9.

Otokunefor, H.C., and Nwodo, O.C. (eds) (1989) *Nigerian Female Writers: A Critical Perspective*, Lagos: Malthouse.

Owen, G. (1988) 'Women and social values in the plays of Trevor Rhone', *Caribbean Quarterly* 34, 3/4: 62–76.

Owen, R. (1991) *Te Awa i Tahuti*, in S. Garrett (ed.) *He Reo Hou*, Wellington: Playmarket, 126–61.

Oyekunle, 'S. (1983) *Katakata for Sofahead*, London: Macmillan.

Pacquet, S.P. (1992) 'Mustapha Matura's *Playboy of the West Indies*: a carnival discourse on imitation and originality', *Journal of West Indian Literature* 5, 1/2: 85–96.

Page, M. (1980) 'West Indian playwrights in Britain', *Canadian Drama* 6, 1: 90–101.

Pallister, J. (1991) *Aimé Césaire*, New York: Twayne.

Parker, A., Russo, M., Sommer, D., and Yaeger, P. (eds) (1992) *Nationalisms and Sexualities*, London: Routledge.

Parker, B. (1980) 'On the edge: Michael Cook's Newfoundland trilogy', *Canadian Literature* 85: 22–41.

Parry, B. (1987) 'Problems in current theories of colonial discourse', *Oxford Literary Review* 9, 1/2: 27–58.

Pavis, P. (1982) *Languages of the Stage: Essays in the Semiology of the Theatre*, trans. S. Melrose, New York: PAJ.

323

BIBLIOGRAPHY

—— (1992) *Theatre at the Crossroads of Culture*, trans. L. Kruger, London: Routledge.

Pearce, A. (1990) 'The didactic essence of Efua Sutherland's plays', in E.D. Jones (ed.) *Women in African Literature Today*, London: James Currey, 71–81.

Pechey, G. (1987) 'On the borders of Bakhtin: dialogization, decolonization', *Oxford Literary Review* 9, 1/2: 59–84.

Perkins, E. (1987) 'Form and transformation in the plays of Alma De Groen', *Australasian Drama Studies* 11: 5–21.

Peters, H. (1993) 'The Aboriginal presence in Canadian theatre and the evolution of being Canadian', *Theatre Research International* 18, 3: 197–205.

Peterson, B. (1990) 'Apartheid and the political imagination in black South African theatre', *Journal of South African Studies* 16, 2: 229–45.

Phelan, P. (1992) *Unmarked: The Politics of Performance*, London: Routledge.

Pine, R. (1990) *Brian Friel and Ireland's Drama*, London: Routledge.

Poliner, S.M. (1984) 'The exiled creature: Ananse tales and the search for Afro-Caribbean identity', *Studies in the Humanities* 11, 1: 12–22.

Pollock, S. (1978) *The* Komagatu Maru *Incident*, Toronto: Playwrights Co-op.

—— (1981) *Generations*, in *Blood Relations and Other Plays*, Edmonton: NeWest, 101–78.

—— (1987) *Whiskey Six Cadenza*, in D. Bessai and D. Kerr (eds) *NeWest Plays by Women*, Edmonton: NeWest, 137–247.

—— (1993) *Walsh*, in J. Wasserman (ed.) *Modern Canadian Plays Volume 1*, 3rd edn, Vancouver: Talonbooks, 237–72.

Porter, D. (1983) 'Orientalism and its problems', in F. Barker *et al.* (eds) *The Politics of Theory. Proceedings of the Essex Conference on the Sociology of Literature, July 1982*, Colchester, Essex: University of Essex Press, 179–83.

Potiki, R. (1991) 'A Maori point of view: the journey from anxiety to confidence', *Australasian Drama Studies* 18: 57–63.

Prasad, M. (1992) 'The "other" worldliness of postcolonial discourse: a critique', *Critical Quarterly* 34, 3: 74–89.

Prentice, C. (1991) 'The interplay of place and placelessness in the subject of post-colonial fiction', *SPAN* 31: 63–80.

Prentki, T. (1990) 'Cop-out, cop-in: carnival as political theatre', *New Theatre Quarterly* 24, 6: 362–94.

Prichard, K.S. (1974) *Brumby Innes*, Sydney: Currency.

Priebe, R.K. (1988) *Myth, Realism and the West African Writer*, Trenton, New Jersey: Africa World Press.

Rabillard, S. (1993) 'Absorption, elimination, and the hybrid: some impure questions of gender and culture in the trickster drama of Tomson Highway', *Essays in Theatre* 12, 1: 3–27.

Rajah, J. and Tay, S. (1991) 'From second tongue to mother tongue: a look at the use of English in Singapore English drama from the 1960s to the present', in E. Thumboo (ed.) *Perceiving Other Worlds*, Singapore: Times Academic Press, 400–12.

Rajan, R.S. (1993) *Real and Imagined Women: Gender, Culture and Postcolonialism*, London: Routledge.

Ramchand, K. (1988) 'Why the dragon can't dance: an examination of Indian-African relations in Lovelace's *The Dragon Can't Dance*', *Journal of West Indian Literature* 2, 2: 1–14.

Rangacharya, A. (1971) *The Indian Theatre*, New Delhi: National Book Trust.

Redmond, E.B. (1993) 'Tess Onwueme's soular system: trilogy of the she-kings – parables, reigns, calabashes', in T.A. Onwueme *Three Plays*, Detroit, Michigan: Wayne State University Press, 13–18.

Reed, I. (1988) 'Soyinka among the monoculturists', *Black American Literature Forum* 22, 4: 705–9.

Reid, C. (1989) *The Belle of the Belfast City* and *Did You Hear the One About the Irishman . . . ?*, London: Methuen.

Reinelt, J. and Roach, J. (eds) (1992) *Critical Theory and Performance*, Ann Arbor, Michigan: Michigan University Press.

Renan, E. (1947) *Oeuvres completes. Edition definitive etable par Henriette Psichari*, H. Psichari (ed.) Paris: Calmann-Levy.

Rendra (1979) *The Struggle of the Naga Tribe*, trans. M. Lane, St Lucia: University of Queensland Press.

Renée (1985) *Wednesday To Come*, Wellington: Victoria University Press.

—— (1986) *Pass It On*, Wellington: Victoria University Press.

—— (1991) *Jeannie Once*, Wellington: Victoria University Press.

Retamar, R.F. (1989) *Caliban and Other Essays*, trans. E. Baker, Minneapolis, Minnesota: University of Minnesota Press.

Rewa, N. (1990) 'Clichés of ethnicity subverted: Robert Lepage's *La Trilogie des Dragons*', *Theatre History in Canada* 11, 2: 148–61.

Reyes, A. (1984) 'Carnival: ritual dance of the past and present in Earl Lovelace's *The Dragon Can't Dance*', *World Literature Written in English* 24, 1: 107–20.

Rhone, T. (1981) *Smile Orange*, in *Old Story Time and Other Plays*, Harlow, Essex: Longman, 161–225.

—— (1984) *Two Can Play*, Lexington, Kentucky: Ket Books.

Rich, F. (1987) Rev. of *Death and the King's Horseman* by W. Soyinka, the *New York Times* 2 March: 13.

Richards, D. (1984) 'Òwe l'esin òrò: proverbs like horses: Wole Soyinka's *Death and the King's Horseman*', *Journal of Commonwealth Literature* 19, 1: 86–97.

Richards, S.L. (1987a) 'Nigerian independence onstage: responses from "second generation" playwrights', *Theatre Journal* 39, 2: 215–27.

—— (1987b) 'Toward a populist Nigerian theatre: the plays of Femi Osofisan', *New Theatre Quarterly* 3, 11: 280–8.

Richmond, F.P., Swann, D.L., and Zarilli, P.B. (1990) *Indian Theatre*, Honolulu, Hawaii: University of Hawaii Press.

Ringwood, G.P. (1984) *Drum Song*, in R. Perkyns (ed.) *Major Plays of the Canadian Theatre 1934–1984*, Toronto: Irwin, 328–83.

Roche, A. (1988) 'Ireland's *Antigones*: tragedy, north and south', in M. Keneally (ed.) *Cultural Contexts and Literary Idioms in Contemporary Irish Literature*, Gerrards Cross, Buckinghamshire: Colin Smythe, 221–50.

Rodo, J.E. (1967) *Ariel*, G. Brotherston (ed.) Cambridge: Cambridge University Press.

Rohlehr, G. (1978) 'The folk in Caribbean literature', in E. Baugh (ed.) *Critics on Caribbean Literature*, Boston, Massachusetts: Allen & Unwin, 27–30.

—— (1990) *Calypso and Society in Pre-Independence Trinidad*, Port of Spain, Trinidad: Rohlehr.

Rohmer, M. (1994) 'Wole Soyinka's *Death and the King's Horseman*, Royal Exchange Theatre, Manchester', *New Theatre Quarterly* 10, 37: 57–69.

Romeril, J. (1975) *The Floating World*, Sydney: Currency.

Rotimi, O. (1971a) 'Traditional Nigerian drama', in B. King (ed.) *Introduction to Nigerian Literature*, Lagos: Africana, 36–49.

—— (1971b) *Kurunmi*, Nigeria: Oxford University Press.

—— (1971c) *The Gods are not to Blame*, London: Oxford University Press.

—— (1974) 'Interview with Ola Rotimi', in B. Lindfors (ed.) *Dem-Say: Interview with Eight Nigerian Writers*, Austin, Texas: African and Afro-American Studies Research Centre, 57–68.

—— (1985) Interview with D. Burness (ed.) *Wana Sema: Conversations With African Writers*, Athens, Ohio: Ohio University Center for International Studies, 11–18.

Rubin, G. (1975) 'The traffic in women: notes on the "political economy" of sex', in R. Reiter (ed.) *Toward an Anthropology of Women*, New York: Monthly Review Press, 157–210.

Ruganda, J. (1986) *Echoes of Silence*, Nairobi: Heinemann.

Russo, M. (1986) 'Female grotesques: carnival and theory', in T. de Lauretis (ed.) *Feminist Studies/Critical Studies*, Bloomington, Indiana: Indiana University Press, 213–29.

Ryga, G. (1971) *The Ecstasy of Rita Joe and Other Plays*, Toronto: New Press.

Said, E. (1979) *Orientalism*, New York: Vintage.

—— (1990) 'Reflections on exile', in R. Ferguson *et al.* (eds) *Out There: Marginalization and Contemporary Cultures*, Cambridge, Massachusetts: MIT Press, 357–66.

—— (1994) *Culture and Imperialism*, London: Vintage.

Saint-Andre, E.U. (1984) 'Political commitment in Nigerian drama (1970–1983)', *Commonwealth: Essays and Studies* 7, 1: 36–49.

Salter, D. (1991) 'The idea of national theatre', in R. Lecker (ed.) *Canadian Canons: Essays in Literary Value*, Toronto: University of Toronto Press, 71–90.

—— (1992) 'On native ground: Canadian theatre historiography and the postmodernism/postcolonialism axis', *Theatre Research in Canada* 13, 1/2: 134–43.

Salutin, R. (1977) *Les Canadiens*, Vancouver: Talonbooks.

Salutin, R. and Theatre Passe Muraille (1993) *1837: The Farmers Revolt*, in *Modern Canadian Plays: Volume 1*, 3rd edn, Vancouver: Talonbooks, 203–31.

Samad, D.R. (1991) 'Cultural imperatives in Derek Walcott's *Dream on Monkey Mountain*', *Commonwealth: Essays and Studies* 13, 2: 8–21.

Sanchez, M. (1976) 'Caliban: the new Latin-American protagonist of *The Tempest*', *Diacritics* 6, 1: 54–61.

Schaffer, K. (1988) *Women and the Bush: Forces of Desire in the Australian Cultural Tradition*, Cambridge: Cambridge University Press.

Schechner, R. (1989) 'Magnitudes of performance', in R. Schechner and W. Appel (eds) *By Means of Performance: Intercultural Studies of Theatre and Ritual*, New York: Cambridge University Press, 19–49.

—— (1993) *The Future of Ritual: Writings on Culture and Performance*, London: Routledge.

Schechner, R. and Appel, W. (eds) (1989) *By Means of Performance: Intercultural Studies of Theatre and Ritual*, New York: Cambridge University Press.

Schipper, M. (1987) 'Mother Africa on a pedestal: the male heritage in African literature and criticism', in E.D. Jones (ed.) *Women in African Literature Today*, London: Currey; Trenton, New Jersey: African World Press, 35–54.

Schulz, L. (1994) 'Theatre for the seven hundred: William Takaku's dream for the National Theatre Company of Papua New Guinea', *Australasian Drama Studies* 24: 47–55.

Scott, D. (1985) *An Echo in the Bone*, in E. Hill (ed.) *Plays for Today*, Harlow, Essex: Longman, 73–137.

Scott, M. (1990) 'Karbarra: the new Aboriginal drama and its audience', *SPAN* 30: 127–40.

Sears, D. (1990) *Afrika Solo*, Toronto: Sister Vision.

—— (1992) 'Naming names: black women playwrights in Canada', in R. Much (ed.) *Women on the Canadian Stage: The Legacy of Hrotsvit'*, Winnipeg: Blizzard, 92–103.

Sebcok, T.A. (ed.) (1984) *Carnival*, Berlin: Gruyter.

'Seditious Drama: The play in the Philipines [sic]: what a recent visitor has to say' (1907) *The Theatre* [Sydney] 1 Feb.: 17.

Selvon, S. (1991) *Highway in the Sun and Other Plays*, Leeds: Peepal Tree Press.

Senanu, K.E. (1980) 'The exigencies of adaption: the case of Soyinka's *Bacchae*', in J. Gibbs (ed.) *Critical Perspectives on Wole Soyinka*, Washington, DC: Three Continents, 108–12.

Senelick, L. (ed.) (1992) *Gender in Performance: The Presentation of Difference in the Performing Arts*, Hanover, Massachusetts: New England University Press.

Sentongo, N. (1975) *The Invisible Bond*, in M. Etherton (ed.) *African Plays for Playing*, London: Heinemann, 7–44.

Seremba, G. (1993) *Come Good Rain*, Winnipeg: Blizzard.

Serumaga, R. (1974) *Majangwa: A Promise of Rain*, Nairobi: East African Publishing House.

Severac, A. (1987) 'Soyinka's tragedies: from ritual to drama', *Commonwealth: Essays and Studies* 10, 1: 26–40.

Sewell, S. (1983) *The Blind Giant is Dancing*, Sydney: Currency.

—— (1988) *Hate*, Sydney: Currency.

Shadbolt, M. (1982) *Once on Chunuk Bair*, Auckland: Hodder & Stoughton.

Shakespeare, W. (1987) *The Tempest*, S. Orgel (ed.), Oxford: Oxford University Press.

Sharpe, J. (1991) 'The unspeakable limits of rape: colonial violence and counter-insurgency', *Genders* 10: 25–46.

—— (1993) *Allegories of Empire: The Figure of Woman in the Colonial Text*, Minneapolis, Minnesota: University of Minnesota.

Shearer, J. (1977) *Catherine*, Port Melbourne, Victoria: Arnold.

Sheil, G. (1991) *Bali: Adat*, Sydney: Currency.

Shepherd, D. (ed.) (1989) *Bakhtin: Carnival and Other Subjects*, Amsterdam: Rodopi.

Shoemaker, A. (1990) 'Swimming in the mainstream: Australian Aboriginal and Canadian Indian drama', *Working Papers in Australian Studies No. 60*, London: Sir Robert Menzies Centre for Australian Studies, University of London, 1–12.

Showalter, E. (1985) 'Feminist criticism in the wilderness', in E. Showalter (ed.) *The New Feminist Criticism: Essays on Women, Literature, and Theory*, New York: Pantheon, 243–70.

Silverstein, M. (1992) ' "It's only a name": schemes of identification and the national community in *Translations*', *Essays in Theatre* 10, 2: 133–42.

Singh, J. (1989) 'Different Shakespeares: the bard in colonial/post-colonial India', *Theatre Journal* 41, 4: 445–58.

Sircar, B. (1983) *Three Plays: Procession, Bhoma, Stale News*, Calcutta: Seagull.

Sistren Theatre Collective (1978) *Bellywoman Bangarang*, unpublished playscript.

—— (1980) *Nana Yah*, unpublished playscript.

—— (1981) *QPH*, unpublished playscript.

—— (1985) *Ida Revolt Inna Jonkunnu Stylee*, unpublished playscript.

—— (1985) *Muffit Inna All a We*, unpublished playscript.

Skura, M. (1989) 'Discourse and the individual: the case of colonialism in *The Tempest*', *Shakespeare Quarterly* 40, 1: 42–60.

Slemon, S. (1987) 'Monuments of empire: allegory/counter-discourse/post-colonial writing', *Kunapipi* 9, 3: 1–16.

—— (1988) 'Post-colonial allegory and the transformation of history', *Journal of Commonwealth Literature* 23, 1: 157–68.

—— (1989) 'Reading for resistance in post-colonial literatures', in H. Maes-Jelinek, K.H. Petersen, and A. Rutherford (eds) *A Shaping of Connections: Commonwealth Literature Studies – Then and Now*, Sydney: Dangaroo, 100–15.

—— (1990a) 'Modernism's last post', in I. Adam and H. Tiffin (eds) *Past the Last Post: Post-Colonialism and Post-Modernism*, Calgary: University of Calgary Press, 1–11.

—— (1990b) 'Unsettling the empire: resistance theory for the second world', *World Literature Written in English* 30, 2: 30–41.

Slemon, S. and Tiffin, H. (1989) 'Introduction', *Kunapipi* 11, 1: ix–xiii.

Smith, F. (1993) Review of *The Black Jacobins* by C.L.R. James, *Trinidad and Tobago Review* June: 26–7.

Smith, R. (ed.) (1976) *Exile and Tradition: Studies in African and Caribbean Literature*, London: Longman.

Smith, R.P. (1972) 'The misunderstood and rejected black hero in the theatre of Aimé Césaire', *CLA Journal* 16, 1: 7–15.

Smith, R.P. and Hudson, R.J. (1992) 'Evoking Caliban: Césaire's response to Shakespeare', *CLA Journal* 35, 4: 387–99.

Smith, R.S. (1991) 'The hermeneutic motion in Brian Friel's *Translations*', *Modern Drama* 34, 3: 392–409.

Söderlind, S. (1991) *Margin/Alias: Language and Colonization in Canadian and Québécois Fiction*, Toronto: University of Toronto Press.

Sofola, 'Z. (1972) *Wedlock of the Gods*, London: Evans Brothers.

—— (1977) *The Sweet Trap*, Ibadan: Oxford University Press.

—— (1979) 'The playwright and theatrical creation', *Nigeria Magazine* 128/9: 68–74.

Sontag, S. (1973) *On Photography*, New York: Farrar, Straus & Giroux.

—— (1978) *Illness as Metaphor*, New York: Farrar, Straus & Giroux.

Sotto, W. (1985) *The Rounded Rite: A Study of Wole Soyinka's Play The Bacchae of Euripides*, Lund, Sweden: Gleerup.

Souchotte, S. (1979) 'Inuit theatre: dramatizing the myths', *Canadian Theatre Review* 23: 32–5.

Sowande, B. (1990) *Tornadoes Full of Dreams*, Lagos: Malthouse.

Soyinka, W. (1973) *Collected Plays 1 [A Dance of the Forests, The Swamp Dwellers, The Strong Breed, The Road, The Bacchae of Euripides]*, Oxford: Oxford University Press.

—— (1976a) 'Drama and the African world-view', in R. Smith (ed.) *Exile and Tradition: Studies in African and Caribbean Literature*, New York: Africana, 173–90.

—— (1976b) *Myth, Literature and the African World*, Cambridge: Cambridge University Press.

—— (1984) *Six Plays [The Trials of Brother Jero, Jero's Metamorphosis, Camwood on the Leaves, Death and the King's Horseman, Madmen and Specialists, Opèrá Wónyòsi]*, London: Methuen.

—— (1988) *Art, Dialogue and Outrage: Essays on Literature and Culture*, Ibadan: New Horn.

—— (1992) *From Zia, with Love* and *A Scourge of Hyacinths*, London: Methuen.

Spivak, G.C. (1985) 'Three women's texts and a critique of imperialism', *Critical Inquiry* 12, 1: 243–61.

—— (1986) 'Imperialism and sexual difference', *Oxford Literary Review* 8, 1/2: 225–40.

—— (1988) *In Other Worlds: Essays in Cultural Politics*, New York: Methuen.

—— (1993) 'Can the subaltern speak?', in P. Williams and L. Chrisman (eds) *Colonial Discourse and Post-colonial Theory: A Reader*, New York: Harvester Wheatsheaf, 66–111.

Stallybrass, P. and White, A. (1986) *The Politics and Poetics of Transgression*, Ithaca, New York: Cornell University Press.

Stam, R. (1989) *Subversive Pleasures: Bakhtin, Cultural Criticism, and Film*, Baltimore, Maryland: Johns Hopkins University Press.

Stam, R. and Spence, L. (1983) 'Colonialism, racism, and representation', *Screen* 24, 2: 2–20.

Steadman, I. (1984) 'Black South African theatre after nationalism', *The English Academy Review* 2: 9–18.

—— (1985) 'Drama and social consciousness: themes in black theatre on the Witwatersrand until 1984', Ph.D. diss., University of Witwatersrand.

BIBLIOGRAPHY

—— (1990) 'Introduction', in M. Manaka, *Pula*, Braamfontein, South Africa: Skotaville, 3–15.

—— (1991) 'Theater beyond apartheid', *Research in African Literatures* 22, 3: 77–90.

Steiner, G. (1975) *After Babel: Aspects of Language and Translation*, New York: Oxford University Press.

Stewart, B. (1991) *Broken Arse*, Wellington: Victoria University Press.

Stone, J.S. (1994) *Theatre: Studies in West Indian Literature*, London: Macmillan.

Storey, R. (1993) *The Glorious 12th*, Victoria, British Columbia: Shillingford.

Strachan, T. (1983) *Eyes of the Whites*, Sydney: Alternative.

Stratton, A. (1991) *Canada Split: Two Plays*, Montréal: NuAge Editions.

Suleri, S. (1992) 'Woman skin deep: feminism and the postcolonial condition', *Critical Inquiry* 18, 4: 756–69.

Sutherland, E. (1967) *Edufa*, London: Longman.

—— (1971) *Foriwa*, Accra, Ghana: Ghana Publishing.

—— (1975) *The Marriage of Anansewa*, Harlow, Essex: Longman Drumbeat.

Suvin, D. (1987) 'Approach to topoanalysis and to the paradigmatics of dramaturgical space', *Poetics Today* 8, 2: 311–34.

Szaffkó, P. (1987) 'The Indian in contemporary North American drama', *Canadian Drama* 13, 2: 182–6.

Tapping, C. (1990) 'Voices off: models of orality in African literature and literary criticism', *ARIEL* 21, 3: 73–86.

Tarlekar, G.H. (1975) *Studies in the Natyasastra: With Special Reference to the Sanskrit Drama in Performance*, Delhi: Motilal Banarsidass.

Taylor, D.H. (1990) *Toronto at Dreamer's Rock* and *Education is Our Right*, Saskatoon: Fifth House.

—— (1993) *Someday*, Saskatoon: Fifth House.

Taylor, P. (1986) 'Myth and reality in Caribbean narrative: Derek Walcott's *Pantomime*', *World Literature Written in English* 26, 1: 169–77.

Thieme, J. (1984) 'A Caribbean Don Juan: Derek Walcott's *Joker of Seville*', *World Literature Written in English* 23, 1: 62–75.

Thompson, J. (1989) *The Other Side of the Dark: Four Plays [Tornado, The Crackwalker, Pink, I am Yours]*, Toronto: Coach House.

—— (1992) *Lion in the Streets*, Toronto: Coach House.

Thompson, M. (1984a) 'Promise and frustration: New Zealand playwrighting since 1975', *Australasian Drama Studies* 3, 1: 122–8.

—— (1984b) *Songs to the Judges*, in *Selected Plays*, Dunedin, New Zealand: Pilgrims South, 147–85.

Tiffin, C. and Lawson, A. (1994) 'Introduction: the textuality of empire', in C. Tiffin and A. Lawson (eds) *De-Scribing Empire: Post-Colonialism and Textuality*, London: Routledge, 1–11.

Tiffin, H. (1987a) 'Post-colonial literatures and counter-discourse', *Kunapipi* 9, 3: 17–34.

—— (1987b) 'Recuperative strategies in the post-colonial novel', in W. McGaw (ed.) *Inventing Countries: Essays in Post-colonial Literatures*, Wollongong, New South Wales: South Pacific Association for Commonwealth Language and Literature Studies, 27–45.

—— (1988) 'Post-colonialism, post-modernism and the rehabilitation of post-colonial history', *Journal of Commonwealth Literature* 23, 1: 169–81.

—— (1993a) '"Cold hearts and (foreign) tongues": recitation and the reclamation of the female body in the works of Erna Brodber and Jamaica Kincaid', *Callaloo* 16, 4: 909–21.

—— (1993b) 'Metaphor and mortality: the "life cycle(s)" of malaria', *Meridian* 12, 1: 46–58.

Tompkins, J. (1991) 'Time past/time passed: the empowerment of women and blacks in Australian feminist and Aboriginal drama', *Australasian Drama Studies* 19: 13–22.

—— (1992a) 'Post-colonialism and Australian drama', *Australian–Canadian Studies* 10, 2: 127–30.

—— (1992b) 'Setting the stage: a semiotic re-reading of selected Australian plays by Dorothy Hewett, Jack Hibberd, Louis Nowra, and Stephen Sewell', Ph.D. diss., York University, Toronto.

—— (1993a) 'History/history/histories: resisting the binary in Aboriginal drama', *Kunapipi* 15, 1: 6–14.

—— (1993b) 'Infinitely rehearsing performance and identity: *Afrika Solo* and *The Book of Jessica*', *Canadian Theatre Review* 74: 35–9.

—— (1994a) '"Celebrate 1988?" Australian drama in the bicentennial year', *Australian and New Zealand Studies in Canada* 12: 103–12.

—— (1994b) 'Oral culture, theatre, text: Jack Davis's theatre', in G. Turcotte (ed.) *Jack Davis*, Sydney: Collins-Angus & Robertson, 48–59.

—— (1994c) 'Re-orienting Australasian drama: staging theatrical irony', *ARIEL* 25, 4: 117–33.

—— (1995a) 'Re-playing and dis-playing the nation: New Zealand drama', in M. Williams and M. Leggott (eds) *Essays on New Zealand Literature*, Auckland: Auckland University Press, 294–306.

—— (1995b) '"Spectacular resistance": metatheatre in post-colonial drama', *Modern Drama* 38, 1: 42–51.

—— (1995c) '"The story of rehearsal never ends": rehearsal, performance, identity', *Canadian Literature* 144: 142–61.

—— (1996) 'Dressing up and dressing down: cultural transvestism in post-colonial drama', in L. Dale and S. Ryan (eds) *The Body in the Library: Post-colonial Representations of the Body*, Amsterdam: Rodopi.

Traore, B. (1972) *The Black African Theatre and its Social Function*, trans. D. Adelugba, Ibadan: University of Ibadan Press.

Tremblay, M. (1971) *A toi, pour toujours, ta Marie-Lou*, Montréal: Leméac.

—— (1973) *Les Belles Soeurs*, trans. J. Van Burek and B. Glassco, Vancouver: Talonbooks.

—— (1988) *Bonjour, Là, Bonjour*, trans. J. Van Burek and B. Glassco, Vancouver: Talonbooks.

—— (1991) *The Guid Sisters and Other Plays*, trans. B. Findlay and M. Bowman, London: Nick Hearn.

—— (1992) *Hosanna*, in J. Doolittle (ed.) *Heroines: Three Plays*, Red Deer, Alberta: Red Deer College Press, 127–91.

Trinh, T. Minh-ha (1989) *Woman, Native, Other*, Bloomington, Indiana: Indiana University Press.

Turcotte, G. (1987) '"The circle is burst": eschatological discourse in

BIBLIOGRAPHY

Louis Nowra's *Sunrise* and *The Golden Age*', *SPAN* 24: 63–80.

—— (ed.) (1994) *Jack Davis: A Critical Study*, Sydney: Collins-Angus and Robertson.

Turner, V. (1982) *From Ritual to Theatre: The Human Seriousness of Play*, New York: PAJ.

—— (1989) 'Are there universals of performance in myth, ritual, and drama?', in R. Schechner and W. Appel (eds) *By Means of Performance: Intercultural Studies of Theatre and Ritual*, New York: Cambridge University Press, 8–18.

Tuwhare, H. (1991) *In the Wilderness Without a Hat*, in S. Garrett (ed.) *He Reo Hou*, Wellington: Playmarket, 53–123.

Ugonna, N. (1983) *Mmonwu: A Dramatic Tradition of the Igbo*, Lagos: Lagos University Press.

Ukpokodu, I.P. (1992) *Socio-political Theatre in Nigeria*, San Francisco, California: Mellen.

Urry, J. (1990) *The Tourist Gaze: Leisure and Travel in Contemporary Societies*, London: Sage.

Usmiani, R. (1979) 'The Tremblay opus: unity in diversity', *Canadian Theatre Review* 24: 12–25.

Uys, P.D. (1989) *Paradise is Closing Down and Other Plays*, London: Penguin.

Van Herk, A. (1992) 'Women writers and the prairie: spies in an indifferent landscape', in A. Van Herk, *A Frozen Tongue*, Sydney: Dangaroo, 139–51.

Van Toorn, P. (1990) 'Discourse/patron discourse: how minority texts command the attention of majority audiences', *SPAN* 30: 102–15.

Varadapande, M.L. (1982) *Krishna Theatre in India*, New Delhi: Abhinav.

Vaughan, A. (1988) 'Caliban in the "third world": Shakespeare's savage as sociopolitical symbol', *Massachusetts Review* 29, 2: 289–313.

Verdecchia, G. (1993) *Fronteras Americanas (American Borders)*, Toronto: Coach House.

Vingoe, M. (1993) *Living Curiosities: The Story of Anna Swan*, in A. Jansen (ed.) *Adventures for Big Girls*, Winnipeg: Blizzard, 25–50.

Visel, R. (1988) 'A half colonization: the problem of the white colonial woman writer', *Kunapipi* 10, 3: 39–45.

Viswanathan, G. (1989) *Masks of Conquest: Literary Study and British Rule in India*, New York: Columbia University Press.

Vizenor, G. (1989) 'Trickster discourse', *The Wicazo SA Review: A Journal of Indian Studies* 5, 1: 2–7.

von Kotze, A. (1987) *Organise and Act: The Natal Workers Theatre Movement 1983–1987*, Durban: Culture and Working Life, University of Natal.

Wabei, T. (1970) *Kulubob*, Melbourne: Heinemann.

Wagner, A. (ed.) (1985) *Contemporary Canadian Theatre: New World Visions*, Toronto: Simon & Pierre.

Walcott, D. (1950) *Henri Christophe*, Trinidad: University of the West Indies, Extramural Studies Unit.

—— (1970a) *Dream on Monkey Mountain and Other Plays*, New York: Farrar, Straus & Giroux.

—— (1970b) 'What the twilight says: an overture', in *Dream on Monkey Mountain and Other Plays*, New York: Farrar, Straus & Giroux, 3–40.

—— (1973) 'Meanings', in D. Lowenthal, and L. Comitas (eds) *Consequences of Class and Colour: West Indian Perspectives*, New York: Anchor/Doubleday, 302–12.

—— (1979a) *The Joker of Seville* and *O Babylon!: Two Plays*, London: Jonathan Cape.

—— (1979b) *Ti-Jean and his brothers*, adapted by M. Gilkes for Video Barbados.

—— (1979c) *Pantomime*, filmed version of play performed in Miami, Florida.

—— (1980) *Remembrance* and *Pantomime*, New York: Farrar, Straus & Giroux.

—— (1985) *Ti-Jean and his Brothers*, in E. Hill (ed.) *Plays for Today*, Essex: Longman, 21–71.

—— (1986) *Three Plays [A Branch of the Blue Nile, Beef, No Chicken, The Last Carnival]*, New York: Farrar, Straus & Giroux.

—— (1992) 'The Caribbean: culture or mimicry', *The Crusader* 17 October: 26–31.

—— (1993) *The Odyssey: A Stage Version*, New York: Farrar, Straus & Giroux.

Walcott, R. (1976) *The Banjo Man*, in E. Hill (ed.) *A Time . . . and a Season: 8 Caribbean Plays*, Trinidad: University of the West Indies, Extramural Studies Unit, 213–56.

Walker, G. (1978) *Three Plays [Bagdad Saloon, Beyond Mozambique, Ramona and the White Slaves]*, Toronto: Coach House.

Wallace, R. (1990) *Producing Marginality: Theatre and Criticism in Canada*, Saskatoon: Fifth House.

Walley, R. (1990) *Coordah*, in *Plays from Black Australia*, Sydney: Currency, 109–66.

Warner, E. (1993) Interview with Helen Gilbert, Jamaica, 28 April.

Watego, C. (1992) 'Aboriginal Australian dramatists', in R. Fotheringham (ed.) *Community Theatre in Australia*, rev. edn, Sydney: Currency, 69–76.

Watene, K. (1974) *Dedan Kimathi*, Nairobi: Transafrica.

Watney, S. (1990) 'Missionary positions: AIDS, "Africa", and race', in R. Ferguson *et al.* (eds) *Out There: Marginalization and Contemporary Cultures*, Cambridge, Massachusetts: MIT Press, 89–103.

Wearne, H. (1992) 'Discourses of disruption and Alma De Groen's *The Rivers of China*', *Australasian Drama Studies* 21: 61–73.

Weiss, J. (1983) 'Québec theatre in the 80s: the end of an era', *American Review of Canadian Studies* 13, 2: 64–73.

Welsh-Asante, K. (ed.) (1993) *The African Aesthetic: Keeper of the Tradition*, Westport, Connecticut: Greenwood.

Whaley, A. (1991) *The Rise and Shine of Comrade Fiasco*, Harare: Anvil.

White, E. (1985) *Redemption Song and Other Plays*, London: Marion Boyars.

White, H. (1973) *Metahistory: The Historical Imagination in Nineteenth-Century Europe*, Baltimore, Maryland: Johns Hopkins University Press.

'Whose voice is it anyway?: a symposium on who should be speaking for whom', (1991) *Books in Canada* 20, 1: 11–17.

Wickham, J. (1979) 'Some reflections on the state of theatre in the Caribbean', *Bim* 17, 65: 16–22.

Wilentz, G. (1992) *Binding Cultures: Black Women Writers in Africa and the Diaspora*, Bloomington, Indiana: Indiana University Press.

Wilkinson, J. (1991) 'Melting the barriers of mind: *The Bacchae of Euripides* as a liberation rite', *Commonwealth: Essays and Studies* 13, 2: 71–84.

Williams, M. (1986) 'The anxiety of writing: language and belonging in New Zealand and Fiji', *SPAN* 22: 93–104.

Williams, P. and Chrisman, L. (eds) (1993) *Colonial Discourse and Post-Colonial Theory: A Reader*, New York: Harvester Wheatsheaf.

Willis, R. (1992) '*Dream on Monkey Mountain*: fantasy as self-perception', in D. Murphy (ed.) *Staging the Impossible: The Fantastic Mode in Modern Drama*, Westport, Connecticut: Greenwood, 150–5.

Winders, J.A. (1983) 'Reggae, rastafarians and revolution: rock music in the third world', *Journal of Popular Culture* 17, 1: 61–73.

Wollen, P. (1987) 'Fashion/orientalism/the body', *New Formations* 1: 5–33.

Workshop '71 Theatre Company (1981) *Survival*, in R. Kavanagh (ed.) *South African People's Plays*, London: Heinemann, 125–72.

Wright, D. (1992) 'Ritual and revolution: Soyinka's dramatic theory', *ARIEL* 23, 1: 39–58.

Wright, R. (1937) *Revels in Jamaica 1682–1838*, New York: Dodd Mead.

Wuest, R. (1990) 'The robber in the Trinidad carnival', *Caribbean Quarterly* 36, 4: 42–53.

Wynter, S. (1970) 'Jonkonnu in Jamaica: towards the interpretation of folk dance as a cultural process', *Jamaica Journal* June: 34–48.

—— (1979) *Maskarade*, in J. Wilson (ed.) *West Indian Plays for Schools*, Jamaica: Jamaica Publishing House.

Yajnik, R.K. (1970) *The Indian Theatre: Its Origins and Its Later Developments under European Influence*, New York: Haskell House.

Yeboa-Dankwa, J. (1988) 'Storytelling of the Akan and Guan in Ghana', in R.K. Priebe (ed.) *Ghanaian Literatures*, New York: Greenwood, 29–42.

Yeo, R. (1990) *One Year Back Home*, Manila: Solidarity Foundation.

—— (1994) 'Theatre and censorship in Singapore', *Australasian Drama Studies* 25: 49–60.

Yeoh, P. (1972) *The Need to Be*, in L. Fernando (ed.) *New Drama Two*, Kuala Lumpur: Oxford University Press, 1–45.

Yerimah, A. (1987) 'Wole Soyinka's experiment: guerilla theatre at the University of Ife', *Odu* 32: 145–59.

Yong, M. (1984) '"Colonial, post-colonial, neo-colonial and at last, a "post-national" drama', *World Literature Written in English* 23, 1: 234–41.

Zabus, C. (1985) 'A Calibanic tempest in anglophone and francophone new world writing', *Canadian Literature* 104: 35–50.

Zambuko and Izibuko (1988) *Katshaa! The Sound of the AK*, Harare: University of Zimbabwe Press.

Zarrilli, P. (1984) *The Kathakali Complex: Actor, Performance and Structure*, New Delhi: Abhinav.

Zimra, C. (1986) 'W/Righting his/tory: versions of things past in contemporary Caribbean women writers', in M. Ueda (ed.) *Explorations: Essays in Comparative Literature*, Lanham, Maryland: University Presses of America, 227–52.

INDEX

INDEX

22, 94; *Henri Christophe* 116; *The Joker of Seville* 89–92, 197; *Pantomime* 36–8, 252; *Ti-Jean and His Brothers* 133–4, 219–20
Walcott, Roderick: *The Banjo Man* 89
Walker, George: *Bagdad Saloon* 284–5
Warner, Earl 82, 92, 281
Weiss, Peter: *Marat/Sade* 17
Whaley, Andrew: *The Rise and Shine of Comrade Fiasco* 161 n. 6
White, Hayden 106, 109, 139
Williams, Patrick and Laura Chrisman 5

Wordsworth, William: 'I Wandered Lonely as a Cloud' 15
Wynter, Sylvia 54; *Maskarade* 89; *see also* The Yard Theatre

yard plays/yard culture 80, 84–5, 92, 98; The Yard Theatre 88, 158
Yeo, Robert, Jothie Rajah, and Simon Tay 179
Yong, Margaret 157

Zambuko and Izibuko: *Ktshaa, the Sound of the AK* 248
Zimbabwean theatre: *see* Zambuko and Izibuko

DATE DUE / DATE DE RETOUR